DIARY (1843–1852) OF JAMES HADLEY

✻   ✻   ✻

A PUBLICATION ISSUED ON THE OCCASION OF YALE'S 250TH ANNIVERSARY

PUBLISHED ON THE FOUNDATION ESTABLISHED
IN MEMORY OF OLIVER BATY CUNNINGHAM
OF THE CLASS OF 1917, YALE COLLEGE

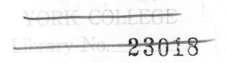

THE OLIVER BATY CUNNINGHAM MEMORIAL
PUBLICATION FUND

The present volume is the twenty-sixth work published by the Yale University Press on the Oliver Baty Cunningham Memorial Publication Fund. This Foundation was established May 8, 1920, by a gift from Frank S. Cunningham, Esq., of Chicago, to Yale University, in memory of his son, Captain Oliver Baty Cunningham, 15th United States Field Artillery, who was born in Chicago, September 17, 1894, and was graduated from Yale College in the Class of 1917. As an undergraduate he was distinguished alike for high scholarship and for proved capacity in leadership among his fellows, as evidenced by his selection as Gordon Brown Prize Man from his class. He received his commission as Second Lieutenant, United States Field Artillery, at the First Officers' Training Camp at Fort Sheridan, and in December, 1917, was detailed abroad for service, receiving subsequently the Distinguished Service Medal. He was killed while on active duty near Thiaucourt, France, on September 17, 1918, the twenty-fourth anniversary of his birth.

JAMES HADLEY, ABOUT 1858

DIARY

---
1 8 4 3 – 1 8 5 2

OF JAMES HADLEY

TUTOR AND PROFESSOR OF GREEK IN

YALE COLLEGE, 1845–1872

EDITED WITH A FOREWORD BY

LAURA HADLEY MOSELEY

25510

NEW HAVEN : YALE UNIVERSITY PRESS

LONDON : GEOFFREY CUMBERLEGE : OXFORD UNIVERSITY PRESS

CONTENTS

ILLUSTRATIONS

FOREWORD

James Hadley was born on March 30, 1821, in Fairfield, Herkimer County, New York, where his father was Professor of Chemistry and Materia Medica in Fairfield Medical College. When he was seven his knee was badly injured in an accident, infection set in, and he was permanently lamed, so that he always had to use a crutch or cane.

He attended Fairfield Academy, and, after finishing the regular course, became an assistant on the Faculty of that school. He entered Yale as a Junior in the fall of 1840, graduating in 1842 with the highest honors. At the time of the first diary entries (1843) he was still studying at Yale, as a "resident graduate," working on higher mathematics and tutoring private pupils. There followed a year in the Yale Theological Seminary and another as tutor in Middlebury College, Vermont. He joined the Yale Faculty in 1845 as a tutor, was appointed Assistant Professor of the Greek Language and Literature in August 1848, and in July 1851 became a full professor. There are fragments of the diary in 1848 and early 1849, but the main portion starts on December 25, 1849, when he was twenty-eight years old, and runs to December 15, 1852, with occasional gaps.

On August 13, 1851, James Hadley married Anne Loring Twining. They had one child, Arthur Twining Hadley, the future president of Yale, who was born in 1856.

James Hadley continued at Yale until his death on November 14, 1872, at the age of fifty-one. He was president of the American Oriental Society, vice-president of the American Philological Association, and a member of the National Academy of Sciences. His field was comparative philology, to the distress of Professor Benjamin Peirce of Harvard, who remarked more than once that he could not forgive Yale College for making the man Professor of Greek who should have been the first mathematician of the country. His *Greek Grammar* was in wide use in America and England for half a century after his death and continues in print today. His "Brief History of the English Language" still appears, with revisions, in *Webster's Dictionary*. He gave lectures on Roman law to undergraduates at Yale and graduates at Harvard, and these, under the title *Introduction to Roman Law,* were issued in 1873 and reissued in 1931. His *Essays Philological and Critical* were likewise published in 1873. They were selected and edited by his colleague and warm friend Professor William Dwight Whitney, who in his preface says of their author: "In extent and accuracy of knowledge, in retentiveness and readiness of memory, in penetration and justness of judgment, I have never met his equal. Whatever others may have done, he was, in the opinion of all who knew him most fully, America's best and soundest philologist."

James Hadley was the son of Dr. James Hadley (1785–1869) and of Maria Hamilton (1793–1873). At the period of the diary his parents were living in Geneva, New York. With them lived James' oldest brother, George, a chemist and geologist, and his sister Mary. There is one reference in the diary to his sister Ann, but apparently she was not customarily a member of the Geneva household. His younger brother Henry Hamilton Hadley, the "Henry" of the diary, was a member of the class of 1847 at Yale, a student in the Yale Theological Seminary in 1848–50 and in Andover Theological Seminary in 1850–51, and a tutor at Yale in 1851 and 1852. Another brother, who died in 1843, is mentioned several times in the diary; he was next younger than James, and bore the name of Hamilton by itself.

Anne (Anna) Loring Twining (November 19, 1816–February 2, 1897) was the daughter of Stephen Twining (1767–1832; Yale 1795) and Almira Catlin (1777–1846). Her father was a New Haven lawyer, and at the time of his death was serving as assistant treasurer of Yale. Anne and her sister Mary lived at 30 Elm Street, opposite the Yale campus. Her brothers Alexander and William and her sister Helen Almira (Mrs. Seagrove William Magill) appear frequently in the diary, along with their wives, husband, and children. Of the latter, Alexander's daughters Julia and Harriet resided for fairly long periods with their aunts at 30 Elm Street.

Further information about James Hadley's life will be found in *Memorials of Eminent Yale Men,* by Anson Phelps Stokes, and in the memoir by his son, Arthur Twining Hadley, in the *Biographical Memoirs* of the National Academy of Sciences, V (1905), 247–254. An account with the flavor of the period is the article by Noah Porter on the death of James Hadley, in the *New Englander* for January 1873. This was also separately printed as a pamphlet, and is most useful in that form, as the pamphlet includes a bibliography of James Hadley's writings and a list, which he had made himself, of his studies up to the age of eighteen (embracing, among other matters, much mathematics and Latin, Greek, Hebrew, Spanish, German, and Italian).

THE YALE OF THE DIARY

In 1849–50 Yale College had an undergraduate body of 386 students. A further 146 were enrolled in Theology, Medicine, Law, and as advanced students in Philosophy and the Arts. The Faculty in all departments numbered 35. Of these, 17 had charge of undergraduate instruction, and others were available for instruction in the modern languages at the student's expense.

The College buildings numbered thirteen, including the President's house and Divinity College. There were four undergraduate dormitories, and impecunious students were allowed to live (and cook) in the recitation rooms in return for taking care of the rooms and keeping up the fires in the stoves. Students were permitted to lodge in the town only when the College rooms were not sufficient to accommodate them all.

The Faculty lived on or close to the campus. James Hadley lived in No. 105 North College until his marriage, when he moved across Elm Street to the Twining house, keeping No. 105 as a study and office. His brother Henry lived in No. 170 Divinity College as a theological student and later as a tutor.

The College day opened with prayers, at 6.30 in winter and at 5.30 in summer. A recitation period followed, and then breakfast. Evening prayers came in the late afternoon. On Sunday, in addition to morning and evening prayers, there were two church services with sermons.

Marks were on the scale of 4.00. Junior and Senior appointments, or honors, began with philosophical orations at the top and descended through various grades of orations, disputes, and colloquies.

Public speaking and debates were a prominent feature of undergraduate life. The Junior class held weekly "disputes," over which, as a member of the Faculty, James Hadley frequently presided. After the reading of essays on the chosen "question," he rendered his "decision," reviewing the arguments brought forward and giving his own opinions on the subject.

Linonia (of which James Hadley was a member) and Brothers in Unity were rival societies devoted to debating and public speaking. They also maintained libraries for the use of their members. The societies campaigned annually for recruits from among the incoming students, each setting forth in a "Statement of Facts" its desirable features and its advantages over the rival organization.

Among the important academic occasions were Junior Exhibition, Presentation Day, and Commencement. Junior Exhibition occurred in the latter part of April. The program embraced some forty items, divided between a morning and an afternoon session. Of these, a dozen were music, and the remainder were orations, dissertations, and poems in Greek, Latin, or English, delivered by the high-ranking Juniors.

Presentation Day, when the names of candidates recommended for the degree were presented, occurred in June or early July, six weeks before Commencement. It was celebrated in much the same way as its successor, the modern Class Day. In 1850 the custom still prevailed of having no recitations for the Senior class after Presentation Day.

Commencement time brought not only the closing ceremonies of the academic year but also the oral examination of candidates for admission. To Commencement of 1850 was added the celebration of the 150th anniversary of the founding of Yale College.

For some time before Commencement, the Faculty received requests from the Seniors to sign in their autograph books, which were embellished, according to the choice of the individual, with engravings of the Faculty, College buildings, and memorials to dead classmates. When signing his name, it was customary for a member of the Faculty to add some motto or quotation. James Hadley's were frequently in Greek.

Undergraduate high spirits had annual outlet in the Burial of

Euclid and the Wooden Spoon Exhibition. On some November night, the Sophomores, escorted by the rest of the student body, would inter the hated Euclid in the woods on Prospect Hill, to the accompaniment of dirges, funeral orations, torchlights, costumes, alcohol, and Faculty disapprobation.

The Wooden Spoon was awarded at first to the biggest eater in Commons, later to the lowest man on the list of Junior appointments, and still later to the most popular man in the Junior class. The presentation ceremony, which began as a burlesque of the academic Junior Exhibition, developed into a leading social event of the undergraduate year.

For reminiscences of Yale life at this period, as well as for photographs of the Faculty, the reader is referred to *Memories of Yale Life and Men,* by Timothy Dwight.

THE MANUSCRIPT

James Hadley kept his diary on loose sheets of paper. The sheets for the year 1850 he bound together a few months later, and that year is complete. The bound sheets, together with many loose ones, survived in a box with other family papers. The loose sheets have been sorted out and arranged, but there are many gaps.

In some instances it is clear, on internal evidence, that the gaps are due to the fact that James Hadley failed to keep up his diary. In other instances it is equally clear that sheets have been lost. There are indications in the diary that a few of the pages written during his courtship were destroyed by him soon after writing.

The manuscript diary, which will be found in the Yale Library, covers the following dates:

1843 February 24–June 4. No pages are missing, but on most days James Hadley failed to keep his diary.
1848 February 27–April 15. May 8. October 14–29.
1849 March 7, 11. December 25–31.
1850 January 1–December 31.
1851 January 1–February 21. February 27–March 7. March 11–March 30. April 1–August 12. September 22–December 31.
1852 January 1–16. May 6–December 15.

For reasons of length, reinforced by those of readability, it has been necessary to omit about a quarter of the extant diary from the printed version. In the period from 1843 through October 6, 1851, the cutting has been confined largely to repetitions of daily routine: recitations, preparation for classes, trivial matters of discipline, academic paper work, correspondence, callers, "10–11½ at Henry's room," bedtime, and weather. Here and there sample days have been left in full to show the normal occupations of the College year. An occasional abstract or discussion of a sermon heard by James Hadley has been omitted, but his religious soliloquies have been retained, as they are necessary to a complete picture of both the man and his day. From October 7, 1851, on (after the return from the wedding trip), the record, though frequently charming, is largely of uneventful social and domestic matters. It has seemed expedient to omit the greater part of these, and to print from this section chiefly the entries that throw light on College or local history or on people in whom the public has had a continuing interest.

With a view to smoothing the reader's way, abbreviations have been expanded, misspellings (save for the most flavorful) corrected, and punctuation and capitalization brought into reasonable conformity with the usage of today. Expansion of abbreviations has not been indicated unless the meaning is conjectural; in the latter case square brackets have been used. Anyone with a technical interest in the forms of a century ago is referred to the manuscript in the Yale Library.

A few notes have been appended to the diary, and the index contains biographical information about people mentioned in the text.

The editor gratefully acknowledges the help and counsel of Morris Hadley, who presumably was the first person since his grandfather, James Hadley, to read the diary, and who proposed its publication, arranged and copied the manuscript, and provided much background material. To Nicholas Moseley, for his assistance, interest, and forbearance, the editor's warmest thanks are also rendered.

LAURA HADLEY MOSELEY

DIARY (1843-1852) OF JAMES HADLEY

SPECIMEN OF JOURNALIZING—1843

FEBRUARY, 1843

Friday, February 24. I enter on the business of journalizing, so often commenced, so often laid aside after a few days' trial, in a very unpretending way and without any high-raised expectations. In these notes I may jot down at random such matters of interest as may from time to time occur either to myself or to those in whom I feel concerned. If in my reading anything curious or striking present itself, it may perhaps find admission here. Of course I shall not exclude my own thoughts, feelings, and opinions, should the caprice of the moment prompt me to record them. This journal is, in short, designed to serve as a kind of omnium-gatherum, and will be conducted on most catholic principles. My former efforts in the same line have failed, I think, chiefly on account of the tedious strictness with which I adhered to a plan originally adopted. Now, as I begin without plan and mean to go on in the same way, I may escape the irksomeness which led to the abandonment of previous attempts. If I do not feel in the humor I shall not write at all, and when I do write it shall be as the humor of the moment dictates. Yet I intend to record occasionally some of my feelings on religious matters, feelings which have never been noticed in my former diaries simply because they had no existence. The truth is that for some years past I have led a miserably godless unspiritual life. My attention has been engrossed by the things of earth. This had become the case to a very sad extent before I entered College, October 1840. But since that time the evil has frightfully increased. I have indeed attended a variety of religious meetings with tolerable regularity and have occasionally borne a part in their proceedings. But this has been a mere outside show, a piece of heartless formality; I have *entirely* neglected the reading of the Scriptures and the practice of private devotion. I have passed through a period of general interest on religious subjects with almost perfect unconcern. I have spent the Sabbath not in its appropriate employments of public and private devotion, but in the ordinary studies or reading of the week. I have given loose to every species of frivolity and buffoonery, indulging in many vulgar and profligate thoughts, and sometimes making light even of sacred things. Of course my whole influence instead of being favorable to religion has been adverse to it, and God only knows how much guilt I may thus have incurred. I do not write in the lust of self-abasement, striving after rhetorical exaggerations of my own misdeeds, but I am using the language of truth and soberness when I say that for several years my whole life has been irreligious. The causes of this state I will not dwell upon, farther than to affirm that, so far as I know myself, College ambition has not been among the number. At length, within the last two weeks the news of a brother's death has roused me to reflection. It seems in fact an authoritative call, which cannot be disregarded without risk of eternal shame. I have commenced studying the Bible and praying to God with such utterance as I can muster; but my performances hitherto have been deplorably feeble, and it is only a strong resolution which can lead me to persevere. May Heaven give me strength for the effort. In truth, how can one expect to shake off in a day the lethargy of years? I feel most thoroughly that without divine assistance I must utterly fail. The great difficulty which I have to encounter is the difficulty of enlisting my own feelings: turn over as I may in mind my own long-continued and aggravated iniquity, my utter pollution and absolute helplessness, I cannot feel them as I ought. But I hope that by dwelling continually and intently on these things I may bring myself to contemplate them with proper emotions.

MARCH, 1843

Sunday, March 5. It is dangerous for a man to felicitate himself on what he is going to do. I expected to write in these pages with some degree of regularity. But more than a week has passed since my first record without seeing a single note or notice. How have I fared in that time? Health good. But what have I done? Alas, but little. Monday and Tuesday last I spent in getting my solutions ready for Mr. Peirce. I sent no solution of the first, nor any of the fourth that deserves to be called a solution. Have read something in the *Mécanique Céleste,* of which however I became tired, and took up DeMorgan's *Calculus,* chapter on the application of calculus to mechanics. Spent some time in reading Bulwer's *Last of the Barons.* In spiritual affairs I have come far short of what I aimed at. I find a prevailing unspirituality, a lack of feeling, a want of interest on religious subjects, which I know not how to

account for. May God help me to overcome this apathy and to
engage earnestly and strenuously in his service.

This afternoon I heard young Dr. Beecher, late President of
Illinois College—nay for anything I know he may be President
of it still, though he has been for some time at the East. He is
about 40 years of age, a middle-sized man, very good-looking, with
a fine high forehead. He preached extemporaneously and with a
good deal of power.

Today I have made my first acquaintance with Dr. Tully. He
called at 8 A.M. to see my roommate, who is unwell, and stayed
about 2 hours. I was much interested in his conversation. Will state
some particulars which I learned from him. Dr. Nathan Smith
was an illiterate man. Never could read a printed book with fluency
—wrote a lecture in New H. but could not read it. Married rich.
Went to Edinburgh and studied there. Came back with the idea
of starting a medical school. Applied to Yale for the countenance
of the Corporation—found he was illiterate and turned him off.
Went to Dartmouth and set up there. Had no assistants for some
years. Little knowledge of chemistry. When Tully was there, had
got Dr. Graves to lecture on chemistry, but sometimes came in and
talked himself. On one such occasion he professed his entire dis-
belief in the alleged marvels of nitrous-oxide gas, saying he had
never succeeded in obtaining it. Tully and Fish (a fellow student
of Tully's) stepped up after lecture and, stating that they had prepared it several times, offered to give Dr. Smith at the next lecture
an opportunity of testing its virtues. The offer was accepted and
the gas manufactured in large quantities. None of the class were
willing to try it lest they should be led to commit some impropriety
in the lecture room. "Well," said the Doctor, "if nobody else will
come forward I'll try it myself." Accordingly Fish administered
it, giving all necessary directions, but out of regard to Dr. Smith
he took care (much to Tully's dissatisfaction) to give but a small
dose. The worthy man, however, was much elated; he got up and
strode about for a minute or two, when, coming to himself, he
exclaimed, "Well, I believe there is something in it after all."

Tully was acquainted with Noyes—tells a story of his giving a
dose of Glauber's salts to a young student who had some slight
ailment. The Doctor's salts had effloresced, and, supposing them
to have become weakened instead of having gained in strength from
this circumstance, he administered a double dose. But, finding out
his mistake in this particular, he gave a strong dose of tartar emetic

to bring up some of the salts, never reflecting on the chemical action which must result from this admixture. The consequence was that the young man was almost killed by the purging.

At Dartmouth Dr. Tully heard a course on anatomy by Dr. Ramsay, of which he speaks in high terms. He became acquainted there with one Sylvester (that he believes to be the name) who went on to Fairfield and started the medical school there. He wrote to Dr. Tully pressing him to take the chair of chemistry, or any other which he wished. Dr. Tully declined taking any. Sylvester then employed Noyes. In 1822 Dr. Tully went to Castleton, a school established by Dr. Woodward, an old acquaintance of his. Says that he never got more than $300 for any course at Castleton. At New Haven he averaged about $250 a course. In 1837 (if I mistake not—the Doctor did not give the date) after the close of the fall term, Dr. Woodward became insane—had manifested symptoms of mental alienation before, but nobody suspected anything. Dr. Tully was president of the Corporation at the time, and except the annual meeting none could be legally held which was not called by him. Nevertheless, at Perkins' instigation (he was the only physician among them, and frightened them by intimating that the professors wished to move the school to Albany), they met and turned out all the professors, but did not inform them of the fact, designing indeed to keep it a profound secret. At the same time they instituted a suit in chancery against Woodward, for whom his children appeared, to recover certain property which had been procured by the professors and was held in Woodward's name. The case was pushed through and the court decided that the property should be given up to the Trustees when Woodward's debt of $600 on the same account should have been paid off by them. The court did not know of any other debts of the same kind, though Tully alone had advanced $800. Well, ignorant of all this, Tully set out for Castleton in the winter following. The course was to commence on Thursday and he arrived in Albany the Saturday previous. Dr. Armsby then communicated these proceedings, which he had privately heard from a young lawyer in Castleton. He had been inclined to consider it as a hoax, and had written to learn more exactly what the truth might be. On Sunday morning they received a farther letter confirming the former and adding other particulars. Dr. Armsby then went on to Castleton and, coming unexpectedly upon the new clerk, got a sight of the proceedings.

The Corporation then met and after some deliberation called in Armsby and questioned him, but adjourned without making much out of him. Before this Dr. Armsby had sent certain of Tully's effects to Granville in New York, 15 miles from Castleton, for fear they might be attached. He was not allowed a key to visit his own anatomical collection. He decoyed a young merchant with him to Granville to drive back horse and sleigh and thus left Castleton on Wednesday morning. Many students were intercepted on their way both here (Granville) and at Albany. It was well ascertained that there would have been not less than 80 students. Some who reached Castleton stayed awhile to plague the new president of the Corporation, an honest farmer, by asking him teasingly what share he was to take in the instruction of the school. At length 30 of them went over to Woodstock, where the Pittsfield Faculty had been lecturing for 2 weeks to 6 students and had resolved to stop in a week if they received no recruits.

Soon after, Tully, who had returned to New Haven, received some letters from Perkins in which he was informed that all his titles and offices excepting one of the professorships which he held were restored to him, and wishing to know the terms on which he would return. Tully's demands were high and the whole thing fell through.

Pittsfield school started by Dr. Batchelder in a miff—sent away from Castleton. Double letters sent by him from time to time in a disguised hand to his old colleagues. Finally ousted from Pittsfield itself.

12 students on the medical catalogue of Yale this year who have not attended a single lecture. Catalogue early.

Tully dislikes Dr. Delamater. Accounts of his intriguing at Sheffield, riding masonry, religion, etc. Similar proceedings of his friend Dr. Ticknor at Salisbury, who ousts Fish.

Note: Dr. Tully has a sad opinion of the progress and prospects of the medical profession. Scantiness of the physician's income. New Haven: Knight, he says, could not support himself but for his surgery. Ives, Beers, and Hooker, who are brothers-in-law, club together and support one another, though not without sparring between Ives and Hooker. Besides them, no other city physician gets more than $300 a year, excepting Dr. More, whom they are doing their utmost to dislodge. Play off Dr. Jewett, worst of all scholars except Peter Parker. Low opinion of Parker. Tully voted against graduating him. Tie among the Faculty, Knight going against him also. Silliman for him. Saved by one vote, the casting vote, Dr. Buel.

Monday, March 6. Visited Professor Stanley this afternoon, and had some not-uninteresting conversation. Read and wrote during the evening. God grant me strength to attend more tomorrow and every future day of my life, than I have this day, to spiritual concerns.

Tuesday, March 7. The world has been surprised of late by the appearance of a very splendid comet. I do not know that it was observed here until Sunday evening. Monday evening at 7 o'clock the cry was, "Heads out," and on looking a fine comet was visible in the southwest near the horizon. Only the train could be seen. Indeed I know not that any nucleus has been observed. Tonight the appearance, which took place at nearly the same hour and in nearly the same part of the heavens, was considerably more striking. It figured as a broad band of white light, stretching obliquely downward at an angle of 45° with the horizon. Its length must have been not far from 25°. The moon was shining brightly at the time within a short distance from the comet, the brightness of which was no doubt much diminished by this circumstance. Had it been otherwise, I cannot help thinking that this appearance would have been among the most extraordinary on record. I am impatient to learn what astronomers make out with regard to its course and dimensions.

Spent the evening in a ridiculous discussion with some friends. Saints protect me from passing another in the same idle way.

JUNE, 1843

Thursday, June 1. Recommence journalizing after a *short* interval or respite of something like 3 months. Singular that my last entry should have appertained to the great comet of 1843, the greatest phenomenon, according to Mr. Walker, ever known, and destined to form an era, before which all other eras must "hide their diminished heads." Certainly of all the remarkable circumstances connected with the present comet, not the least remarkable is the series of publications made by that gentleman relative to it. Gathering inspiration from his subject, or rather "catching its humour," he has pursued a most erratic course, taking up his position successively in every quarter of the heavens, as though he considered the entire firmament as created for the especial behoof and full proprietorship of Mr. Walker and the Philada High School. I am disposed, notwithstanding the undeniable inaccuracy of his earlier calculations, and a certain slippery way, occasionally betrayed and not eminently adapted to secure confidence, I am disposed, I say, to put some faith in his last results. Professor Stanley is quite incredulous, or was so on Saturday last. He thinks it unaccountable that the carefully corrected parabolic elements of Mr. Walker should give an inclination differing by 12° from that of the hyperbolic elements, which are said to account even better for the observed position. It seems to me, however, a sticking fact that the sum of the squares of the errors is on the hyperbolic orbit only one hundredth of what it was on the parabolic. So says Mr. Walker, and as he has now acquired a good deal of experience in these calculations and has besides very respectable coadjutors, may we not believe him? But I feel disposed to dwell pretty thoroughly on Mr. Herrick's question, "Where is the centre of gravity of the comet of 1843?" We must of course in our calculations take the apparent middle point of the nucleus, but can we trust our result? We can assign no other point with any greater probability, but after all what probability belongs to the one we take?

Friday, June 2. I am in the middle of a very troublesome cold, the only severe one I have had for a twelvemonth. I was attacked on Monday. Tuesday my nostrils and fauces felt as if on fire. Wednesday the burning sensation disappeared, but I became hoarse, and had unpleasantly copious ejections from the nose. Thursday, same symptoms aggravated. Friday, somewhat less hoarseness, and less mucus, but a tickling in the throat and a disposition to cough. It came on with great violence, and had it not been for applications of cold water, hot water, and fleshbrushes, would have proved a serious affair.

I am at present pretty well occupied in teaching. I have four pupils. 1. Taylor, a young man who, after preparing for Harvard, applied for admission here into the Sophomore class. Deficient in mathematics; had read enough but, not reviewing, had forgotten much; has a decided aptitude for mathematics, and will be able to enter in the course of 4 or 5 weeks. Recommended to me by

Professor Kingsley, who called in on Tuesday to inquire about his progress. 2. White, from South Carolina. Studied at Charleston High School and Charleston College. Wishes to enter the present Freshman class when they become Sophomores. Good in mathematics, but far from thoroughly grounded in the languages. He seems to be industrious and persevering. Introduced to me by his cousin Mr. Brickell of the Sophomore class. 3. Babcock, from Washington College. Applied at close of last term for admission into the Freshman class. Deficient in mathematics; commenced under Hubbard of our class, but recited only twice; began with me about a week before the term opened and had 7 recitations; knew only the four simple rules of algebra and those very imperfectly. I took him through "fractions," and tried to initiate him a little into the mysteries of simple and quadratic equations, but he is not an apt scholar and is lazy withal, so that my success was not conspicuous. He applied for admission and was again rejected. He is required, besides the algebra, to catch up with the class in geometry; they read the first book of Euclid last term. He can do it if he will work, but I have my fears, and unless he pulls up, I will have nothing to do with him. 4. Hayden, a member of the Freshman class. Became mystified in geometry, does not understand it, and cannot get the lessons. He has recited only once. Will get along I think. Sent to me by Professor Thacher.

These are my pupils: of course considerable time is occupied in hearing them. Indeed during the present week I have accomplished little else. Half knocked up by a bad cold, I have felt by no means in the mood for vigorous study. The immortal Boz has solaced many of my weary hours. I have read his *Pickwick Papers,* at least the last 4 volumes (the first volume could not be obtained). Wonderful book—is it not better than any of his subsequent productions? It is less diluted certainly. To me, indeed, its fertility of thought and humor seem quite miraculous. As soon as I get a little clear of this cold, I shall go on with Cournot's *Integral Calculus,* after which I shall probably read Poisson's *Mécanique.* I mean to attend also to German. If I can get an opportunity to acquire an accurate pronunciation I shall avail myself of it. Indeed if I had but this, I think it probable that I might have taken the optional class in German during the present summer. They were expecting to recite to a Mr. Werner, a native German, but he has left New Haven; and they are now instructed by Professor Woolsey, who was, however, averse to the task.

Professor Olmsted called on me this afternoon, and mentioned that Dr. Dunbar of Natchez had just arrived at New Haven bringing with him a nephew named Suchet (such I conjecture to be the spelling: the pronunciation was *Sooshay*), a young man who wishes to enter the next Freshman class, and desires to obtain an instructor in the meantime, that is, until Commencement. I consented to take him, but made no particular arrangements. Professor Olmsted wishes me to keep an account of his recitations, and report to him. If discipline be necessary, he undertakes to administer it, for which I feel greatly obliged to him. He very kindly invited me to take tea with him, an invitation which I at first accepted, but afterwards reluctantly excused myself on the ground of my cold. I had a slight attack of colick or flatulence this afternoon, for which I took a few drops of laudanum with entire relief. I judged it best, however, to refrain from supper.

I learn today that Mr. Walker has abandoned his hyperbola, and come back again to the ellipse. I have not, however, seen his paper.

As for Babcock, he comes on very indifferently, and I think I must advise him to wait until Commencement, and join the class which will then be entering College.

Saturday, June 3. Dr. Dunbar called here this morning with his nephew Mr. Suzette. He is a man of pleasing manners, and apparently much interested in the success of his young relative. As regards the latter, he told me privately that he is prone to dejection and discouragement, distrustful of his own powers and timid to a fault; he has received his education from a private teacher, a very critical one, says the Doctor. Under him he has read all the books required for admission into College, but protests that he has forgotten all he ever knew.

My cold today is somewhat less troublesome; there seems to be, however, a disposition to cough, which I do not quite like and of which I must if possible rid myself.

Have been reading recent numbers of *Fraser's Magazine,* the *Dublin University Magazine,* and the *Westminster Review,* all for May 1843. In the first two, find absolutely nothing worth reading. In the third, there is a clever article (by G.G.) on the early legends of Greece. The author contends very strongly that we have no Grecian history previous to 776 B.C.—that the accounts of the Argonautic Expedition, the Theban Wars, the Siege of Troy, etc. *may be* founded on actual occurrences or *may not,* we cannot tell which, much less separate the true from the false or use them as materials of authentic history. He therefore censures alike those who have put upon them an allegorical interpretation, as did Anaxagoras and Metrodorus, and those who, like Thucydides, Polybius, and Strabo, have arbitrarily changed them, by retrenching improbabilities, putting new colors on the events, professing thus to have determined the actual grounds on which they rest. He insists much on the ease with which fictions wholly groundless arise, and gain extensive currency even at the present day.

The same Review contains an article on the philosophy of Spinoza. (Benedict Spinoza, a Jew of Amsterdam, lived about the middle of the 17th century; early proficiency; abandons Judaism, but never embraces Christianity; earns a scanty subsistence by polishing lenses; refuses liberal offers of support; dies at the age of 45. Attracted by the Cartesian philosophy, but does not receive it; holds to a reality called by him *noumenon* as the basis of all *phenomena;* this *noumenon* he denominates *substance,* and considers it as God—makes *extension* and *thought* attributes of *substance;* his agreement with the transcendentalists—Kant, Schelling, Hegel; called by Novalis, "a God-intoxicated man"; those who study ontology become almost universally pantheists.)

Sunday, June 4. Had a hacking cough this morning, for which took several spoonfuls of dissolved tartar emetic; sickened myself more than I had intended; was obliged to keep my room during the forenoon, but went out and heard Dr. Fitch in the afternoon.

✳   ✳   ✳

FEBRUARY, 1848

Sunday, February 27, 1848. If I should be called suddenly or soon out of this life, it may be a satisfaction to my friends to know that for some weeks past I have been making serious endeavors to lead a godly life—endeavors, alas, how weak and imperfect, "but that which I have done, may He within Himself make pure." It is my most ardent longing to escape from the dominion of the earthly and the sensual; to dwell habitually in a spiritual world; to look beyond the objects of time, uncertain in attainment, uncertain in duration, but certain not to last long and equally certain not to satisfy the soul even while they last; to fix upon that which is fixed in itself; to plant myself upon a foundation which shall be firm in prosperity and in adversity, that prosperity may not be embittered by harassing alarms and adversity find the soul without resource or solace; to obtain that hope which shall be an anchor to the soul both sure and steadfast; and thus to merge the temporary in the eternal; to live less as a mortal than as an immortal being; to face continually the solemn realities of the invisible world; that the chances and changes of time, contrasted with eternal fixities, may sink into nothingness, that death itself may make but little change to a mind that cares little for all it terminates, and has long been familiar in thought with all it ushers in. May God help me to attain these objects of my most fervent wishes and petitions. Amen.

Monday, February 28. Recitations as usual. Shall soon commence reviewing the *Gorgias*. Weather dull; slight snowstorm in the evening. My cold rather freer; looseness of bowels occasioned by Dr. Tully's prescription, pills of morphine and veratrine with aloes, of which I have been taking 3 or 4 a day for nearly a week, but which have only just broken out. Shall discontinue them. German with Henry at evening. Very sleepy. Bed at 11. Received an invitation to a party at Mrs. Devereux's on Thursday evening. Shall not be able to attend. Meeting of Philological Society. Sorry; should like to become acquainted with Mrs. Devereux.

May God forgive my forgetfulness of him and enable me to act with more constant reference to his will and his glory.

MARCH, 1848

Tuesday. Made notes for decision on Irish repeal.

Wednesday. Evening, called on Miss Field. Staid too late, as usual.

Thursday. Meeting of Philological Society at Professor Porter's. Tennyson's *Princess* read between 11 and 1.

Friday. Heard Miss Bacon's recent statement of the MacWhorter case. Written with great vehemence of style and some ingenuity —no names mentioned. Dr. Taylor attacked with excessive bitterness; compared to a certain John King of London who endeavored on false pretences, by threatening to circulate slanderous reports, to extort money from a lady. Miss Beecher's statement on the same subject I was also allowed to read—a rather old-maidish production, not without ingenuity, very incorrect in style, and somewhat flighty as to matters of fact—and marked a certain fussy and fidgety air which is exceedingly characteristic. Both productions have very little that is at all explicit on the course of circumstances and relations as between the parties prior to the grand explosion in February or March 1847.[1] Shown to me by Hodges.

Notes for decision on suicide of Cato. Preparatory lecture by Dr. Taylor.

Saturday. Saw Dr. Bacon's protest. Talked with Larned and Mac-Whorter on the Baconian movement. Sermon by Professor Porter.

Sunday, March 5. Communion. Some devotional feelings, but much distracted by wandering thoughts. May God make me more spiritual. Learned Galatians, chapter 5. MacWhorter in the evening. Curious history of Miss Bacon.

Wednesday, March 8. Wrote a letter to Mr. George Hill of Washington, substitute poet of ΦBK Society. In evening called on Miss Field with copy of Horace Bushnell's Alumni Address on Progress of Morals. Talked on ideas of future state. I discouraged attempts to conceive definitely the modes of existence which belong to it.

Monday, March 13. In afternoon, committee on College laws, first session, at ½ past 2. Members: President, Professors Olmsted and Thacher, and Tutor Hadley. Divided out the business. Broke up at 4. Prayers for first time at 5½ P.M. Tomorrow morning at 6.

Tuesday, March 14. Afternoon, conversation with Mr. Thacher, and at 4 with Professor Stanley on Leverrier's recent letter to Mr. Maury in reply to Professor Peirce. Leverrier seems to have Peirce on the hip as respects one or two things. In evening wrote something on the West Point School for question tomorrow.

Wednesday, March 15. In evening called on Miss Larned and Miss Field. Read to latter Henry's Junior Exhibition speech, which she was much pleased with. Also some ludicrous prose and poetry from the *Democratic Review* for March 1848. Home at 10 and soon after abed.

Thursday, March 16. Mr. Eustis examined today and installed over Chapel Street Church. Sermon by Mr. Thompson. Charge by Dr. Bacon with oblique countercharge to Mr. MacWhorter. Did not attend the exercises.

Friday, March 17. Afternoon, conversation with Mr. Stanley: proposes to republish Dalby on Spherics, has not time to write a treatise himself. Says that Mr. Peirce never charged Leverrier with overlooking the variation in the elements of Uranus. It was Mr. Mitchell who did this. In evening attended church meeting. Mr. Woolsey spoke on importance of deep convictions of sin. Hubbard, Senior, followed in a very noble spirit. Attended meeting of "Our Society" at Mrs. E. E. Salisbury's. Went down at 8 o'clock, first male creature on the ground. Broke up early, before 10. Did not get around among my friends. Was presented to Mrs. Devereux and apologized for my absence a fortnight since.

Saturday, March 18. Question on policy of Puritans towards the Indians—feebly discussed. Undertook to talk about it with no previous preparation, succeeded very badly as I deserved. Afternoon, tutors' meeting. Went to call on MacWhorter. Stumbled into wrong house and got half way up stairs, but turned back precipitately by hearing a piano and seeing a feminine, incompatible with character of Stag Hall. Stopped in at Pease's. Great news from France—émeute and abdication. Tutor Goodrich came in, and Robert Fiske. In evening, sermon by Mr. Porter, thinly attended—many gone to Exchange to hear General Sam Houston. Tried to draw up a chapter of laws on location of students. Long talk with Hurlbutt, who is wallowing in gloomy deeps of despondency. Said what I could to guide him onward and upward, but God knows how miserably fitted I am to act as religious mentor to any man.

Monday, March 20. Committee on College laws at 2½ P.M. Professor Olmsted reported, and President Woolsey. No time for me, though I had spent the forenoon in drawing up a chapter on location.

Tuesday, March 21. Called on Larned in the afternoon. Read me something on the scrimmage, fragments of an impartial statement.

Wednesday, March 22. In the evening cut the Connecticut Academy, and called on Miss Field. Brought Tennyson's *Princess* on the tapis, talked about it, read from it. At last left the book and came away, some time after 10 o'clock.

Thursday, March 23. In evening Mr. Thacher called in and read his notice of Tyler's *Tacitus, Germany and Agricola*. A very judicious piece. After some general praise, points out by a critical examination of a few pages the very serious inaccuracies which deform the book. Very different from the honeyed review in the *Bibliotheca Sacra,* which professes to emanate from an association of teachers, said association consisting probably (as Mr. Thacher suggested) of Professors Lincoln, Tyler, and Robbins, whose works are reviewed in the article.

Friday, March 24. In afternoon attended Whig meeting. Heard Mr. Thompson of Indiana, an inaccurate but humorous and pointed and effective speaker. Tom Corwin I saw, and heard him say a few words, a dull heavy-looking man. Did not go to hear him in the evening. Great jam, they say.

Saturday. Afternoon, called on Dr. Forbes, MacWhorter not being in. Had some interesting conversation on the French. Called at Pease's and got last number of *North British Review,* which I read the rest of the afternoon and through the evening, except time spent in hearing a sermon of Professor Porter after tea, on Galatians 2.20. "We should live by faith in the son of God as our example, our Savior from sin and death, our ever present helper." God enable me so to live, for Christ's sake. Amen.

Sunday, March 26. Spent much time in prayer, not without feeling. Dr. Fitch preached in the afternoon his sermon on Lazarus and Dives, beautifully written, badly listened to. In evening read some little in Greek grammar. Conversation with Henry. I wish that I might have greater seriousness and spirituality in my conversation, so as to make some definite religious impression on such as come within the circle of my influence.

Monday, March 27. Lesson in forenoon. Heard Walker read his Junior Exhibition piece at 12. Conversed with Hubbard on Chinese language. At 2½, committee on College laws. Reported a chapter on location. Mr. Thacher on matriculation, etc. In evening talked with Henry—with Gilman on his difficulties with Brace.

How difficult I find it to carry into particular action, into study and business and amusement, into the things which I say and do, the spirit of a Christian—a feeling of God's presence, accompanied by the love and gratitude and devotion which such a feeling should inspire.

Tuesday, March 28. Read Mr. Webster's speech on the loan bill, a very brilliant affair. Notes for a decision on pulpit and bar as theatre for eloquence. Received piece of Greek poetry from Hurlbut. Not very Greek and not very poetical.

Wednesday, March 29. Before breakfast, made Hurlbut go over his piece and translate it—many inaccuracies. In forenoon Mr. Kingsley gave me some account of Dr. Jarvis' late article in answer to himself, filled with ridiculous blunders. Faculty meeting. Bowie brought up for intoxication. Singular case—pleaded guilty before Civil Court and not guilty before us. Tutor Hurlbutt got the mumps. Quite prevalent.

Attended political meeting in the evening and heard Horace Greeley and Cassius M. Clay. The former spoke well, the latter poorly—very poorly, in matter and manner.

Thursday, March 30. My birthday, but did not much notice it. A busy time. Should have thought and prayed more on such an occasion. Remade the first stanza for Hurlbut's poem. Got a first lesson in *Electra* in afternoon. In evening Mr. Brace gave me a singular explanation as to his relations with Mr. Emerson. At 8 went to call on Miss Field. Most agreeable conversation. Came away at 10.

Undertook to engage in religious exercises, but soon fell asleep and did not wake up till 12½. Bed at 1.

APRIL, 1848

Wednesday, April 5. Called in evening on Professor Salisbury and then on Miss Field. She will leave New Haven on Monday, not to reside here any longer. I have taken great pleasure in her society for the last two or three months, and shall feel her absence very sensibly.

Sermon by Henry Beecher.

Friday, April 7. In the evening notes on question, Constitutional power of Congress to exclude slavery from territory newly acquired.

Saturday, April 8. Interesting news from Europe. Disturbances in Austria.

Last of the disputes. Rather poor. Failed in the decision.

Afternoon, Faculty meeting. Some time at Henry's room talking on οὐ and μή, playing on flute. Some time at Pease's. Philological conversation with Sobieski.

Evening, sermon by Professor Porter.

Sunday, April 9. Election day in France. Heard Dr. Bushnell at Centre Church in forenoon. Admirable sermon on "first love," from Revelation 2.5. Dr. Fitch in afternoon—quite heavy—I or he. In the evening went to North Church, thinking that perhaps Dr. Bushnell would preach, but he did not and Mr. Dutton did.

Monday, April 10. Important news from Europe by *Hibernia*. Dispersed a party of ball-playing Sophomores at 3 P.M. Faculty meeting at 2 to nominate tutors. Selden cannot come. Davis, Harrison, and Talcott nominated.

Thursday, April 13. Hurlbut's poem, the second time, considerably more correct, especially in metre—rather prosaic. I wish he had written in prose. It would have lightened my labor. Called on Miss Twining; talked about Upham's *Interior Life,* which she recommended and offered to lend me. Called on Miss Larned, but found that she left the place a week ago, when Miss Dutton's school broke up.

MAY, 1848

Monday, May 8. Here occurs one of those long blanks which are wont to diversify—I was going to say disfigure, but that is a matter of taste—the diaries of men who have not the patience of Job or the perseverance of the Grecian princes before the walls of Troy. Examination week, which followed immediately after my last record, was a busy time, though interrupted by what students generally regard as a holyday—the annual state fast, appointed as usual for Good Friday, which this year falls unusually late. Monday, April 24, I conducted the Berkeleian examination in Greek, the President being prevented from doing so by considerations of delicacy, as his nephew was one of the candidates. Of the two men, Winthrop appeared to have made the more thorough and careful preparation, Colton to possess the more of general knowledge about Greek and Latin. They were declared equal, and drew lots for the precedence, which fell to Colton. Junior Exhibition, on Tuesday, April 25, went off respectably—two very fair poems by Waring and Finch. From Tuesday to Friday, read *Jane Eyre* and *Wuthering Heights*—the first excellent—the second much inferior, showing decided power, but stuffed with a complication of savagery and brutal wickedness, at once repulsive, unartistic, and unintelligible. On Friday Henry returned to Geneva with a son of Dr. Bacon in his company.

Since then I have finished up on the *Gorgias* and commenced preparing for the *Prometheus,* which I am to have next term, as Hurlbutt will take optics. I am engaged in reading diligently on the Greek theatre.

OCTOBER, 1848

Saturday, October 14, 1848. A broken day—a good deal of leisure, ill improved. Little addition to my article on Dr. Owen, to whom, by the way, I ought to write my acknowledgments for that copy of his *Thucydides* which I ought to have received but have not. Mem., ask him where he sent it. Should have called on Willard to enlist his aid in cataloguing the Theologs, but forgot it. Afternoon in the libraries with Henry. Occupied some time in looking up authorities on Platonic Logos and Trinity, notions which, if they exist at all in Plato, exist, I suspect, only as rudiments scarcely to be recognized. The apostles found a developed doctrine of the Logos—post-Platonic—did they find a developed Trinity? Henry is to write an essay on this subject so far as it relates to Plato. Evening, settled some old scores. Called at Miss Dutton's to see Miss Larned, went thence to MacWhorter's, read the first half of Miss Bacon's testimony, and got home quarter to 12. Pennsylvania sure for the Whigs. Ohio doubtful, but probably Locofoco.

Faith raises the mind to higher objects, widens it by introducing a world invisible and eternal, gives unity to our whole existence by bringing the narrow present and the boundless future into mutual connection, action and reaction, withdraws us from actual imperfection to ideal perfection, and so gives scope for feelings of love, reverence, devotion, which earthly objects never could call forth.

Sunday, October 15. Dr. Fitch in the morning on faith in spiritual and invisible realities—an excellent sermon. Wrote a prayer on that theme. Mr. Dutton on the sanctifying power of the Atonement compared with that of the law—better than I ever before heard him do. Read some of Dr. Arnold's Rugby sermons—very admirable in matter and in manner. Plain handling of school matters— the peculiar circumstances, views, feelings, temptations, faults, follies, vices of a large public school—in this respect worthy of imitation. May I be sedulous to learn the evils of College, and having learned them, to rebuke them not harshly but plainly and unsparingly. Our College a very different place from his school—less of the small boy—more of the man—yet alike in some important particulars, especially in mutual influence and in dread of a somewhat corrupt public opinion.

Wrote to Honorable Ashbel Smith, substitute orator, and Dr. O. W. Holmes, substitute poet of ΦBK, apprizing them of failure of principals.

Monday, October 16. Made tolerably good speed with my review, which lacks but a page or two more. Hope to finish it tomorrow if not prevented by meeting of the Oriental Society.

Thursday, October 19. On Tuesday finished up my article, which will fill nine or ten pages of the *Bibliotheca*. Sent it off to Professor Edwards with a request that he would act his pleasure as to printing it, and that, if he chose to print, he would make any alterations he might think advisable.

Wednesday afternoon at 2 o'clock we had our Faculty meeting. At 3 went down to Professor Salisbury's to attend meeting of the Oriental Society. Found Dr. Robinson, Dr. Owen, and Professor Turner (W. W.) from New York, Professor Edwards from Andover, Dr. Anderson from Boston, Dr. Jarvis from Middletown, Reverend Messrs. Bingham, Brown, and Calhoun, missionaries, and one or two others beside our New Haven people. Society organized, Dr. Robinson in the chair. Corresponding secretary presented some interesting communications from missionaries abroad. Others read by Dr. Robinson, some especially on recent exploration of Dead Sea. Dr. Jarvis then proceeded to disinter the mummies, and continued his Artesian processes until after 6 o'clock, when he was induced to defer the remainder until tomorrow morning. Society adjourned at 6½, after an invitation to Professor Salisbury's parlor for 7. As it rained quite hard I did not leave during the interval. Had a pleasant evening—conversation with Dr. Owen, Dr. Anderson, Professor Edwards, Mr. Brown, etc. Dr. Owen appears to be an amiable and excellent man—afraid he will be a little hurt by my article. Gave Mr. Brown that old notification of election into the Philological Society and got off pretty well with it.

This morning met again at 8½. Conclusion of Dr. Jarvis, confined

to half an hour. President Woolsey on Grecian kings of Bactria.
Professor Salisbury on cuneiform inscriptions. Professor Edwards
on study of Hebrew in a collegiate course, when eleven o'clock approached and I was obliged to *tortle*. On the whole a very successful
meeting, and full of encouragement for the future.

Saturday, October 28. Condemned to hopeless mediocrity—
longing to fly, yet lacking wings to fly with—scorning the vile
earth, yet doomed to crawl forever upon it—haunted by yearnings
never to be satisfied, aspirations never to be realized. For I have
neither wit nor words nor worth, action or utterance. Without
elocution to set off feeble talents, without talents to compensate for
imperfect elocution—without the powers of memory, even, which
are indispensable to the production of a scholar. What can I do?
Earthly hopes fade from my view. To me this world holds out little
that is attractive. My hopes, aims, longings, comforts, everything
must center in another. Is this seeking heaven because earth is not
to be secured? Perhaps—and I ought to be ashamed when I find
it necessary to set such considerations before my mind. But so it
is—woe is me for my inconceivable frailty. This world is all too
apt to swallow up my thoughts, and I am compelled to leave no
means untried for detaching myself from its vanities.

Have just been reading a very brief notice of Owen's *Thucydides*
in the *Biblical Repository*, written probably by Professor Lewis.
It makes me fairly ashamed of my own. It is so much neater and
clearer and more businesslike than mine. Still I think his eulogies
are overstrained. In particular he commends that habit of pointing
out the beauties of an author, and telling the student what he ought
to admire, which has on me an effect closely analogous to that of
ipecac. I believe that the judgments of my article are right, that I
praise and blame in the right places, but I mourn over the feeble-
ness and meagerness of the article to which they belong. Well, fugit
irrevocabile verbum. Better luck next time.

Called on the Miss Twinings, and staid till nearly ten, though
thinking that I was just upon the boundary of nine. The mischief
was that they sent for Dr. Bushnell's late ΦBK, which made abun-
dance of reading and of talking, so as quite to drown the voice
of clocks and the soft footfall of passing time.

Sunday, October 29. Why should I not lead a larger and broader
life, less confined within narrow metes and bounds, less fettered
by custom and convention, above all less subject to the galling

bondage of fear? Oh, for a noble boldness, for a spirit of personal independence, founded on a consciousness of worth, of worth as an ever-subsisting centre of intellectual and moral action. Oh, for a spirit of free and fearless enterprise, that shall scorn all bounds but those of duty and propriety and shall adventure unrestrained into the infinite of thought and feeling and activity. Truly I believe that cowardice is at the bottom of all evil—the perpetual bans and curse—a malison upon it. Fear it is, as Bulwer says in his noble *Zanoni,* that bars the entrance to a higher life. The dastardly spirit halts at the threshold, and, fearful of unknown evil, misses the unknown good. And cowardice is lazy, dreads the rushing tide of industrious effort, shuns to encounter the perplexities of deep searching thought, flies from the dangerous novelties that meet the eye of original investigation. Oh, I feel this miserable laziness through my whole nature, this vile disposition to rest satisfied with things as they are, to say what other people say, and do what other people do, and think what other people think, only because they say and do and think it, not because the reason and conscience that God has given have viewed it face to face and recognized it as congenial.

MARCH, 1849

Wednesday, March 7, 1849. Seven weeks from the beginning of the term. We have reached the meta and are just at the point of turning. As for me, the article on Tennyson, the result of much toil very ill expended, is off my hands; prize translations, too, a tedious affair, are well nigh dispatched; and the Freshmen, who are now in the twelfth book of the *Odyssey,* will commence reviewing next week. So that I am likely to have more than usual leisure. Now there are matters, enough of them, that claim attention, nay vociferously demand it. There is the system of analysis for Greek verbs, and the short synopsis of dialectic peculiarities, which ought to be finished up. There are the etymological productions of Georg Curtius to be read through and inwardly digested. There is Bopp's *Comparative Grammar* to be served in the same way. Then there is the Sanskrit, which has been lying perdu ever since that execrable *Princess* came upon the tapis. And the Anglo-Saxon, too, hardly yet opened, but presenting from afar a most inviting field. And Döderlein's Latin and Greek *Etymologies,* which I propose to ransack. And an essay for the Philological Society, shall it be on *will* and *shall* in English, the origin and history of their use as auxiliaries, or on Umbrian and Oscan remains? And Chladni on meteorites to be searched and extracted from for Professor Olmsted, and—and—and forty other things, many of which I shrewdly suspect will never leave the limbo of projects to assume fixed place in the daylight world of facts. But meantime there is a matter not yet mentioned, yet more pressing than any of these. For next term is hastening on apace, and the vast field of ancient history lies before me. Now I must not teach it in the same slipshod way as last summer, when I slipped along in the shabbiest manner possible. But if anything is to be accomplished, I must begin now, and work steadily on from day to day, so that every day shall see some progress made. Now Roman history comes last in order, falling on a time when I shall naturally be "laziest of myself." I must therefore start it first and make the thoroughest preparation on it. I have taken up Arnold and propose to drive him through, looking also at Michelet and Schmitz and Niebuhr. Beyond the Second Punic War, I must try to get hold of Ferguson, look at Mérimée for the Conspiracy of Catiline. For the Civil Wars and the Reign of Augustus, make use of Hoeck, and getting over the first century as I can, plod on the rest of the way with Gibbon. And now that something may be done, I intend every day to write on Roman history. It may be only a line, a hint, a query, but no day must pass without a word recorded.

And so for the beginning.

[Notes on Roman History follow, through April 11, 1849.]

*   *   *   *   *   *

Sunday, March 11, 1849. Live Godward, that is the true direction of my being, and in that direction with the help of God I mean to look from henceforth and forever. Great words, not lightly to be uttered, not in a spirit of misplaced self-confidence, or vainglorious self-righteousness. I know my own inconceivable frailty, and sure I am that unless the current of my days shall suddenly dry up, there lies before me many a fall, many a lapse from God and duty, many a cause for shame and penitence. O God, strengthen thy servant, and as far as may be let him escape those wretched consequences of a corrupt and fallen nature. But what I mean is this, that having put my hand to the plough I hope by God's good grace never to look back, that in the midst of besetting temptations and sins, I will yet look forward, that I will bate no jot of heart and hope, but still bear up and steer right onward. This is my hope and this my fixed resolve (so far as fixed resolve is possible to such a feeble creature), that my own sinfulness and my own sins shall not discourage me from the attempt to lead a truly spiritual life, that I will never abandon the effort for a genuine self-culture, that I will cling to the dream, if dream it be, of a higher life. Purity, holiness, conformity to God in will and character, a life in which the human is irradiated and interpenetrated by the divine—these things float before my mind invested in celestial glory, they seem infinitely captivating, I have no words to express the charm with which they are surrounded. But alas my nature is completely unpractical—expression, realization, are and always have been out of my power. I have no means in the outer world by which I may give shape and substance to my ideas. I live in an atmosphere of hopes, longings, instincts, aspirations, but when I strive to seize upon them, to give them fixity, they vanish like the shades of the dead from the embraces of Aeneas and Ulysses. The external world of form and action is so wholly different from the ideal one, so hard it is to bring it under the categories of the soul, that I am often driven well nigh to despair. So many things imperfect and uncouth to produce a constant chafing of the spirit. So many things to say which you are conscious of saying badly, so many things to do which you are conscious of doing detestably, that life becomes a burthen, and the discouraged soul, oppressed with the feeling of its weakness, sighs for deliverance from this life-long struggle with imperfection. And in my own case there is added to all these things the galling sense of personal deformity —outwardly as well as inwardly I am a thing misshapen and unsightly. I send a thrill of pain through everyone who looks upon me. Everywhere ridicule or pity. Oh, to be as others are. To be passed in the streets without exciting thought or notice in the passers by, to be an undistinguished unit in the private party or the public assembly, seem to me at times the most desirable of earthly blessings. I know well, in my own experience when looking on others like myself, the recoil of feeling with which men look upon the deformed, and the thought that I am awakening the same sensation in others is frequently all but intolerable to me. But God forbid that I should murmur. What have I deserved: how light are the inflictions of his hand when compared with the sins by which I have provoked his anger and incurred his chastisements.

Meantime, amid all imperfection and confusion, there are two points at which I mean to aim—one, to feed my soul as much as possible with the best spiritual aliment, to dwell perpetually on great and noble thoughts, to fill my mind with ideas and images of purity and truth and beauty, to keep constantly before me the highest standards of intellectual and moral excellence—and secondly, φυγεῖν τὸ αἰσχρόν, to shun as a pestilence all contamination of baseness and impurity, to abstain from all thoughts and actions inconsistent with the ideal perfection of a beautiful and holy life.

Dr. Hawes in forenoon on "Tragywyddoldeb." Gordon Hall in afternoon on "Ye are not yet entered into your rest." Both very good. Young ministers, however, should be rather sparing of hortatory sermons, which come best from gray hairs. Youth is the season of intellectual activity, the golden time of invention and imagination. Most great discoveries made in youth. A great mind forms its view and picture of the world: it does not coincide with the common traditional view, and the result is a discovery. But the picture and the view once formed abides, presents only its original departures from the established system, yields no farther revelations.

Read in Dr. Bushnell's "Preliminary Dissertation on Language."

DECEMBER, 1849

'Tis easy to talk of persons—but when we have continued it long, we are apt to feel ashamed of ourselves, as if we had been engaged in small business. Mere gossip is contemptible. Details in and for themselves are worthless. If they are strange, whimsical, and humorous—if they are ingenious and subtle, provoking to explanation, yet baffling the research—if they are characteristic, displaying remarkable modes of activity and feeling—if they are the exponents of striking and important truths—then they are tolerable, even desirable. Nay, I am ready to admit them, though with some reservation, where they are merely supplementary, giving completeness to an interesting view which as yet you know only in part, giving fixity and definiteness to ideas which might otherwise float loosely and vaguely through the mind. But in general, may Heaven deliver us from gossip. Conversation that does not go beneath the outward surface of things into the subsoil of principles is not worth conversing. A truly active mind will strive to generalize and formulize. What a magnificent philosopher is Sancho Panza: he lives not in the concrete but the abstract, goes beyond the phenomenon and states the law, reduces life and action to principles, digests all particulars under broad generalities—categories which he pours out abundantly in pithy forms of saw and adage.

December 25, 1849. Christmas. Tuesday. Sitting up for spreers, not altogether without effect. McCormick, Sophomore, found drunk. Gaylord, Battles, and Este excited. A medical student, Green, of this city, flourishing a dirk and uttering drunken braggadocio, arrested; dirk extorted; gent greatly collapsed; engaged to take the Temperance Pledge, if they would promise to say nothing about it. John Grant promised. Hurlbutt and others refused and made off, whereupon Green complained that they were going away too promiscuous. In his bravado declaring that he was a Sophomore of Yale College and that if anybody touched him he would put seven inches of cold steel into his vitals. He added, "One man's blood will lie at my door—but what is *one* man's blood at my door?"—expecting probably that he should some day get into extensive practice as a doctor.

Got to bed a little after three A.M. Lay till nine. Not much sleep the last two hours. At home during forenoon in offices. Rather fine dinner at Tontine. Back at half past two. Commenced letter to Mary. 4 to 5, in College Library. Intending to go to Mr. Brewer's during the evening, received invitation to tea there. Found Miss Field, lively as ever and full of interesting experiences. Off at 9. Exegetical spree on nuts and apples at 170. Did not stop to partake. Loitered away an hour in Tutor Hurlbutt's room. Bed about 11. Cold day and growing colder—somewhat cloudy—high and chilly wind, which subsided in the evening.

Do not like controversy; it is too partial, deals wholly in particulars, does not allow a system of truth to produce its proper effect as a system. Its triumph is to prove that a collection of bricks, set up, say, in the form of an arch, can have but little of solidity or strength, because every single brick could be split by a smart tap of the hammer.

Wednesday, December 26. Dollar to Moses. Henry off to New York at noon, to stay several days. Gave him orders for a few books —think I must not go to New York myself this next vacation for fear of buying too many. Faculty meeting, 3 to 5, with much un-

YALE COLLEGE IN 1843

The buildings shown are South College, Athenaeum, South Middle, Lyceum, North Middle, Chapel, North, Divinity College, and, in the foreground, the President's house.

NEW HAVEN GREEN, LOOKING EAST, ABOUT 1843, SHOWING THE TONTINE

finished business. Sanskrit recitation as usual. Connecticut Academy at Mr. E. W. Blake's. Professor Twining present; gave an interesting account of a settling of land at Cleveland, Ohio; expects to prevent any recurrence of similar difficulty by pile driving, grading, etc.

Thursday, December 27. At evening, dressed up and went out at 7½. Called at Professor Olmsted's. Heard the severest remark which Dr. Dwight ever made to a student in Professor Olmsted's hearing: a member of the class having made a rather impertinent remark, the Doctor took a pinch of snuff and, with a manner indicative of pain and displeasure, said, "Young man, you are hasty."

Friday, December 28. Butler tells me that Mr. DeLucy proposes to take a family of young men as boarders, with French as the exclusive language of the conversation. Butler thinks of going into it, and wanted to know whether I would like to. I said, "Yes, if all things—company, board, price, etc.—agreeable."

Sanskrit at 6½. Professor Salisbury proposed to me to spend some time during the vacation in making a list of his books published in the East, to send abroad as a guide to an agent in making collections on his account. Agreed.

Went thence to Exchange Hall to hear the *Creation* by Musical Association, Miss Jones, and Italian Opera orchestra (50 cents).

Saturday, December 29. At 10 got order on New Haven County Bank for $280, my salary for the term, but have not yet presented it. Reporting at 10; not quite finished. Faculty meeting at 11 to 1 and again 3 to 5. Disposed of Christmas outrages, matriculation, and so on. Denny, Fellowes, McKnight, Perkins, and Mansfield to be sent away from the Freshman class. N.B., must dispose of the second-division men myself in the absence of Dwight. Officiated at prayers. No tea. Called on Whitney at 7; concluded to recite by ourselves next week when Professor Salisbury cannot hear us; to take up the Wortbildung. Fixed the time at 6½ on Monday evening, forgetting just then the meeting of the Professors appointed by the President for the same time, which will likewise keep me away from a sociable at Mr. Blake's on same evening, that is, if the conspiracy to get me out, of which Butler speaks, would, apart from said Faculty meeting, have the desired and desirable effect.

At 8 called on the Twinings. Professor at home, deep in railroad calculations. Too much of Roman Catholicism—too long altogether—*must* reform.

Monday, December 31. Calls of students, to get off before the end. We close tonight, giving up the New Year's day, and excusing pretty early to allow them to get home before it is over. Ought to have had some more definite rule. Faculty meeting at 2 to 4. Euclideans dispatched. After tea at the President's, a meeting of the Professors. Much talk, no conclusion. If Dana would only take it, a happy riddance. Further inquiries to be made. Back at 9. Concluded not to go to the sociable at the Blakes—must call in tomorrow and apologize. Can I get anybody to go with me?

JANUARY, 1850

Tuesday, January 1, 1850. Up at 6½. From 7 to 7½ receiving prize translations. Breakfast at 7½ for the first time since September. During A.M. talked with Thomas about his scholarship—with Goring about a fight with the townies on the night of Friday, December 21, in which he was one of the College champions. Could not catch Denny, Fellowes, and McKnight. The last has sloped for New York—turn him over to Professor Olmsted. He has informed Mr. Fellowes, Senior, as to the decision of the Faculty in the case of his son. Gorham called and presented his bill, $9.43, which I paid. He is going to give up his shoemaking from ill health—tells me I have a piece of cork at his shop. Called on Knevals and paid up for the year, $132.88. Grand dinner at Tontine—out at 2½. Called on Whitney to recite the Sanskrit. Could not find him in, though he was so, turning over a new leaf preparatory to his single New Year's call. Spent the afternoon in vain attempts at poetizing —Muses unpropitious. College Library at 4. Read *Literary World*.

No tea. Drest and went out at 7 agreeably to orders received from Mr. Butler, who said I must call at the Twinings' and the Blakes' they were so near—no excuse if I didn't. I told him I could say they were so near that I could come in as well any other time. Called first at the Twinings'. Professor goes to Middlebury on Thursday. Anna gone to President Day's. Mrs. Day sick. Next at the Blakes'. Saw Miss Henrietta go in just before me, a sign that I should find at entering no one whom I knew. Miss Mary was in the room, to whom I was never introduced, and did not even know her by sight. She was good enough, however, to recognize me and introduce me to two other ladies in the room. Henry Blake there, and Butler, looking at a beautiful German *Cid*. Miss Henrietta came in by and by, and had a charming talk with Butler about pictures, showing on her own part a delightful perversity of taste, avowed and gloried in. Left at 8, and went to the Brewers'. Found Miss Field and sat till 9½—pleasant conversation. Back to College with Seropyan. A little Sanskrit—rather obfuscate. Bed at 12.

Keep me, O my God, this year which I begin today, or such part of it as thou hast appointed me to live, that whether living or dying, it may be to thee. Oh may it be, may all my life be, in thee—hid with Christ in God—swallowed up in a divine life—lost in the current of infinite goodness, holiness, and love.

Wednesday, January 2. Up at 8. Breakfast. Met Butler as I came away. He goes to New York this morning. Next, to Professor Salisbury's. Looked about among the books until the Professor came in at 10, when I set to work and catalogued with abridged titles a large part of the works published in India. Returning at 12¼ found that Henry was just back from New York. Brings me Smith's *Dictionary of Biography and Mythology,* Carlyle's *Heroes in History,* and Longfellow's late volume, all for $16.00.

Thursday, January 3. K. Twining brought in 1st volume of Mrs. M. A. G. Schimmelpenninck's *Memoir of Port Royal*—looked over about an hour—a heavy book. At 7½ went down to hear President Hopkins' lecture (.25) on method—ingenious in its distinctions between method and order, method and means, method and manner. Told a good story of Dr. Bellamy saying to a certain Reverend Mr. Bell, "Bell, you don't know how to preach." "Why not?" "You are like a fellow fishing that whacks his line into the water and says, 'Bite you dogs, you.'"

Saturday, January 5. P.M., Port Royal *Memoir.* Finished the volume after a sort, doing very well for the Mère Angélique, but very shabbily for her niece Angélique de Saint Jean and almost nothing for the dying De Saci. Returned it [to the Twinings] and received the second volume. Staid again for two hours, which *must* not be repeated.

Sunday, January 6. At breakfast fell in with Macy. Has given up the idea of entering at New York Seminary and will settle down here. Chance for studying Chinese. He thinks Andrews' recent essay ingenious and plausible in some particulars, but wrong in many and in not a few ridiculous and absurd. Some time at Henry's room. Took away books for study of Gospel history with reference to my notion of a Freshman Bible class: DeWette, Neander, and Robinson's *Harmony*. Henry will accompany me in the study.

Conversation with Henry as to prospects. He has thought of giving up theology after this year, and studying history, polity, or something of that sort in class or club with Mears or others. I advise a continued course of theology, some time at Andover—vigorous pushing there—acquaintance gained with men, ideas, and modes—subsequent study of theology, especially exegesis and ecclesiastical history, while tutor—perhaps exegetical exercise among seminarians in reference to any possible contingencies. Sed absint spes longae. God grant that we may live our time of life industriously and faithfully and piously, that the end, come when or how it may, find us ready and willing to depart. May we form our plans in deep submission to his will, and resign them without a murmur if in his Providence they come to nought. May we place our faith and hope not in this life but in the life to come, not in man but in God, that we may put ourselves beyond the reach of disappointment, that we may defy the power of change and death and may be able always to say, In te Domine speravi, non confundar in aeternum. And, O God, grant that we may be blest of thee in all our intercourse with each other, that we may be each to each agents and ministers of good.

Monday, January 7. Coming up at 2¼, found at Henry's room Professor Low of Geneva, or late of Geneva, for he has thrown up his place in the College and is on his way to his father's at Concord to spend some time there. Much interested in what he said as to his reasons for this step. Essential immorality of students in the College and of their Governors—want of principle in the administration. President Hale. Salaries back—deficit of $750 in his case —doubtful as to his getting it. No immediate hope from Trinity Church. People there rather averse to the College. Don't like the way they managed the $6000 a year which they used to receive from the state. President has found a claim of $15,000 against the Protestant Episcopal Educational Society, but not likely to get it. Not easy to see what the College can do.

Tuesday, January 8. Received word of Hyde's death. Much surprised; did not know that he was dangerously ill. After dinner called on Mr. Hyde, Senior; very pious man, mourning, yet rejoicing.

Spoke of his son's triumphant death. If I could feel thus concerning myself, how gladly would I die today. Yet this wish, I suspect, is dictated quite as much by an indolent dislike for the toils and duties of life as by any better reason.

Wednesday, January 9. Funeral service for Hyde at 9. Dr. Fitch very good. Thence in procession to cars—more Freshmen than I had supposed, upwards of 20, I should think—some of other classes. Professor Thacher to lead. Brings good word of Mr. Stanley, who will be down, he says, next week. Up at 10. Pretty hard work on the Sanskrit, 20 pages of those peculiarities of verbs—no joke—to say nothing of reading lesson doubled. Pleasantly interrupted in afternoon by call from Henry Field, who sat about an hour—on his way from Colchester to New York. They want him to settle at Colchester but he has not made up his mind to do so. Twining in to talk about a Society, *not secret*. Letter to Mary, long one. Set aside the beginning made on Christmas—less formally religious, but not without a "looking that way," as Mrs. Fry says. May God always enable me to look that way. Horribly belated; left off writing at 1½ but did not get through with ablutions etc. until 2½.

Great company today at Tontine—parties interested in a case of $50,000 arising out of a railroad contract, connected with settlement of Mr. Bishop's (of Bridgeport) estate. Quite overrun. Hard to get anything to eat.

Thursday, January 10. An inefficient day, too late last night. Evening, long lecture by Mr. Giles on conversation. Rather disappointed—not the felicity and finish which I had expected. As for depth of matter, I had *not* expected that. (Topics for conversation alone—health—weather—politics—dollar. English journalist maintained that accidents were special dispensations of Providence for benefit of newspapers. Argument, more of them during recess of parliament. Madame de Staël, experiment on—placed a dummy at her side, to whom she declaimed with great volubility and afterward expressed herself charmed with the elegance of his manners and the suggestiveness of his conversation.)

Read Longfellow's late volume. Sounds a little like echoes of his former self.

Friday, January 11. Rainy, with much ice—perilous walking. Going to dinner with umbrella up was really frightful. In evening, when the rain had slackened and indeed nearly ceased, it was much better. Dressed, and about 9 attended meeting of the Our Society agreeably to invitation of Miss Twining. Very small gathering.

Mrs. President Day died about noon of a catarrhal fever—not considered as in very serious danger until yesterday morning—happy in the near prospect of death. My God, enable me so to live that in the same place I shall have cheering memories and cheerful hopes. May the work of life be done and well done.

Saturday, January 12. At College Library some time both forenoon and afternoon. Conversed with President Woolsey. Read *Literary World*. Very ably written. In evening called on Professor Olmsted and Miss Twining.

Biography is excellent reading. But then there should be enough of it, to present all forms of excellence. He who confines himself to a single great life is apt to imitate a model perhaps least of all suited to his character and circumstances, apt also to imitate the very things which are least of all to be imitated. He swamps his own individuality and makes himself ridiculous. Here as in a thousand other things it is safer to trust the resultant action of many combined forces than the single influence of one overmastering impulse. A single biography may produce onesidedness and eccentricity: many biographies can hardly fail of giving breadth and scope to the character. They at least teach one to appreciate and admire the most diverse manifestations of virtue and nobleness. In biography we are to seek power rather than guidance, motives rather than models, propulsion rather than paragons. The subject should be not our fugleman but our trumpeter. The biography of the Lord Jesus Christ stands far apart from all others, and should not be comprehended under the same categories. Yet even here it is not so much the particular actions that we ought to regard (many of these are wholly impossible for us) as the spirit which those actions breathe and show.

Monday, January 14. Afternoon, at 2½, funeral of Mrs. Day. Long procession of carriages. O God, let me profit by all this experience of mortality around me so as to see myself ever on the brink of the grave: let me walk in the cypress-shade of life, secluded from the glare of earth, but receiving gleams of light from that upper world of which I hope ere long to be a denizen.

Absented myself from recitation in Sanskrit to hear Fanny Kemble—7½, at Temple (50 cents)—crowded house. She read

Twelfth Night, a fortunate selection for me, as I happen to be particularly familiar with that play. She read superbly, I was delighted with everything.

Returning to Henry's room, had a talk with Mears on naturalness and conventionalism in elocution, in which I tried to show that very much in speaking, reading, etc. is and must be arbitrary and conventional, and that we cannot guide ourselves by considering what is natural in the abstract, but must consider how far that naturalness accords with the conventionalisms, fixed and, for the time at least, unchangeable conditions, in the audience.

This forenoon MacWhorter came in and laid down upon my table a copy of Ticknor's *History of Spanish Literature,* just published, declaring that he had concluded it would be for the greatest good of the universe to leave it here, as a memorial of himself "unsmashed up to date," January 1, 1850, his 28th anniversary of birthday. A noble present, for which I did not know how to thank him, as I never can muster the words for anything, but I suspect that I showed by actions how much it delighted me.

Tuesday, January 15. Finished that tedious Valentine of 120 lines—rather bungled at the end—wanted really another stanza which I was too lazy to add. Read the *Winter's Tale* from 12 to 1 and again in P.M. in College Library, locked in there by Lyman Baird, Mr. Herrick having gone off on a pleasure excursion. In evening went with Henry to hear Mrs. Kemble (50 cents). Her Perdita was exceedingly beautiful, the play less interesting than *Twelfth Night.* At Smith's Hall, and a good audience—say 250.

Wednesday, January 16. Read *King Lear,* and in evening heard it read by Mrs. Kemble at Temple (50 cents). Very full house— one woman fainted. The reading was superb.

Commencement of our term. Dwight not yet back, will be here next week. Professor Stanley has come on, looking much as usual, though he appears to be still quite feeble.

Saturday, January 19. 7–8, with Miss Larned. 8–10, at the Twinings'. They speak well of this Panorama of the Rhine, now on exhibition; must go see it. Concluding dream of *our* series. 10–12, Henry's room. Wickes back—no books. Sold off $1,800 for $25.

Proposed the Bible class to Dowd.

Sunday, January 20. Dr. Bond of Norwich in A.M., fair. David Trumbull in P.M., quite a spirited performance—want of taste—fine fellow.

Talk with Mr. Whitney, Senior, who came here yesterday, on views and prospects of his son. Quite bent on philology. Thinks of studying here till summer or fall, then going to Germany and staying for 2 or 3 years, believing that when he comes back he shall be able to find eventually some place suited to him. Seems to have much faith in modern philology, and in its ultimate extension in this country. Father a liberal and enlightened man, though not a man of education.

Wednesday, January 23. Hard at work on Sanskrit during all the leisure of the day. Particulars on causals, desideratives, etc. pretty hard to remember. Faculty meeting at 3. Application of Freshman in regard to a society which is to be secret from the undergraduate classes but open to the Faculty (that its members may not be excluded from the benefactions of the College) granted with much difficulty by a majority of one vote. Dissentients, Kingsley, Olmsted, Stanley, Root, and Backus. (Hurlbutt?) Affirmants, Porter, Thacher, Hadley, Grant, Talcott, and Silliman with hesitation. The understanding on which this point is conceded to be written out by me. Threatened with a cold—opium and warm water treatment.

Thursday, January 24. Professor Putnam of Dartmouth came in just before 11. Went with me to my recitation. 2d division, a broken lesson, did not read and comment. Talk with Putnam about books on general philology and Sanskrit, both of which he thinks of attacking. Staid till 1 and called again in afternoon, $3\frac{1}{2}$ to 4.

Friday, January 25. Tough lesson in Sanskrit. It will not be convenient for Professor Salisbury to hear us next week. Whitney and I shall go on by ourselves. Cold somewhat more threatening. Took but one meal during the day, a light dinner. Swallowed a Dover in four doses. From 10 to 11 at College Library; took out Kuinoel on Synoptic Gospels. Henry has got Strauss and Olshausen from Professor Gibbs. I take DeWette, Olshausen, and Neander; he Kuinoel and Strauss.

Saturday, January 26. Cold likely to blow over. Had breakfast and dinner, but missed supper. In evening saw Professor Twining. Says they are pretty much run out at Middlebury College. President Labaree at Boston soliciting funds, which nobody gives him. Rest of the Faculty at Middlebury with, say, a student apiece. Henry's room, 10 to 11. Fisher there and Benton, droll fellow and very shrewd.

10 cents at Dow's for 6 Dovers.

Sunday, January 27. Cold a little more menacing owing to imprudence last night. No breakfast. Funeral sermon from Dr. Fitch. Mentioned the recent deaths in the families of Professors Gibbs, Goodrich, Silliman, and President Day; gave no particular account of the deceased; went on to prove the doctrine of immortality. In the afternoon, necessity of diligence in striving after heaven. My attention not so constant as it should have been, as my thoughts were apt to wander off on my approaching Bible exercise. Met the class at my recitation room immediately after afternoon service. Some 15 of them present. Talked nearly an hour on preliminary matters, and then half an hour longer on the Proem of Luke. Bungling, yet voluble. Hope I conveyed the impression that this study of the Bible seems to me a very serious matter. May God help me so to conduct it as to advance the spiritual interests of all who attend it, theirs and mine.

Wednesday, January 30. Talking with Twining about EΔ Society among Freshmen. Faculty at 3. Meeting of examination committee at end. Appointed me to report a bill. Evening at President Woolsey's with Professor Beck and family, guessing proverbs, etc. Professor Beck given up at Harvard.

FEBRUARY, 1850

Saturday, February 2. Evening at Twinings'. Just saw Professor Twining. Leaves on Tuesday. Has found a way of saving the country, but did not say what it is.

Sunday, February 3. Communion, after a beautiful sermon by Dr. Fitch on heaven. Art thou traveling thitherward? I know not. But oh, my God, give me strength to travel daily Godward. Bible class at 4. Annunciation of birth of John Baptist. Wretched—a perfect bungle. Well, there is this comfort about it, I shall now feel easy in my mind; I shall feel that I have done my worst, that I have no chance to lower my reputation and may possibly improve it. But do thou, O Lord, forgive me for thinking thus of my own reputation, when I should be thinking only of thy glory and the priceless souls which Christ has died to save.

Just as I was going down to tea, Hyde came into my room with a fellow whom he introduced as Mr. Cook, a graduate of Harvard and tutor of mathematics in the College. I had my doubts as to his identity, for he showed less of the Cambridge polish than any other man I ever saw. His manner was boisterous and embarrassed. It grew more quiet, however, as he went on, and he appeared to me a man of good mind as well as a very good-natured fellow. He was on his way to Washington to spend the long vacation of 6 weeks. Had not heard of Professor Beck's resignation; says Mr. Lane will succeed him. Passing through here he found Mr. Hyde's name on our Catalogue as tutor in mathematics and rushed around to his room. Hyde took him to me, we went together to sup at the Tontine, and after supper I took him to Mr. Stanley. Here we sat till 8½, when we adjourned to my room. He left at 9—starts out for New York early in the morning. Told me some interesting things about Harvard. Talk with Henry till after 10. Little time for Greek and Sanskrit.

Wednesday, February 6. P.M., Faculty meeting. Kellogg, Junior, set aside, intoxication and attendance at Burial of Euclid. Meeting of Professors to talk about expediency of celebrating semicentennial in 1850.

Saturday, February 9. Officiated in Chapel—some disturbance in outset—beggar or crazy man in the house, I believe. After tea, sat an hour with Mr. and Mrs. Larned. From 8, with the Twinings. Was charged with having in one case used flattery in setting up Miss Twining's knowledge of German above my own. The reproof was beautifully given, but I was shamefully self-willed and refused all acknowledgment. Amende honorable next time. Good ghost story: A man saw a ghost several times by night under a bridge which he had occasion to pass. Mentioned it to two friends and engaged them to come and see. Fearing it might fail and he be laughed at, he dressed himself as ghost and took his place. They come. "See, there's the ghost." "Yes, two of them." Man turns round, sees the real ghost beside him, mozies with velocity.

Sunday, February 10. Bible lesson. Studied carefully, did better than last time. Yet I fear the thing will prove a failure. I bungle everything so shockingly that it must be very dull for the fellows. If they fall off I shall know how to excuse them. I should be glad, however, if before that I could say or do something which should give them an impulse toward God and good that never might be lost.

Monday, February 11. Spent much time with Dr. Siljestrom of Stockholm, who is examining our educational institutions. Took him to my recitation at 11, 3d division—a good deal flustered. To Dr. Taylor's at 2. Tutor Hurlbutt's in natural philosophy at 4. After tea, to Professor Silliman's, where I left him at 7, and went to Professor Salisbury's, with very little of a lesson. Fortunately Whitney had recited nearly everything. Salisbury spoke very freely with us, wishing that if we preferred going on by ourselves we would do so, or if any plan of occasional help would answer that we would take it. He does not shrink from the labor—thinks the exercise has been of service to him—but wishes us to follow our own preferences. We must go on with him, I believe. It is better on the whole for us. We often get new views from him, and the responsibility of the recitation is useful. But beside that, it is better for him; it is in the line of his profession, and makes him feel that his profession is not profession merely but likewise practice. It gives him the discipline of teaching, which every teacher knows to be invaluable. It gives body to his department, and actual active existence, making it a concrete somewhat and not a mere name or abstraction, as some are apt enough to suppose of a Sanskrit and Arabic professorship. It lays a foundation for future effort of the same kind, presenting an example of regular and thorough instruction in these subjects which may not be without influence on others who feel a vocation for similar studies.

Wednesday, February 13. Simons, Freshman from Longmeadow, died this morning after an illness of some two weeks. He entered at the beginning of the term from Amherst and had attended only a few recitations when he was seized with the mortal sickness. Three students boarding together were attacked at the same time with what appeared to be a dysentery—probably poisoned accidentally by something in their food. Kent was able to get home, but word has just come that his life is despaired of. Hedges is still sick here, likely to recover. In Simons' case the disease was aggravated by erysipelas, which resulted in mortification. He was an amiable young man, religiously educated, and, though not a professor of religion, died in hope. Requiescat in pace. A funeral service was held at the house, 15 Grove Street, at 12 o'clock, followed by a procession of the class to the cars. This is the third member of the class who has died in New Haven. May we all heed, O Lord, the admonitions of thy Providence.

2 to 3, drew up plan for our future examinations, which after Faculty meeting I presented to the committee on examinations. Mr. Thacher wishes to have at the close of every term a written examination from printed papers, but I feel convinced that we are not yet prepared for it.

Thursday, February 14. 12 to 1, in College Library, looking at modern doctrine of tenses in Hebrew—article in Jahn's *Jahrbuch,* 1849, 2d Heft. Spent some time on same subject in P.M. Meeting of Philological Society at 7 at President Woolsey's—pouring rain. Present, only Murdock, Salisbury, and myself, with Whitney. Larned, whose turn came round, sick with quinsy. Saw him at 2. After some conversation on metaphysics, in which I was much pleased with the remarks of the President, I took hold and tried to say something about the Hebrew tenses—afterward something about Moeso-Gothic representation of Greek characters and indications thus afforded as to old pronunciation of Greek A.D. 350. Back at 9½—bright starlight.

Friday, February 15. With Professor Larned from 1½ to 2½. Slowly recovering from his quinsy. Talked about Fred Perkins, who has kindly come up to enlighten us here on College government. Only think of it! An undergraduate in age and sent away in disgrace a twelvemonth since—the fellow has some talent, but tenfold more conceit and presumption. He had a talk with Hurlbutt, who I suspect did not manage it very well, and with the President, whose conversation he professed to be greatly pleased with.

Saturday, February 16. Called to see Miss Larned—out. Mrs. Brewer—the family will leave for Middletown the first of April. Miss Twinings—to 9½, quite an improvement. At Henry's till 10¼. At MacWhorter's till 11½. Fisher there. Larned came in. Has been at Boston for Canal railroad; prospect fair, he thinks. Mac told a capital story about having his bed "Scotched" by Fisher and Whittlesey, the night of Mrs. Devereux's party.

Sunday, February 17. Worried through the Bible lesson. I wonder that anybody will come to hear me. They will soon drop off I think—myself last of all, for I am resolved not to give up the ship, but hold on as long as one man remains. Called on Mrs. Larned after tea. Professor nearly well, will be out again tomorrow. Spoke with General Kimberly, so that after a year of eating opposite to him, we may at length begin to bow to one another. Mr. Willis came in. He certainly keeps himself very close, and is passing, I fear, through a bitter experience. Wrote the long-delayed letter to Emerson, and did up twenty of my tracts on the Greek verb.

Monday, February 18. Went to see Young of my division, who has the erysipelas; feel somewhat anxious for him. Tried to find a *Sartor Resartus,* but failed. Got Mr. Thacher's *Latin Excerpts*—34 cents—ought to give them to us. New cap, $1.25. Settled with Tuttle for shoes, $3.50.

Tuesday. Called on Hubbard (Dr.), who gives a more favorable account of Young than I had anticipated.

Great crowd this evening at Tontine. Whig State Convention.

Wednesday, February 20. Tontine still full. Convention not particularly harmonious. Foster of Norwich for Governor. Gave $1.00 to Moses.

Saturday, February 23. At Backus' from 3 to 5. Settled up prizes for 3d division. Made great guess. "Well, gents," said Backus, "you have given the first prize to ——, the 2d to —— and ——, and now who do you think has the third?" "Stop," said I, "I think I can guess." But the moment after I was inclined to regret the venture. I knew from Backus' manner that it could be no first-rate scholar, but then to make a selection among five and twenty second-, third-, or fourth-rates was no easy matter, as there was nothing at all peculiar or distinctive about the translation: this however was partly a help—two or three men who occurred to me I set aside, on the ground that their translations would have something peculiar. At last I thought of R and was near giving his name, when the association of place brought up one who sits near him in the recitation room and I came out with the name of P. "Well! I give up," says Backus, greatly to my surprise. "You must have known something about it." "Not a bit," said I. "Never thought of him in connection with these prizes until a moment since."

Moeso-Gothic at Whitney's, 6¾. Called on Miss Larned at 7½. Afterwards at the Twinings'. From 10½ to 12 at Mac's.

Ludicrous description of Fitch emulating Coxe in story-telling, sawing air with arms and legs in perpetual circumgyration, and persisting whether anybody listened or not.

Sunday, February 24. Bible lesson—the circumcision of John and prophecy of Zacharias—rather hard. Two long sermons from Dr. Cox, that in the afternoon the most impressive. A succession of unconnected brilliancies is apt to be rather tiresome. Introduced at dinner to young Russell, the elocutionist, who is giving a series of lessons to the Theologs. Appears to be a very pleasant fellow.

Symptoms of colic. Took grain of opium in Dover—settled the hash but left me rather sleepy and dumpish.

Russell said that once when he remarked to a young man that he thought he had seen him somewhere—"Very likely," was the answer, "I have been there often."

Tuesday, February 26. At College Library, 12 to 1 and 3 to 4, looking over journals. Interesting article on Homer's theology by Blackie. Foolish one by Bonnycastle on Homeric scansion.

Attended Russell's *Hamlet*-reading. Rather wanting in intensity and force, but simple and tasteful—beautiful voice. Chapel crowded, gallery closed.

Wednesday, February 27. Meeting of examination committee after adjournment of Faculty. Settled on term examinations, oral at first, and biennial examinations, written. Details still back.

Longish talk with Henry about going to Andover, which I advise.

Thursday, February 28. Fast for Colleges. Church meeting in P.M. Rhetorical Chamber. David Trumbull spoke well. For the rest rather heavy—Dr. Fitch hitchy.

Wrote to Reverend Josiah Clark, new principal at East Hampton. Advise the extension of his preparatory course in Greek and greater variety of authors.

MARCH, 1850

Friday, March 1. Beginning of Spring, a day of all weather. In evening went out to see Miss Field, but she had not come, though momently expected. Called at Professor Olmsted's.

Russell left this afternoon. Good fellow.

Settled for board at Tontine, $14.00.

Saturday, March 2. Excused myself from the Twinings', and spent evening with Miss Field charmingly. At 10½ went over to MacWhorter's. Found him very hoarse, from riding in cars near window which Mrs. Devereux, intent on good air, kept wide open.

Exclaimed at parting, "Samivel, beware of vidders." Home at 12¾. Only one light in the College front—at 170 Divinity College.

Monday, March 4. Found that I had a most unmistakable cold. Commenced a course of opium practice. Excused myself from the Sanskrit recitation to take tea at Mr. Brewer's. Staid till half past 9, though I had made an appointment for 9 o'clock. Miss Field wanted to consult me about the propriety of an application on the part of young Brewer for a remission of his tuition. She feared that it might involve the idea of degradation or dependence. I assured her that it did not in the feeling of College, and advised the application. Went to Dwight's room to hear prize translations of 2d division. First two very capital—the best performances of the kind, it seems to me, that I have yet seen in my acquaintance with Freshmen.

Promised Miss Field a call at Brooklyn in the beginning of our vacation.

Wednesday, March 6. Sanskrit not hard. Recitation at 6½. Came home in a severe rainstorm not very favorable to my cold. It had been snowing, and the ground was covered with half an inch of slush. Opposite Governor Baldwin's my crutch slipped, and down I came on hands and umbrella. A man who was passing came to pick me up with, "Oh, my dear Sir, have you hurt you?" "No," said I, "only my umbrella." One of its rafters was broken, a compound fracture, for the sharp stump protruded through the integument of silk.

Professors at 4 to consider Mr. Dana's proposition about inviting Mr. Silliman to hold on. Meeting favorable. Not so well perhaps for Mr. Silliman, but some relief to us, who find ourselves in something of a fix.

Thursday, March 7. Moeso-Gothic, very heavily. Had no breakfast and dinner. Butler concerned; came round to see me at 1½. Kind-hearted man and real Christian, I believe. Went out to tea, thence to Whitney's room, and thence with him to Philological Society at Professor Salisbury's. People tardy about coming. Present, Hadley, Larned, Murdock, Porter, Salisbury, Thacher, Woolsey, and Whitney. (Kingsley—bad cold.) President told about Blumenbach, who disliked Hospitirers, shaking out piece of fur tenanted by bugs with, "Weg, Hospitirer." And about Hermann saying of old rationalists that they had taken "miracula" from New Testament and substituted "monstra."

Professor Larned read dissertation on the structure of the oratorical period, with reference to Demosthenes' "De Corona" founded on Latin of Dissen. Free conversation on variety of subjects quite interesting and instructive. Adjourned at 9¾ to meet next at Porter's. Went to Whitney's room to recite Moeso-Gothic but his fire had gone out, so put it over. Hour and a half at Henry's room talking on social reform, next question in Rhetorical Society. Joking with Benton.

Friday, March 8. Hoarser. HOur Society at Salisburys', did not attend. Butler did, uninvited.

Saturday, March 9. To Twinings' at 8. Gave satisfactory exposition of Schiller's "An die Freude"—never got so clear a view of it myself. Tennyson—very pleasant. Stopt awhile at Henry's room. Much obfuscated by cold, terribly hoarse. At home, wrote in some autograph books, and abed at 12½.

Sunday, March 10. Bible lesson on double sense in prophecy. Professor Gibbs, if there, would have groaned in spirit.

Clark called up in evening to talk about inspiration of Sacred Scriptures. Ticklish subject, but held to orthodoxy.

Bacon has preached two quarter-century sermons today. Very fine, they say. Avows himself a learner. Speaks slightingly of metaphysical theology and dogmatical controversies. Defends his non-visitation and his writing for periodicals.

Tuesday, March 12. At Pease's from 7 to 8½, at first reading *Bothie of Toper-na-Fuosich*—clever, very—and afterwards talking with Sobieski, which I don't quite like. He is ingenious and instructive, but always assumes on the part of his auditors a familiarity with his Ideankreis and his Kunstsprache, which are very artificial and make him horribly puzzling.

Tried to see MacWhorter to inquire about Miss Beecher's forthcoming publication—queer thing, that—but could not find him. Have made two attempts lately to see Richard Willis, who left his card at my door on Saturday—but unsuccessful.

Wednesday, March 13. Signed a petition for cheap postage. Called on Mr. Knevals and ordered coat, $24; vest, $5½; pants, $9½; neckcloth, $1½; shirts, 6 at $2½ = $15. Sum total, $55½. After Sanskrit tried, but in vain, to see MacWhorter. Spent some time copying out mottoes. Henry came in from Rhetorical Society. Question on

propriety of agitating social reform—fellows generally moderate.
Fisher at Washington. Mears and Benton disabled by Henry
Barnes' oysters last night, his farewell spree. Was to leave for Philadelphia today. Started letter to George at 12, finished at 1½. Had
just got letter from him dated Geneva; he is going to work at the
crutch, wants to know about this one.

Friday, March 15. Bought *Bothie of Toper-na-Fuosich* at Pease's,
.75. Tennyson's *Poems* at Fitch's, $1.50.

Tried to see MacWhorter, but he was off to the beehive. At
Henry's room saw California papers. Heard some of Webster's great
speech in Senate—use-up of Dix and Niles. Talk with Benton about
underground railway.

Saturday, March 16. Called on Miss Larned. Afterward at Twinings'. At 10½ on MacWhorter. Staid till 12½. M. told me about
Miss Catherine Beecher and her forthcoming book (stereotyped)
on the MacWhorter case. Observation of Mrs. W[oolsey] that there
was an engagement between Miss Beecher and Miss Bacon by
which the former was to furnish the literature and the latter the lies.

Sunday, March 17. Bible lesson, rather heavy. After tea, called on
Mrs. Larned and staid till General Kimberly came in—nearly nine.
Came home and started Sanskrit. Henry came in and sat above an
hour. Says that Dr. Bacon preached this P.M. a mystical sermon in
which he was understood to affirm a direct intuition of God by the
soul in religion, a divine consciousness—beautiful isn't it? This
man is determined to lay hold of ideas everywhere and feed himself
and his hearers with them, in defiance of logic be it chopped never so
fine. Young man didn't hear the sermon, heard of it.

Wednesday, March 20. Auction sale of Mr. Sobieski's books this
afternoon, 2 o'clock, at Boothe's in Temple. Attached for debt by
Gorham, druggist, who had heard of executions as ready in Hartford. Did not attend—afraid I should buy—was rather sorry I did
not. Might have got a *Nibelungenlied* cheap, also Richardson's
Dictionary and Eberhard, *German Synonyms*.

Discussion on comparative importance of dogmatic and exegetical theology. Nemesis of Gibbs.

Thursday, March 21. Long talk with Henry on his subject before
Exegetical Society, scriptural idea of a Church. Urged this point:
Congregationalists admit an authority of the Congregation—not

mere moral influence but fettering free activity of individual—official—belonging to Congregation as Congregation without respect to their wisdom or piety—they so interpret the scriptural passages which assert the authority and efficiency of Congregations. Why then should they adopt a different interpretation for those which assert the authority and efficiency of Episcopi, Presbyteri, and Diaconi? Congregationalism to be consistent should be Come-outerism —assert the absolute independence of the individual.

Question of last night. Benton and Fisher not so well as usual. Mears very good though Butler thinks otherwise. Hyde had no chance. On dogmatic side, only Howard and Riemensnyder. Former spoke well. Doctor started at 10 and kept it up till nearly 11—better than usual. Adroit and plausible. Defence of philosophy, which however he uses ambiguously, sometimes for right-thinking, sometimes for scientific system, mixing up sophistically. Denied mysticism and mystery in Bible, with the old fallacies. Made exegesis the foundation, dogmatics the superstructure, but shied the great point of dogmatic interpretation, denying it in some statements but leaving room for it in others. Shied also the great question how the undeniable dangers of the dogmatic tendency are to be avoided.

Monday, March 25. Still cold. Ordered coal, ⅛th ton, with charcoal, 1 bushel. 95 cents, paid. Lost the *Tribune* of Saturday, which did not come. Sorry; it contained Littlefield's overwhelming testimony in the Webster trial. Cross-examination today. There can be no more doubt after this in any mind that Webster was the murderer.[2] Sanskrit at Whitney's, 6½; finished 12th book, a long one. Whitney has a younger brother here on a visit. Returning home at 8, tabulated my Sanskrit verbs, a long-hanging job.

Tuesday, March 26. Coal brought in at 3. Read Mr. Poole on perfect intonation in *Silliman's Journal,* at College Library from 12 to 1, and afterwards borrowed the numbers from Professor Stanley. The article has excited a great deal of discussion in the city, a certain Mr. Ives, ex-organist at St. Paul's, having taken up the cudgels for the wolf. Gave my name for a letter to Professor H. D. Rogers, State Geologist of Pennsylvania, requesting him to lecture here on music (especially the euharmonic organ). He has been lecturing on meteorology in Boston, where he fell in with Mr. Poole and became much interested in his doings.

Wednesday, March 27. Connecticut Academy in evening. Heard that Dana, at whose house it was, would talk, and so went with Whitney. About a dozen there. Dana on the Pacific Ocean. Volcanoes around it—islands in it—parallel ranges S.E. and N.W. transverse range—compared with great lines of coast—islands' extent (80,000 sq.), coral 19,000, 25,00[o] of dry land—land strip with central lagoon—few plants—rest volcanic—few active volcanoes—etc. Volcanoes not safety valves. Very interesting and valuable.

Thursday, March 28. Read Mr. Poole's article and received a call from him in the afternoon—a bright fellow, very confident and positive. Speaks contemptuously of the theoretical works on music; has read them all, he says.

Friday, March 29. Fast day. No recitations. Up at 7½. Breakfast, no dinner. Dr. Hawes in Chapel, on fixed moral principle, forenoon and afternoon. At 3 had another call from the Pooles, who sat till 5. Interesting conversation. Showed a drawing which represented the mechanism of his organ.

Evidence for defence in Webster trial, plausible but unsatisfactory.

Saturday, March 30. Mr. Poole's article. Bible lesson. Webster case. Heard Fisher read Merrick's plea. At 8–11 at the Twinings'. To 11! That is quite too strong, my dear young friend. You must stop that, and luckily you have a chance, for this evening it was proposed that I should come in on Sunday nights and study the Bible. I hesitated much at the time, alleging, what was very true, that I was afraid of spoiling them all by mad neologisms. But I have concluded to accept the proposal; one must not throw away a chance of studying the Bible. So Saturday shall be exchanged for Sunday evening, and sport for earnest: for I am determined to act the parson—at any rate not to act the trifler—and make myself seriously useful instead of wasting my own time and other people's. It was a hint most certainly, and a truly good and rational one for which I have to thank the giver.

At Henry's room to 12½. Then to bed.

Sunday, March 31. Dr. Fitch recommencing his course, on the existence of God. Rejects immediate intuition and goes into the old argument from causality, which can never satisfy the soul of man, though it may perhaps satisfy his intellect—but? Mr. Van Lennep, missionary from Constantinople, in the P.M., on excellence of God's moral law. Neatly written but not strong. Did not go out to hear him at Monthly Concert. Bible lesson much as usual. Carefully studied but bunglingly presented.

No dinner. At supper time had nearly reached Tontine, when I remembered that I had promised to bring down to Butler at tea a paper which he had lent me in the morning. I went back to my room for it, but Butler did not make his appearance at table. Had not come back from West Haven, where he went to preach for Mr. Wright. The paper was a number of the *New York Herald* containing the evidence on Forrest's side in his petition for divorce. I ask pardon for reading it on Sunday. 'Tis a miserable story, and if half of it is true, Catherine Sinclair must be one of the most shameless women. It is not overpowering passion for one which leads her astray, but a swinish lust which fastens indiscriminately on every object that presents itself. Dick Willis is a good deal implicated. Very sorry to hear it, but glad that I do not hear it concerning a professor of Yale College. "Quam paene vidimus." In this respect we are more fortunate than Columbia, where Professor Hackley comes in for his share.[3]

APRIL, 1850

Monday, April 1. Calhoun dead, a great man fallen. Webster to die, a felon's death. Miserrime—yet he showed his meanness to the last, charging his counsel with incompetence. Read *North British* article on Müller's doctrine of sin. Very good. Saw Salisbury at College Library; is to be engaged this evening; will start us again on Wednesday. Sanskrit at Whitney's in evening. Afterwards with Whitney to Exchange Hall to hear Professor Rogers on music (25 cents), a beautiful performance. Very complimentary to Mr. Poole, who was present to enjoy it. From 9½ to 11 at Henry's room, reading new number of *Bibliotheca Sacra*. Contains Morris' article on Welsh bards. From 11 to 11½ at my own room—no fire—looking over Greek lesson for morning, for they are now reviewing in the 13th book and I have to get my lessons. Bed at 11¾. *Very early.*

Paid board at Tontine, for March, $15.50.

Yesterday and today, pleasant weather.

At College Library, 12 to 1. Selected a passage from one of Sir William Jones' prefaces for prize translation. Defence of writing Latin.

Tuesday, April 2. Charles Hammond at breakfast. Also Beach—gave quite a feeling account of his uncle's death—very sudden. At Mr. Thacher's room, 12–1. Talked about Dick Willis. Carried prize Latin to printer.

Wednesday, April 3. College Library, 12 to 1, looking at article on dual in Indo-European languages in Jahn und Klotz *Jahrbuch,* by Silberstein, a poor affair. Thinks the dual passed over from Shemitish to Indo-European. Bristed's article in *Literary World* on Felton's *Birds of Aristophanes,* very good-natured. Defends non-expurgation against Anthon, on ground that it is essential to a just idea of heathen antiquity, as compared with Jewish and Christian, that the wrong side should be made to appear. Good idea. Critique on Hawthorne's *Scarlet Letter*—must get that book. Query, also *Twice-Told Tales* and *Mosses from an Old Manse.*

Sanskrit and recitation at Salisbury's, 6½–8. Stayed to look at Magians and Azazel in Winer's *Realwörterbuch.* A good deal of talk on Webster case. Salisbury says that he always made an unpleasant impression on those who came into contact with [him]—unkind in his family—irritable and fussy.

Friday, April 5, 1850. Called on Miss Larned. She goes to Thompson tomorrow. Henry's room, 8–10, gossiping on theology. Fisher and Benton there.

Contributed $2.00 for colored meetinghouse. Paid.

Saturday, April 6. Sent note to Twinings promising call tomorrow evening on new basis.

Received suit from Knevals: left in entry and picked up by students, who, finding no owner among themselves, at last brought them round to me.

Sunday, April 7. Fitch, animated sermon if not new, in P.M. New Testament and Bible class. Magi—hard matter—difficult to believe. Strauss' objections very forcible. After tea called on Mrs. Larned, who says that Miss Elizabeth Baldwin wishes to be acquainted with me. When she becomes so she will wonder that she ever wished it. "Comfort thyself—what comfort is in me?"

At 7½ at Twinings'. Read *North British Review* on Müller's *Lehre von der Sünde,* then talked till 10. Agreed to look a little at Jewish sacrifices. Was told that no insinuations were intended last Saturday evening and that I did not need to consider myself excluded the evening before. Shall not change my plan; the Saturday evening meetings had run themselves out. We will see what can be made of Sunday evenings.

Monday, April 8. P.M., considered subject of examination with Hurlbutt. In evening, talk with Henry about miracles.

Winthrop brought in his Greek poem—rather tough—no more poetry than an old shoe.

Concert of Musical Association this evening. Wanted to attend but could not. Crowded house.

Wednesday, April 10. *Tribune* enlarged—good article by Greeley —read from 2 to 3. Faculty, 3–4½—matriculation of Freshmen. Professors, 4½–5. Communication from President on part of Prudential Committee as to Dr. Fitch, satisfactory? Meeting on the subject at President's, Monday evening at 7.

Saturday, April 13. Moeso-Gothic at Whitney's, 6½ to nearly 8. Then alas for the weakness of poor human nature. Back at 11 and went at Hengstenberg and Bähr. Ablutions etc. Bed at 2¼.

Sunday, April 14. Fast all day. Bible lesson. Jesus in the temple among the doctors. Last lesson in the term. Heard Henry on double sense. Sharp.

At Twinings', 7½ to 9½, talking about Azazel etc.

Tried, but in vain, to find MacWhorter.

At Henry's to near 12, with Benton. Talk about moral system.

In Chapel, P.M., Mr. Bliss of Boston. A foolish sermon eulogistic of Puritans. Heaven save us from our friends.

Monday, April 15. At tea found Tutor Brace. Left him at 7 to go to the President's to attend the Fitch meeting. Expected to return in half an hour. Held on 3 hours. Porter and Thacher expressed themselves pretty strongly. Olmsted less so. Silliman, Larned, and Kingsley (with whom I agreed) more favorably. President said nothing, yet hinted at the true difficulty: want of visible proof of a warm and zealous piety. I presume that nothing will be done.

Broke appointment with Brace, whom I had agreed to see again during the evening, also with Whitney for the Sanskrit, and besides with Winthrop, whose piece I was to recriticise at 9. A little time in preparation for examination.

Bed at 11¾. Winter-bitter weather.

Thursday, April 18. Last recitation. Started examinations—went pretty well. Examining committee very slim, only Avery, Grant, and Love, with President Day.

Friday. More of the same, tolerable. Had Grant present at one session and Thacher at another. In evening, at Dwight's to make out results and report, 7–9½.

Saturday, April 20. Finished up examination, last session, 8–10. Avery and Love in for a short time. Making out results, 10–11. Do not turn out anybody. Brownson advised to leave. Faculty meeting, 11–12½. Sophomore instructors ferocious. Hinman, Johnson, McKissack, and Niles to go, latter in part for insolence and disobedience. Hinman and McKissack undetected Euclideans—an excellent riddance. No money from Treasurer.

P.M., giving out sentences, and getting in prize translations. College Library, looked up genealogy of Prince of Condé (le Grand), also reason for sharping up 6th and 7th of ascending minor scale.

Dressed. 8–10 at Twinings'. Off to Mac's—not to be found. Returning, in brown study, opposite Dr. N. B. Ives' hailed by two men walking very unsteadily. Was going to push by but could not. Found them out as Mac and Larned, afflicted with rheumatics. Adjourned to Mac's room. Staid to 12½, talking chiefly about Bushnell's views. New Haven West Association are to meet at the instance of Fairfield Association to overhaul him on Wednesday next.

Sunday, April 21. Fitch—paid him better attention than usual. No Bible class; fellows many of them gone. 7½ to 10, at Twinings', winding up on the ceremonial of the great Day of Atonement. A foolish talk about personal matters, which confirms me in a resolution previously taken and observed *occasionally* not to talk about myself. Looked out passages for Berkeleian examination tomorrow.

Monday, April 22. Getting ready for departure. From 10 to 12, examined for Berkeley [Prize], Camp and Sanford. Scanned badly, otherwise tolerable. Best on *Cyropaedia*. Camp rather the best in President's opinion and mine. Did best also in Latin in afternoon. Receives the prize.

At Treasury, check on bank for $130, certificate of deposit for $150. College Library witnessed signatures.

After dinner went to bank. Settled with Pease. *Tribune* for one year, $6.50. Watch guard, 12½ cents.

Lisle thread gloves at Knevals'.

Settled for washing, $4.25. Board, $11. Got in new shoe from Tuttle's at last moment.

Tuesday, April 23. Up at 5½. Carriage round at 6¼. Lowering morning. At New York, Florence's. Well accommodated—rowdy place. At Lockwood's purchased Chénier's poems, .87½. At Radde's, inquiring price of some books. At Chassell's—busy. Bought umbrella, 45 cents, but had little occasion to use it. Over to Brooklyn. Passing Crittenden's Seminary was quite overwhelmed by a bevy of schoolgirls just coming out about 2 o'clock. Made my way to Noyes', a longer walk than I had supposed. Noyes rather sick— pleasant talk. Returning at 4, called at Mr. Crittenden's, but Miss Field was absent. Left my card. Went over to New York. Supped at Florence. Called again on Miss Field and staid with her till nearly 8 o'clock.

Pretty tired; went early to bed at 10.

Expenses of the day: fare to New Haven, $1.50; porterage, .25; bussing and ferrying, .45; umbrella, .45; Chénier, .87½; supper, .31.

Wednesday, April 24. Up at 7. Shaving, 6 cents. Breakfast at Mercer's, 18 cents. At Garrigue's—De Wette's *Einleitung in das Neue Testament* sent to New Haven on Monday to Mr. Hillhouse. *Indralokâg*, by Bopp, translation and commentary, out of print. Schneidewin's Pindar—will send. Bought *Peter Schlemihl*, German and English, for 75 [cents]. Looked over Appleton's assortment and left memorandum.

At 12, by Fulton Ferry to Brooklyn. With Noyes until 3½— better today. Projected visit to the Atlantic tomorrow. With Miss Field from 4 to 5. At Appleton's bought as follows:

Bopp, *Comparative Grammar,* 3d [edition,]	$2.63
Humboldt's *Cosmos,* American edition, 2 v.,	1.62
Views of Nature, Bohn,	1.25
Somerville, *Physical Geography*	1.25
Hawthorne, *Scarlet Letter*	.75
Twice-Told Tales	2.00 ?
(*Mosses from an old Manse*—out of print)	
Carlyle, *Sartor Resartus* etc., Harper,	1.25
Irving, *Mahomet,* 2 v.	2.25
Hengstenberg, *Egypt* etc.	.75
Browning's *Poems,* 2 v.	1.75
Annual of Scientific Discovery	1.12½
Southey, *Life and Correspondence,* Harper, 2 parts	.44
	——
Paid $18.00	$18.18

Memorandum. Inquire again about Hawthorne's *Twice-Told Tales*. Think it is a mistake for $1.00.

Had a mind to get Yonge's *English-Greek Lexicon*. Must when I go back. Thought also of getting Count Hamilton's *Fairy Tales*. (Spratt and Forbes, *Travels in Lycia*. Lane's *Selections from Kurân*.)

Hengstenberg, *Authenticity of Pentateuch and Daniel,* and Olshausen, *Commentaries,* not to be had. Appleton thinks of taking the Clark agency.

Felton's *Birds of Aristophanes,* missing. H. Miller's *Footprints of the Creator,* ditto. 6 copies sold already.

Had previously purchased *Moneypenny,* .50, and *Onyx Ring,* .25, of Lockwood.

Supper at Mercer's, .25. Back at Brooklyn. With Miss Field, 7½ to 9½. Ran over in great haste to Noyes. Found him in bed. Thinks himself too weak for the Atlantic expedition. Has arranged the matter with George Howard.

Off in haste to Fulton Ferry, just in time. Rode up in omnibus to Florence. Packed books. Bed at 12.

Beautiful day, followed by a most delightful moonlight evening. No dust.

Bussing etc., 52 cents.

Thursday, April 25. Up at 5½. Walked down to Duane Street pier. Saw Henry with Camp. Back to Florence's. Rode down to Garrigue's and looked around again. Rather think of getting *Die Gegenwart,* 3 volumes, $2.00 per volume. Spruner's *Ancient Atlas,* 29 maps, for $6.62½. Not very much theology. Not all of *Exegetisches Handbuch zum Alten Testament*. Did not get that but must. Hengstenberg on Revelation, Volume 1, just out. Winer, *Biblisches Realwörterbuch*. At Düsseldorf Gallery from 10 to 12, 37½ cents (.25 admission, .12½ catalogue). A beautiful collection; should like to see it again. 1 to 3½, with Howard to see the Atlantic at foot of Canal Street. Very grand. Saw De Vinton.

Breakfast at Mercer's, 31 cents. Dinner at Florence, 31 cents. Saw John Grant at former. Bussing today, .12½.

Porter hire, .25. Fare in hack, .50. Paid fare to Geneva, $6.50. Off for Piermont at 4. Pleasant night carriages.

Friday, April 26. Rode with Edward Cooper from Binghamton to Owego—lives at Astoria—place in custom house—is to undertake Quackenbos' *Literary American,* and drive it of course. Says the *Literary World* is to be given up; its advertisements have been free and its subscription list not sufficient to pay expenses. Invited Mary to spend summer with him at Astoria. At Owego saw Camp and Platt. At Elmira looked for Henry but did not find him. At Jefferson, 9 o'clock. On boat, blacking shoes, .12½, grog, .06¼, porterage, .25. An uncommonly beautiful spring day.

At Home at 12½. Dinner, unpacking books, cutting leaves, etc. Saw Reverend Mr. Curry, Mr. Rumney and Robert Rumney, Mr. McDonald, tutor in Geneva College. Read in Bopp's *Comparative Grammar.* Asleep at 11.

Father quite unwell. George lecturing. Rest as usual. Number of students in Medical College, 70+, in Academy, 40. Vacation begins today, closes when ours does.

Saturday, April 27. A.M., wrote to parentals, as to examination etc., eight letters. P.M., read aloud *Bothie of Toper-na-Fuosich* all the way through. On the whole a very clever book, though the hexameters in many places are desperately hard.

In evening sat up with George, talking about poetry, Professor Webster, and Poole's euharmonic organ until 12½.

Sunday, April 28. Mr. Hogarth in morning. Mr. Douglass (Episcopalian), son of late Professor Douglass, in afternoon. Read in Exodus, rapidly and cursorily. In evening read Hengstenberg, *Egypt and Books of Moses.* Talk on theology.

Monday, April 29. Read aloud 200 pages of Hawthorne's *Scarlet Letter.* Read from Chénier's *Poems.* Head shampooed, 20 cents.

In evening explained Poole's organ to Reverend Mr. Curry. Wound up with a little Sanskrit.

Tuesday, April 30. *Nala.* Chénier. Read aloud the remainder of the *Scarlet Letter.* Browning's minor poems. Wonderful copiousness of expression.

Pistol shooting with George and Henry. Shoe mended, .25. Sleepy in evening. Keeled up at 9. Bed at 10.

MAY, 1850

Wednesday, May 1. *Nala.* Chénier. Browning ("Pippa Passes"). Ticknor's *Spanish Literature.* 130 pages read aloud.

In evening, Hungarian (olim Moravian) Singers with Henry and Mary, George despising such amusement. Good audience. Stoepel did well. Krausz dolorous as ever. Lovarny most unfortunately hoarse—has been ever since last winter—afraid she will spoil her voice.

Concert, 50 cents.

Thursday, May 2. Not much Sanskrit. Ticknor. Humboldt on steppes. Out on new pier—sagged. In afternoon, up to Mr. Brown's. Returning met George and Henry. Pistolling. Evening, read and lounged.

Friday, May 3. Not much Sanskrit. Ticknor. Weekly and daily *Tribune.* P.M., commenced a sermon on hidden life.

Saturday, May 4. Ticknor. Spent much time reading Bopp, English translation, Volume 3, on participles—interesting. In evening read *Onyx Ring.*

My journals are growing to be wholly material, absolutely void of anything like ideas. So let it be. When I started them this last time, I resolved not to hamper myself with rules or restrictions, which might become a troublesome, perhaps an intolerable, burthen. I was to speak only when the spirit moved. If ideas came, craving admission and imploring leave to express themselves, they were to be heartily welcome, but I was not to trouble myself with chasing them when they were shy and silent. This has certainly been their prevailing condition of late. I hardly know how to account for it that when I am at home I lead so unspiritual a life. It is a continual disappointment, for being with those who of all on earth are dearest to me, I would rather be in a state to do them good and to receive some good myself.

Sunday, May 5. Leviticus. Hengstenberg, *Egypt and Books of Moses.* In A.M. heard Mr. Hogarth. Meant to attend Episcopal Church in P.M., but Henry was reading aloud *Foreign Quarterly* on Morell's *Philosophy of Religion,* and I stopped to hear. We commented a good deal, think the review not entirely fair, but some points pressed with much force, particularly Morell's omission to treat of sin and its remedy.

Late in evening read *Onyx Ring.* Full of noble thoughts and feelings. Very interesting speeches. Walsingham to Collins on art. Collins to Thomas on politics. Fowler to Collins on religion.

Monday, May 6. Took more serious hold of the *Nala* and read 40 pages. In evening attended Monthly Concert—not very full (25 cents). Was afraid I should be called on, and was so busy with thinking what I should say as to lose much of the proper enjoyment of the season. I had nearly made up my mind to speak at any rate when Mr. Hogarth somewhat abruptly closed the exercises. I should have said, we are too apt to think this work our own, human not divine. Hence we are too much elated in success, depressed in adversity. We must not indeed be indifferent, we must desire the immediate advancement of God's kingdom, and lament all that impedes or seems to impede it. But this feeling may be excessive and lead to fretful impatience or paralyzing despondency. For God does not carry on his work as we should expect. For reasons which we can to some extent divine but never fathom, he works slowly, through long alternations of success and failure. So with all world-enterprises: wherever it appears otherwise it is only appearance; there may be a sudden crisis but there has been a long preparation. Thus with the establishment of God's kingdom. Do not deny that there is much to encourage us—great motion and activity—not surprising that some expect the millennium at once. Not so I. In my opinion we do but see the dawn, and the sky will be lowering and overcast many times ere we reach the serene brightness of the perfect day. We begin to make some impression here and there in the phalanx of the enemy, but his strength is yet unbroken, and he will [deliver] many a stroke and often drive us backward over the plain ere we gain the final victory. Yet even in defeat we can strike, and every stroke has its worth. If only for our own sake it is well worth while to keep up the contest, how much more if but a single soul is won over from sin to holiness. If all missionary effort for a half century should but save one soul that would otherwise perish, who shall pronounce it a failure? We must not despise the day of small things: the small things are really great and appear small only because we expect too much. It would be pleasant no doubt to live in a great world crisis and see the sudden revolution, but this is not optional with us. We stand in the posts where God has placed us—we do the work which God has set us. We must do it faithfully and joyfully, whether it be to fire the train that shatters the mountain, or by long and heavy toil drill out the hole that is to receive the powder.

Tuesday, May 7. Read 45 pages of *Nala*. More of *Moneypenny*—rather slim—a very distant imitation of Dickens. One tolerable thing: "He was not exactly seedy, but was ready to go to seed."

From Hood: "In fact, he did not find M.D.'s worth one D—m."

Wednesday, May 8. Read 35 pages of *Nala,* with some reviewing. In evening Henry read to me and George some of his collection of facetiae—the best perhaps that of Dr. Mason, who, when some scorners recommended the devil's turnpike as particularly comfortable and easy, reminded them that there would be a hell of a toll to pay.

This plan of collecting jokes is not amiss—a man needs to be armed at all points. Yet for my own part I have determined not to be a story teller. It requires more capital than I possess or ever shall, and even with the most copious resources a man is terribly apt to repeat himself. If I attempt the anecdotic it shall be not aggressively, but so to speak in self-defence, to bear my part and not be overborne in anecdotic conversation. Still, as a matter of theory, and without reference to my own imperfections, I look upon this anecdotic style as the true ideal. There must be a basis of fact ever present—the actual, the concrete—to support the principles and abstractions which discussion may present. Abstractions alone are unsatisfactory; they furnish a diet too concentrated; dilution is absolutely indispensable. Circumstances and details must be thrown in, however dry and indigestible, on the same principle as that by which the Esquimaux is obliged to mix sawdust with his train oil.

If you find a man free and wild in speculation you are not therefore to conclude that he is without settled faith. It is not perhaps the homeless man who makes the most adventurous and erratic wanderer, but the man who has a quiet home to which he can retreat when he so chooses. The comet dashes out fearlessly into the infinite void, trusting in the powerful attraction of the central sun to bring it back again into the cheerful realms of light and warmth. In this way firmness itself may put on the appearance of vacillation. You see the wandering out-door life of a man, but know little or nothing of that fireside which forms the center of his activity and life. So in the spiritual world, the intellect may be mobile precisely because the heart is fixed. If I feel and know that nothing can draw me from the love of Christ and the blessed truth of his Gospel, I may all the more freely go abroad in other systems of belief and feeling. I may even at times put myself in the position of their votaries, seeing with their eyes and judging with their judgments, and seeking to recognize and appreciate that element of truth without which no falsehood could gain currency among men. I may not say so much about Christianity—why should I?

You and I both hold it; 'tis a thing presumed and taken for granted in all our conversational discussions.

Thursday, May 9. *Nala.* Read some of Hawthorne's tales. One very striking of a Reverend Mr. Hooper, who shrouded his face in a black crape veil, which he never removed through life, to the horror of the community. Tale illustrates what I have often thought of, the secrecy which hides the inmost nature of every man—the necessary isolation of the individual—the impossibility of perfect confidence—"We are each one a centre of repulsion."

Friday, May 10. *Nala.* Weekly and daily *Tribune.* More of Hawthorne.

It may be necessary for a man to live unnaturally. We cannot float down the stream, for its course has been perverted and it flows towards a tremendous cataract. We must struggle against it for life or death, and in this fierce strife with wind and wave we cannot confine ourselves to those motions which are free, easy, simple, and natural. We must make many which are constrained and jerking. We lead a scrambling life and must make the best of it, patient, not murmuring.

Saturday, May 11. *Nala.* Ran over yet more of Hawthorne. What I like most about this writer is that he is much more than a mere story teller: a series of incidents merely as such has no interest for his mind. Fertile in details, he cares little or nothing for mere detail. His ideality is extraordinary. Every tale of his is constructed upon an idea (using the word in something of its etymological sense—a form of thought or of imagination). It is the working out of the idea, often with wonderful richness of fancy and invention.

Sunday, May 12. Wrote two prayers. Read Hengstenberg on *Egypt and Books of Moses.* Heard Reverend Mr. Curry in forenoon, a sound sermon on parable of talents. Came out against tobacco (I have doubts in regard to the soundness of his views on that head). Mr. Curry is a very ingenious practical optician, a successful grinder of lenses and maker of microscopes. He has accepted the charge of the Congregational Church, lately so called—now North or Second Presbyterian Church. The Society it is said have accepted an old offer, once refused, of Mr. H. Dwight, to give them $1000 on condition of their organizing a Presbyterian Church. In afternoon at 4 went to the Episcopal Church and heard Reverend

Mr. Bissell—a good sermon, though abruptly terminated, from 2 Timothy, "I have finished my course etc." Idea: assurance of salvation the last result of a Christian life.

Monday, May 13. *Nala.* Shall not be able to do up all I wished with this. In afternoon heard Professor Bryan's Introductory at Medical College, on races of men—splurging affair. It struck me that Morton's measurements of cranial capacity do not as yet amount to much. The number of heads examined is too small for a general induction. Besides, it seems important to know something in regard to sex, size of individual, condition of life, etc. I am pretty skeptical as to this whole matter, though I am inclined to believe that intellectual and moral culture do in the long run improve the physical appearance. Bryan is inclined, as he says Morton is, to assume original diversity. To me it seems all but incredible that the race should have been united in the year 2348 B.C. in the person of Noah; the unity if it exist must be thrown back to an earlier date.

Call from Reverend Mr. Curry in evening.

Tuesday, May 14. *Nala.* Chénier. In evening took tea at Reverend Mr. Curry's with George. Mrs. Curry a very striking woman. At half past 8 went over to the Hodges'. Found H. with the two young ladies. Mrs. Hodges came in at 9. Came away at 9½.

Hairdressing, .18¾. Charcoal and hair oil, .25. *Tribune,* .03.

Wednesday, May 15. Repairing crutch by George. Saw Professor Olmsted on his way to Chicago. He had but a moment to stop, and after a word with Father and George I went with him to the cars, where I saw his son Lucius and Mr. Samuel Barnum, with a very pretty Mrs. ditto. Mr. Olmsted thinks of being absent the first 2 or 3 days of the term. Make arrangements for the astronomy recitation.

Saturday, May 25. Traveling is a sad breaker in our regular habits, and in this instance, at least, journeying and journalizing have not gone hand in hand. Thursday, May 16, was the last full day of my sojourning at home. I read a little in the *Nala,* copied out a few extracts from Chénier's poems, tried, but in vain, to see Mr. J. C. Strong, and about 6 o'clock went with Mary and Henry to a little tea party at Mrs. Hodges'. Here we met Mr. and Mrs. Hogarth, Mr. and Mrs. Van Vranken, and Mrs. Curry (Mr. Curry had gone to Rochester). We had intended to come away at 8, but did not get tea until that hour, and in fact did not leave till about 10. Had some pleasant conversation with Mr. Hogarth.

Next morning up early and packed my trunk before breakfast. Off at 11½ with Henry, and stopped at Schenectady about 7 P.M. Left trunk at hotel and went to Foster's. All well. Staid here Saturday and Sunday. Saturday, saw Professor Pierson and Professor Tayler Lewis. Amusing account from Professor Gillespie of his experiences with the Rochester rappers, whom he had that very day consulted professionally at Albany. Was informed that he was 53 years old, had been married 5 years, and had lost a child—rayther astounding information.[4]

Sunday, heard Reverend Mr. Taylor, Dutch Reformed Minister, in the forenoon and Mr. Thomson of Buffalo, Presbyterian, in the afternoon. Mr. Thomson is visiting a brother who resides in Schenectady and is far advanced in a consumption.

Read Bunsen's report to British Association, 1847, on relation of Egyptian language to Semitic and Indo-European. Excellent; must read it again. So also Charles Meyer's report on Celtic languages—likewise ethnological articles of Prichard and Meyer in same volume. Monday morning, up very early, a little after 3, to take train which regularly starts at 4. Mr. Lyman came to call me up, and Foster walked with me to hotel, but the train proved a slow coach and did not get in until 6½, which made us too late for the morning boat. Dined at the Stanwix Hall—rather shabby place. Rained all the forenoon, but I contrived to call on George Shepard and Henry S. McCall. Latter married about a year ago, comfortably settled, active in new Congregational Society. At 3½ P.M. went on board the *Jos. Belknap,* which brought us to Poughkeepsie at 9. Thence to New York by the cars, a beautiful moonlight ride. Out at Canal Street and walked up with carpet bag to Florence at 1 A.M. Good night's rest in fifth story. In morning, after reclaiming trunk and breakfasting, went over to Brooklyn. Spent three hours with Noyes. Afternoon, an hour at Putnam's; found Hengstenberg on authenticity of Pentateuch but not Olshausen on New Testament. An hour with Miss Field at Mr. Crittenden's, and again two hours in the evening, very agreeably spent. Gave her a copy of Bacon's quarter-century sermon, together with my Chénier. Their term in the Academy closes about July 10 and reopens September 1.

Wednesday morning, called at Garrigue's and paid for De Wette, *Einleitung in das Neue Testament,* $1.34. Bought of Radde, Johnson's *Hitopadeśa,* $2.50, *Locman's Fables* by Rödiger, $1.00, Freiligrath's *Gedichte,* $1.75, and Goethe, 40 Bände in 20 for $20.00.

Spent 2 hours with Noyes. Returning, packed up and took cars for New Haven at 3. Arrived at 6.

Supper at Tontine. Filled with shad eaters. Talk with Henry —with Root, who takes Freshman Greek. Examined Lyons from Williams College—hard. Talk with Hurlbutt.

Thursday. Started the history. Met optional class in afternoon; are to have the *Birds* of Aristophanes, Felton's edition. Gave them for next lesson article on Greek comedy in Smith's *Dictionary of Antiquities.*

Friday. Faculty meeting at 2. Recitation in logic to Professor Porter substituted this term for disputation—better for the class though worse for me. Optional class at 5. Gave them some of Müller's ideas on origin of Greek drama. A little colicky in evening —corrected by opium.

My traveling expenses this time have been $13.77. Thursday, May 16, lent Henry 15. Paid Mother for washing, $1.00. Wednesday, May 22, paid Chassell for razor strop and soap, .79. Spent for books, as above, $26.59. Thursday, May 23, Moses for waiting, $1.00.

Saturday, May 25. After tea called on Mrs. Larned. She spoke to me from Mrs. Whitney about boarding with Mr. DeLucy, and "parlez-vous"ing. I am sorry for Mr. DeLucy and should be glad to help him, but I do not know about undertaking this matter at present. I am so busy that I should scarcely be able to give the French the time necessary for any real improvement. Besides, I find that I am becoming attached to the Sybarite life of a hotel. Called on Miss Larned, or tried to. She was out. Saw Miss Thacher. Called at the Twinings'. Had stumbled on Mrs. Twining at the President's, and on Professor Twining, just in from New York, as I was going to supper. They have broken up from Middlebury, and are going to reside at Hudson, Ohio. They leave on Monday. Miss Anna Twining had not seen the advertisement in the *Independent,* which I had the pleasure of pointing out to her. She thinks that Dr. Bacon feels angrily and bitterly toward the College.

Sunday, May 26. Dr. Fitch in forenoon, on what subject I am utterly unable to say. Wonderful unimpressiveness and evanescence about his writing. In afternoon, David Trumbull on use of early persecutions, very able and interesting. In evening, at Professor Porter's, heard Professor Twining read his essay (written 1833) on person of Christ and unity of Godhead. Drawn out with great ingenuity and force of argument. He denies bipersonality of Christ, as not contained in Sacred Scriptures and contrary to their teachings. Regards Christ as a divine soul appearing under forms and conditions of humanity, agreeing essentially with Dr. Bushnell. As to the Trinity, he holds it in the full tritheistic form, starting with diversity of attributes, which, he says, implies diversity of being; treating the unity of substance as a nullity; and taking his stand on moral unity, which he thinks sufficient to vindicate the language of the Old Testament. That language, it is true, did not express the full truth as to the divine nature, but its impression on the Hebrews was on the whole more true than would have been made by the New Testament doctrine if then revealed. He also held to the official subordination of the divine Son to the Father.

Monday, May 27. In afternoon had a call from MacWhorter, talked about his new experiences. Call from Whitney, who has just come on. He waited for his brother until Saturday, expecting to spend the Sunday with him in Northampton, but was disappointed—and in consequence did not get away until today. Saw him again in evening. He had talked with Mr. Salisbury, who is just back from meeting of Oriental Society in Boston and must steer off again in a few days; doubtful whether he can hear us this term. Made arrangements for recitation by ourselves every morning from 8 to 9. Moeso-Gothic on Tuesday and Friday, Sanskrit the remaining days of the week.

Tuesday, May 28. A pretty full day. Saw George Bushnell at breakfast, talked with him about doctrine of Trinity etc. Says he can get no clear idea of the interior consciousness of Christ. Easy to believe—the subject is wrapped in mystery. One objection perhaps to Twining's view [is] that it does not sufficiently recognize the duality of the phenomena. This divine soul which he says manifests itself under the conditions of humanity, does not in all respects conform to these conditions, has, for example, a knowledge of the hearts of others which passes the utmost reach of human power. On the whole I am inclined to adopt the doctrine of the

Church, and say, here are human predicates and divine predicates, here is a being at once Man and God. But (I would add) not Man and God in apposition (juxtaposition), but Man and God in mysterious inexplicable interfusion: the human steeped in the divine, the divine leavened with the human. However, I have no wish to hold on even to this with too great tenacity—why should I?—can I lay my hand upon my heart, and say, I have found the perfect "light and truth" of this matter?—but, like Jansen, I am ready to take back whatever the Holy Papa shall condemn and to make whatever modification he in his wisdom shall direct.

Studied Sanskrit, beginning of *Hitopadeśa*.

Mr. Dana called in the afternoon to propose that I should undertake to furnish the *American Whig Review,* by request of Dr. Whelpley, the editor, with an account of the services rendered to science by Yale College, said account to accompany a portrait of Professor Silliman. I pleaded off as Dana and Herrick had done before me, alleging want of time—though a more important reason was want of knowledge—and recommending (1) Professor Kingsley and (2) J. G. E. Larned.

In forenoon it grew suddenly hot, but a cold blast swept over us in the afternoon, and in the evening we had a thunderstorm. I started up a fire, which made me stupid, but after sleeping an hour in my chair, I roused up, soaked my feet to dissolve out a cold, and at 11½ went to bed.

Wednesday, May 29. Drew Jones' *Hitopadeśa* from College Library—very incorrect translation. Faculty at 3. Examination of delinquents to be in writing—relieve us and aggravate them.

Henry came in to say that according to Herrick the Library funds for theology are more than enough to pay for books recommended. Tried to think up some new ones. Some time at Library.

Evening, at 10½ Talcott roused up Hurlbutt and me to assist in apprehension of an "inebriate" near South College, but before we got there the bird had flown.

Thursday, May 30. Steady pulling at Sanskrit, Moeso-Gothic, Aristophanes, and Greek history, my four regular studies. My College duties occupy me in lessons and preparation about 36 hours a week, or 6 a day. College business, such as reporting, attending Chapel, hearing excuses, occasional examinations, etc., perhaps 6 hours more, making 7 in a day. With Mr. Whitney I spend 6 hours in recitation and ought to spend 24 in preparation. This would make 12 hours a day of regular business. Now meals must occupy two hours or so. Newspapers, letters, occasional conversation, calls, etc., the thousand drains upon a man's time, are but scantly provided for by two more. Then say 1 hour for dressing and the like —and there remain 7 for sleep, which I must try to keep intact though I shall be in danger often of infringing upon them. May God assist me in all duty, and forgive all shortcomings, and graciously accept my work with all its imperfections and its failures as work done unto himself.

JUNE, 1850

Saturday, June 1. From 11 to 1 in College Library looking again at collection of works on general philology. Noticed particularly Lhuyd, *Archaeologia Britannica,* which contains an Irish vocabulary and may be used in studying the language. By the way, must drive the College to get an Irish lexicon, O'Reilly and O'Brien— also *Myvyrian Archaeology of Wales.* From 2 to 4, holding examination of Freshmen delinquent in April—absent and conditioned—12 of them.

In evening called at Twinings'. Spirited controversy as to a certain Mr. Jenks, a quondam Baptist missionary in China, reported by Mrs. Macy (like her son, perhaps a little censorious) as one of those good men who think more of their books and their work than of their wives. Mr. Jenks, it appears, returning with his wife on account of her sickness (he hesitated some time about coming out with her), neglected her on the voyage and took so little heed of his child that the mother, anticipating her approaching death, commended the boy to the Captain's charge. On the night of her decease he sat up with her till 1 o'clock, when, feeling that he could do nothing more for her, he went to bed. In the morning he found her cold and breathless. He called the Captain and with obvious emotion said, "See there, she's dead—I don't know when she died." For 2 or 3 days he seemed much affected, but about 6 months after consoled himself by a second marriage. The Captain thought him a very pleasant man, but wondered much that he should so neglect his family. This I attributed to his want of practical dexterity, and an imperfect aesthesis which failed to show him the proper relation between feeling and action, between the love he cherished for his wife and the forms of conduct by which that love might be most naturally and appropriately manifested. (2 other points. 1. A man's work and books *are* more important than his wife. 2. A solitary death is best. Death of Cavendish. Bryant's "Thanatopsis," "And what if thou depart unheeded of the living etc.")

Sunday, June 2. Fitch in forenoon. Eustis in afternoon. Latter made me think of Bacon speaking before a concave mirror, so placed as to pour the sound of his voice with magnified intensity upon my ear, while the sense was made wholly undistinguishable. Did little today, and had very little of that feeling which is appropriate to the Lord's day generally, and in particular to the monthly celebration of the Lord's Supper.

Monday, June 3. Miss Beecher's new book, *Truth Stranger Than Fiction,* announced in *Tribune* with great flourish of trumpets (query, by Frederick Beecher Perkins), covering a broadside of the paper. It seems to be, like Miss Bacon's manuscript statement, directed more against Taylor than anybody else, and will trouble the poor Doctor, I fear, a good deal. On the whole, I incline to think, contrary to my first opinion, that this publication is a politic move for Miss Bacon. First, it will raise the wind, an important object for one deep in debt and cut off from old sources of revenue. Second, it will certainly annoy the enemy, and thus afford revenge, which, as Becky Sharp says, if not Christian, is at all events sweet. Third, it will bring to many who have heard only the MacWhorter statement, a forcible and plausible and to many convincing representation of the Baconian side. Fourth, it cannot be fully answered. For suppose that MacWhorter appeals to the evidence. It will be said by the Baconians that the evidence is not fairly given, and to show that it is, will be difficult, at least so as to convince sympathizers. And fifth, it will call out that sympathy, public and spontaneous, which, in the absence of proof positive against her, waits upon one who can show herself off as a wronged and suffering woman, trusting and betrayed.

Nor can it be said, on the other hand, that it will give the matter a much greater notoriety than it had before.

With the best judges, however, the book will injure Miss Bacon by creating an impression unfavorable to her delicacy and simplicity of character.

Had a long talk with Fisher about President Wayland's new notions, college education, etc. etc. Bed at 12. (Paid $5 for Aeolian piano of College choir.)

Wednesday, June 5. Finished up reporting. Wingfield diddled.

Evening, at 9, called at Professor Porter's, to mention meeting of Philological Society tomorrow evening. Met him as I was coming away from his house. He had been attending Brother Gilman's matrimonial graduation, not as a bachelor, but as Master (perhaps).

Went to MacWhorter's room by previous arrangement with Whittlesey, to discuss the meeting of our class. Found Larned. Pretty rheumatic, poor fellow; he has been kept indoors for five weeks. MacWhorter came in soon after, grumbling at Barnes, whom he found at the Blakes' and was prevented by his persistent stay from enjoying the confidential chat which he had hoped for. He gave an amusing account of Miss Beecher's late circular to the clergy. The MacWhorter party do not intend replying to Miss Beecher.

By and by, Fisher came in. Talked about Dr. Woods—the 5 oysters which he purchased for Mrs. Woods when indisposed, at 6¼ per dozen. Offered a shilling and wanted 10 cents change. Also the hat story—how he went to a store and was poking about among the 3-dollar hats, but chanced at last to ask the price of a better article, to which the vender replied, 8 dollars, but added a request that the Doctor would take it as a present. The Doctor did not appear quite satisfied, and, on being prest, suggested, "Couldn't you let me have this (a 3-dollar tarpaulin) and give me $5 in money?"

At last in came Whittlesey, and on organizing, Larned in the chair and Fisher delegate from Brown, Mr. Hadley was constrained to accept the appointment of class Secretary Pro-tem, as vice of Dr. Forbes, and received the book, accompanied by a neat speech from Mr. MacWhorter. The latter gentleman and Mr. Whittlesey were appointed jointly Purveyors General to the class, and it was agreed that the great gathering take place on Wednesday, August 14, at 9 P.M. A circular of invitation to be drafted by me, printed, and sent off to every member. Class of '42 then adjourned, and some of the old evidence etc. in the MacWhorter case was brought upon the tapis, especially the testimony of Alexander Clapp, which could hardly be improved upon. Adjourned a little after midnight.

Thursday, June 6. Meeting of examination committee at 9. Main points reviewed to be submitted to Faculty, and, if approved,

communicated to students. Details talked of, but nothing settled.
4 to 5, with Mr. Gray, an Englishman, professor at Hagerstown or
near by in Maryland, at an Episcopal college. Mr. Woolsey came
in with him and staid through the hour. Mr. Gray is a Rugby man,
an old pupil of Dr. Arnold. Said he was once flogged by the Doctor
for having said, on hearing a bad joke from one of his comrades,
that that was Munronian wit. Mr. Munro, an assistant, heard the
remark and reported it, much to the discontent of Master Gray.
Adjourned my optional class, having had no time to study the
lesson.

Philological Society at Porter's in the evening. Present, Gibbs,
Hadley, Larned, Murdock, and Porter. The last read on Thiersch
(H.W.J., son of grammarian, orthodox and Irvingite). His views
as to language and style of New Testament writers: thinks even
those born in Palestine were always more or less bilingual, that
they had a good knowledge of Greek, that the Hebrew or Aramaic
coloring came not from that language being more familiar to their
minds and so influencing their expression, but from intentional
reference to Old Testament Sacred Scriptures, either in Hebrew
or in Septuagint, and imitation of its forms, an imitation founded
on religious motives and varied according to subject matter of
discourse.

Friday, June 7. Whitney flunked on the Moeso-Gothic this
morning in order to escort his newly married friend and so forth
(i.e., the lady) about our College premises—very opportunely for
me, who had not read a word of the lesson. Worked away, not
very efficiently, at the regular things until 12 o'clock at night, when
we abluted and went to bed.

Saturday, June 8. From 9 to 12 at meeting of examination committee. Settled these points: Term examinations to go in as $\frac{1}{10}$
in the term averages, and to be visited once a year by a committee
constituted as heretofore. Biennial examinations, at beginning of
Junior year on studies of Freshman and Sophomore years, and near
end of Senior year (in 3d term, 2 or 3 weeks from beginning) on
studies of Junior and Senior years, each of these to count in making up appointments as equal to study of one term, each by printed
papers of questions to be answered in writing. Sessions of $2\frac{1}{2}$ to
$3\frac{1}{2}$ hours, and no lessons on the day of any session. No reëxamination. Absentees from Junior examination allowed to stand it next

year, and so of Senior examination. Mutual assistance to be highly
penal. With some other points of less importance.

12 to 1, with Nelson of my class. Did not at first recognize him,
but soon found him the same good-natured, stumpy, self-important
person as 10 years ago. He is soon going to Wisconsin to lend out
some $50,000 of his father's money.

Evening, at Twinings'. Coming back, stopped at Henry's and
had a talk about morals and religion, their relations and reactions,
which interested me a good deal and which I would report here
if I had time.

Sunday, June 9. Fitch, A.M., "No peace to the wicked." P.M.,
murder of John Baptist. Analysed thirty pages of Bähr's *Symbolik,*
on sacrifices. Many excellent ideas, but as regards the general
significance of sacrifices, he appears to me at once defective and
unsatisfactory. As to the symbolical meaning which he gives the
act, the surrender of an animal (sinful) nature to death (removal),
I am inclined to doubt whether it can be found in it at all, at
least, whether that idea was really connected with it in the Hebrew
mind. It is inconsistent with that typical character which even
Bähr concedes to the sacrifice, for no such symbolism can be
imagined in the great sacrifice of him who was offered up as a lamb
without spot or blemish. And here we see that the victim was not
regarded by the Hebrews as unclean either ceremonially or sym-
bolically, but as pure and incorrupt and so a fitting type of him
who died, the just for the unjust, that we through him might have
life. The language just quoted, it appears to me, contains the idea
of substitution, which so far as the New Testament is concerned
cannot be "abgesprochen." I should be inclined therefore to find
it in the Old Testament and to reject Bähr's symbolic view as
inconsistent with it. His language as to the sacramental character
of the act, I confess I have not been able yet to understand with
clearness.

Discussed the subject at Twinings' in the evening. Staid later
than I otherwise should, on account of the rain, which fell "strom-
weis," with vivid demonstrations of an electrical character.

Monday, June 10. Paid subscription to *Yale Literary Magazine,*
$2.00. Read a good deal in Grote's *History of Greece,* Volume 8—
wonderfully interesting. I *must* have the book by next October
at farthest. His account of Callicratidas is superb, and all the finer
for his strong anti-Spartan feeling. Had a call in the evening from

Mr. Henry Field, who sat about an hour. He is at present preaching in Guilford, substitute for Mr. Hall, who has gone to Europe and will return in the fall. We talked a good deal about church and Churches—agreed very well. I said that being comfortably settled here among the Congregationalists I had no intention of quitting the camp, but if I were going to live as a professional or literary man in New York City I should probably join the Episcopalians. Mr. Field declared that he was at present among the Congregationalists and had no present intention of leaving them, but he did not like their system. He should be as liberal as he pleased to other people, and if the Congregationalists were offended he should take up his hat, bid them a polite good-by, and go over to the Episcopalians.

Tuesday, June 11. Gave a lot (κλῆρος) of old clothes to a small boy, nomine Edward Downing, for the benefit of the Downing family; the father is sick, he says, and unable to work. Sent off $2.00 to Mr. W. W. Greenough, 14 Merchants Row, Boston, being one year's tax for American Oriental Society.

Wednesday, June 12. Faculty meeting, 3–5. President not in at first, so that for about a quarter of an hour we had a stand-up meeting in the entry. Resolved to change the old Presentation Dinner into a cold collation on a liberal and handsome scale. Reported from examination committee, but no action taken. College Library, 5–6. Talk with Gibbs about Park's recent sermon in Boston. It seems to me as though this separation of theology of feelings and theology of intellect was meant to be of use to him in the theological warfare which he anticipates—with which at any rate he is threatened. May it do him good service. It is true; there is no reason why it should not be useful.

After tea Henry came in with a letter from George, giving an account of his geological, carbonaceous explorations in Pennsylvania, with complaints of bad hotels and boorish people. Read Grote on Sophists and Socrates. He says a great deal of truth and says it wonderfully well, but, as in Macaulay, one desiderates the moral and religious view.

Thursday, June 13. Starting Roman history. Make a good deal of talk about Origines. I do not suppose that much will stick, but it may give them an impulse. It will serve to show at all events that I take some interest in the subject, and regard it not as mere dry formula, but matter of thought and feeling.

Friday, June 14. I forgot to note down among the proceedings of yesterday a conversation which I had from 10 to 11 P.M. with Larrowe of the Freshman class. He was to have been examined before this time on his Greek, which he omitted last term, but the thing has been deferred on account of his lectures before the Young Men's Institute. He has been holding forth on astronomy and geology, and has taken occasion, it appears, apropos of the latter subject, to deny the original unity of the human race. Some of his audience thought this doctrine in conflict with the teachings of Scripture, and wished him to add another lecture to his course in order to set forth their consistency. I gave him the indulgence which he desired for his examination and added some advice as to the topics and arrangement of his lecture, which I should like to write out here if I had the time for it.

Henry bought me some oil at Olmstead's, a gallon for $1.37½, which he is to charge on account.

Sat up till 12½, having slept, that is laid me down and tried to sleep, from 2 to 3 in the afternoon. I have some thought of experimenting on this matter, to see whether this long vigil of 17 or 18 hours cannot be advantageously divided by a short interval of sleep, but at first I shall be likely to find it rather difficult to overcome these old habits which make me wakeful in the afternoon.

Saturday, June 15. Bought of Pease, *The Village Notary,* by Baron Eötvös, from the Hungarian, price .25.

Read more in Bähr. I agree with him that the idea of holiness and sin—as absolutely moral qualities and as complete polar opposites, placing God and man in opposition to each other—that the idea of this great moral antithesis in the distinctness and prominence which it has in the Mosaic system is quite peculiar to that system. I am not sure that it appears so trenchantly even in Christianity. Certainly we do not find in the latter that strenuous avoidance of all outward defilement which in the Mosaic institution was the analog of inward holiness. It may be said, however, and with justice, that this attention to outward purity was important chiefly as a means of moral culture, and ceased naturally when the moral idea had become so strongly established as no longer to require its support.

In evening at Twinings'.

Sunday, June 16. Dr. Fitch in forenoon on unity of God; in afternoon, new sermon, on day of Pentecost, very workmanlike, unexceptionable, and unimpressive.

Read Bähr and discussed it in evening. Something very strange about pantheism. It is the shadow of the truth, dogs it and haunts it everywhere. Everything in the true world system has its analog in the pantheistic. Everything in pantheism may be adopted in a certain sense by the true and devout believer. I am by no means a pantheist myself. I regard the system as untrue and dangerous, yet I do not regard it as mere haphazard. It must sustain some definite relation to the truth, run someway parallel to it through a great part of its course. I was struck with this when noticing how in the religious systems of the heathen world God was represented as suffering for man, as being made a sacrifice, as giving up his life for creatures—expressions all of them which belong likewise to the Christian system. There is a difference, it is true, and a wide difference, between them—the difference of moral and physical, God and nature. Yet the parallelism is very curious.

Monday, June 17. Read Arnold's *History of Rome* in the evening. Bed at 12½. Am keeping up my afternoon siesta. I get no sleep, but considerable rest, which keeps me alert through the evening, but I do not consider myself as having tasted yet the economy or even safety of the plan.

Tuesday, June 18. Whitney goes to Northampton today to meet his brother Josiah, who is just starting for the West. He will be back in two days. Our next recitation is to be on Friday, 4 pages, a double lesson in the *Hitopadeśa*.

Wednesday, June 19. Not much done today. Good deal of time spent in offices. O Lord, how long! Let me not thus wait and languish for thy presence. I see very clearly that all indulgence in known sin or baseness is incompatible with the enjoyment of God. Help me, O Father, to attain to purity of heart and life. And suffer me not to lean too much on others. Let me live habitually with God and my own soul, regarding these as my only permanent connections, my companions through eternity. I believe that this feeling, instead of making me egotistical or selfish, will give me a tenderer interest and warmer sympathy for others. Thou shalt soon part and perhaps forever—that will be the thought—attest thy feeling, show affection, give happiness, now or never.

Interesting half hour's talk with Henry Field.

Faculty from 3 to 5½. More about the cold victuals on Presentation Day. It is to be a stand-up affair and called a cold dinner.

Report of examination committee called up again and principal points passed.

After tea called on Salisbury to ask him to read a paper at next meeting of Philological Society. Answer dubious. Next on Kingsley to borrow Niebuhr's *Lectures*. Stopped awhile at Henry's. Looked at Everett's Bunker Hill speech. Talked about Roman history. Home at 10. Studied till 12, when I grew sleepy in spite of my siesta.

Thursday, June 20. Bought a ream of French paper for $1.75. I did not want it and was loth to take it, but there were pressing motives of charity, so I yielded. At dinner saw Brace and spent half an hour with him and Mrs. Brace—a charming woman. In evening saw Whitney, back from Northampton. Added one or two to the Gliddon jokes, as the query, "Whether the Rochester rappings or the Boston unwrappings be the greatest hum," and the assertion that Gliddon had fulfilled his promise, "for the critter was a d—m-sell, as he predicted."

Friday, June 21. Willis says he heard Liszt play Bach's fugues in a beautiful classic style, giving the sub-base with his fingers, a marvellous feat of musical legerdemain. Dreyschock, another Hungarian pianist, plays very difficult music with the left hand alone. Is that any better than Signor Blitz? I trow not.

Sent my draft of circular invitation to Benham's press, by Mac-Whorter and Whittlesey. We strike off 150.

Saturday, June 22. Our respected legislators adjourned today—may peace go with them. We shall now have quieter times at the Tontine. Evening at Twinings'. Carried with me *Tribune* containing Mr. Clark's recent address before students of Union Theological Seminary. Moonshine. I must write out my notions on the subject.

Sunday, June 23. Mr. Dwight of Constantinople this morning, an interesting account of progress in the missionary operations in Turkey. Analysed Bähr on sacrifices, and went over the ground as usual in the evening.

Monday, June 24. Made out paper for Woolsey examination. Took 8 copies myself and am to have 3 from each of the instructors of the class. 17 applicants this year—preposterous. 8 from the 2d division, so poor that it doesn't know its own wretchedness. I am to come on, Wednesday morning at 8 in Rhetorical Chamber.

In evening, chat with Mr. Stanley from 8 to 10. I wish I could spend more time with him; his solitary, feeble, melancholy condition is sorrowful to think of.

Tuesday, June 25. Reporting from 9 to 10½, a tedious job. Began my Sanskrit at 12¼, but Hurlbutt came in, and talked till 1½—much exasperated against the President and Thacher. Perhaps he has some ground of complaint, yet he shows himself very unreasonable and quite incapable of judging properly the characters of men. At 10 in the evening Hyde came in and invited me to Mad. Bailey's. Returning stopped in at Henry's room, found a large crowd. Heard Fisk tell his ghost story. Had a long talk with Benton about Joslin, Owen, Loomis, Marshall, etc. Home at 12. Stopped to look at the moon, which is now at the full or a little past it. The sight was certainly not altogether unpleasant. It suggested funereal associations, and one who like myself walks on the shadow-side of life can have no objection to that. Yet it is not the pleasantest view of death which is called up by moonlight; it brings before you the final condition of the body not the soul. It is the cessation of an old activity, not the commencement of a new one. You have the pallor of the corpse, the stillness of the grave, the humid coldness of the narrow house—but the free motion, the regenerated life of a soul awaking to a consciousness of its immortal power, there is nothing at all of this.

Wednesday, June 26. The moonlight had a baleful influence on me last night, and I now hate it worse than ever. It transposed me into the world of illusion, from which I did not escape till after six this morning. I have the faintest recollection of hearing the prayer-bell. It was not the hearing of a man awake: the sound of the bell mixed itself with my sleeping thoughts, and then—a plague upon that pale-faced moon, may the Thessalian hags drag her down from the summits of the sky forever—and then came the thought, "It is Sunday morning." I must have thought that, I am sure, for when at length I awoke in genuine earnest, the impression was yet strong upon my mind. Is it nearly eight o'clock, I said—and started up to see half past six—and just then the melancholy truth flashed upon me. Fairly diddled. Slept over for the first time in five years. Well, it cannot now be helped, but in future beware of the moon-beams.

At 8 A.M. commenced the Woolsey examination with 17 present. Respited by Mr. Larned from 11 to 11½. Saw Mr. Gilman in College Library. He goes again, not alone, tomorrow. At one called in the papers—had not set quite enough. On my way to the Tontine met George, just from New York. Has finished his Pennsylvania explorations, reported to his employers, got his $100, and has come on here, I hope to spend several days with me.

Faculty meeting at 3. Took up report of examination committee but progressed backward. Kingsley opposed to our whole scheme. I should not be very sorry if he knocked in the head our plan of written examinations, which will prove, I fear, a splendid failure. So he says, and it is to that he opposes himself. The great question was as to the time of holding the first biennial examination. The Faculty disapproved our recommendation, but could not agree on anything else.

Called on Whitney and arranged it that he should let me off for a few days, going on in the meantime by himself till he finishes up the first book of the *Hitopadeśa*. We are then to start together in the *Bhagavadgītā*, probably the latter part of next week.

At 8 went with George to Connecticut Academy at Professor Salisbury's. Very good attendance. Subjects of discussion: Paine's gas and coal mines. Fine treat to strawberries and cream. Back at 10. Cording bed, an operation that wouldn't have occurred for a century if George had not come. Turned in at 12½.

Thursday, June 27. Saw Larned this afternoon. He is just getting about again after his long confinement with the rheumatism, is going to Thompson to recruit. Talks of making me publish the Phi Beta Catalogue. I did not refuse, but I believe I must do so. There is not time now to set on foot the necessary inquiries. With all exertion on my part the work would be very imperfect, the more so as I have not the least capacity in the world for statistics. And besides, I have not time for it. I should be obliged to give up my Sanskrit with Mr. Whitney, and that I will not do. I would not do it at any rate, and for an imperfect unsatisfactory affair still less.

Attended Mrs. Fitch's party in the evening—rather warm work.

Mrs. Trumbull looking very finely, David much as heretofore. I did not very much enjoy it, partly no doubt my own fault.

Friday, June 28. From 9 to 10 at Whittlesey's room, arranging the distribution of our class circulars. Whittlesey, MacWhorter, and myself divide the business between us. Started on the prize papers; great difference between the best and the poorest, much more than last year. Dressed for the President's levee, and went down at 8½. Many of the Seniors absent, attending initiations. A goodly number of ladies, well sprinkled in—altogether a free and easy and genial time. Some music by Mrs. Larned, Mrs. Wilcox, Mr. Willis, and several of the Seniors, as Ludden, Camp, Ripley, etc. Came home in a pouring rain, rather soaky. Washed up with great care, got my history lesson, and went to bed at 12½.

Have been reading the proceedings of the General Association of Connecticut at their late meeting in Litchfield. Much struck with the superiority of Dr. Bushnell. He towers high above the men around him; Hall, Atwater and Smith speak well, but are insignificant when compared with Bushnell. He is not only ingenious and eloquent, he is wise, noble, mild, and Christian. He has determined, it is plain, not to be read out of the Church, not to quit his present connexions, and the reason too is plain: it is his deep spiritual feeling, his sense of human depravity and his perception of the need of an Atonement. He cannot join the Unitarians, and he will therefore stay with the Orthodox; and to do that he will be forbearing and conciliatory. His manner certainly had a powerful influence on the Association: it disarmed in great part the severity of his opponents.

Saturday, June 29. Nearly finished up the Woolseys. Some time at the College Library, looking over journals. Mure's *Literature of Greece* out, in 3 volumes, bringing the subject down to 560—rather heavily written, I should think from the extracts of the *Athenaeum*. A Sanskrit drama lately acted with great success in Paris. Query, what one.

George and Henry off to West Rock with Wickes and Barnes—a steaming time. At evening bought of Pease 50 envelopes, .18¾.

Drest and called at Twinings'. Anna has been spending the week at Dr. Hewitt's in Bridgeport. Dr. Hewitt is displeased with the *Independent's* report of the proceedings of the General Association in Litchfield, which he complains of as being partial to Dr. Bushnell.

Is well satisfied with that of the *Evangelist*. Dr. Hewitt is much exercised with the rappings, has preached upon the subject. Denounced the whole thing as the work of the devil, and proposed to excommunicate all who believe in it. Strong-ish that, yet something of a come-down from the old Puritan times.

Called at Henry's. Hear that I am placed on the matrimonial list. Alas, no purity, however immaculate, is secure from calumny. This particular reproach emanates, it is said, from Reverend Mr. Richards (class of '46). Not engaged perhaps, but as good as so, and to—"Angels and ministers of grace" etc.—an awful world we live in. "Oh, Mrs. Jones, it *does* make us think that we are all accountable creeters."

JULY, 1850

Monday, July 1. Called on Mr. Stanley at 12. While we were talking, Mr. Thacher came in. Agreed to meet tomorrow at 3 P.M. to settle Woolsey scholarship. Called with George on Whitney and looked at Boehm flute—very ingenious. Settled for board at Tontine, $19.50. Had drawn $30 from Treasurer to pay it.

Discouragingly warm today, but I complain not. What a fool I should be to complain of anything. "In glowing health—in boundless wealth"—that is, never sick, or only enough so to make me feel the enjoyment of health, never pinched for cash, enough for all my wants and with a trifling balance in my favor at the end of the year. Father and mother living, kindred kindlier and friends friendlier than I, with a position of respectability and usefulness, mounted on the heights of intellectual and moral culture—what cause for grumbling? I know not, yet still I live in the shade, subject to a sort of melancholy which I have never yet succeeded in "anatomizing," feeling that the very joy of the world is steeped in sadness, that there is a half-heard knell in its laughter. This seems to be nature with me, and it is not unpleasant; it is not moping and, if I can help it, never shall be. O my God, enable me to hold fast my confidence in thee, to rejoice in thy presence, to feel the security and exultation of those who are rooted and grounded in thee.

Tuesday, July 2. Replied to B. A. Smith on Greek Readers—rather in their favor—speak for variety—experience of many different styles. Reporting from 9 to 10½, a long and heavy job. Hillyer's case to be ignored until after Presentation Day. Met at Professor Stanley's at 3 to settle Woolsey scholarship. Davies found to be first in Greek, second in mathematics, third in Latin. On the whole, far superior to Lewis and Whiton, who came next. Lewis was first in mathematics by a long chalk but low in languages. Whiton first in Latin, second in Greek, but shockingly down in mathematics. On the whole it has turned out well. Davies is a fine scholar and, with some drawbacks, a fine fellow—so at least I regard him. I believe that on acquaintance he would develop some peculiarly excellent and amiable traits of character. Faculty meeting at 4, to finish up examinations. Mills and W. R. Bliss stuck, but worked through. In evening, finding it comfortable weather, George and I sallied out, called on Miss Larned, and afterwards on Professor Olmsted, who as it happened was not in. Stopped at Henry's room and talked till 10. Bed at 11½.

Wednesday, July 3. Presentation Day. Caught in rain at Tontine. George walked through, getting pretty wet, and brought me down an umbrella. Ordered a suit of clothes at Knevals'. Exercises in Chapel at 10. Poem by Adams, very so-so. Hillyer's oration uncommonly brilliant and striking. Collation at 1¼. Handsome speech by the President, well got up and went off admirably. Faculty at 3. Case of Hillyer stated and deferred. Freshman collars rather too conspicuous at prayers. At Miss Twinings' small social circle in evening.

Thursday, July 4. The usual clanging, cracking, and crashing. Day mostly overcast and damp, but on the whole well adapted for its uses. Lighted a fire in the morning to dry the atmosphere of the room. At 12¾, out on the Green, heard peroration of Declaration of Independence read by Honorable Mr. Boardman, followed by exordium of H. B. Harrison. Finding that the latter was likely to get on successfully, notwithstanding some hoarseness, I went to Tontine to dinner. Quite a crowd.

In evening, fireworks, more brilliant than anything of the kind that we have before had here. Back at room at 9½. At 10½ alarm of fire in Lyceum. Started out and ran over to Thacher's, whom I roused, but on getting back heard the cry of "All out." Some squib thrown into Johnson's room had fallen on his bed and set it blazing. His room was broken into and fire put out without much trouble or damage.

Friday, July 5. Call from Mr. Thacher, 12 to 1. Mr. Sophocles, 2 to 4, quick, sharp, and mocking as ever. Preparatory lecture by

President at 7, on consecration to Christ, from Revelation 4.9,10,11. Discussion with Henry on the question of conflict of laws, pending before the Porter Rhetorical Society. "What is best judgment on a moral question," does it imply exhaustive investigation? No, to be determined by practical considerations.

Ice cream and strawberries from Seniors in other entry, brought round by Welch, consumed with George's help. Cake reserved to be given to Professor Paley.

Saturday, July 6. Mr. Sophocles again in the morning. Read *Evangelist*. Report of proceedings of Litchfield General Association. Somewhat fuller for Hall and Atwater, mentions that the latter sunk his voice to a solemn tone, but after all makes no essential change, does not destroy the obvious and splendid superiority of Bushnell. In afternoon tried to get Thierry's *Merovingian Era* from Linonian Library, but it was out. Evening at Twinings'.

Sunday, July 7. Communion Sunday. Less attentive than I could have wished; wandering thoughts, or rather vacuity of mind. Yet, O my God, let not the occasion pass without effect; give me a new consecration unto thee. Enable me to set the Lord continually before my face; to labor and to endure as seeing thee who art invisible. Oh, give me a calm and quiet spirit, tranquil and collected, ever fixed on thee, ever intent on those eternal things which cast in shadow all the mightiest concerns of earth and time. Make me sensible to the sorrow of others, heedless of my own, ashamed to waste the treasure of my feelings on the stings and brushes of a moment. Make me hopeful, trustful, and triumphant in thee and in thy grace. Make me active in thy service. May an inward impulse urge me ever forward in the way of duty and of life.

Studied Bähr and talked it over in the evening. George making preparations for departure tomorrow.

Monday, July 8. George off at 9½. Will spend a few days in New York, and start for home at the end of the week. Have had a long and very pleasant visit with him. At 12 called on Whitney and made arrangements for taking up the *Bhagavadgītā*. Talked about Meyer on Celtic languages, ingenious but obscure, and audacious in speculation.

Tuesday, July 9. Sleepy in evening. Went to bed at 10 o'clock, a thing unheard of. Some beautiful verses in *Tribune* from Tennyson's *In Memoriam*.

Wednesday, July 10. Faculty meeting. Case of Hillyer—confessed intoxication—degree not to be withheld or deferred—appointment not to be withdrawn—could only secure the requirement of a confession—by far too little for such a man. Examinations deferred to a special meeting, Friday, 2 P.M. Professors' meeting for question whether Mr. Dana should with his consent be now appointed professor on an understanding that he commences when his engagements with Government permit—agreed. Question proposed by President whether tutors shall hereafter be appointed for *two years*—agreed doubtfully.

At evening drest and went out, to call on Miss Elizabeth Baldwin —not at home. Over to President Woolsey's—staid to 9½. Talked of President Taylor's death and changes likely to be made in Washington and elsewhere by that event.

Thursday, July 11. Professor Olmsted's last lecture on optics. Supposed that Winthrop would get only a half lesson in optional Greek, but the rogue went over the whole, which left me in a somewhat awkward fix. I looked as wise as I could and heard him through, and he was good-natured and did not trouble me with questions. My class has dwindled. Downie went off early to swell the ranks of practical surveyors under Mr. French. Cone was sent off from College about the middle of the term for irregularity in attendance upon exercises. And now Potwin is gone this week, recruiting at home, so that Winthrop alone, the inexpugnable, remains.

At College Library from 4 to 5. Whole batch of *Revue des deux mondes*.

At 7½ went with Whitney and Gibbs to Philological Society at Professor Salisbury's. Present besides, Larned, Murdock, Porter, Thacher, and Woolsey. Salisbury on cuneiform inscriptions of Darius Hystaspes at Nakshi Rustam. Translation and analysis. Interesting to Whitney and me, as Pandits—to Gibbs also as philologer in general—less so to the rest.

Next meeting of Philological Society at Gibbs', Thursday, August 8. Thacher to explot.

Friday, July 12. At evening tried the Baldwins again, but without success. Called on Miss Larned. Loafed in Henry's room with Benton.

Saturday, July 13. Some time in College Library, reading the *Satyricon* of Petronius Arbiter—ingenious and witty, but pretty hard. Bells tolling from 12 to 2 for funeral of President Taylor. Looked over some collections of funereal poetry, also looked at Retzsch's illustrations of Schiller's "Bell Song," very beautiful and interesting. Evening at Twinings'. Some talk on feminine depend-ence and R. D. Dana, from whom I ventured to dissent without knowing what his opinions are.

Sunday, July 14. Dr. Fitch in A.M., "God is a spirit." William Kingsley in P.M. on "Nobleness of Christian life," interesting to me, but I am afraid not altogether acceptable to the audience. There is a lack of breadth and dignity, both in thought and manner, which interfered a good deal with the effect of the sermon. Yet the sub-ject was one which engaged my attention, and the thoughts were excellent and just.
Studied Bähr and talked it over in evening.

Monday, July 15. A hot heavy sleepy day likely to be followed by others yet more abundant. Washed off in the evening and got to bed a little after 12. Pretty soon heard a great crash of windows—Mr. Hurlbutt's, as it proved in the morning.

Tuesday, July 16. Excused some of my division to go to Monson, Massachusetts, to attend the funeral of Holmes, a classmate of theirs who has just died after a long illness. Reporting from 9 to 12 and then left unfinished. Talk with Mr. Thacher at 12 about examina-tions. The Faculty at their meeting on Friday have concluded to hold the first biennial examination at the end of summer in Sopho-more year. In my view this action is the death doom of our plan. It imposes an intolerable burthen both on Faculty and on students. I am much ashamed of my negligence in forgetting the appointment for that meeting, which lost me the opportunity of opposing, as I should have done, pro virili parte and I believe successfully, this most unfortunate alteration in the plan of the committee. Thacher seems for once to have lost heart. He was discouraged by my absence, and by the apparent reluctance of the President to assume the re-sponsibility of the scheme, which arose I doubt not from a desire not to bias the action of the Faculty. He was disheartened also by the opposition of our senior brethren, Silliman, who does not really know what he wants, Kingsley, who looks with natural suspicion on our newfangled notions, and even Olmsted, who has just discovered that he never was in favor of this plan but was overruled, it appears, in committee.

Finished *Birds* of Aristophanes with Winthrop, the sole survivor of my class, who looks half dead himself and was obliged, mirabile dictu, to ask excuse from recitation for tomorrow morning.

Talk with Hyde, who told me a most amusing story about the jealousies of Hurlbutt, Root, and Grant toward himself. "He thought himself too good for them, did not often visit them, did not go with them to post office, etc., and, horresco referens, wanted one of them to quit the tutorship in order to furnish him a place." Tantaene animis caelestibus irae?

Wednesday, July 17. Talk with President about our examination business. Faculty meeting at 3; no great progress. (Henry, tutor.) Bought a cap, $1.25, ordered shoes at Tuttle's. Call from Mr. Herrick after tea. Corrected proof of Triennial Catalogue for class of 1842.

Thursday, July 18. I felt unwell yesterday and more so today, though I went through with the business of the day after a fashion. Took half a Dover in the evening and went to bed at 10.

Reading *Bibliotheca Sacra*. President Woolsey on Champlin's Aeschines. Very thorough and learned. Beecher (Dr. Edward) on anthropopathism—unsatisfactory. Splendid discourse by Park— theologies of intellect and feeling.

Friday, July 19. Awoke at two o'clock, and heard the rain dashing in at the open windows of my room with a great howling of the wind. After that I lay in a not uncomfortable state, as one partially under the influence of opium, at once asleep and awake, waking sleepily and wakefully sleeping. I heard every stroke of the clocks amid the roaring of the storm, until the bell at 5½ started me out of bed. It was raining violently and continued to do so until after 8 o'clock, so that, partly afraid to encounter it and partly obfuscated by the narcotic, I concluded to give up breakfast. At Whitney's from 8 to 9 in Moeso-Gothic. A good many boughs have been blown off from the elms and other trees about. We shall hear of mischief from this storm. I dragged along in a dull enough fashion through the day, and slept all the evening from 8½ onward. Took a ½ Dover and went to bed at 11.

Saturday, July 20. P.M., looked awhile at an old problem in Legendre's *Geometry* (Davies edition)—to find a right-angled triangle from the hyp. and diff. of lines from acute angles to centre of inscribed circle. Some teacher (I know not where) has written on express to Fiske for a solution. It was much easier to me now than when I first tried it years ago at Fairfield Academy, when Hoyt, who showed it to me, solved it so ingeniously.

Evening at Twinings'. Moonshine in garden—a not unpleasing illusion. Attacked not wholly without reason for incommunicativeness. Had said nothing of George's visit.

Sunday, July 21. Dr. Fitch in A.M. "I love them that love me." Treated the love of God too much as matter of calculation. The loveliness, inherent and essential loveliness, of piety, as well as hatefulness of the opposite, which should have stood in forefront, were hardly noticed. A genuine utilitarian view of the subject. Trumbull of my class in P.M., on future state of righteous. Ingenious and interesting but not without unprofitable speculations about the acuteness of saintly optics and the number of celestial senses.

Bähr on species of offerings. Evening exercise much interrupted by conversation, not exclusively upon religious subjects. (Called on Mrs. Larned.)

Monday, July 22. Received a letter from James G. Gould, Augusta, Georgia—to get a man for a vacant place in their high school —teacher of mathematics and physics with salary of $1200 per annum. Talked with John Grant and afterwards with Miller, class of '47.

Tuesday, July 23. Mr. Willis back. Has been in New York for a few days, making arrangements for the publication of a book of sacred music. Saw Mr. (Baron) de Margueritte at Tontine. Gives a concert here on Wednesday night, bad time. News of Margaret Fuller's death—particulars very affecting. I never fancied very much either the woman or her writings, yet I had so often seen her name a star, had thought and spoken of her so frequently, that it strikes me now as if an old familiar friend had gone, by a most tragical catastrophe. I feel a sort of shame and sorrow for the harsh and contemptuous speeches which I have so often made about her, and would gladly recall them if I might. I truly believe that she was good and noble; and her end, melancholy as it is, has a depth of tragic pathos which makes it almost enviable.

Wednesday, July 24. Our 11 o'clock recitation was given up for the funeral celebration in honor of General Taylor. The Faculty and students have generally had the last place assigned to them (not occupied by them) at our civic processions—an insult probably at first, perpetuated through carelessness. Better arrangement this time by Mayor Aaron Skinner's influence: Faculty and students immediately after town authorities. Many of the students attended, few of Faculty. The firemen, unwilling to follow students, went forward with military escort. The terminus of marching was the Centre Church, where an oration was pronounced by E. K. Foster, Esquire. Though an original Taylorite, I attended no part of the exercises; a warm and dusty day, a crowded church, a long address were scarecrows.

Guns fired from 6 to 7 and bells tolled. A torchlight procession of firemen in evening, ending in a sort of uproarious jollification, rather discordant with the occasion. I attended Madame de Margueritte's concert, 30 or 40 people, in Smith's Hall, hot and ill ventilated. Madame had a bad sore throat—was bled, I understand, in the afternoon—sang hoarsely and with difficulty, but seemed to be a good singer. Mrs. Voorhies so and so. Mr. Saroni, pianist, good. Some byplay, it is said, between him and one of the West Indian Miss Bartletts, who is engaged to him, having jilted a former betrothed in his favor. But I did not see it. Most striking circumstance a bird that came in and went sailing about the room, to the great discontent of Dr. Wheat, who lunged at him with a hat whenever he came near. Doctor afraid perhaps that the bird would be in his hair. Off at the recess, about 9 o'clock, leaving 25 cents' worth behind.

At Faculty meeting, appointed examination committee with right of nominating assistants.

Subject of tutors up. Decided to take another from class of '47, but could not settle on the man. Deferred to next week.

Letter from Noyes, announcing his engagement to Helen McGregor Means of Boston, and signifying his readiness to bear such ridicule as may be forthcoming. He will be in New Haven at Commencement time.

Heigh ho—Brace, Long, and now Noyes—our old bachelor company is quite broken up. I remain "the last rose of summer left blooming *alone*." Or rather I may say,

> For now the whole round table is dissolved,
> Which was an image of the mighty world;
> And I, the last, go forth companionless,
> Among new men, strange faces, other minds.

Thursday, July 25. An epistolary day: finished letter to Mary; wrote one of congratulation to Noyes; one of inquiry to Foster, asking when he is to be expected in these parts; and one of advice to Mr. A. C. Felton, West Brattleboro, who had written to the President in regard to his preparation for our Freshman class.

Had a talk in evening with Norris of Brooklyn, who wishes to enter next Freshman class. He fitted with Benjamin W. Dwight, graduate of Hamilton College. Has read a good deal of French and German but not enough of Greek, and appeared quite anxious as to his success. He seems bright but not very deep, and withal a little conceited. Bed at 11+.

The difference between a poet and a wit is that the one sees congruities, the other incongruities. Of course each of these implies its opposite: a man who perceives fitness cannot be insensible to unfitness, and vice versa. The difference consists in the greater or less prominence which is given to these two phases of thought. Tennyson is principally occupied with congruities, and when he takes a look at the other side, as in his "Amphion," he does not fail indeed, but his success is not distinguished. In this walk he is surpassed by Thomas Hood, who has the keenest eye for incongruity, who is therefore a most admirable wit, while in poetry, although not wholly wanting, he is far from reaching the front rank. The highest may include both these faculties in an equal and extraordinary degree.

Forgot to mention that in forenoon I talked with Thacher, Stanley, President, Olmsted, about our examination matters and it was agreed to divide each class into 9 sections, and to have sessions of about an hour and a half each, keeping in the men through all the time, and perhaps carrying the questions two or three times round.

Friday, July 26. Hair cut and shaved, .18¾. Abed at 10 for a wonder, but I had not felt quite well during the day and had once or twice assumed the recumbent.

Saturday, July 27. After tea saw Charles Doolittle of Utica—met him in the street—here with mother-in-law, wife, and child—goes out on Monday.

At Twinings'. More moderate. Away by 10 o'clock.

Sunday, July 28. Spent much of the day with Doolittle, who seems a really fine fellow. Introduced me to his baby, of whom he spoke in the highest terms, and to his wife, whose appearance impressed me strongly. There is a great deal of sweet and quiet dignity in her manner. Mrs. Sherman, the mother-in-law, had been reading Miss

Beecher's book at Brattleboro. Took Doolittle with me to Chapel in afternoon. He was not much pleased with the Doctor's sermon on the widow of Nain. It is perhaps the least successful of Dr. Fitch's descriptive series; its want of pathos, considering the subject, is truly wonderful; the feelings of the widow on hearing the words, "I say unto thee, arise," were downright bathos. Read some in Bähr and expounded in evening.

Monday, July 29. Whitney went to Guilford on Saturday and spent Sunday with Mr. Henry Field. Our recitation therefore did not come till 2 P.M. Read a little in Mrs. Somerville's *Physical Geography*. Lent Miss Twining the four *Foreign Quarterlies* which I have received this summer.

Henry Field is going up to Haddam to see his sister Mary. Utinam adessem.

Tuesday, July 30. In evening had a talk with Miller. His friends are willing that he should go to Augusta, Georgia.

Wednesday, July 31. Reporting at 9. Some sharp shooting between Thacher and Hurlbutt, in which the latter avowed his intention to give as good as he got. Is it worth while to aggravate him? For my part I cannot help pitying a goodhearted man and a good scholar, who is completely blinded by notions and gropes stumblingly among objects dimly seen and incorrectly apprehended.

Wrote to Gould, mentioning Grant and Miller, with criticism of each. Mentioned also Kellogg and Bonbright. Faculty at 3. Talk of tutors. Nominated Aitchison and Blodget in that order. I voted for the opposite one, declaring that Blodget had gained on Aitchison all the way through College, and was probably ahead of him by this time. Talk about Burial of Euclid. Inclined to haul off without saying much about it, referring to the law whenever questioned and punishing such as we detect, but making no grand combined demonstration as last year.

At tea Mr. Willis gave me his experience of the Ahnfrau of the Hessian family—die weisse Frau—a signal instance of a good ghost story spoiled by vigorous investigation.

AUGUST, 1850

Thursday, August 1. From 10 to 11 examined Camp for Clark scholarship. No competition, Tupper having given out. Camp is a very fine fellow, bright and quick, but not a very painstaking scholar, and his performances show a lack of finish and felicity which surprises me. I think Tupper would have run him hard.

Afternoon and evening, calculated averages for last term—all three divisions of Freshman class—it ought not to have lagged thus far behind. Warm work this hot weather. We had a heavy shower in afternoon, which as usual only made it hotter than ever. Plenty of winged creatures by the lamplight, though this year we have had fewer than common, especially of moths, which are generally the most troublesome. One moth flew in, so large that it seems to me I never saw a larger. Then in came a bat and went sailing about the room. I caught up an old cap and began to make passes at him. While I was thus engaged, flew in two more—the unclean birds —and whizzed about in most unpleasant proximity to my head. At last I brought one to the floor, and having mastered him, thrust him squeaking out of the window. The other two in the meantime had thought it expedient to decamp, and rid me of their hateful presence. Why should they haunt me thus? I am no Edgar A. Poe to delight in the company of these night fowl. "He might have soared in the morning light, but he made his nest with the birds of night." Bed at 11.

Mr. Storrs of Brooklyn (lately here, called on Taylor) loquitur: "Sell a human being! I would as soon think of selling an angel." Dr. Taylor: "I would sell an angel quick, if it was for the greatest good."

Friday, August 2. At College Library from 12 to 1, reading Jahn's *Jahrbücher*. Interesting article in *Tribune* on French papers, by C. A. Dana.

Preparatory lecture in evening by Benton, extemporaneous, not uninteresting. He felt rather nervous about it, and made some apologetical remarks as we were coming away. I asked him to my room, where he staid till nearly ten. We talked chiefly on European politics. My view is that monarchy in Western Europe is doomed, that it must fall before many years. What is the basis of a throne? Loyalty, attachment to the person, respect for the person of the monarch. But what is the basis of loyalty? There must be some ground for respect and attachment—there may be several. The sovereign may be respected for the power he wields, but in England he wields no power. That which in theory is conceded to him, he is in practice restrained from exercising; he cannot veto the decrees of the Commons; he cannot select his own ministers. He may be respected for his virtues and abilities, but in most living sovereigns these are not conspicuous, and if they were, it is not enough that a king should be a gentleman, a Christian, a man of genius. He must be a king too, he must have an opportunity to display these good qualities on a great scale and with most beneficent results. But how is that possible for a powerless king? He may be respected as the constitutional head of the government. Ay, but then he must be so in fact and not in name merely. Suppose we Americans should ordain that Bishop Gobat of Abyssinia shall be the head of our government but shall have no more real power over us than before, what would be the practical effect of such a resolution? I can think of only one ground beside. He may be respected as the remnant and representative of what has been great and glorious and powerful in the past; history and tradition may support him. They do support the king of England, and, in a people who establish so strong a connection between the present and past, this may continue for some time. But even here it must at last be seen that the past is represented only in form and name, not in substance and reality: it is only the corpse of departed greatness, which, mummify it as you will, cannot forever rule the world. Even in England, a king who should attempt to restore the basis on which rested the throne of William the Conqueror or Henry the 7th, would only show how unsubstantial is his own, and, by seeking to be a king, would prove himself to be none. Royalty in England is a shell, which may hold together, hollow as it is within, and make a fair appearance so long as it remains untouched, but on the first rude shock will fall to pieces. This of England. But all Western Europe is tending in the same direction; it is in fact the universal tendency of constitutional monarchy, which ought not to be regarded as a permanent polity, but rather as a transition form. I cannot wonder at the King of Prussia for his resistance to a Constitution; he saw and saw rightly that it is in essence incompatible with monarchy, that the popular acclaim which hails a new Constitution is the far-off death-knell of the old monarchy.

Saturday, August 3. Carried watch to Olmstead's to have it cleaned. Going away from dinner, was stopped by a gentleman who announced himself as Professor Chace of Brown University. He wished to inquire about Porter of my class, as they think of appointing him Professor of Applied Chemistry in Brown, on their new organization. I spoke very highly of Porter, explaining his indifferent scholarship in College, stating the favorable opinion which we entertained of his talents, and saying what I knew of his success as an instructor in Delaware College.

The Professor had intended to stay over Sunday, but was unable to secure satisfactory lodgings at the Tontine and concluded to leave in the night-boat for New York. I sent Fisher to him, and heard from Fisher that he took him to Dr. Taylor, who in a conversation on College studies spoke after his fashion rather slightingly of the physical sciences, Professor Chace's own department of instruction. The Professor vindicated his department, and Dr. Taylor, who smelt the cat, allowed the subject to drop. Professor Boies, it appears, has resigned, and is going to Europe.

After tea, talk with Fisher on pantheism etc. Most sultry evening, collar utterly collapsed, yet trusting to the darkness made my appearance at the Twinings', or should have done so had there been any light in the room. Professor Silliman came in soon after, and kept up a running fire of gossip and gallantry in his fine though not faultless way. Miss Anna confided to him some matters as to the "Brothers Hall" (that is to be), which I as a Linonian was not supposed to hear, and of course cannot repeat. Afraid, however, that my presence might operate as a check to prevent confidences, I took my leave at 9, and stept over to Mac's room. Found Whittlesey. Read *New York Herald* on the Beecher book, which is again out of limbo, attached for $25, bought in for $50, and now advertised in the secular papers. Bennett's notice is unprincipled in tone, but takes a sensible view of the expediency of publication, and is particularly severe on Kate Beecher, whom he dubs busybody general.

Saw Tennyson's *In Memoriam* for the first time. Mac came in about 10, and showed us his famous letter to Clapp, describing Miss Bacon's note of invitation at the outset of their acquaintance. Really a very innocent affair, contains no imputations on Miss Bacon, though humorous enough on the singularity of his introduction to her.

Talked politics and what not till after 12.

Sunday, August 4. Communion. Spent much of the day in religious meditation, and hope that I gained something, that my thoughts and hopes and feelings may hereafter be more constantly religious. Lord, strengthen thy servant, arm him for action and for suffering, attune his soul to harmony with thee; may the chords of his heart vibrate in unison with all that is pure and noble and holy. Deliver me from the devices of my own imagination—from perverted ingenuity and specious plausibility and imposing soph-istry, from overstrained refinements, from mazing subtleties of reason, from misguiding analogies, from the illusions of a perverse corrupted nature. May I walk before thee in simplicity, seeking for thy direction and in childlike faith submitting to thy teachings. Give me the wisdom not of earth but of heaven, the wisdom that cometh down from thee, the light that illumines without dazzling, the clear daylight of divine truth shed abroad over the calm and peaceful soul.

Read from Baxter's *Saint's Rest*. Negativeness of heaven. Baxter enlarges, not formulizes.

Read Hall's vindication of himself against charges of *Independ-ent*. Not satisfactory, that is to say, he has not shown and cannot show that in his remarks on the *Independent* in the Litchfield General Association he correctly represented the position of that paper. His attempt to show that the Association acted in direct contradiction to the views of the *Independent* is a failure except on one point, the right of remonstrance as between Associations, where the *Independent*, or Dr. Bacon, stands on extreme ground. Hall is more pettifogging in his way than I should have expected to find him. I had thought him rather a fair, candid, and straight-forward man.

Tuesday, August 6. Thacher has a plan for an 8-weeks vacation from July to September, giving two weeks to each of the other vacations, the winter vacation to include the holidays. He says that President Day has no objection and that President Woolsey will not make any if President Day does not. There may be some trouble about details, but I go for the plan. Success to it.

From 4 to 5 examined Potwin and Winthrop on the *Birds*. They did very well. Excellent and faithful men, both of them.

Read some in Goethe's minor poems—wonderful variety, and freshness and freedom.

Wednesday, August 7. Examination, 4 sessions of an hour and a half each—going three times round—on Greek history, Roman Republic, and Roman Empire. Generally quite well, but the absentees rub hard. Sanskrit with Mr. Whitney at 12. Went without dinner, feeling rather out of sorts—a little tendency to a diarrhoea. There has been a good deal of this abroad within a few days past.

Finished up the *Bhagavadgītā,* a book which has given me much pleasure and some instruction, which however I have at present no time to criticise.

Thursday, August 8. Mr. Brewster last evening inaugurated his new (Washington) Hall with a discourse (discursive as usual, they say) from Park Benjamin. I did not go near it.

Again 4 sessions of examination, which were rather a weariness to the flesh, as I felt somewhat unwell and was therefore absent from supper. Moeso-Gothic with Whitney at 12 M. Finish up in one lesson more, which may come perhaps on Saturday. We have not read much of Moeso-Gothic text this term, but have been perusing the grammar, especially the syntax, together, talking freely on all points and questions suggested by that perusal.

Friday, August 9. Last session of examination at 8. At 10, in Hurlbutt's room, Hurlbutt, Porter, and myself to talk it. More than 20 below average and sentenced to reëxamination on something or other, several on all. Absenteeism.

Faculty from 11 to 1 and again 3 to 5 P.M. Case of Jones, who was with Dean (?) when the latter insulted a woman in West Chapel Street some evenings since. Concluded to urge a legal prosecution —arrest of Dean, Jones to be called on as witness—in order to bring out name of principal offender.

Hurlbutt impracticable about Greek grammar in our examination at Commencement of candidates for admission. Queer fellow. The only view which he can take of the matter is that Thacher examines in Latin grammar specially and solely and that therefore someone should do the same for Greek grammar.

Subject of terms and vacations taken up but adjourned till tomorrow morning at 8 o'clock.

President consulted Professors in regard to Mr. Grant. Thought best that something should be said to him, directly or indirectly, and as gently as possible, expressing our view of matters. ([Vote:] 6/4.)

At evening took a glass of soda, the only nutritious material appropriated during the day.

Saturday, August 10. Went down to breakfast at 7, but, not finding it quite ready, sheared off. Sent round for most of the fellows in my division who came off halting at the examination. Saw Battles, Burnham, Cone, Griswold, Lincoln, Solomon. Remaining yet to see Estabrook, Jenks, Loomis, and Spencer. The first it appears cleared out without leave on Friday; he dodged his optional examination altogether, went well on other things.

Faculty at 8. Settled in regard to Jones that he should be held as particeps criminis, and cut off from College unless justice could be satisfied by the detection and punishment of the principal offender, whom of course he can if he will make known to us. In regard to terms and vacations, the Faculty voted unanimously (Kingsley, who would have said No, being absent): 1. that it was desirable to have a change; 2. that the change ought to secure two points, Commencement earlier in the summer and Christmas and New Year in vacation. Three plans were brought forward: a. Commencement third Thursday in July, with 8, 2, and 2 weeks respectively for the summer, winter, and spring vacations; b. Commencement last Thursday in July, with vacations of 7, 2, and 3 weeks; c. Commencement first Thursday in August, with vacations of 6, 3, and 3 weeks. The last was supported by Stanley, Grant, and Dwight. Porter and I preferred the first but were ready to acquiesce in the second, which seemed likely to prevail and which did thus secure 9 voices. The President seemed not averse to it, and I am really in hopes that it may be adopted. I afterwards drew it off for him in a clear synopsis to be laid before the Corporation.

Went over to Dow's and took a dose of Castor oil, rather bunglingly administered in a measuring glass. I did what I could with brandy and syrup of sugar but it was a rather nauseous dose. It operated somewhat gripingly and not very copiously—how should it, copiously? for I had eaten nothing during 48 hours and drunk nothing either except that glass of soda. I contrived, however, to read the *Tribune* and Goethe's *Faust,* to examine Wingfield satisfactorily on history, to have a talk with Grant, which was interrupted by the incoming of my classmate Sherman, and lastly to take tea at the Tontine. Found Mr. Willis there, who much to my satisfaction did not appear to have observed my two-days-and-upward absence.

At 8 went over to the Twinings'. Was obliged to acknowledge my reasons for premature departure last Saturday evening, to say peccavi and promise amendment. Root was identified as the man who informed against me that George was here in New Haven. The attempt to ascertain whether the same George was a professor proved a failure.

Sunday, August 11. Read Tennyson *In Memoriam,* which I bought last night of Pease, 75 cents—all excepting 50 pages of advertisements in the end, which vexed me as much as it is worth while to be vexed in a world like this. Like a great deal of Tennyson's poetry, it needs to be read over and over. It is wonderfully full and deep, and to many will seem a revelation of their own inward experience.

At Trinity Church in forenoon heard a preacher, to me unknown, who pronounced a most ingenious and interesting discourse from the text "Rejoice with trembling." He contrasted the religion of comfort which prevails nowadays with the terroristic religion of former times: both wrong, but the first probably more mischievous and fatal than the other. Both are partial, present but one aspect of the truth. Catholic doctrine unites them, preaching terror as well as comfort, and showing itself here, as so often elsewhere, paradoxical. Is he a Massachusetts man reacting against predominant tendencies there? It looked so, yet here at least it might seem a sort of internal opposition to a style of preaching prevalent in his own Church.

In the afternoon, Dr. Fitch, an interesting subject abstractly and dully treated, yet not inferior to the other baccalaureate sermons which I have heard from him. How a man can contrive to be so unimpressive on such an occasion is more than I can understand.

At Twinings', 8–10. Solved the sphinx riddle of my character, presenting in "skepticism" the master key which opens all its mysteries, the latent principle which accounts for all anomalies. Met the Reverend Mr. Blanchard of Lowell, who was pathetic on the subject of early marriages.

Monday, August 12. Started examination at 9, adjourned at 12½. Resumed at 2 and continued till 6. Conducted in a very businesslike way; we pushed hard and worked fast. I examined in the forenoon 23 candidates for Freshman standing. In afternoon, occupied chiefly with Sophomores and Juniors. We turned out 39 Freshmen, not including Sibley and Drake, of whom the first will certainly be admitted, nor Fellowes, who applied for Sophomore and was told he might enter Freshman. Three more have been admitted before, in whose examination I participated, and one at least, perhaps two or three, examined by Professor Kingsley alone.

Tontine crowded. Get my meals a half hour after the time. Morris in the evening. Has been a year at Auburn, will stay a year longer. Not much spirit of study, too much practical religion. Speaks well of Mills, highly of Hickok and Hopkins, not so well of Few Smith, whom he regards as a good scholar and a man of talents, but of frigid nature.

Tuesday, August 13. At 9 started again with our examination, which we carried on till near 5 in the afternoon. Counting Sibley and Drake, together with White, Hill, and Shurtleff and one at least (name unknown) examined solely by Professor Kingsley, we should make out 73 Freshmen. 6 have been admitted Sophomore, 4 Junior.

At 8 received salary of Mr. Herrick, $240 in check on New Haven County Bank.

At dinner saw Benner, Bushnell, and Scudder, Dana, Northrop, Brace, Gilbert. Noyes and Emerson appeared at the examination room. Latter called upon me at my own apartments. Call from Reverend Mr. Eustis as to corresponding secretaryship of Phi Beta Kappa.

Fellows coming in pretty thick. Call from Long in the evening. Abed at 12.

Wednesday, August 14. Up at 6½ to reclaim a cane which I had left yesterday at the examination room.

At 8 looked in upon business meeting of ΦBK. Seward elected orator, but on protest of Southern gentlemen withdrawn. Orator for next year, ——; substitute, George Hillard. Poet, Alfred B. Street; ——, substitute.

Alumni in College Chapel at 9½. Deaths by Dutton. Procession down to Centre Church. Long and interesting address by President, feebly delivered, except peroration, which was noble and pronounced with great animation. Up at 1. After about half an hour marched by classes into the tent and sat down to a dinner on the whole very well got up. Went away at 3½ to examine a student for Freshman. Returning at 4½, heard part of the after-dinner speaking. Best thing a very handsome offhand performance from Bates of Missouri. A humorous poem from John Pierpont very well read. Good speeches from Dr. A. H. Stevens of New York and Judge Gould of Georgia. A good one also, rather too long, from Daniel Lord of New York. Felton and Bacon I missed. Bacon spoke, they say, slightingly of the dispute between Taylor and Tyler, as having a difference of only one letter in their names and still less in their theology. He talked of the College as having a powerful tendency, from the way in which it was conducted, to make men Episcopalians. Do not know precisely what he meant, but guess that he thinks our instruction dogmatical.

A little talk with Noyes till 6½.

At Henry's room from 7 to 8. Cut the ΦBK, Andrews and Holmes. Went up to the Philosophical Chamber at 10¼, where the fellows soon came in from ΦBK. Marched in procession to Union Hotel and sat down to cold supper with tea and coffee. Mathews near by, quite uneasy, said 'twas late, must go to business: on his motion, Peters appointed chairman. Hadley, secretary. Whittlesey acted, reading names, I taking notes. Went through the roll, getting some things quite too imperfectly. Mathews presented resolutions as to Parker, to be sent to his widow. Referred to me to draw up resolutions in case of Higginbotham and send them to his friends, if I can find who they are. Adjourned, to meet again in August 1855. Vain attempt to procure publication of details. Sang "Auld Lang Syne" and adjourned. Much more decorous than could have been expected—in fact, remarkably well for class of 1842.

Back with Eaton. At room just about 3 A.M. Soon went to bed, but lay awake for some time in serious conversation. Eaton, however, got up and made off about daylight.

A most admirable day, lowering at first, and cold and cloudy for most of the time throughout, but free from rain. The performances went off in the most comfortable and congenial manner.

Our supper cost me $1.75. The class turned out, all things considered, wonderfully well. Of 98 surviving members, 46 were on the ground during the day and 42 present at the supper. The class of '47, which graduated 124 members, had no larger number for their masters meeting.

Thursday, August 15. A cold and rainy day. I rose at 7½ and went without my breakfast, for which in fact I felt no manner of appetite. Staid away from Commencement exercises, forenoon and afternoon. Went off, they say, very well, better than was generally expected. Richards appears to have carried off the palm.

Examined several fellows during the forenoon. Have now 76 names on our Freshman list.

In the evening dressed and went to President's levee, at about 9 o'clock. Immense crowd. Staid about 5 minutes and then came off. At Henry's room till 10 o'clock, when I came home and went to bed.

Received from Pitts three dollars to be handed over as subscription to the committee for erecting a new Linonian Hall.

Friday, August 16. Saw MacWhorter and Bushnell at breakfast. Mac showed me Miss Beecher's circular to women, in which that respectable portion of the community are requested to combine against a man who says that he was courted by a woman, and against all who uphold him, even if doctors of divinity or presidents of colleges. Saw Benner at my room. Had an interview with Mr. Harvey Peet of New York, painful both to me and him. Was obliged to say that I should vote against the immediate restoration of his son. A pleasant half hour with Noyes, who is going East; will be gone 4 Sundays, beginning with the next. Wrote a letter of condolence to Mrs. Anna C., widow of the late Charles Collins Parker, enclosing resolutions of the class as proposed by Mathews. Also another to the friends of Jesse Alexander Higginbotham, with resolutions drawn up by myself as directed by the class. Reclaimed the class book from Whittlesey's room, collected statistics in regard to several of the fellows. After dinner had Sherman at my room from 2 to 3, copying residences of the classmates. Afternoon spent in miscellaneous reading. Evening, called on Mrs. Larned. Staid till 9½.

Saturday, August 17. Worked at my essay on the verb εἰμί, which must be copied for the press. Spent some time both forenoon and afternoon in the College Library. Interesting articles by Curtius in *Zeitschrift für Alterthumswissenschaft* on Oscan and Umbrian grammar. MacWhorter rushed in impetuously about 10½ and haled me off to Whittlesey's room, to translate certain documents which he had received early in the morning from a Don Whiskerando that interrupted his morning slumbers to bestow them. They proved to be a diploma, letter, etc. associating him as a foreign correspondent of the Academy of Science and Belles Lettres of Palermo in Sicily. I do not know precisely what to make of it, but I suspect that the society empowered Mr. Forresti and Mr. La Fata to recommend American associates, and that these gentlemen enquired of Dr. Forbes in New York or of somebody else who was intimate with Mac, and were told of him as the most distinguished man in New Haven, and hence the papers.

At evening received the great brass key with which, like St. Peter, I am to bind and loose the entrance to my vacation paradise. Got numbers of *Edinburgh* and *London Quarterly Reviews* at

Pease's. Visit at Twinings'. Talk at Henry's with Fisk and Camp until 12.

Camp is going into 170 next year, with the understanding that I am still to retain my old loafing place. Our furniture, too, will remain there, as well as some part of our literary treasures.

Sunday, August 18th. Up at 7½. At Trinity Church in forenoon; heard a preacher whom I know not, very moderate. At Centre Church in afternoon; Parson Ludlow, pious, earnest, and out of taste as usual.

Bähr on sin offering and trespass offering—explained in evening.

Monday, August 19th. Finished up my article on $\epsilon\grave{\imath}\mu\acute{\imath}$, sum. At the cars from 10½ to 11 looking for Foster, who however did not make his appearance. Call from Mr. Whitney; agreed to correspond.

Went over to Geological Lecture Room, to look after the *Savants*. They had already started at 2½. Professor Olmsted, when I entered, was reading on the subject of lightning and lightning rods, brilliant and pointed as usual, followed by Henry, who gave a lucid and interesting account of some experiments of his own. Next Agassiz in a curious dissertation (extemporaneous) on the resemblance in face and feature between men and fishes. His drawing is wonderful.

B. Silliman, Jr., on the knobs in certain Niagara rocks, ascribed to tadpoles, pollywogs, etc. Fine little speech of Agassiz. Marks of rain drops in rocks.

Loomis on houses electrically excited, not uncommon, ascribed to friction of shoe leather on carpets. Interesting discussion in which quite a number participated. At 5½ adjourned.

Dressed up a little and at 6½ went to Professor Gibbs' as per invitation received in the morning. Present, Mr. and Mrs. Klipstein, Dr. Mason, Professor J. A. Porter, Professor Fowler, Mr. Whitney, Mr. Selden, with a number of ladies—non descripts—quite unknown to me. Circular arrangement of party, black coats all together in one lune, particolored dresses in another. After listening awhile to Professor Fowler and Dr. Klipstein, I got beside Porter, but soon perceiving an accidental opening in the enemy's line—viz., a vacant chair between Miss Anna Gibbs and the rest of the feminine line—I charged gallantly to the spot and carried it triumphantly. I then began to talk quite energetically, but not without misgivings that my stock would fail me, when

Mr. Gibbs was good enough to introduce me to a Miss Martin, sister, as it appeared, of Reverend Mr. Martin, class of 1837. She talked with great vivacity and spirit, and we kept up a lively fire across the front of Miss Gibbs, who sat between us and said nothing —my fault: I should have appealed to her and drawn her out: I am quite ashamed of my negligence. About nine there seemed to be a movement, and I with most unusual gallantry inquired of Miss Martin whether she was provided with an escort. She said no, but she needed none, as she was staying at Mr. Gibbs'. I did not express the relief I felt, but asked how long she was to remain in New Haven. "Several weeks—until colder weather." I expressed a hope that I might see her again. "She should be staying at Mrs. Lee's boardinghouse." So I bowed myself out. Spoke with Mrs. Gibbs in the entry, apologized for Henry, who is tarrying in Jericho until his beard is grown; he has been a shaveling through the summer, but is now donning his winter shag. I did not mention this fact to Mrs. Gibbs, but alluded to the necessity under which he unexpectedly found himself of attending a friend at the cars. Foster, however, did not come, and I begin to fear that some necessity may keep him away altogether. After a short stay in Henry's room, I returned to my own and betimes went to bed.

Tuesday, August 20. This morning the Association divided itself into two sections, one of Geology and Natural History, the other of Physics and Chemistry. Heard Agassiz on eggs, but went out to look for Foster, who was nowhere to be found. Returned to the physical section and heard Lieutenant Davis and Professor Peirce. The latter thinks that a Virginis probably, though by no means certainly, has an orbital motion around a body invisible. From 2 to 3, made out averages. At 3, general meeting of Association in Chapel. Professor Henry on mechanical powers—lively discussion —and Dr. Page of Washington on electromagnetism as a motive power. Has made a machine of 4 horsepower at least—this statement confirmed by Professors Johnson and Henry. At 6½ adjourned.

Hailed by Henry, who said that Foster had just come and was settled at Mrs. Hazard's. Went on to tea, where I saw, but did not speak with, Wadsworth. I forgot to mention in my journal for Saturday, that he saluted me after breakfast on that date, and told me that he had been here, though too rheumatic to go about, during the whole of last week. He has been here several times, he says, within the last few years. When asked why he had not sought me out, he returned very unsatisfactory answers. Was going up to Hartford, to be back this week. In the reading room after tea found Professor O. Root of Hamilton College, rather the worse for wear, had a cold and headache. Off to Mrs. Hazard's and brought away Foster to the Tontine to see him. After some talk we all adjourned to Mrs. Hazard's, where I staid talking till after 9. Coming back, gave Mr. Dwight the Freshman averages of my division for the second term of the year, all but Griffith, whose average in geometry Mr. Backus had neglected to hand me.

Abed at 10½. Rainy in evening. Soda at Dow's, 5 cents. Idem last evening, 5 cents.

Suffer me not, O Father, to forget thee and thy presence. May my thoughts be continually turning towards thee. May I feel that earth with all its fortunes and its interests, its hopes and fears, its mirth and earnestness—that all these rest in thy being, and that I myself rest in thee, and so resting may abide secure forever. May a simple, natural, unquestioning piety be the habitual condition of my heart. May I cling close to thee, the rock, the enduring and permanent one, and thus bid defiance to the storms around me. Against time may I take refuge in the Eternal, against change in the Immutable, against chance in Providential Wisdom, against death in Him who has brought life and immortality to light in the gospel of his Son.

Wednesday, August 21. At 9½ went over to Cabinet and found Root exploring there. Soon after saw Professor Dwight of Hamilton College. Heard Agassiz on crustacean jaws. Crossed over to physical section, and heard from Professor Mitchel a remarkably clear and forcible statement of his method for measuring right ascensions and declinations. Method itself rather shaky, I suspect. Rogers commenced an exhibition of Poole's organ, when, finding that I knew all and more than all he had to communicate, I left precipitately. There were 3 sections this morning, that of Chemistry and Mineralogy having been set off by itself.

Afternoon session rather heavy, had not patience to sit it through. After tea, had a long talk with Wadsworth on front steps of the Tontine. He graduated at Union in 1838, with no very high opinion of the College, taught two hard-working years at Canajoharie, New York, spent two years in Princeton Theological Seminary, going out in 1842, the year of my graduation here, settled in Troy until last January, when he went to Philadelphia. He has given up his poetry, neither reading nor writing the article, did not know that Tennyson was a great poet, has been accustomed to laugh at his wife for admiring him, but on my recommendation promised to read a little of him. Showed his depoetization still more by the very matter-of-fact, commonplace, and prosaic advice and counsel which he was kind enough to give me on the subject of matrimony. Left him at 8 and went to Henry's room. Paid Henry for paying my washing bill, $4.62.

Staid away from Mr. Squier's lecture on volcanoes of Nicaragua, as also from Professor Shepard's party, to which in fact I had no proper right.

Thursday, August 22. Talk with Bonbright, who is going to teach in Madison, Georgia. Long one with Grant, who is to leave us—takes it more comfortably than I had feared. Heard Professor Peirce on fundamental principles of dynamics—sorry I did not hear the whole. It made a great impression on Hackley, who called attention to the $\int Pdp = 0$ as a most novel and important discovery. At end of forenoon a most spirited discussion on Professor Mitchel's new method for right ascensions and declinations of stars. Peirce led off the opposition and spoke well. Walker talked rather favorably. Hackley and Bond, Junior, took the other side. Bond spiteful. Hackley as mean as he could possibly show himself. Mitchel responded with great energy and confidence, which made more impression on the unlearned than on the scientific portion of his audience. Bache poured oil on the troubled waters; he was most excellent and happy in all he said. Perhaps complimented Mitchel too highly. Peirce deprecated the game of brag and hoped that all might be done in a scientific spirit. Committee of reference appointed with Peirce as chairman.

P.M., some time in College Library, looking at natural philosophy. At general session heard Gould, Dana, Agassiz, and Jewett—latter on stereotyped titles for library catalogues. Saw Whitney off. Saw Root and Foster. Introduced to Stephen Alexander, who is staying with them at Mrs. Hazard's. After tea, long talk with Willis on Chapel steps with full moon rising before us. Conversation mainly religious. Went to College Street Church and heard most of Professor Henry's lecture—excellent.

Friday, August 23. Interesting papers by Bache on tides, Coffin on winds etc. Shepard is coming out with a number of new mineral species to replace those which he has lost. In afternoon, interesting paper by Alexander of Princeton on extension of Bode's law. Bond talked without much consideration on a method of making lenses achromatic without using different kinds of glass. After he sat down, Gould, who happened to have at hand a copy of Brewster's *Optics,* showed him the whole thing in print. All he could say was that Brewster spoke of eye pieces while he himself referred to object glasses. Miss Baldwin, happening to sit near me about the close of the session, gave me an invitation on behalf of her mother to take tea with them. Mr. Gould of Cambridge to be there; beside him, only their own family and visitors. The discussion on galvanic wave time, the last business of the afternoon, had commenced. Mr. Gould and Mr. Culmann had spoken. Professor Loomis was speaking. Dr. Hare rose to speak, when I sloped. Had just time to don a change of habit, none to nap a two days' growth upon my chin, and in such wise presented myself. Saw a Miss Perkins, sister of Perkins, class of '48, who talked with great spirit. Went over to Professor Salisbury's to look at Professor Bailey's microscope. Had a good deal of talk with Mr. Gould. He is well acquainted with J. D. Whitney and speaks of him in the highest terms. Says that in the difficulty with Jackson, the latter was all in the wrong; that if anything in Whitney's course was censurable, he (Mr. Gould) is entitled to half the blame. Speaks contemptuously of Hackley, who I doubt not richly deserves it. Came away at 8. Cut the evening session of the Scientifics.

The Savants had a party at Mr. Hillhouse's. Miss Baldwin was kind enough to give me an invitation, and even proffer me a place in their carriage, but I declined.

Saturday, August 24. Association from 10 to 1. Physical section finished up, 18 articles presented mostly by their titles. Mr. Redfield in 10 or 15 minutes defended his views, which had been roughly attacked by Dr. Hare the evening previous. Bache stated his difficulties. Davis attested the superior accuracy of Redfield's data. Alexander Fisher. Olmsted on monsoons caused by burning canebrakes—noticed by Bache and Henry in a very flattering manner. Henry gave some account of old experiments on dynamical electricity, oscillatory movement in discharge of Leyden jar. Bond exhibited his spring governor—very ingenious. Saw Root: says that Foster went to New York with Alexander at 10 A.M. Have seen very little of him. Root will stay over Sunday to visit Bristol mineral locality on Monday. Settled with Pease, 8 dollars for Reviews and 50 cents for *Initials*. Last general meeting of Association in afternoon at 3. Guyot on meteorological observations in New York state (the "great" state, corrected by him to the "large" state, of New York) under direction of Smithsonian Institution, arranged and superintended by himself. Complimentary resolutions. Concluding speech by Professor Silliman, containing some historical notices, the usual lurry about "word and works" with the usual shadiness about the reconciling exegesis, and the usual delicate allusions to the ladies—five allusions at the very smallest calculation.

After tea had an hour's talk with Wadsworth on Scientifics, Agassiz, original unity of race, inspiration, etc. etc. He talks well, but it strikes me rather curiously to find myself able to cope on equal terms, at least so far as mere strength of intellect is concerned, with one whom my latest recollections represent to me as so immeasurably superior.

At Twinings'. Talked on Tennyson. Glad to find that Lieutenant Davis is a reader and admirer of the poet.

[*Crossed out heavily:* Staid preposterously—till 11 o'clock—which if I do again, and except under the pressure of necessity, I will subject myself to a pecuniary forfeit, of 1 cent for the first 5 minutes, 2 for the second (10), 4 for the third (15), and so on, doubling for every additional 5 minutes after 10 o'clock—the sum to be given to the Orphan Society here or to some other objects of —— which may seem to have greater claims, and to be over and above the sum which I should otherwise apply in the way of charity.]

Sunday, August 25. Woke up early, or rather was awaked by a great storm of rain, beating in at my windows. The water fell continuously and copiously during most of the day, keeping me from breakfast, from church in the forenoon, almost from dinner. It was rather as a matter of principle and duty that I mustered resolution to go down to the Tontine. Returning, stopped at Henry's, who told me of Dr. Bacon's forenoon sermon—extemporaneous—intended specially for the Scientifics, Agassiz, etc., who were there—side blow as usual against Taylor—liberal in tone—held that, though the Sacred Scriptures are infallible, our interpretation is fallible and must be modified to answer the demands of science. True, if you mean exegetical science, but if you mean astronomy, geology, physiology, etc., most false. Every tub on its own bottom. If Moses calls a thing black, the fact of its being white does not prove that he meant white when he said black.

Attended at Episcopal Church and heard Mr. Pitkin, who preached a very sound, well-ordered sermon. Professor Bache and Professor Coakley were present—whole number perhaps 50, some ladies among them, which must have required a good deal of resolution as it both rained and blew violently. The wind eventually prevailed and toward the end of the afternoon gave us a fine clear sky.

I feel today the reaction of the last 3 weeks. Could hardly bring my mind to any settled occupation. Read, however, Bähr on consecration offerings, and expounded in the evening.

Talk with Henry from 7 to 8. He thinks of joining Trinity Church here, before going to Andover. I interposed no objection. I think in fact that it is his best course. His own free, spontaneous disposition in this matter, prompted by no solicitations on my part (though that perhaps is a thing for me to be ashamed of), yet his independent resolution to profess himself a Christian, gives me the utmost pleasure. May God enable us both to honor that profession by holy and consistent lives.

Took over *Jane Eyre* and the *Initials* to Twinings'. Back at 10 to Henry's room. Read in the *Edinburgh Review*. Finished up article on the Gorham case.[5] Read on Goethe, a fine article, severe but just, and on Mérimée's history of Pedro the Cruel—story very well told. Henry went to bed at 12. I sat till one, when I blew out the light, went home in a glorious moonlight, and abed without a lamp.

Monday, August 26. After breakfast took my article on εἰμί to Professor Salisbury's. Called at Mrs. Hazard's to see Root, but he had gone already. Got into Hurlbutt's room and obtained the examination papers of the late Junior class, which I averaged so far as my own division are concerned. Wrote letters to the parents or guardians of that respectable fraction of my men, 10 in number, who are liable to reëxamination in whole or in part at the opening of next term. Shaved and went to supper. Had a talk with Wadsworth, interrupted by the incoming of Mr. Root, who has got back, laden with spoil from his day's expedition. At Bristol he obtained from a German chemist some specimens of their vitreous copper, which he would have thought fine, had he not seen some

very much finer, which were not to be had either for love or money.
It is Dr. Nott's mine, but whether the Doctor is responsible or not
for this peculiar tightness is more than I can say. Root promises
some good specimens for George, will bring them to Geneva, early
in next week. On his way back he stopped at Chester, visited the
baryta mine, and picked up some interesting things. I introduced
him to Wadsworth, who at first seemed rather shy and at last broke
out with, "When you sent me off from Hamilton College." Root
owned that he was tutor at the time of Wadsworth's dismission,
but denied that he had any share in that business. Dr. Dwight,
he said, had declared, "I am the College." He was crazy then and
had become crazier since. Was living in New York City, nobody
could tell where. Those who wished to see him called at a certain
bookstore where he was usually to be found at a particular hour
of the day etc. At my instance we adjourned (Root and I) to Henry's
room, where we sat till 10, when Root took his leave. Returning
home I wrote report of class meeting, till 11½, when I abluted,
and got to bed at 12. Went to sleep, thinking over the cause of the
Harvest Moon, but without making much progress in the explanation. (Toothbrush at Dow's, 40 cents.) Waistcoats and gloves at
Knevals' on credit.

Tuesday, August 27. After breakfast, finished up report of Class
meeting. Went to the cars at 9½, and at 10 saw Root off on his
way to New York. Returning, received from Mr. Herrick the $95
which I had on deposit in the College Treasury. Filed letters and
sorted papers, made an auto da fe of the refuse. After dinner, drew
my salary, $240, from New Haven County Bank. Bought of Pease:
Southey's *Life and Correspondence* by Harpers, Parts 3 and 4, 50
cents; Bryant's *Letters of a Traveler*, $1.25; *Mosses from an Old
Manse*, $1.00; Dyer's *Life of Calvin*, $1.00; Grace Aguilar, *Vale of
Cedars*, 75 cents—in all, $4.50.

Returning, found Egleston of New York City, a Pittsfield pupil
of Mr. Brace, rejected a year ago and since studying with Mr.
Dudley in Northampton. He now applies again for Freshman class.
I examined him in Greek and marked him 2¼. He seems to have
been pretty industrious, but he has a shockingly bad memory and,
what is worse, has not the heart even of a chicken—pa and ma I
fear have brought him up too tenderly.

Packed my trunk for the greatest part. After tea, paid my bill
at Tontine, $13.50. Tried to see Wadsworth, but failing of that,

left my article on Tennyson for him. He has been accustomed to laugh at his wife for her admiration of Tennyson; in this particular at least she is certainly the better half. Talk with Henry. Directed him to pay up for *Independent* to end of next year, December 31, 1851. Pay to Pease, money to be refunded if pay has in the meantime been sent on from home. He makes a good suggestion that our folks should take the semi-weekly *Tribune* in place of the weekly *Tribune* and the *New York Observer*. Wrote journal. Abluted and to bed in good season. Prospect of a fine day tomorrow.

Wednesday, August 28. Up at 6½. Finished packing and arranged matters in my room in a leisurely way. At 9 called on Miss Anna Twining. Carried last *Edinburgh* and *London Quarterly Reviews*. Received the *Initials,* which she had finished before supper yesterday. Her sister left last evening for Bridgeport. She expressed the hope that I might find out something about "our folks" and especially about the supposed Home Missionary. The Tennyson (*In Memoriam*) I left, thinking that of all our folks George alone would care for it and that he would probably obtain a copy.

At 9½ the carriage came from Tuttle's (25 cents). I locked up room door and entry door and left the keys with Henry. Fare to New York, $1.50. Started at 9.50. The rain of last Sunday had not lost its effect, and the dust was for this route scarcely noticeable. Toward New York it was worse. The sand blew up in clouds, and on arriving at the city washing and brushing were more than mere luxuries, they were necessities. To obtain them however was not so easy. At the Broadway Hotel (.37½), where I stopt, their rooms were all occupied, and they told me that the city was unusually full and that all the hotels were crowded. I cleaned off a little (.05) in the barroom and then sallied forth. Had a mean dinner at the Saracen's Head in Dey Street for .18¾. Mem., beware of Turks and *Tartars*. Called on John Chassell and had a pleasant chat. Looked round Appleton's Bookstore; tried to find Doyle's; examined some of the cheap bookstalls; glanced at Garrigue's establishment (Garrigue himself gone to Europe). Encountered some temptations, but escaped them all through the conviction that I could not without a good deal of trouble open my trunk to insert any new thing.

Supped at Broadway Hotel, very tolerably—good glass of porter. Away to Castle Garden to hear the opera of *I Puritani* performed

by the Havana Company. Got there just at 7, when the doors were
opened (ticket, .50; libretto, .25). The people were coming in fast,
and at 8, when the music struck up, an immense crowd had assembled, filling the whole room—3000 I thought—the papers
estimated 5000. Steffanoni, whose benefit it was, received very flattering testimonials of approbation from the audience, but her
singing did not please me. I could not see that it showed much
either of taste or execution. Her voice is strong but not clear, and
her style inferior not only to that of Laborde and Pico but to that
of Truffi even: so at least it seems to me. The men, on the other
hand—Salvi, Badiali, and Marini—all have fine voices, and sing
well; not with very much taste perhaps, but in that, it may be they
were only accommodating themselves to their audience. It was
plain that the people valued noise above everything else; a loud
blast always brought out a round of applause, and a stunning duet
between Badiali and Marini, with a perfectly deafening warwhoop
on "gridando libertà," was most enthusiastically cheered and en-
cored. This however was partly political, the "sovereigns" (tyrants)
being always taken with the name of *libertà*. The libretto was
lamentably poor, absurd and dull enough to be beneath criticism,
almost below contempt. Between the first and second acts came
an instrumental duet, Arditi on the violin and Bottesini on the
double bass. Both played well and were warmly applauded by the
audience, who, however, appeared to admire more than anything
else the really surprising rapidity and dexterity with which Bottesini handled his clumsy instrument. Yet is it not a waste of ingenuity and effort to do with immense labor and difficulty in the
double bass what is so much more easily and perfectly effected on
the violin? The performances were very long—it was more than
half past ten when the second act closed. I was tired and sleepy,
so I worked my way out of the throng, and rode up to the hotel.
(Bussing, .12½.) By good luck I got a room in the extreme apex
of the roof, the 7th floor of the house, where I found a comfortable
bed and had a reasonable snooze. I settled my bill, = $0.94, before
retiring, or rather, mounting to my roost. Whole expenses of the
day, $4.18.

Thursday, August 29. Called up at 5½. Called a hack. Paid the
porter .10. Hack fare, .37½, with which the gentleman-driver was
very much dissatisfied, and finding me immovable (I had inquired
at the hotel), he intimated a doubt as to my gentlemanly character,

which I thought it not worth while to vindicate. Embarked on board Piermont boat, and started off at 6½. Fare to Geneva, $6.oo. A fine day and on the whole a pleasant ride, though 350 miles is a tedious journey, take it how you will. The valley of the Delaware seems to me scarcely so beautiful as I thought it on my first survey; on the other hand the Chemung valley interested me more than before. At Elmira found Mr. Hogarth returning from a large Synodal meeting just held in that place. On taking the boat at Jefferson he introduced me to Professor Hopkins of Auburn, the professor of ecclesiastical history of whom Morris spoke to me in such high terms. He was Moderator of the Synod and presided with uncommon acceptance. Our conversation was soon interrupted by a how d'ye do from my classmate Robinson, just getting back to Penn Yan. I asked Robinson to make out a written account of himself in chronological order, for the use of the class secretary. He promised to do so and let me have it next week. Pretty soon Reverend Mr. Cannon came up and informed Robinson that Geneva College had a prospect of 30 or 40 Freshmen for the next year; this he had heard from Mr. Kidder, a trustee. I struck in and had quite a talk with Mr. Cannon, who appeared very pleasant and interesting.

The new boat is a fine one and made excellent time, so that we reached Geneva at about 9½. On getting home, however, the people were all abed and lights blown out. George was not long behind hand, but came in undress to undo the door, and after lifting my trunk upstairs, took me downstairs, where I ate with vigorous appetite. I had eaten very little during the day: a miserable piece of pie at Port Jervis, with two cakes that were not bad, a couple of wretched peaches at New York, and a decent apple on Seneca Lake, to say nothing of a cup of coffee which I bought but did not drink at Lanesboro and a glass of soda beer which I took at the bar of the boat—total expense, 23 cents.

Father and Mother have been at Meadville, Pennsylvania. Will perhaps return by end of the week.

Upstairs, some talk with George, and abed at 11½.

Bought on the way a Railway Guide, price 12½ cents. Whole expenses of the day, $6.85⅝, of the trip, $11.03¼.

The weather has been as fine as it possibly could be.

Friday, August 30. Journalized. At 11, Father and Mother back from Meadville, Pennsylvania. They did not go to Cleveland, having heard that it was sickly there, and being both, I suspect, a little homesick. In the afternoon and evening did a good deal of talking, and not much beside. Attended the lecture preparatory to the Communion by Mr. Hogarth. Text from Colossians 1.21,22. Three things to be considered by Christians, and especially with reference to this ordinance: 1. their past state toward God as aliens and enemies by wicked works; 2. their present condition as reconciled in the body of His flesh through death; and 3. their future destiny, to be presented holy, unblamable, and unreprovable in his sight. We are not to wait till death for sanctification, but to expect it here from steady use of the means of grace and constant performance of Christian duties.

Prepare me, O Father, to celebrate the redeeming love of Jesus Christ, thy son, through whom I am reclaimed from enmity, reconciled to thee, and made fit for thy presence in heaven. And enable me so faithfully to serve thee, to overcome the evil of my own heart and become conformed to thy perfect image as revealed in the person of my Savior, that having passed the period of wardship, I may enter in full-grown strength and love on the possession of the inheritance which thou has promised, as heir of God, and joint heir with Jesus Christ, to whom be glory evermore.

In afternoon announced Henry's intention of joining the Episcopal Church, which seemed to occasion more of satisfaction than regret.

In evening talked of Professor Webster's execution, this being the fatal day.

Read in Mrs. Somerville's *Physical Geography*.

Saturday, August 31. Wrote letters to A. E. Stevens, 4 pages, and to Henry, 5. This occupied the forenoon and small part of the afternoon. Went out at 1½ to mail the letters, but could not find the post office; it has been removed to the vicinity of the Franklin House. Was going down there, but the south wind blew along the street, raising such clouds of dust that I gave up the enterprise in despair and put the letters into George's hands. Paid Seeley 25 cents for his porters who took me and my luggage up from the boat on Thursday evening. In afternoon and evening read Mrs. Somerville's *Physical Geography*.

SEPTEMBER, 1850

Sunday, September 1. Prepared for the Communion by a written exercise, in which I endeavored to set before my own mind the benefits for which I am indebted to Christ and him crucified. Mr.

Hogarth preached eloquently and impressively on the perpetuity of the Eucharist. Communion service in the afternoon. Felt that I am to be among the children of the light, enjoying the light of God's truth and the light of God's countenance, that I am to walk in light, clearly, openly, and cheerfully, that I am to shun the darkness, of deceit, of doubt, of gloom, and to put away the unfruitful works of darkness. Oh that I may set the Lord always before my face, and live amid the light and hope and joy of his immediate presence.

At 3½ went to Episcopal Church. Sermon by Mr. Bissell—"the wages of sin is death"—plain spoken and evangelical. Read a little in Dyer's *Life of Calvin,* a book rather destitute, I fear, of philosophic insight.

Heavy rains, commencing at 6 o'clock and continuing for several hours. Will lay the dust, which has been troublesome. Abed at 11. Contribution box, 25 cents.

Monday, September 2. Continued raining all last night and great part of today. Read Mrs. Somerville's *Physical Geography*. At evening attended Monthly Concert with Mary—quite interesting. Mr. Hogarth presses matters on in a very businesslike way. Interesting intelligence from India that a Hindoo changing his religion cannot be excluded from the civil privileges of caste, that is, within the dominions of the East India Company. Contributed 25 cents borrowed from George.

Tuesday, September 3. Pleasant day. Read Mrs. Somerville. The book is not very well done. There is a lack of thorough digestion and careful finish. Trimmed my beard a little in the afternoon, for an evening at Mrs. Curry's—only our people. Mr. Curry was away at Lyons. His sister Miss Curry, from Kentucky, has spent the summer here, taking lessons in music and drawing—soon to return home. Came off at 9. Missed Hodges, who had called to see me. He goes tomorrow morning.

Wednesday, September 4. Read Mrs. Somerville. Spent a good deal of time with Professor Root of Hamilton College, who came according to promise on the noon train, as a guest of George's this time, rather than mine. Vain effort to purchase a daily *Tribune;* read it, however, at Franklin House. Have caught a hard cold most decidedly—soaked my feet in the evening.

Thursday, September 5. Root still with us, a very fine man,

full of quiet power. Hard rain in afternoon. Calls from Mrs. Titus and Mrs. Hargan in evening.

Friday, September 6. Root left us this morning in the cars at 11, having previously examined the circulation in a frog's foot as exhibited by George with a microscope of Chevalier's belonging to the College. Mr. Curry went down with us to the cars. Told of a fellow at Lockport who had committed some offence for which he was disciplined by the Church and brought to confess. "Finally, my brethren," said he, "I am a great sinner—*and who isn't?*"

Caught a glimpse of my classmate Beach, and obtained his chronological biography. Mrs. Hargan at dinner. Has Miss Beecher's book, recommended by Mrs. Hodges. Knows Miss Bacon, and dislikes her. Reading Mrs. Somerville. Read over some old decisions for Mary's benefit. It is a fine exercise, this writing of decisions; one ought to get a list of questions and do up one in a day regularly.

Heard a letter addressed by George to James Hoyt, who wrote him from Greenfield enquiring the most expedient way of laying out $100 for minerals. He wishes to get some for his school in Talladega, Alabama. Is to be in New Haven about the 15th inst. His address in New York City, where he will spend some time, is 109 Henry Street. I must call there to see him. After mentioning and criticising other methods, George suggested that Father would put him up a fair cabinet on reasonable terms.

Read the weekly *Tribune*. New correspondent, the Princess Belgioioso, in poverty and exile. She writes well but does not seem to know precisely what ought to be said.

Old woman's distinction between poetry and blank verse.

"I went down to the mill dam

"And when I got there I fell down $\begin{cases} \text{slam" = poetry} \\ \text{whop" = blank.} \end{cases}$

Sunday, September 8. Head scratched, a scurvy job. Reverend Mr. Cannon preached very well in forenoon. I contributed $1.00. Mr. Hogarth in afternoon, not so clear as usual.

Attended Episcopal Church at 4, and heard Reverend Mr. Bissell. Not much interested in the sermon, my fault perhaps quite as much as the preacher's.

Wrote a prayer. Sang in the evening.

Monday, September 9. In forenoon bought bottle of hair oil, 16 cents. In afternoon, call from my classmate Robinson of Penn

Yan, who brought me a written account of his experiences. I showed him over the College, and then went down with him to call on John C. Strong: but Mr. Strong, it appears, has gone to Buffalo, not much regretted, I fear, by the good people of this borough of Geneva. Robinson invited me to call and see his wife at the Temperance House, but I suspected that the baby of five weeks might be a little troublesome, and so declined. They were to leave in the cars at 4, en route for Oswego, to attend the meeting of the American Board.

Returning home, stopped at *Gazette* office and purchased daily *Tribune,* 3 cents. Spent some time at bookstore. Bought *Woman's Friendship,* by Grace Aguilar for 75 cents, Dickens' *Household Words,* numbers for August 17 and August 24, 12½ cents, and case of pencil leads, 5 cents. Letter from Henry. Has settled for the *Independent* to December 31, 1851. Delay in the arrival of the paper at Geneva accounted for by the fact of its being sent from Pease's at New Haven; to be sent hereafter from New York. Henry says that Mr. Pitkin, concerned for his spiritual welfare, advised him to put himself under the tuition of the Church, meaning by the Church here Arthur Cleveland Coxe and other Apostolicats of Hartford. Henry replied that such a course, involving on his part an entire change of purposes and plans, required mature consideration. He says he *shall* consider it fully, very fully indeed.

At evening, talk with George about his introductory course on geology at the approaching preliminary term in Buffalo.

Wednesday, September 11. Read Mrs. Somerville. In afternoon went over to College and looked about in Anatomical Museum. Walked down town with George and tried to find a daily *Tribune,* but without success, the steamboat had not come in. We proceeded to the landing and waited awhile for the boat, but she did not make her appearance.

In evening called with George on Mrs. Hodges, found her at home. The young ladies out, attending lecture. Came in by and by, greatly alarmed, and not without cause, at Mr. King's big dog, who had jumped out upon them by the way.

Thursday, September 12. In morning took my watch to Mr. Barnard's, who did but little to it. Went to railroad office to find out about the car-times at Utica. Unsuccessful there and at the *Gazette* office, but found out at Franklin House. Broom brush, .125. Home, fluting. Mrs. Somerville. Shall not do as much as I intended with the book. In afternoon called with Mary on Mrs. Curry, sat about an hour. Evening, read Goethe's *Wahlverwandt- schaften*. Sleepy. Up till 11½ with Father, who was busily engaged with the tail of *Woman's Friendship*. The fire went down, the room grew cold, and I crept off to bed in the dark, stumbling about so as to alarm Mary, who cried out, "George, are you sick?"

Friday, September 13. Packed. Gave George $200 to be deposited with Sidney Shepard. Received acknowledgment. Paid Mother for towels and washing, .94. Left in the cars at 11. Porter, .25, nuts, .06. Fare to Syracuse, $1.625. Thence to Utica, $1.50. Large influx of American Boarders. Saw Drs. Cox, Hough, formerly of Middle- bury, Adams of Boston. Utica, 4½. At Baggs', excellent supper. Doolittle out. Professor Prentice's at 7½. Mrs. Prentice and Jane at a party. Miss Emily tending a wounded student. Professor soon came in—an hour's talk—promised him a Yale Triennial—he proposed a correspondence—but? He gave me an account of initia- tory examination at Harvard which he attended in July. Superior to ours in organization and thoroughness. We cannot come up to it, must compensate by strictness after the formation of the class.

Now on hand, $118.04.

Saturday, September 14. Up at 5½. Bill at Baggs', $1.50; por- terage, .25. Good breakfast. Cars at 7. Herkimer at 8. Ticket, .50. Sallied out. Saw Michael Hoffman, one of the Turtelots, Harvey Doolittle, Andrew, the old Doctor, about the house and better than I had expected. Driving out with Andrew saw Col[onel] Bellinger. Dinner with him and Mrs. Doolittle, the latter an old schoolmate of Mary's at Pittsfield (Mary Bain).

Newport stage at 1, 50 cents. Beautiful drive over plank road. Saw the Franklins at Middleville. Mr. and Mrs. Chassell, as I feared, not at home—gone in their own conveyance to attend meeting of the Board at Oswego. Lucinda and William cordial. Mr. Gris- wold of Rome at supper. Over to Newport with William. Saw Elkins and his family—living in a beautiful place near the old Willoughby property. Back to Mr. Chassell's and abed at 11½.

Sunday, September 15. Heard Elder Brown of Newport, fore- noon and afternoon. Spent afternoon, evening, and night with Elkins at Newport in multitudinous talk.

Monday, September 16. Long talk with Wilson. Some old pas- sages betwixt him and Taylor illustrative of greatest happiness theories. Some old books for College Library at New Haven. Saw old Mr. Yale's lock shop and his son's picture studio. Back at Mr. Chassell's. After dinner, with William to Fairfield. Saw Mr. and Mrs. Bradley, Philander Griffin (assistant in the Academy. Principal, Mr. Weed from Hamilton, Madison County, brought thither by Dr. Mather's influence), Eb. Porter, just recovering from fever (his father in same situation, his mother worn out with watching and fatigue), Dr. Sweet, Major May, Mr. Morehouse, Martha Bryan, very pale and thin (mother sick abed), Miss Maria Tallman. Back at 6. After supper Gaylord Griswold came in. While we were in full tide of talk, about 9 came Mr. and Mrs. Chassell. Mr. Chassell talked about his health encouragingly, and fought over his old battles at Dartmouth.

Tuesday, September 17. Interrupted at prayers. Off in stage, James Johnson, driver, 50 cents. At Herkimer, .25 for porterage. Off at 11 in mail train, $1.90. Schenectady at 3. Foster at home, family well. Little Agnes has had whooping cough and inflammation of the lungs, and for a time was hanging betwixt life and death. From 7 to 9 with Tayler Lewis, talking of his theory of metre. He rejects triple time, reducing it to common by means of assumed pauses; trochees and iambi = dactyls or anapaests with one short time omitted, so that iambic verse is a staccato anapaestic.

Wednesday, September 18. Up at 7. From 10½ to 12½ with Tayler Lewis, talking on miscellaneous subjects. From 2 to 3 with Cousin Romeyn—quite too much of the naso suspendis adunco— no special right on his part. Promises well. Porterage at Givven[']s, .25. Fare to Albany, .50. Off at 7. Off in *Hendrik Hudson* at 8½. Fare to New York, $2.00. Staterooms all engaged. Turned into berth at 11. Slept very little. 5 cents for liquor.

Thursday, September 19. Up at 4½, into New York at 6. Porterage, .20; hack, .50. Broadway Hotel at 7. Washed. Stept over to American Museum to get a Jenny Lind ticket. Got into the crowd and squeezed up. Ticket $5.00. Up to Westermann's and bought Müller's *Neueste Fortschritte der Physik* for $1.75, to be sent to Foster by Mr. Stephen Vedder of Schenectady with Westermann's Catalogue. Read over their lists; not so good for philology and theology as Garrigue's. Called at Parker's, 10½, and breakfasted, 19 cents. Saw John Chassell. Back to my room, up four pair of stairs, and drest. Down to see Spenser Shepard. Not at home. Called at Gowans' Bookstore. Saw Malte-Brun for $5.25. *Encyclopaedia of Geography*, $3.75.

Talk with Cousin Spenser. Bought umbrella of John Chassell, 40 cents. Warren Green not at Sands', found him at home, No. 6 Prospect Street, Brooklyn, at dinner. Cordial invitation to stay, which I declined. Over to Mr. Crittenden's. Miss Field not in, left card.

At Castle Garden, talk with Mr. Morley. 25 cents for Jenny Lind words. Preposterously early; whiled away time from 5½ to 7, when people began to pour in. My seat rather hard. Sleepy during the last part of the performance. Off at 10. No carriages to be had. Walked up and went to bed in a heat. No use for my umbrella. 10 cents for blacking shoes. .06 for bussing etc.

Friday, September 20. Up at 7. Breakfast at 8 at Parker's, .25. Over to Garrigue's. Bought *Die Gegenwart*, $8.00; *Exegetisches Handbuch zum Alten Testament,* $14.00; Keil's *Josua*, $2.00; Latin religious songs of Middle Ages, $1.125; Tholuck on relation of Old and New Testaments, .75. Did not pay for them. Settle in December. Whitney came in with his brother Josiah—to sail in the *Washington* at 3 P.M. Off to see James Hoyt at 109 Henry Street, his father-in-law's. Found his wife. Agreed to meet him at 8 to-morrow morning. Back at hotel, drest. Over to Brooklyn. Talk with Noyes. To Mr. Crittenden's—Miss Field at her brother's in New York. Away to Squire Mann's. Carried far away to foot of Court Street by carelessness of bus driver. Got back to Warren Street, 66, where the people live. Angry at Mary. Henry to be labored with. Supper there. Returning, drest, and went up to 87 East 17th. Found Miss Field ill with whooping cough. Saw her brother Mr. Cyrus Field and his wife—pleasant visit from 8½ to 10¼. Back to hotel. Journalized. Abed at 11½. Bussing etc., .48.

Saturday, September 21. Breakfast, .25. Up at 8½ to see James Hoyt. At 10 came down with him and looked around at Appleton's, Newman's, and Westermann's. Added Spruner, *Ancient Atlas,* $6.625, to my list at Garrigue's. At 2½ to Mr. Pratt's to dine by Hoyt's invitation. Down again at 4. Over to Brooklyn, met Noyes. Sauntered back to New York. Looked at daguerreotypes. Talked till 6. Drest and rode up to Spenser Shepard's. Saw Mrs. Shepard and little girls, Charley, and at last Mary with John Bain. Over to Mr. Cyrus Field's. Miss Mary no better. Saw Mrs. Brewer from Middletown. Mr. Stone, brother-in-law of Mr. Field. Come over in *Pacific*, shortest passage of 10 days and 5 hours. Back and abed. Porterage etc., 54 cents.

Sunday, September 22. Breakfast at Lovejoy's, .25 (Parker and Mercer closed). Drest and over to Brooklyn. Heard Noyes, truly pathetic sermon. Little talk with him.

Dined with the Manns and attended Mr. Storrs' church, but heard somebody else, rather heavy. Supper at Warren Green's with John C[hassell]. Went with them to hear Henry Ward Beecher. Great crowd. Sermon, what I heard, for I was terribly sleepy, lively and entertaining.

Over to New York. Tried for a bath, but in vain. Shaved moustache, etc. Horribly bitten with mosquitoes, this whole time in New York. My face will not recover from its wounds in a fortnight.

Monday, September 23. Breakfast at Parker, .31. At Gowans' bought *Encyclopaedia of Geography*, $3.75, and Fuss, *Roman Antiquities*, $1.25. At Garrigue's ordered Max Müller's translation of *Hitopadeśa*. Packed. Looked at cheap bookstore on Fulton Street near Herald Buildings. Crowd attracted by Jenny Lind. Looked in at Bartlett and Welford's, saw Johnston's *Physical Atlas*, $12.00, Herschel's *Astronomy*, $1.75. Bill at Broadway Hotel, $2.25. Porter, .16. Hack to cars, .50. Fare to New Haven, $1.50. Porter at New Haven, .375. Express train in at 6. Supper at Tontine. Unpacked etc. Abed at 12.

Traveling expenses for the trip	$20.30
Add Jenny Lind ticket	5.00
and books for myself	5.00
Foster	1.75
	32.05
Started with	121.475
Balance on hand	89.425

Tuesday, September 24. Up at 7. After breakfast, at examination room. They commenced this year with unusual expedition on Monday afternoon. Worked pretty steadily through the day—a toughish batch of fellows. Meeting at the President's at 7½; subject, vacancies in the Faculty. Root and Grant have left us, and Mr. Stanley is too ill to go on. His symptoms have become quite threatening; has short breathing, hectic cough, and night sweats;

will probably go abroad for the winter, i.e., if his friends can prevail upon him to do so. For the gaps here, Hyde, of course, stops one. My brother will not turn aside from setting his face toward Andover. Aitchison will not pledge himself for two years, and Blodget has not yet made his appearance. Some talk about Hodges and Miller. Concluded at last to offer Aitchison Mr. Stanley's place without pledges, and to see Blodget when he comes on.

Wednesday, September 25. Continued examination. About 35 Freshmen admitted—in all perhaps 115 or thereabouts. Examined this afternoon in my own room. After tea called on Mr. Woolsey, and obtained copy of Bullion's *Greek Reader*. A little while with Mrs. Woolsey.

Tutors at a loss about their studies. Hurlbutt and Talcott go with the Juniors. Dwight and Backus want to take the Freshmen again. This would leave Hyde, Aitchison, and Blodget with the Sophomores, all new to the class and two new to the tutorship. Some of the Faculty remonstrated, and a meeting was held at 12½ to consider the matter. It was expressed as the general preference of the Faculty (aside from any special circumstances or conveniences) that one of the old instructors should continue with the class. Dwight, however, was immovable, and Backus yielded. With the utmost regret he consented to take Sophomore Greek. Being assured, however, by several that the vote of the Faculty was not to be construed as imperative, or binding on honor and conscience, he went back again to his Freshman mathematics, which on the whole I believe to be for the best. He would have been unpopular with the Sophomore class, I fear, if he had stuck to them another year. Dwight and Backus will meet with the Sophomore instructors through the term, and give them the lights of their experience.

My friend Mr. Butler has packed his duds for Brooklyn, and leaves tonight in the boat. He will probably go to Europe in the spring. I am heartily sorry to lose him.

Story from Mrs. Woolsey about the mutual admiration society, how on the appearance of the *In Memoriam* they dropt in one after another at the Ticknors', Longfellow, Sumner, etc., each with his "Tennyson has done for friendship what Petrarch did for love." At last one of the house came in, caught up the book, and cried, "Ah, *In Memoriam* out. Tennyson has done etc." Lieutenant Davis in repeating the remark gave it *Plutarch* for *Petrarch*.

Anecdote told by Professor Kingsley. Dr. Brodhead, over 100, at a public dinner turned to Dr. Dwight and said, "Dr. Dwight, I have something to tell you." "Ah, what is it?" "I remember, when you were a tutor, you came to Saybrook and preached there. I heard you and didn't like you." "Very probable, but what didn't you like?" "Why, you came there and preached up the doctrine of disinterested benevolence, and that I didn't like. I wrote to Dr. Dana that there was a young man, a Mr. Dwight, who was making quite a stir there with his preaching of disinterested benevolence, and Dr. Dana wrote back that he was glad to hear Mr. Dwight was a young man, for when he got to be an old man he would know better."

Dr. Dwight used to say that he wondered the people didn't get up and go out of the church when he preached some of his earliest sermons.

Thursday, September 26. A good deal of examining. We have at last got 120 names on our list. Met the class at 11 and gave them their lessons. At 4 heard my first recitation in Greek, *Odyssey,* xix, first 13 lines. Talked a good deal.

A cold rainy day. Clinton Camp arrived in the afternoon. I know not how the plowing match throve. Yesterday was a fine fair time for the agricultural and horticultural exhibitions.

Friday, September 27. Colder today and more rainy, a dull time for our 120 Freshmen, who however are not yet all on the ground. 7 absentees thus far. Examined a Wadham, who failed in Latin and Greek both and was rejected. Between 12 and 1 at College Library. Article on Latin nouns in *io* with special reference to *religio,* which I must look at farther. It is by Volckmar in *Zeitschrift für Alterthumswissenschaft.* Evening, borrowed a pail full of coal from Brother Hurlbutt and started up a fire. Read Curtius on Greek verb and *Encyclopaedia of Geography.*

Saturday, September 28. In afternoon examined Woodward—rather scantily fitted in Greek. His father, Judge Woodward from the Wyoming Valley, with whom I had some conversation in the evening, appears to me to be a remarkably sensible man.

Looked over my tract on analysis of verbs, to see what changes are requisite. Noticed nothing in the system itself, only two or three points in the conjectural explanations, as the future of liquid verbs, and the Aeolic aorist optative. Examined Volckmar on Nouns in *o* and *io*. Think he has proved that *religio* cannot come from *religā-ò,* but still hold it derived from the primitive whence *ligāo,* which probably signifies "to adhere"—Sanskrit *lag,* or perhaps *rang'.*

At Twinings' from 8 to 9. Came away in very tolerable season. At Hurlbutt's from 9½ to 11½.

Sunday, September 29. In the morning, Hyde called and said that he must either preach at Eustis' in the afternoon or send a hand, that he had but one sermon which he considered as at all fit to preach there, and about that he had a good deal of hesitation, as it crossed the Taylorite track, incidentally but pretty sharply, in several places. He was afraid of appearing somewhat petulant if he took the first opportunity of preaching in New Haven to attack the doctrine of our schools. He read me the most critical passages. They were excellent in all respects, and I strongly advised him to come out with the sermon. I was very desirous to hear it, but could hardly venture to quit the Chapel on the first Sunday of the term. Tried to hear Dr. Fitch, with but indifferent success. Read Bähr on Nazarites and expounded in evening, or rather, read it out of the book. Not quite satisfied with his view; doubt whether long hair can properly be regarded as a symbol of holiness; should view it rather as a sign of full unchecked physical development, while the abstinence from wine is intended to secure the mind in its highest clearness and energy, so that both together give us the consecrated *man* in his utmost natural perfection, so that in his vow he consecrates to God not simply himself, but himself in his best estate.

Symptoms of a cold, so, after looking over lesson for the morning, took a pretty thorough hot bath and went to bed at 12½.

The Germania Musical Association have been thronging the Tontine for several days. They gave concerts at Brewster's Hall on Friday and Saturday evenings, and a grand sacred concert this evening, but with what success I know not. They make a singular appearance with their sandy moustaches and their Dutchy lingo. Yet they are intelligent in look, and behave themselves with propriety.

Monday, September 30. Examined Harris and Gibson. The first admitted, the last rejected. 122 now on the list. Sophomores nearly as many—they are threatening to beat us. Reëxamined Hall for Sophomore. He was rejected on his Greek last Wednesday and told that he could not enter without a satisfactory examination on his

Iliad, 6 books. He has read them all since then, though sick for two days of the interim—Sunday I hope was one of the sick days —and came up for examination last night. He translated quite tolerably, though still rather backward in his grammar. Will be able I think to sustain himself in the class.

My cold progressing, rather painfully raw last night. Hot bath and wet sheet—the last, as I had everything to do myself, could not well be managed in a satisfactory way, and I doubt whether it was of any real benefit.

OCTOBER, 1850

Tuesday, October 1. Examined Baldwin—well fitted. Drew Petermann's *Armenian Grammar* as also Aucher's from College Library. Had drawn on Monday volumes Homer, Eustathius, in Odyss[eam], Volume 2, and Terpstra, *Antiquitas Homerica*. Visit from Hurlbutt in evening.

Cold advancing. Bath and wet sheet, this time, I am confident, decidedly injurious.

Wednesday, October 2. Hoarse enough, but worked through my recitations with some difficulty. Hengst examined and allowed to try for four weeks—the deficiency in Greek. Mahlon Long here, at the request of Dr. Reily of Harrisburg, to see about his son, a pupil of Mr. Long's and one of our great rejected. Mr. Long is not really displeased at his rejection, as he told the father that, though his boy might perhaps get in, yet it would be better for him to spend another year in preparation.

Freshmen seated and Seniors not. Danger of a collision, which was happily prevented.

Statements of facts (so called) at Exchange Hall. Linoes last, who kept the Freshmen in after 5 o'clock, so that they came stringing in at prayers through the whole reading. People that can't lie more concisely deserve defeat, which our men experienced in this case—how bad a one, I don't quite know.

Thursday, October 3. 8 to 9, with Mahlon Long. Wrote and distributed invitations to Philological Society. Some more time at College Library, looking at Volckmar on Latin nouns in *o* and *io*. With Long again from 6 to 7. Then to Professor Gibbs' to attend meeting of Philological Society. Present, Gibbs, Hadley, Kingsley, Larned, Murdock, Porter, Salisbury, Thacher, Woolsey. Thacher on Tyler's *Tacitus,* Part 7, Book 5. The question on the derivation of *religio* arose of itself and gave me an opportunity to bring out my recent reading. Some talk about Brown and Union.

Home at 10. Talcott came in and talked with me for a while about grammatical points (tenses), then showed me a preposterous essay by William Mosely, who proves conclusively that the tragic choruses are to be scanned by sevens, heptads of syllables, sung each syllable by a different singer, on the successive notes of the musical scale (the very tune the old cow expired on—tragic truly), and that they have no such thing as regular feet of any sort. Talcott staid till 11¾, after which I swallowed a half Dover and turned in forthwith.

Philological Society next time at President Woolsey's; ipse exploteraturus.

Friday, October 4. Examined Gaylord in morning. Afternoon, some time in College Library looking over German books to find something for Miss Twining. Pitched on Wieland's *Abderites,* but did not draw it till next day. At 5 o'clock Daggett came in and began putting up the new shelves—quit at 6. In evening Henry and I concluded to sequestrate some of the boards as too rough, Henry to come over to meet Daggett tomorrow morning at 7½ for that purpose. Dovers at Dow's, 10 cents. Wrote to Faculty of University of Alabama informing them that their application for a branch of the ΦΒΚ has the sanction of our Alpha. At the same time wrote the other Alphas informing them of the fact. Ought to have done it a year ago, but shamefully forgot it. Eustis is now corresponding secretary, but I think it not right that he should suffer for my negligence. The business was not even now voluntarily undertaken by me, but pressed upon me by Olmsted.

Failed of attending preparatory lecture, which comes now at my supper time.

Saturday, October 5. Wrote letter of recommendation for John Grant, who has set up school in Newark, New Jersey. Daggett job finished. Henry and I put up the books, which occupied us from 12 to 1 and then from 2 to 3½ or 4. At 6½, to Dwight's room, for reporting. Drest and went over at 8¼ to Twinings'. Carried Wieland's *Abderites* and read a little. Saw Mr. William Twining, professor in Wabash College, a clear, positive, upright, and severe man, much like his brother Alexander, who, by the way, has fallen out with the railroad company he served, has thrown up his commission, and is now lying on his oars in Hudson, Ohio.

Sunday, October 6. Communion Sunday. Thoughts wandering to the ends of the earth. O Lord, may my roving spirit find its home in thee. Like Noah's dove, after long flying over the waste of waters, may it come back wearied to the ark of thy love and alight upon thy hand and nestle in thy bosom.

Dr. Fitch in the afternoon on "worshipping the Lord in the beauty of holiness," with special reference to the proprieties of public worship in God's house—a fine sermon, preached three years ago. Gave Henry my cane to be repaired. Have worn away an inch of steel within the last two years. Made out my marking book for the term, 134 names. Three have not yet come on, Harrison, Pierson, and Janin, of whom the first two are welcome to stay away.

Monday, October 7. Some time in the College Library, reading *Athenaeum*. A cold day, followed by an almost wintry evening. Borrowed some coal of Henry and started up a fire. Henry read part of his dissertation on Canticles—ingenious and forcible, but after all I have my doubts about this rifacimento business. It seems to me as though we never should have any fair understanding of the Hebrew history. Hurlbutt came in and held on till nearly 12, when he quit and I went to bed.

Ordered ton of coal and 8 bushels [of] charcoal, $7.40. Charged in account. To be delivered on Wednesday.

Tuesday, October 8. Call from Cyrus Pitts, detained here by the sickness and death of Dr. Hotchkiss and of his aunt. At evening settled for stove etc., $2.75. Bought *In Memoriam* of Pease, .75. Amazing sleepy. Tumbled into bed at 10½. No recitation in the afternoon as the President addressed the class in the Chapel. Philological conversation with Mr. Sobieski; some ingenious things.

Wednesday, October 9. Got in my ton of coal this morning, with rather less of inward swearing than usual in such inflictions. Nearly everything movable was transferred to the bedrooms and the floor carpet overlaid with an upper carpeting of daily *Tribunes*, which were pasted together where the carriers were to tread upon them. Altogether the thing was successfully managed, though the charcoal dust was pretty near choking me. A half hour in the College Library looking at Klotz on the Latin language—must draw the book and examine it more leisurely. He holds to the mixed origin, a Greek element superinduced by the Pelasgic aborigines on the

Celtic or Germano-Celtic Sicelians—the latter element originally the predominant one. 12 to 1, washing and dressing.

At 2 had my supplementary examination in history. The whole class not informed, I suspect. Only 8 present, of whom only one, Munger for a wonder, did tolerably. At 4 went into Faculty meeting. Jones case up. Decided to inform his uncle of the circumstances and advise him to remove his nephew from College. Was appointed to assist Mr. Hurlbutt with the Catalogue. Election of tutors—up for ten minutes—no conclusion. Meeting tomorrow at 2.

Evening, settled with Henry. *Independent* till Jan. 1, 1852 = $2.67. Oil, $1.42. Postage, .35. Cane repaired, .38 = $4.81. Paid him $4.75. Forgot to mention on Monday that my books came safely from Garrigue. Charge of 25 cents paid.

Shaved, drest, and went out calling. Miss E. Baldwin not at home. An hour with Miss Larned. A half hour with Miss Julia Olmsted. Back at Henry's room. Talk with Hyde and Fisk. The latter told a story of an old woman on a steamboat, furnished with a life preserver, was sleeping very comfortably early in the evening. About 11 the boat stopt a minute for some purpose. The old lady waked up, thought they were going to the bottom, rushed in great agony out upon deck, grasping her life preserver and crying, "Who'll blow me up? Who'll blow me up?"

Went home and looked over Greek lesson. Abed at 11½.

Thursday, October 10. 12 to 1, in College Library, talking with MacWhorter. Forgot to attend Faculty meeting at 2, though I had made a note of it in the morning. Hair cut, .125. Made some notes on obsolescence of laws, with reference to fugitive-slave question. Lesson in Greek on old Cretans, interesting. Read *North British Review*.

Friday, October 11[, and Saturday, October 12]. Had some touch of colic even in the morning, but went on ignoring it until evening, when it became too decided for any such treatment. Staid away from supper and commenced taking Dovers, half a Dover at a time. Went to bed at 8½, but as the pain did not cease, got up again about 10 o'clock, vomited, took a third Dover (a whole one this time), which proved effectual. Slept wakingly but delightfully, as a man sleeps under the influence of opium, feeling himself sleep, until 2½, when I thought it necessary to get up and stir about, in order to wear off the nausea, which after heavy opium drugging is occasioned by the slightest effort. Studied a little, read more, slept more still. Had some nausea and made several essays, but unsuccessful ones, towards emesis—when at last the bell rung and I went off to recitation. It had rained during the night, but was making ready to clear off. Felt very flighty during the recitation, as in fact I did even at the 11 o'clock exercise. Examined Stanton, one of two survivors in the *Isaac Mead*, a schooner recently run down by a steamboat in the Sound. He seems to have a pretty good mind, but is terribly rusty with his Greek, which he has not looked at, he says, for several months. Was writing on very quietly on obsolescence of laws, when Backus came in and reminded me that I was losing my memory; we had agreed, it appears, to report at 10 o'clock on Saturday morning. Went over accordingly to Dwight's room and reported.

From 12 to 1 in College Library. They have been purchasing Clark's (Edinburgh) translations of foreign theological works. In the afternoon took it easy, with reading newspaper, shaving, dressing, getting ready for prayers, etc. Saw Professor Johnson at College Library. Drew Bunsen's *Egypt*, Volume 1, and was reading it at 7 in evening, preparatory to calling on Miss Baldwin, when Henry Field came in. We sat talking in a very pleasant way, and I had given up the Baldwins and was beginning to think of giving up the Twinings, when Mr. Field rose to go. He said he supposed the ladies would all be occupied with their teachers' meetings; he had thought of calling on Miss Twining, but supposed he should not find her in. I told him he probably would and offered to bear a part in the quest. It proved successful and we held on (I was waiting for Mr. Field) till 10 o'clock. A rather interesting serio-comic conversation, in which I made a most disgraceful figure and was thoroughly ashamed of myself. I was fidgety, dogmatical, and positively rude, interrupting others, contradicting them, saying unmeaning things with a puzzling appearance of meaning something, making allusions to matters known only to a part of the company, implying often more intimacy with the ladies than I have any right to claim, and putting them certainly in an embarrassing position. I was really worse than usual last night, a consequence perhaps of the opium eating of the night before. Yet in these points I am always bad enough, and would fain amend. Read Bunsen sleepily till after 12, and then abed.

What a terrible thing pain—physical pain—is, all conquering, all destroying. God be thanked for deliverance from it, for ease and quiet and comfort, for all of blessing, for all of good. Benedictus sit Deus.

Paid Daggett for bookshelves, $6.00.

Sunday, October 13. Dr. Fitch in forenoon on omniscience. In afternoon, broke over settled principles—we should not be aware of their existence, if we did not sometimes run against them—and turned my back upon the Chapel. Went over to College Street Church, not to hear Brother Strengthy himself—my principles are proof against all such temptation—but because Mr. Henry Field was to preach there. Unluckily I chanced to overhaul him at the door with Mrs. Strong, to whom he introduced me and bade me walk in with her. Of course there was nothing for it but compliance, so there I was, stuck close under the pulpit, with scanty opportunity to watch the graceful motion of the notes, waived à la Français, and quite losing the minister when he stept down, as he often did, from his pedestal. His subject was prayer. The sermon was written in a *pathetic* style with much elegance and taste, and great fullness of matter. It moved easily and nimbly on from point to point, with little of the show of method, and perhaps not quite enough of the substance. To me however it was *very edifying*. Read Bähr on jealousy offering and ceremonial on occasion of a murder by an unknown author.

After tea called on Hyde. Talked about Field, whom he likes well, about fugitive-slave law, etc. At 7½ went over to Twinings' and expounded. She proposed to take up Daniel, to which I acceded. With Mr. Field she professed herself much pleased. She had never seen him to such advantage as on the evening previous. I was glad to hear it, for I knew not exactly how some things might have appeared: if I were to criticise my friends, which no man ought to do, I should fear that the Fields are a little worldly—even with Mary, who is charming, I have at times half felt it. Heard from Miss Twining an encouraging account of her success in the education of her twin nephews. She has been instructing them in geometry during the vacation, with result surpassing expectation. Reclaimed two numbers of *Foreign Quarterly*.

At Henry's till 11½, gossipping: there is fear that the Seminary will become Taylorite again this year. Henry half regrets that he is not to stay and fight it out. Bunsen on hieroglyphs till 12½.

Monday, October 14. Saw Mr. Stanley after dinner, looking very thin. He panted much after mounting the stairs, and had a troublesome hack. He sails on Wednesday in the *Zurich* for Havre; will go from Havre over land to Marseilles, and thence to Italy—Nice, Naples, Sorrento, or Palermo, staying wherever he can make himself comfortable. May God prosper him—with life, if it may be —if not, as there seems too much reason for fearing, with a fair outlook, good hope, and good harbor for the life to come. I wish I knew what he thinks of death and how he stands affected to the powers on the other side. It was not easy for me to maintain the gay and debonair, when seeing a man whom I regard with so much of respect, gratitude, and love, wasted to a shadow, and apparently on the verge of the shadow-world. But that perhaps is no bad position after all.

Tuesday, October 15. At College Library, read Winer on prophetism, an admirable article. Carried my tract on Greek verb to Mr. Hamlen's—to be printed within a fortnight. Read on authorship of Homeric poems, and made remarks at the recitation.

In evening, talk with Hyde about fugitive slaves. Long call from Hurlbutt, who staid till 12½.

Wednesday, October 16. Read Ihne on Homeric question in Smith's *Dictionary*. Winer on John Baptist. Talk with Mr. Jones about his son, who is doing quite poorly. Shaving and dressing— cut face and finger. Late dinner, nearly two o'clock. At 3, Faculty meeting. Hodges appointed tutor in case Kinne declines. Second warning to Webster, Sophomore. Talk about Townsend's Building.

To Professor Salisbury's at 4 for meeting of American Oriental Society. Quite a roomful. Tail piece of Mr. Turner's article on Modern Syriac. Adjourned at 5¼. Called on Mrs. Larned, who has just recovered from an illness which kept her prisoner for several days. Saw her mother, Mrs. Battell, with Mr. and Mrs. Eldridge of New Bedford.

At 6½ to Henry's room. They have adjourned their fugitive-slave discussion, so that Henry is completely cut out, will have to fire his obsolescence of laws elsewhere. Went over with him to my room, where Hurlbutt presently came in and soon after Hodges from Pittsfield. I had telegraphed him on Monday, or rather tried to do so. Hurlbutt wished it, as Abbe had refused and Kinne it was thought could not come. The President consented and I put the question, "Could you, if appointed tutor, come at once?" Hurlbutt took it to the office, but found that there was no telegraph station at Pittsfield. The message ought then to have been withheld and Hodges corresponded with by letter, but Hurlbutt, at whose expense it was done, had it telegraphed to Springfield and thence forwarded by mail. It came to hand last night, and Hodges, quite taken aback and not knowing what to make of it, thought it his safest course to come down here. I explained the circumstances of the case and made the best I could of a somewhat awkward job.

Over to Professor Gibbs' at 8, though invited to come at 7. Found quite a gathering, by no means confined to Pundits. Some ladies. Practised a rigorous self-devotion and consecrated my efforts to the gentlemen of the morning-land. Talked with Mr. Turner, Professor Andrews, Mr. Saropyan, Dr. Hoisington, Professor Robinson, Mr. Stoddard, etc. Mr. G. P. R. James was present but I did not speak with him.

Thursday, October 17. Orientals at 8½. Dr. Hoisington, very interesting abstract of a Tamil translation with commentary of an old Sanskrit devotional poem. Dr. Poor on the Batticotta Seminary; much what he gave us in the Centre Church, and crammed with oddities. Mr. Walker on the Bakĕlĕ language. Mr. Steele on that of the Dayacks in Borneo. Dr. Beck on Oscan and Umbrian, which I lost, being obliged to go out at 11 and adjourn my division. Stopped some time at Henry's to talk with Hodges, and did not get down again until 11½. Dr. Anderson of New York pleaded off for want of time from his geological account of Palestine. Dr. Robinson made some statements in regard to recent contributions to sacred geography from Lynch, Schulz, Ritter, etc. Professor Gibbs on original unity, philologically considered. Stated the analogies of the Indo-European languages, especially internal inflexion, and for the rest appealed to the argumentum ad ignorantiam—a queer performance which nobody touched. Adjourned to 3 P.M.

Saw Mr. Turner at dinner and invited him up to my room, where we sat talking till 3.

At the Oriental Society, Mr. Salisbury read extracts from a good article of Mr. Brown's on Chinese culture, and commenced some remarks on the recent progress of investigation as to cuneiform inscriptions, when I was forced away to my 4 o'clock recitation. At 6 I went over to the Twinings', agreeable to an invitation received in the afternoon through Professor Twining, who has got back from Lowell. Found Dr. and Mrs. Poor, Dr. Hoisington, and that is all, I believe. Pleasant time till 8 o'clock, when I went off in company with Dr. Hoisington. He says that he has made some beginnings in lecturing on India, and partly promises to come here before he gets through. Called at Mr. Baldwin's and sat till 9 in very agreeable conversation.

Returning, found that Kinne had been heard from, two letters in one day. He says that he wants to come, but cannot fairly get away until a substitute is provided. Will be detained till some time next week, perhaps longer. I thought it important that the President should be consulted forthwith, and marched off to his house accordingly. I knew that the surviving orientals had been invited to his house, but had intended myself to stay away, nor had I understood what sort of a gathering it was to be. Arrived there, I found that it was a smallish party scantly filling two rooms and mostly seated. Of course I had no way but to march in and salute Mrs. Woolsey, who planted me forthwith by Miss James. This young lady I judged to be somewhere between 15 and 30 (16 I hear is the real number of her summers). She is tall, straight, black-eyed, somewhat cast-iron in appearance, converses with great ease, promptitude, and decision, with a certain forward swing and a peculiar dead-setness of manner, but with uncommon vivacity and intelligence. I was seated on a low chair, at least a foot beneath her; her stature made the difference of another foot; her straightness, with my curvature, increased it by a third; and then her bold and energetic manner, contrasted with my timidity and hesitation, gave her a superiority which made me feel somewhat strangely, as if I were a woman and talking to a man. She got rid of me at last, and I contrived to exchange some words with the President, who scarcely knew what to say. Agreed to a Faculty meeting tomorrow morning at 9 o'clock. At my own room, saw Hyde, who expressed his willingness to go to Colchester if desired and confer with Kinne.

Friday, October 18. Faculty meeting at 9. Hodges nominated as tutor without conditions. Hyde to go to Colchester, see Kinne, and send word back by telegraph. Timothy Dwight in the meantime to hear his recitations.

Examined Reily and Peny. Reily is Mahlon Long's pupil from Harrisburg, a pleasant little fellow, but without grammatical conscience: 3¼ in mathematics, 2 in Greek (by grace of Tutor

Hurlbutt), 1¼ in Latin. Consented to try him. So with Peny, who had 2 in mathematics and 1½ in Greek and Latin, but was admitted Sophomore a year ago.

Saw Professor Norton in afternoon. Consented to let the Catalogue stand as last year, distinguishing between present and past members of his department. Sleepy in early evening. Talk with Henry. Long call from Hurlbutt, who staid till 11 and showed that unaccountable mixture of sweet and bitter which belongs to him beyond every man of my acquaintance.

Saturday, October 19. At College Library, 12 to 1, looking at Winer *Realwörterbuch*. Drew Richter, Schmelzle's *Reise nach Flätz,* and from Linonian Library the translation of it by Carlyle in his *German Romance*. During forenoon was constantly expecting a telegraphic message from Hyde; on going to report left at my door a card referring to No. 170. Was again at my room just after 12, and again set up the card at leaving. Returning at 2 o'clock found that the telegraph carrier had been there, shaken the door to get in, and thrust his paper under it, without heeding the direction on the card. The message was, "Kinne is bent on coming next week Trustees consent." Camp went down immediately and telegraphed back, "All right." Charge, 20 cents.

Advanced 10 dollars to Hodges to cover his expenses in coming down. He went off at 4½. Some time with Mr. Hamlen, talking over the Catalogue. Some time at College Library.

At tea had a talk with MacWhorter and George Bushnell. The latter has come down on an exchange with Eustis. Dwight Foster, he says, is sick with a rheumatic fever—wife, too, quite feeble. Spoke of fugitive-slave law, which Mac says is constitutional and ought to be obeyed, Bush says is unconstitutional and ought not to be obeyed, and I say is constitutional and ought not to be obeyed—three different opinions, none of course the right one. Mac says that James' lecture last evening on modern civilization was interesting, delivered too with scarcely any aid from notes. He seems to have followed Guizot and contradicted him to cover up the imitation. His course consists of six lectures. At Twinings' from 8 to 10. Mr. Jones is a sentimental personage, *remarkably sentimental*.

At Henry's from 10 to 12, nearly. Swopped lamps—even—a good bargain, proposed by him. Bought of him a neck kerchief for $2.00 and half a ream of paper for 50 cents.

Sunday, October 20. Dr. Fitch in forenoon. "God's will can be known and ought to be known." An hour long. Undertook to give the external evidences of Christianity, which were too much compressed to be effective, and yet swelled the discourse to an immoderate extent. Mr. Dutton in afternoon. "Our rock is not as their rock, our enemies themselves being witness." A very good discourse. Studied history of John Baptist and expounded at 4 in Greek Recitation Room. Some dozen of the Freshmen had come together. I had only mentioned it the night before and had ordered that no public notice should be given. Talked with a good deal of freedom, and not without hope that in my efforts I should have the presence and the blessing of God. After tea read Hengstenberg on Prophets in *Kitto*. At 7¾ went over to Twinings'. Came away at 9½.

Henry at my room read his *first sermon,* on opposite phases of religious character, the moral and the sensitive—their extreme types, their relation to each other, and the practical duty both of the Church and of the individual as regards them. Beautifully written, though not precisely according to homiletic rule; no text, a deficiency which I supplied by suggesting Ephesians 4.13 and 16.

Tuesday, October 22. Found this morning that there was a passage in my Greek lesson which I had overlooked the night before and could not explain at once in a satisfactory manner—no way but to dodge it as well as possible. Henry went off at 10½, having before given me a cushion. He takes my little Greek Testament, leaves certain monies to be collected by me. From 12 to 1 in College Library, looking at *Kitto's Journal.* In afternoon read Richter. From 4 to 5, as Mr. Silliman was addressing the Freshmen, I went to College Library and read Ewald on Prophets.

Wednesday, October 23. New number of the *Bibliotheca Sacra.* Article by Mr. Tracy on infinites to show impossibility of infinite series of finite existences, ingenious and plausible, but radically unsound. Answer it, say in the *Independent?* Had given notice to the Seniors that the delinquents in history, some 9 or 10 in number, must come up for examination at 2 o'clock in the Senior Recitation Room. Only one made his appearance, Mead, who wanted to get off, on the ground that he had a brother in town. I held on to him, however, and questioned him among other things on the civil wars of Pompey and Caesar: he wanted to know if that was the war with the Carthaginians.

Spent some time in afternoon and evening with Mr. Moore, a graduate of Princeton and late tutor in Delaware College, who has come on here to reside as teacher and guardian to a young man, son of Mr. Prescott Hall of New York. He intends also to pursue studies of his own in the natural sciences and the mathematics. He brings letters from Mr. Charles Long, only they have not yet come. Mr. Herrick was trying to get him a place to live in, which, as his wants are somewhat peculiar, is just at this time no very easy matter. Mr. Herrick called upon me in the evening to report progress, or rather want of progress, and I took occasion to consult him on some questions propounded in a letter from Foster, in behalf of a certain Schenectady family, who have a notion of coming down here to take boarders. Read further in *Bibliotheca Sacra*. Well-written article by my friend Mr. Whitney on Greek and Latin verbs. Interesting account of Dr. DeWette.

Thursday, October 24. Wrote an epistle general of recommendation for Brother Hurlbutt, to be used by him as occasion may serve for getting private pupils or others in New York. Carried over to Hamlen's my tract on analysis of verbs, the proof which had been given me on Wednesday, revised and corrected. Called on Talcott to see about Catalogue. Faculty meeting at 2. Nothing of especial consequence. Adjourned at 3. Went to work on the descriptive part of the Catalogue, which beside the remainder of the afternoon took up much of the evening. Prepared cards for use in the recitation room. (Borrowed Mure from President Woolsey by Camp.)

Friday, October 25. Conversation on the Catalogue with Professor Thacher and Tutor Talcott. Hurlbutt has already transferred his seniority to the latter. Went to tea in the midst of a pouring rain. Abed early, about 10 o'clock. Undertook to read Mure in bed, had been reading him before, but soon gave over. My position was not very comfortable; the cord which George strained so in the spring had snapped, and I felt myself gradually sagging floorward. I did not, however, reach the floor in the course of the night, and early in the morning engaged Mr. Andrews to get a new cord and string the bed anew.

Saturday, October 26. Letter from Henry at Andover, unexpectedly early. Answered it at night from 10½ to 12½ at considerable length.

Hurlbutt quit at 12, leaving with me his class book etc. for

Kinne. The latter came on at the same time. Dwight takes 102. Backus 21. Kinne 37.

Call from Mr. Moore, 7 to 8. Called at Twinings'. Away at 10.

Matches and pencils at Gorham's, 17 cents.

Sunday, October 27. Dr. Fitch in forenoon on love of God. Afternoon, love of man. The latter a new sermon, much less of the happiness jingle which rendered the former quite distasteful to me. Sunday School lesson on baptism of Jesus by John. Was a good deal perplexed with the discrepancy of the evangelical accounts, and, not having gained a very clear idea of the points, spoke with some embarrassment. In the evening, more on the prophets, looking out the references in Winer. Away at 10.

Monday, October 28. Call from Hyde. Talk on utilitarianism. Call from President, offering me the location business, which I declined in favor of Mr. Thacher. At work on the Catalogue. Called on Mr. Moore and took his name for analytical department. Introduced him to Professor Norton. At evening finished letter to George and wrote to Foster. Read in Mure's *Literature of Greece*. Rather humdrum, especially on classical and romantic, where he altogether overlooks the spiritual element of the latter.

Tuesday, October 29. Drest and went out in the evening. Called on Miss Larned. Tried Miss Baldwin, but in vain. Spent an hour at the President's.

Wednesday, October 30. College Library, 12 to 1. Talking about M.A.'s, which tutors nowadays have to pay for, if they take them. I gave my experience: how President Day sometime in January 1846 brought me a document which he said he had found in his room belonging to me. I did not ask him what it cost, indeed I supposed that being an officer of College I should of course get it free of charge. That was the common understanding of the tutors in those times, insomuch that Mr. Long, who had been appointed tutor but had not yet come in, was greatly surprised and somewhat chagrined that Mr. Day accepted the V which he proffered him. Nowadays, however, they withhold the sheepskin until the cash is forthcoming. They might keep it for me till the day of judgment. The M.A. is no honor at all. It certifies indeed that a man has been B.A. 3 years earlier, but the first diploma certifies that. It proves also that a man has paid 5 dollars to the College, but that only shows him 5 dollars poorer than he was before, and for ought that appears it may have been the last 5 dollars that the poor fellow had, and may leave him absolutely penniless, or, if it were borrowed money, even worse. It is notoriously no certificate either of application or attainment. If it had been from the first what it now is, it could not have come into use, and being what it now is, must ere long go out of use or change its form to something significant. Hyde has not taken it, nor my brother, and will not, I am thinking, unless it is given to them.

Faculty meeting at 3. Complaints against the Sophomores on account of their conduct in the Chapel and otherwheres.

Thursday, October 31. Finished Schmelzle's *Reise nach Flätz.* Spent some time on Armenian grammar, which I have a mind to resume and carry forward with such speed as I can make. From 12 to 1 in College Library, looking over proofs of Catalogues. After 2, stopt some Seniors from footballing on the Green. Talk with Hyde about genitives.

NOVEMBER, 1850

Friday, November 1. In evening, preparatory lecture from Mr. Porter. Stayed away from supper to attend it. After it was over had a call from MacWhorter, who stayed till 11. Hyde was with us for a while, and afterwards Blodget. Much interesting talk: but as luck would have, I fell at length into a preposterous discussion on some points of Taylorism and got more excited than was reasonable. When shall I learn not to agitate matters that I care anything about, with people that differ from me? As for Mac, he was cool as a cucumber, and made the mildest possible use of his victory. He is a very grand fellow. What a pity he should be so much of a Taylorite. Blodget is a little inclined, I should think, to recusancy. He has too much moral depth and earnestness for "the system" of *endaemonism,* as Kant calls it. Dwight has still more of the same feeling, and does not hesitate to express his opposition to the system.[6]

Saturday, November 2. Settled for board, $19.50. Gave my boy one dollar; he is very attentive and good-natured. Made out averages for some of our Freshmen, for all who appeared to have fallen below two, and compared notes among ourselves. We were to have done it at 10, but not being quite ready then, we met for the purpose at 3. The upshot is that for seven men of my division I must send the cry of danger to their anxious friends. Dwight also has seven cases. Backus is more fortunate: he has only 2. Some time at College Library; Olshausen on temptation of Christ. Drew *Foreign Quarterly Review,* Volume 2, from Brothers Library. It contains a fine article on Wieland, which I read and at 8 carried to Twinings'. Found Professor Twining of Wabash College returned from New York with his wife, who has recovered the use of her voice. They start on Monday for the West. At Camp's till 11. Reading Mure in bed till half past twelve.

Paid Mr. Andrews for carpet, bed cords, cording, etc., $1.50.

Sunday, November 3. Communion today. Could not hear very much of Dr. Fitch's sermon, though it seemed to me a good one. Mr. Egleston preached in the afternoon, an interesting discourse on the self-betraying power of sin. Bible lesson on the temptation of Christ; got on better than I expected. After supper, long gossiping conversation with Dwight. Read in Bunsen's *Egypt* and afterwards Wieland's *Abderites,* returned to me by Miss Twining —the latter in bed, which soon sent me to sleep about 11 o'clock.

Monday, November 4. Writing letters of warning to the parents and guardians of our dullards. Serious talk with Wells. Woodward back. Some talk with Aitchison and Blodget and afterwards Dwight about the conduct of the Sophomores in prayers. It is perfectly heathenish. Suggested that we may have to call upon the religious men of the class to help us in this matter.

Tuesday, November 5. Received a long letter from Henry, which I read to Hyde, and had some talk with him about Jouffroy's system of morals. Copied off the notes of my journey from Geneva to this place in September last, which I made at the time roughly in my memorandum book.

Wednesday, November 6. In the morning, while I was revising the proof of the Catalogue, President Woolsey came in and made a change in the sentence on public worship, to show that students can only go out of Chapel to attend the worship of other denominations to which their parents belong. He spoke of the Euclid affair, as being about to come off very soon, perhaps tonight, and raised the question whether it were worth while to say anything about it to the Freshmen. As for speaking in the Chapel, with the only effect of bringing the authority of the College into open contempt, by exciting immediate and successful defiance and disobedience, he was decided against anything of the kind. I could not at once make up my mind to talk to our class and am now glad that I did not.

From 12 to 1 in College Library, committee on Catalogue. In the afternoon, news of the New York election, more favorable than I had expected to the Whigs.

Faculty at 3. Some cases of disorder reported from the Sophomores, but not well prepared for us. Crawford suspended till beginning of next term, for disobedience, kicking at door of Blodget's recitation room after express prohibition to the class. An hour's talk on the Euclid business, with the same result as heretofore, that is, with none at all.

At tea found MacWhorter. Talked over Miss Beecher's recent letter to editors of newspapers, pressing her book on the attention of the public. Discussed the question whether any disclaimer should appear on the part of the College, to intimate that we do not own the soft impeachment; decided that it would seem a little ridiculous. It was held, however, that a publication of the evidence taken by the committee of investigation, properly certified, might at some future time be justifiable and expedient.

Saw Bellamy at supper table and judged from something that he dropt that the Euclid was to come off tonight. Mr. Herrick came in about 9¼, to say that he had heard of it at the concert of the Derwort family. But Kinne, who was then at my room, thought that it could not be, as the Societies were still in operation. Kinne soon went out to hear Taylor's decision on the constitutionality of the recent fugitive-slave law. Came back at 10 and said Taylor had been reading Judge Grier on the subject. Kinne still thought the Euclid would not come tonight. Talked of espionage etc. After he went out, Talcott came in about 11 and said it was going on. He had been making some explorations, had on a great broad-brimmed hat, which quite disguised him. Unfortunately those whom he saw entering the hall were more effectually disguised than he. He had tried to raise some tutorics, but without success. We concluded to go to bed, and did so accordingly. I seem to have been catching cold, and so washed off my feet in warm water, to give the thing free vent. Abed at 12. The noise of the procession, the music and the shouting, swelled up soon after and then died away in the distance, and I sunk into a sound sleep.

Thursday, November 7. Called on Aitchison to ask him to send P. A. Clarke to my room. On Chapman to purchase his Hengstenberg on Daniel, but he was unwilling to part with it. Journalizing. Arrangements for meeting of Philological Society. Call from Professor Gibbs to reclaim his Bähr. Clarke came at 12½. I told him I was sorry to see him pushing out of Chapel the evening before. He disclaimed the charge and referred me to others sitting in his seat. Read in Bunsen's *Egypt*. Greek lesson in afternoon. At 3, called on Dr. Murdock and sat for half an hour. After tea, called at Pease's. Looked at Stuart on Daniel, an ugly looking affair, yet I believe I must have it. Got my number of the *London Quarterly*.

Philological Society at 7 at President Woolsey's. Six members on the ground, Messrs. Gibbs, Hadley, Kingsley, Murdock, Salisbury, and Woolsey. President Woolsey read some papers on the derivation of words in the Old French, particularly on "bachelier," leaving, however, the etymology uncertain. Adjourned at 9½, to meet next at Professor Kingsley's, Professor Gibbs to operate.

Story of Marquis de Chateaulieu, who traveled in this country in the Revolution, of a place in Virginia where he dined. Various articles served up, all in same dish, and when he went to bed found the same crockery again.

At levee of British minister in Washington some years since, a Tennesseean M[ember of] C[ongress] named Anderson was found in a side room, easing himself at the fire. Worse than Sausage Sawyer.

Old Mr. Hillhouse, when member of U.S. Senate, hung up his cloak in a little closet outside of the door, but going to seek it found it missing. Some days afterwards saw it on the back of a western Judge, claimed it, was denied—turned down the collar and there sure enough was James Hillhouse at full length.

All these stories alluded to in former articles of *London Quarterly Review*.

Friday, November 8. At Pease's purchased Stuart on Daniel, $2.50. Pütz, *Ancient Geography and History*, $1.00. Mediaeval ditto, .75. Spent some time looking at Pütz. Think I shall introduce it next summer. Election news. Hunt likely to come in after all. Found myself (name given in full) badly scalded in explosion of steamer *Telegraph* near Wilmington, Delaware. She was on her way from Philadelphia to Baltimore under too great press of steam when she blew up with frightful destruction. In the evening, read Stuart on Daniel, chapter 1. He says Judah was the oldest son of Jacob, a fair specimen of his accuracy. He is utterly unmethodical, and full of a ridiculous fussiness, as unscholarlike as anything that can be imagined.

Wrote a long letter to Henry. Had a call from Blodget, who says that McFarland and Bromley were both drunk on Wednesday. In the last case the proof is ample; in the first not so, but his father will remove him by the advice of Professor Porter.

Saturday, November 9. It turns out that I was not scalded, but James Headly or Harley or Harder; for all three names appear in the paper. Had some admonitory conversation with Warner and Wells of my division. At College Library in afternoon looked at Olshausen on John 1.1–18, beautiful in spirit, but a little misty like his author.

In evening saw MacWhorter at tea, and had a call from him after it. He came up with Sobieski and read me a paper on perfect moral government to show that extreme punishment was necessary as a sanction under such a system: but he destroyed the interest of the question to my mind by drawing a broad line of distinction between a perfect moral government on the one hand, resting everything on the idea of authority and requiring extreme punishment as highest proof of the Governor's attachment to law, even though such a sanction were not the most likely means of securing holiness—and on the other hand a perfect government employing all means of influence in the wisest way to accomplish the great ends and aims of government. Talked about Park's argument against eternity of matter. Mac agreed that it was unsatisfactory. Sobieski started on Beckerism, acknowledging it to be his hobby, castigating us pretty severely for our unphilosophical tuition in grammar, and urging me to read Becker's 27 pages of Introduction, which I promised to do at the first convenient opportunity. Invited him to call frequently upon me, but meantime sent them both off with a polite congé at 8½, and went over to Twinings'.

Sunday, November 10. Studied John 1.1–18 and expounded it at 4 to Bible class. Dr. Fitch in morning on immutability of God. In afternoon, Professor Conrad of Wittemberg College (on German field) about Catholic Christianity, from which, as it seemed, Catholics were to be excluded; on the necessity of schism (among Protestants) to a perfect Church; with a text 15 verses long and a sermon to match, containing a little of everything and not much of anything, all done in a sort of inventory style, piling clause on clause and epithet on epithet.

Looked a little further at first chapter of Daniel and expounded in evening at Twinings'. Coming back at 9½, staid at Camp's room (part of the time with Clark and Hutchins) until 11 o'clock.

Monday, November 11. Made a beginning, a small one, in calculating averages for last term. Returned *Foreign Quarterly,* Volume 2, to Brothers Library: they call in their books today. Drew Grote's *Greece,* Volume 2, and Sharpe's *Egypt* from Linonian Library. Read Sharpe's Preface. Not a very original or critical writer, I should think. At 5 drew out Wieland's *Oberon* from College Library. Ran over two or three fairy tales which are contained in the same volume. At 7½ carried the book to Twinings' and went down to hear the Derwort family—"Student's benefit for Master William." A very pretty brood they are. I have been admiring them at the Tontine for three weeks without knowing who they were. They seem very much at their ease before an audience, and play with a good deal of execution on their violins and violoncello—without much expression, like all children, though the eldest, who is approaching her teens, is not altogether without style.

Back at 9½. Talk with Hyde on matters of discipline. Read Grote on Doric migration.

Tuesday, November 12. Talked with Gallup about Bromley. He saw him after prayers on Wednesday evening, and thought that he needed the assistance which he evidently received. King came in to say that he had decided to leave the class: he was going, he said, to ask Mr. Dwight to pull off his name: and then, as a pathetic finale, he added, "The fellows 'll miss hearing me make flunks after this." Wells came in on much the same errand in the afternoon—a happy riddance. McConihe at 5½ called upon me and had a crying spell over his shortcomings.

Between 12 and 1 called in at Hyde's to report Gallup's testimony. Found Blodget there. They were examining McFarland, and kept it up with much spirit for three quarters of an hour—rather suspicious evidence.

At tea saw Mr. Willis, who has at length fairly got his book to the light, and has come up from New York to establish himself again in New Haven. In evening read *New Englander,* new number, just out. Review of *In Memoriam* by Mr. Tarbox; is kind enough to endorse *our* article. Elaborate article by Morton in opposition to Mr. Agassiz. Long diatribe by Thompson on fugitive-slave law. Read myself asleep over Grote; my fault, not his; he is wonderfully interesting.

Wednesday, November 13. Read Grote. Wells called to say that he had concluded to withdraw. (Thompson.) Faculty at 3. Bromley dismissed, a good riddance. In evening called at Dr. Wells'—very pleasant people.

Thursday, November 14. Read Petronius Arbiter, *Satyricon,* in College Library. Could hardly feel the force of Niebuhr's praise. Talk with Professor Olmsted about Wade, advising his removal from the Freshman class. Sorry he's under Olmsted's wing; we shall have to wait for end of term, might otherwise bluff him off at once. Spoke to our divisions about keeping their seats in Chapel. Call from Mr. Linsley of Brantford to find a school teacher—$18 or $20 a month. Call from young Edward Olmstead to talk about Wells.

In evening, paid year's subscription for *Yale Literary Magazine* ($2.00) to McCall, who came in to deliver first number of Volume 16. Wonderful age for College magazine. Wretched number; only one or two pieces which seemed tolerable.

Friday, November 15. Read Mure; especially, at evening, his long chapter on the age of alphabetical writing—very able, though his proof I think lags when he comes to Homer himself. His parallels in respect to omission are hardly satisfactory—his argument on θεῶν ἐνὶ γούνασι κεῖται proves too much—and the case of Bellerophon is at least doubtful. The absence of any allusion to writing is an argument against any large interpolation.

MacWhorter at tea. Has been for several days in New York. New books on theology and metaphysics in College Library: Tuch's *Genesis,* Movers' *Phoenicians,* etc.

Saturday, November 16. At Pease's got last numbers of *Edinburgh* and *Westminster Reviews.* At 8 called on Twinings. Report of Jenny Lind concert on Wednesday afternoon, or *morning* as they call it, at 1 P.M. Half a canto of Wieland's *Oberon* etc.

Reading *Edinburgh* on English language. Aelfric in his English Grammar, or Saxon rather, gives *species* by *hiw* (= huc) and *person* by *hat.* Horne Tooke from Athenaeus: "Grammarians would be the greatest fools in existence if there were no physicians: εἰ μὴ ἰατροὶ ἦσαν." "*To* plant = *do* plant." Horne Tooke. Hume on wherewith, -unto, etc.: "The only tolerable decent gentleman of the family I think is *wherein:* and I should not choose to be often seen in his company." Gawain Douglas on Caxton's *Aeneid:* "that it was no more like Virgil than the devil was like St. Austin." Jeremy Taylor: "contrition of the serpent." Johnson's network: "anything reticulated or decussated with interstices at equal distances between the intersections."

Johnsonism: "Deity is my pastor; I shall not be indigent. Thou anointest my locks with odoriferous unguents; my chalice exuberates." 23d Psalm.

Sunday, November 17. Dr. Fitch in morning on perpetuity of material universe, a shining sermon, though I have no confidence in his exegetical methods, or the conclusions at which he arrives. Studied John 1, and expounded in my Bible class. Full attendance, about 25 I should think.

After tea sat down to study Daniel, but soon Hyde came in and presently Moore, who staid till 8, when I turned them out and went over to Twinings'. Staid till 9½. Talked about the propriety of my preaching. Read *Edinburgh Review* (Lyell).

Monday, November 18. Began this morning criticising translations. Read in *Edinburgh Review*—Panizzi. Received a long and very interesting letter from Mr. Whitney at Berlin. Received Stieler's *Hand Atlas* from Garrigue, price $13. I did not mean to order it, though I remember asking to look at it; it was not then in the shop, but was expected soon. I suppose they understood me to order it. Shall send it back unless Camp wishes it.

Saw Sobieski at tea. He is determined that I shall know something of Becker, will call in on Thursday evening to talk it over. Speaks disparagingly of Whitney's article, and in fact I doubt not thinks us all a parcel of ignoramuses. He is a gentleman in his manners, but whether a good fellow at bottom?

Tuesday, November 19. Call from Mr. Cowperthwaite (& Co.), bookseller of Philadelphia, who, having received Mr. Dwight's letter of warning, has come on to spur his boy forward up the hill of science. He brings with him a daughter somewhat older than Joseph—and if only half as handsome, a very pretty girl—in whom he has great confidence. She is to be settled in the same house as a sort of monitress to keep him steady. For the rest, the instructors of the class are to communicate if necessary with Miss Cowperthwaite; the danger is that the arrangement may itself create the necessity.

12 to 1, in College Library, reading periodicals. In afternoon wrote to Mr. Garrigue explaining my reason for returning Stieler, and promising to settle with him at end of term. Paid Camp 50 cents for express charges both ways.

After prayers dressed, and at 6½ went out to sup with Dr. Wells, who had invited me to meet a gentleman from Georgia, a Mr. McAllister, cousin of the McAllister who was for a time member of the class of 1849. His cousin, he says, is doing great business in San Francisco. Mr. Silliman, Mr. Norton, and Mr. Hillhouse were at tea. With the latter I talked awhile on mathematical subjects and received from him a friendly invitation to call at his house and look at his library. After supper, I excused myself, and finding at MacWhorter's room that it was not quite ½ past 8, called at Mr. Salisbury's to deliver Whitney's messages, intending to go afterwards to Governor Baldwin's. But Mrs. Baldwin and Elizabeth came in while I was there, saving me the necessity of an extra call. Left at 9½ and spent an hour talking in Camp's room. Letter from Henry. Speaks highly of Phelps and poorly of his own success in skeletonizing. Thinks their debates a hum, and the Library itself not all that he expected it to be.

Had a talk in the afternoon with Mr. Thacher about our approaching biennial examination.

Apples, .125.

Wednesday, November 20. To Professor Salisbury's at 8, having received an invitation for 7. Expected a large crowd. Small party for the young ladies who are staying there. Most of the time spent in games, in which I was victimized most shockingly, and tired out into the bargain.

Thursday, November 21. Made out my first examination paper in Greek and carried it to Hamlen's. Tried to find Mr. Baird to get my crutch head mended—the ivory plug has come out, leaving a ghastly gap—but Mr. Baird has removed to 37 Green Street. Conversation in evening with Mr. Church, who called with Professor Silliman. Will withdraw his son until end of next term, to study with Mr. Hurlbutt in New York. Drest, and about 9 went with Dwight and Backus to the Blakes'. Wedding party, general smash. Back at 11. Read sleepily till 1 o'clock and then tumbled off to bed.

Friday, November 22. Working on my second Greek paper for examination, and on a mathematics paper: but Mr. Thacher came in about 3 P.M. and said the examination would not commence under two weeks. At College Library, 12½ to 1. Saw Professor Andrews; his *Dictionary* nearly out. Distributed Catalogues at 12. In afternoon Townsend came in to speak of his doings last Wednesday evening, when he helped keep the Sophomores out of Chapel until after the reading commenced. Appeared to be pretty thoroughly frightened. Talk with Tutor Kinne on same subject at 6. In evening began two letters, one to Whitney and one to Henry. Wrote a page of each, and then slept most of the time till 12, when abed.

Saturday, November 23. Had a letter from Henry, with his first skeleton, and Professor Phelps' criticism and reconstruction. Read and talked them over with Hyde. At 8 to Twinings'. Back at 10½; should have come earlier, but Miss Mary came in at 10. Willis back from New York.

Sunday, November 24. Dr. Fitch, A.M.: God incomprehensible. Mr. Love in afternoon: heavy doom of Galilaean cities. Bible lesson, John 1.35 to 2.13. Near thirty present. Talked rather hobblingly.

Studied Daniel 2, and expounded from 9 to 10, waiting till that time for Miss Mary.

Finished up letter to Henry, giving my own reconstruction of his sketch.

Monday, November 25. Call from Professor Goodrich. Inquired if I was a voter. Answer, "Yes." He said some of the people were dissatisfied with several nominees of the regular ticket, particularly Mr. Hollister, Grand Juror of last year, on account of their unfaithfulness on the license law. Showed me a Reform ticket, and wished me to vote it. I acted accordingly, depositing my vote at 12 o'clock. Returning to my room, met Mr. Gordon, class of '49, who sat with me nearly an hour. Says Webster of '48 is dead— consumption. Foote, of his class, unsteady etc. Spent a good deal of time in reading Grote. At tea, a new and more sociable arrangement of our company at one long table, instead of two parallel ones. Read *Westminster Review* on *Mahāvīracharita* of Bhavabhūti —so-so. Read it in bed. Asleep by midnight.

Tuesday, November 26. My old friend Mr. Tutor Nooney has, it seems, been getting into office in California, as Superintendent of Public Instruction. Professor Stanley has arrived in Havre, at least the Honorable D. D. Barnard has, and Mr. Stanley was with him.

In evening studied Becker, went over nearly the whole Introduction. Had some talk with Henry Colton, a foolish fellow. Myself foolisher to care anything what he thinks or says. He endorses Taylor with great emphasis, and is severe on his last winter's adversaries.

Wednesday, November 27. Went round in search of a boy to act as water carrier, William Grant having left me in the lurch for a week past. Called on Miss Boardman to see Mrs. Kinney, but she has gone up to York Street; found her there. She has been sick with dropsy about the heart, but is now better. Could recommend no boy. But in afternoon I made arrangements with Mr. Andrews, the sweeper, whose boy is to do the business.

Saw MacWhorter after breakfast. He spoke of the party last night at Mr. Kingsley's—talking in one room, dancing in the other; that is as it should be. He did intend to have some Thanksgiving doings with Larned, Sobieski, and me, but Taylor has insisted on his going up to Springfield. At College Library drew Ahrens on dialects. Faculty at 3. Subject of examinations. Mr. Thacher reported a plan for the biennial. I was appointed a committee for the term examination. Some conversation with Mr. Woolsey after the meeting. In evening attended meeting of Connecticut Academy at Gibbs'. A queer communication from Judge Dutton on scientific aspects of real estate. A good deal of interesting and instructive conversation.

Thursday, November 28. Thanksgiving. Continued my letter to Whitney. Dr. Fitch at 11 on tendency to universal peace, in regard to which the newspapers bring telegraphic news by the *Europa* of a bloody collision between Austrians and Prussians, showing apparently that the millennium has not yet come. At half past one went down to dinner. Expected a tedious time, and wished to make it as short as possible. Found Mrs. Larned opposite, with Mr. J. G. E. Larned and Miss Sophia, and with them two young ladies of Miss Dutton's school. Lost my turkey, but found some pleasant conversation, and after dinner, being invited to Mrs. Larned's room, spent two hours there very agreeably. Professor Larned has gone to Thompson for his family potluck. Did not eat dinner enough to spoil my supper.

Friday, November 29. Blodget and Kinne reported their doings on Wednesday night. Several of the tutors were up and cruising round till 3 A.M. Olds found drunk. A drunken fellow entered 108 Crown Street, where there seemed to be several carousers; who they were, could not be ascertained. But inquiry this morning showed that it was the room of Boardman, formerly member of the class now Juniors—nephew of Judge Boardman, who has not yet returned from Ohio.

Sent off 16 Catalogues[,] with Triennial for Mr. Prentice of Utica. Saw Coe at College Library. He has left Middlebury, Vermont; is to be settled in Danbury of this state. Becker on prefixes.

Saturday, November 30. Paid William Grant 28 cents for bringing water. MacWhorter at dinner, just returned from Springfield. At Twinings' in evening—staid too long.

DECEMBER, 1850

Sunday, December 1. S. E. Dwight, D.D., formerly president of Hamilton College, died yesterday morning in Philadelphia— disease, softening of the brain, probably long and gradual, reducing him at last to hopeless imbecility. He was a man of some ability, but always singularly wanting in sound judgment, almost in common sense.

Monday, December 2. Drew up rules for the biennial examination and submitted them to Mr. Thacher. Carried them to Hamlen with second Greek paper and first mathematical. Copied out a piece from Keble's *Praelectiones* for Freshman prize translation. Letter from Henry urging me to come there next vacation— MacWhorter, too—no bad idea.

Fine article in *Tribune* on German War.

Congress starts today.

Tuesday, December 3. Afternoon, sleepy over Sharpe's *Egypt* —no great wonder. Evening, drest and went to party at Professor Goodrich's, at 8¾. Rainy out, lively enough within. Saw Mr. Edwin Hall, and his bride, Miss Malan that was, of Geneva. Coming up at 11, stopt at Camp's, found Timothy Dwight. Talked till 12½ on the failings of our friends.

Wednesday, December 4. Gave my division a rating for the noise they made when I adjourned them yesterday afternoon. Mr. Dwight was absent, attending the funeral of his uncle, and at his request I informed the division that the recitation would be omitted; they took it rather uproariously, for which they took it rather severely of me this morning.

Faculty at 3. President at Danbury, preaching ordination sermon for Mr. Coe, late of Middlebury, Vermont. Disciplined Olds— second warning and letter home.

Evening, called at Mr. Baldwin's and spent an hour and a half with Mr. and Mrs. Dwight Foster. Blodget and Camp came in while I was there. Foster is still pretty much crippled with his rheumatism, though improving.

Thursday, December 5. Philological Society at 7 at Professor Kingsley's. Present, Gibbs, Hadley, Kingsley, Larned, Murdock, Thacher, Woolsey. Professor Gibbs read first some remarks on *bachelor* as derived from *bas chevalier,* and then on the different classes of adverbs, and their character as objects of the verb. Meet next in February at Dr. Murdock's. My turn to officiate.

Hyde came into my room and sat till 12. He talks strong of spending our short vacation in Andover. Camp came in and staid till same time. Wrote a little on my sermon.

Friday, December 6. Read in Sharpe's *Egypt.* At evening felt an incipient colic, staid away from supper. At last, about 8 o'clock, took two Dovers at once and went to bed. It did not seem to have much effect; the pain continued until 10, when I got up and swallowed another Dover, which proved effectual. Dozed delightfully until

Saturday, December 7, two o'clock in the morning, when I felt that I must take measures to recover from the opium. Started up, built a good fire, trimmed my lamps, vomited a little, read Bunsen a very little, dozed in chair a good deal, till 6½, when I was able, though half nauseated and pretty flighty and almost absolutely voiceless, to work through the recitation hour. Felt able to go down to Tontine, notwithstanding the rain, which has for several days been nearly incessant: and having got down a little breakfast found myself sensibly better for it.

Talk with Hyde and Blodget about subjects for Sophomore prize compositions, which Professor Larned has entrusted to their discretion. Mr. Larned has gone to New York, where he went on Wednesday last, called there by the critical illness of Mr. Humphrey's child. Mrs. Larned has been there ever since.

At 11 distributed pieces for prize translation. Call on Professor Olmsted to talk about Wade, who has concluded to withdraw. He alluded pleasantly to our shaggy gills, and said that old people ought not to expect that young people should have the same tastes with themselves: he was in favor of freedom—a declaration which was kindly intended and kindly received. I explained that my reason for non-shaving was a dread of the continual martyrizing of the razor. He then told me that all difficulty on that score might be obviated by an application of sweet oil previous to lathering, or better still by the use of a soap containing his peculiar compound of lard and rosin, 3 of lard to 1 of rosin. Returning to my room I immediately tried the sweet-oil practice, with quite satisfactory results. After dinner, quite a talk with Camp about Greek verbs. At my room had another call from Mr. Seeley of Rochester, who brought another problem, less absurd than the one he before showed me, yet evidently indeterminate. He thinks of joining the Freshman class at the end of this term or the beginning of the next. Drew *Nathan the Wise* from College Library. Read DeWette on John 3.1 etc.

Called at Twinings'. Read in *Nathan der Weise*. Talked strange nonsense de meipso. How far is dignity of appearance a possibility in one so shabbingly and bunglingly made up? With Hyde from 11 to 12. Several of our folks on the *qui vive* for discoveries.

MacWhorter at tea. Spoke of some articles by Porter, contributed to *New York Observer,* on conflict of laws. Must look them up. Said he saw Sam Strong at Springfield. Samivel alluded to the last year's Middlers as tending to neology and Germanism.

Sunday, December 8. Rogues are in luck. A window-breaker last night, with the greatest odds against him, made his escape by the narrowest chance. May the good people have their turn next time.

Studied Daniel 3 and went over it at Twinings'. Miss Anna leaves soon for New York with her niece; is to stay at Mr. Johnson's, No. 27 Gramercy Park; to be absent from one to two weeks. Home. Wrote two pages of my sermon.

Monday, December 9. Call from Mr. Thacher in the evening, to talk of the examination: thinks his paper too long: suggested to me the propriety of shortening: inquired about the drawing of the figures etc. Wrote further on my sermon, but grew sleepy and gave up soon. In forenoon, call from Mr. Finney, half brother of Davis, Freshman—a great traveler, who has not only made the tour of Europe, but gone over the length and breadth of India, in the employ of the East India Company.

Tuesday, December 10. Saw Mr. Finney again at breakfast; he was to leave in the forenoon. After criticising translations from 9 to 10, went up to Chapel Attic, to relieve Mr. Thacher for a time in superintending the examination of the Juniors. Much struck with the silent and orderly appearance of the men. It was my paper, Greek of Freshman year—proved to be just long enough.

Fine for books from Linonian Library, 25 cents.

Wednesday, December 11. Made out my second mathematics paper and carried it to Mr. Hamlen. Corrected proof of that and second Greek paper. Faculty at 3. Senior optionals. President and Professor Porter to lecture in the forenoon, balance of the forenoon being allowed for voluntary study.

Dr. North: some of his eccentricities. Collisions with Aiken, Capron, Smith, and Twining and others of the Sophomores. Conclusion, to make peace all around. Staid away from prayers.

Evening, saw MacWhorter at tea. Went to Pease's with him and looked at a communication to the *Knickerbocker* on Miss Beecher's book, signed R. and supposed to be by Russell—very probably; it is poor enough for him. Saw subscription list for Union meeting, good names. Returned to room. Sermon and Bunsen.

Thursday, December 12. At Philosophical Chamber, drawing figures for Talcott—examination in Freshman mathematics. Kinne drew for his room, Rhetorical Chamber. Mr. Thacher, in Chapel, used the cards. Paper well contrived, just matter enough—perhaps a little too easy.

In evening, number of *North British Review* at Pease's. Attended first Institute lecture, 25 cents. Prosy statement by Professor Dalton. Dashing address by Professor Mitchel of Cincinnati on the moon. He feels the strangeness of things; they do not become commonplace to him. Came home at 9 with Mr. Moore, who sat till 10½ and borrowed my last number of *New Englander*.

Friday, December 13. Examination of Juniors in Rhet[oric]. Mr. Thacher came in at 10 and showed me Mr. Larned's papers.

Sermonizing. Gave John, waiter at Tontine, $1.00. He is a very good-natured faithful boy.

Conversation with Blake of my division, who has concluded to leave—my fourth loss. Started out in the evening to see the Blakes and talk the matter over, but finding a carriage before the door, I passed on. Stopt at Mr. Baldwin's and inquired for Mr. Foster— he had gone this day to Worcester. Signs of a gathering there (it was the beehive, Miss Larned told me) and I decamped. Called at the President's, but Mr. and Mrs. Woolsey were at meeting of book club, somewhere. Called on Miss Larned and found her in, being too ill with a cold to attend the beehive.

Saturday, December 14. Finished up my sermon. Call from Hyde, who was to preach at Mr. Cleaveland's church, and was a little afraid of offending people either by speculation or new schoolism. Afterward concluded to let Mr. Bullard preach at Cleaveland's, and go himself to Northford.

Called on Miss Mary Twining. She has not yet heard from her sister.

Read Professor Koeppen's testimonials, forwarded to Professor Olmsted in hope of obtaining an appointment in this College.

Sunday, December 15. Studied and expounded the remainder of John 3d. Good attendance still. Oh, if I but knew what to say to them. Professor Fowler in afternoon, on progressive nature of sin; much reliance on *facts*. In evening, call from Professor Thacher, who sat for about an hour. Spoke of a note to Mr. Woolsey's Historical Address, which will speak of the wants of the College—quite plainly.

Read my sermon to Miss Mary Twining.

Monday, December 16. Started the complementary sermon on divergence of character. I am afraid it will appear that the best ideas and expressions have been used up in the first.

Tuesday, December 17. Continued sermon. Mr. Woolsey wanted to know on behalf of the *New Englander* committee whether I would contribute an article on Mure's *Literature of Greece* for the February number, that is, if they find a publisher, which is matter of some doubt. I said that I would try. Announced order of examination.

Calculated averages in history for summer term; took about two hours. Drest and went at 9½ to Mrs. Whitney's party. Spoke with

Miss Baldwin, Miss Mary Dwight and Miss Clarke, and Mrs. Blake. Just enough people there, and everything admirably managed. Very pleasant for the lovers of such things. Came away at 11¼ in advance of the company. Fine full moon etc.

Wednesday, December 18. Sermonizing. Call from Professor Fowler—wants me to let him know from time to time what matters of interest and importance may come out in the philological world.

Catalogue of Hamilton College from Root. Not quite so full this year—two lower classes, 19 each.

Letter from Henry. Wants me to bring certain of his duds when I come to Andover. Gives some of Park's ideas about inspiration. Read the letter to Hyde.

Faculty at 3. Discussed individuals, but took no action of any importance. President gave us all round copies of his Address. Fine note at end on wants of the College.

Talk with Blodget in evening. He will maintain his independence of mind in the Seminary.

Up pretty late doing nothing.

Thursday, December 19. Drawing figures for Junior examination on mathematics of Sophomore year. I had forgotten all about it until last evening, and was then going to ignore it, but Mr. Thacher caught hold of me at 8½ and pressed me into service. Drew for Talcott and Kinne, and indeed for Thacher too, as cards for conics came up missing—figures only four and very simple. Sat for Mr. Thacher from 10 to 10½ in examination room. This was the last session of an examination much dreaded, and the fellows cheered a good deal as they came out. They got together after tea on the State House steps and, notwithstanding the rain, kept up a tremendous pow-wow for an hour and a half.

Had our last recitation at 11, and gave out notices for examination. No books to be brought in at Latin and Greek recitations; a new notion adopted at Dwight's suggestion.

Received from Mr. Herrick, by order of President, the ten dollars which I advanced to Hodges for his expenses when here in October. President took some pains, I thought, to show me that he does not share in the suspicion with which some of the older brethren appear to regard our attempts to enforce a tolerable standard of scholarship in the Freshman class.

First session of term examination at 3; continued till near 5. Canfield absent, agreeable to my advice given in morning to Mr.

William Thompson Bacon. Gave each man six marks: for translating, and commenting twice round, scanning, and reciting grammar. So-so.

Evening, counting recitations of Freshmen during the term and
calculating averages of first division. No small job with so large
a class.

Friday, December 20. Continued examination. 6 hours at it;
rather tedious.

Our last night's snow having turned to rain has covered the trees
with a fine frosting. Tonight is cold and clear, and, with the full
moon overhead, furnishes famous sleighing, of which our people
are not slow to avail themselves.

Saturday, December 21. Six hours more of examining. Dwight
and I met from 7 to 8, to talk over the part (⅓) who are finished
up. The men have done tolerably well, several of the hardest cases
having saved us the trouble of examining them by quitting in the
course of the term.

From 8½ to 10 at Twinings'. Miss Anna not yet returned from
New York. 10 to 11½ at Hyde's room. Several of the tutors there.
Some apprehensions of disorder, one third of Sophomores and
Freshmen having got through with their examination. Concluded
at last to break up and go home. Splendid moonlight on ice-covered
trees and snow-covered ground.

Sunday, December 22. Studied and expounded John 4. Dr. Fitch,
forenoon and afternoon, good sermons, very imperfectly heard.
There is something strange about the man's style, an *unction*, I
should say, which prevents it from sticking anywhere; it slides
smoothly over the mind and passes off without finding a lodgment.
Evening at Twinings'. Looked at Professor Porter's articles in *New
York Observer* on conflict of laws; very fair and thorough, and with
some explanation and perhaps extension of the doctrine of *passive
disobedience,* I could adopt its formulas.

At Camp's to 11½. He is going to Washington on Thursday, to
stay he knows not just how long, according to circumstances. Thinks
of giving up the privateering business, which has taken up so much
of his time this term. Some talk of a Hebrew exercise with me,
very informal, so managed as not to seem any encroachment on
Mr. Gibbs.

Monday, December 23. Examination from 9 to 1, finished. Meeting of our Freshman corps at Mr. Dwight's, 2 to 3. Faculty, 3 to 5.

Tuesday, December 24. Up at 6½. Receiving prize translations from 7 to 7½. Finished communicating results of examination. Examined for admission two pupils of Camp's, Marmaduke and Shackelford, from Missouri, very slenderly fitted, but Camp thinks they will do. So we let them in with conditions.

At 12 went over to draw my salary of Treasurer, $266.66, with a deduction of $7.21 for coal. Had it cashed at bank. Called on J. G. E. Larned and paid him $3.00 contributed by Cyrus Pitts for a Linonian Hall. Larned talked some of leaving New Haven. Some hope of situation as instructor. Talked of getting up a Greek class, with Harrison, MacWhorter, etc., and wanted me to join it. Answered favorably. Settled with Mr. Pease, *Tribune* for 6 months, October 26 to April 26, $3.25. After dinner, settled with Tuttle, $7.13, and with Knevals, $107.81, and with Dow, $2.95. Interview at 1½ with William Thompson Bacon in regard to his nephew. Loafing in Dwight's room. Talk with Wing about study, Chinese etc.

In College Library, *Literary World*. Talk with Blodget. Lyman on inaccuracies of Professor Peirce.

MacWhorter at tea. Talked of a great fight with Joe Larned, George Bushnell present as bottle-holder. He went after tea to our grand Union meeting, which I voted a humbug and magnanimously cut. Settled at Tontine, $12.50. Purchased 100 envelopes, .25. Had paid Mr. Andrews in the morning .25 for his boy's services, also $4.29 to Mrs. Levere for washing. Wrote letters home for Baldwin, Drake, Hallock, Russell, and Thompson of my division; had already written for Lathrop in forenoon.

Wednesday, December 25. CHRISTMAS. Up at 7¼. To breakfast at 7½, a half hour too early, Christmas, it appears, being a sort of Sunday. I did not wait, however, but swallowed a hasty meal and returned to my room. At 9 came in Seeley of Rochester, the man who has brought me two or three absurd mathematical problems, cut from old newspapers, and wished to be examined for the Freshman class. Took him at 10, and tried him in a perfunctory way; marked him 1½. Dwight had him afterwards and marked him 1. Can't come in.

Mr. Olmsted gave me an invitation to a Christmas dinner, a family affair, which of course I was obliged to decline. Packed my trunk. Read Pindar, 1st Olympiac, with Dissen's commentary. To dinner at 1½, it having been promised at 1. It came at 1¾. Very good, but I am becoming more and more convinced that I have no special taste for grand dinners. Ordered carriage at Tuttle's. Called at Blodget's and gave him Bokum's *Introduction,* as he talks of studying German during the vacation.

Off to the cars at 4, 25 cents. Ticket, $1.50. Started at 4½. Got behind time and had to wait for everything that passed, that is, for two or three trains from the west. At Bridgeport we took in the Housatonic passengers, who had come in too late for the express train. Our three cars were thus pretty well filled. As we passed on from village to village, we took on board a crowd of Christmas revellers returning to New York from their holiday in the country. Fires were started in the baggage cars and many people accommodated there. Yet at last they overflowed, could no longer get seats but were obliged, ladies even, to stand up in the mid-alleys. In at 10. Drove to Broadway Hotel, 50 cents, made .625 by a piece dropt upon the pavement. Went to bed directly, No. 92, up two pair of stairs, fair room, ill-lighted. Unpacked trunk. Abed at 11½.

Thursday, December 26. Breakfast at Parker's, 19 cents. Cap at Genin's, $1.50. Settled bill at Garrigue's, $34.95. Called on Spenser Shepard and John Chassell. Bought of John a clothes brush and portable inkstand, .625. At Mrs. Beman's a pair of woollen gloves, .625. Called on Warren Green, at Sands'; invited me to dine with him tomorrow at 2. Over to Brooklyn, found Noyes and took dinner with him. He starts tomorrow for Boston, to be married on Tuesday, December 31, at 12 M. Ceremony to be performed at the house of Mr. Robert Appleton, a brother-in-law of Miss Means, at 95 Boylston Street, 3 doors beyond church. Mr. Appleton sick; doubtful whether they can have any company, yet Mr. Noyes invited me to call there and ascertain the fact.

Over to Mr. Crittenden's. Miss Field in the country, will not be back till next week.

To Mr. Mann's. Did not see Mary, recently confined. Mrs. Mann gave me the Fairfield news: Mrs. Bryan died December 2, and Martha soon to become Mrs. North.

Back to New York at 5½. Journalizing. At 7 went to Niblo's to see the Ravel family; fine pantomime; beautiful tight-rope dancing

by Leon Javelli; 50 cents. Room crowded when I got there, a half
hour before performances commenced. Knevals (Sophomore)
made room for me, and thus I got a comfortable seat. Talk with
Henry Field. He had seen Miss Twining in an omnibus. Is making
arrangements with Harpers for the publication of his book on
Irish Rebellion of 1798.

Bussing, .30.

Friday, December 27. Breakfast at Parker's, 25 cents. Called at
76½ Chatham Street to see Hurlbutt; he had gone out to Medical
College. Stept into Westermann's and looked about, bought Andersen's *Märchen*, $1.25, for Miss Twining. Up to 23 Gramercy Park;
she had gone out shopping. Mrs. Johnson invited me to call tomorrow morning. Went to 15 East 17th Street to see Dr. Owen;
find that he lives in 112 West 23d. Went to Cousin Spenser's and
sat for an hour. Better pleased than heretofore with Cousin Mary's
appearance. Dined at 2 with Warren Green. An hour with Hurlbutt. At 5 went over to Jersey City, corner of Grove and Mont-
gomery Streets. Saw Mr. and Mrs. Fink, took tea and had a sociable
of two hours with Nancy, wonderfully pleasant. Off at 9. With
Hurlbutt till nearly 12. Bussing etc., 40 cents.

Saturday, December 28. Breakfast at Parker's, 19 cents. Call on
John C[hassell]. Drest and up town. Overhauled Metcalfe (class
of '49) in bus. At 23 Gramercy Park, sat above an hour with Miss
Twining. At 112 West 23d, Dr. Owen not in. To Cousin Spenser's,
dined etc. Down town at 4. Called on John C[hassell] and took tea
at his boardinghouse. Snow which commenced falling at 4 turned
to rain at 6, or rather to drizzle. Walking in slop, caught cold.
Concluded to take a bath. While preparing, Hurlbutt came in.
Went with him to 76½ Chatham Street and sat till 10. Hurlbutt
invited me to attend an anatomical exhibition of an Englishman
(Goadsby) on Monday evening. Promised to introduce me to
Parker and Clark, their great guns. Should like to be there, but
believe I must see Noyes married.

Went to Phalin's and took a bath, 25 cents. Good accommoda-
tions. Bussing, .25.

Sunday, December 29. Frozen and slippery. Got over to Pilgrim
Church and heard Storrs, text, "Let us not be weary in well doing
etc."—animated and animating discourse. Dinner at Mr. Mann's.
He gave me a copy of Storrs' Thanksgiving sermon on obedience

to law, of which he thinks very highly. P.M., service at Dr. Storrs' church. Sermon by assistant rector, Mr. Denison, long and sulphurous: "the wicked made for the day of evil."

Tedious walk to 6 Poplar Street. Supped at Green's. Being tired with walking in slippery places, excused myself from attending church in the evening. Green came over with me to New York and sat awhile. Bed at 9. Cold getting on comfortably.

Monday, December 30. Breakfast at Parker's, .25. Bought Tennyson's *Poems* for Cousin Mary at Putnam's for $1.50. Meant to leave them with Spenser, but he had gone up the river. Carried them myself to 12th Street, read several of the pieces, dined there. Back at 2. Bus, .125. 3 cents for change on a dollar. Paid bill at hotel, $3.00. .125 to porter. .50 hack to boat. 5 cents to porter. On board *State of Maine* for Boston by Fall River route. Fare, $4.00. Stateroom, $1.00. Supper good, 50 cents. For toothpick, 10 cents. Newspapers, 6 [cents].

Tuesday, December 31. Good night's rest from 9 to 4. Cold morning, comfortable in cars. Coach to Adams House, 25 cents. Good room and good breakfast. Looked about at Little and Brown's, and then at 11½ went to 95 Boylston Street. Mr. Appleton sick. Welcomed by Mrs. Appleton. Small company assembled, among others Mr. Means of Groton, brother of the bride. Ceremony by Mr. Dexter. Kissed the bride awkwardly, chatted with her pleasantly, count much on future acquaintance. At dinner found myself side by side with President Labaree. Visited antiquarian bookstore in Cornhill—great throng—talk with Dexter. Bus back, 6 cents. Evening at Museum, 25 cents. *Apostate,* poor tragedy. Booth, no great shakes. Warren, fine comedian.

JANUARY, 1851

Wednesday, January 1, 1851. Probably the first New Year in my life when nobody has wished me a happy New Year. After breakfast was roving about—met Professor Andrews. Visited Revere House. Walking back met Fisher. Went with him to State House, to Adams House, to Old South Church, to Little and Brown's, where I bought Didot's Herodotus, $5.00, and Niebuhr's *Lectures,* 2d edition, $5.50. Fisher, who had gone out to get news of legislature, came back, reporting that, from union of free soilers and democrats, the organization would probably be effected without difficulty. With him saw Mr. Smith, teacher formerly in Worcester, now in Cambridge. Assistant in his school is Mr. Gray, the flogged (ὁ μαστιγιστός) of Dr. Arnold, whom I met last summer.

Saw Bangs, Whittlesey, Scudder, Huggins, Macy, Wickes, Willard, etc., most of them in Old South Church, where we repaired at 12 and sat till after 2. Word was then brought that the houses had been organized, but that the sermon was deferred till 11½ A.M. tomorrow. This was in compliance with a request from Professor Park, unable on account of weak eyes to preach in the later afternoon. After dinner, to 17 State Street, Scudder's office. Spent an hour with him and Whittlesey. Evening, reading Niebuhr. Sleepy. Bed at 10. Wickes returned to Andover. Bus, 11 cents.

Thursday, January 2. Up at 8. Breakfast. At Ticknor's bookstore with Fisher. Little and Brown's. At 11 to Church (Old South). Saw Walker, Byington, Hyde (N. A.), Cutler, etc. At 12½ the dons came in and exercises began. Sermon from 1 to 2 hours 20. Very brilliant and powerful—on indebtedness of state to clergy. Fine allusions to capital punishment as the demand of true humanity. Principles applicable to fugitive-slave law fully and fairly stated in the most admirable way, without any application.

Dinner at 3. Settled bill, $4.00, at Adams. Read Pindar. Off at 5. .25 to porter. .25 for hack. .55 fare to Andover. Saw Buck. Talk with Whittlesey and Walker. Arrived at Andover, took stage for Mansion House. Henry came in presently. Went to his room. Wickes there. Fisher and Whittlesey came in. Read Park's vindication in *Bibliotheca Sacra* against Hodge—a crusher. Back at 10. Unpacked. Shaved. Abed at 11½.

Friday, January 3. Heard Park at 11. Lecture on divinity of Christ—very handsome. Phelps at 3. Plan of sermon criticised—ingenious and skilful. Introduced to him. Between 1 and 3 went into Library and Reading Room. Introduced to Mr. Robie, the Librarian. At dinner found President Labaree—a flying visit, to leave in the evening. At 7 called on Professor Edwards. Engaged to dine with him on Monday.

At 8 went to Professor Park's and sat for upwards of an hour in pleasant conversation—very easy and unpretending. Henry did the agreeable to Mrs. Park. Saw Mr. Wellman. Engaged to sup there on Monday.

Declined engagements for Saturday on account of a project we have of going over to Lawrence to look up Reverend Silas Blaisdale, said to be a teacher there and believed to be a cousin of ours on the Hadley side.

Began reading my sermon to Henry, but broke off in the middle on account of his quite excusable sleepiness.

I am stopping here at the Mansion House—a pleasant room— plain substantial fare—everything very comfortable.

Saturday, January 4. Called on Mr. Taylor and sat from 11 to 12. We had declined two or three engagements on account of our proposed trip to Lawrence, but the day proved to be snowy and blowy —not very severe, but worse than we cared to encounter upon a quest so uncertain.

Afternoon at Henry's room. Talk with Whittlesey on utility. Finished reading my sermon to Henry.

Evening at Fisher's room, in manifold talkings, with accompaniment of apples, crackers, and raisins.

Sunday, January 5. Sat in Professor Park's pew, and heard a sermon from Professor Emerson, a half-century sermon, a curious performance, plenty of pudding but very little of yeast. He resuscitated Washington and set him jogging over the country to see the various novelties that have sprung up since his decease. To be continued in the afternoon, but a quarter of a century at a time was enough for me. I staid at home and wrote a letter to Mary. I understand that Mr. Emerson assumed to prophesy, and assembled a great religious convention at New York in the year of grace 1900, including among other lions a converted Pope. Evening, at Henry's room. Heard his piece on the doctrine of primitive holiness, an ideal state.

At my room, read Niebuhr and Tennyson.

Monday, January 6. Finished letter to Mary and carried it over to the bookstore, the place of deposit for mailable matters. Saw there the January number of *Brownson's Quarterly*. In noticing the *American Almanac* he says that Protestants introduce their heresies even into pure mathematics, yet in general the book may be commended as useful and valuable. In referring to Miss Beecher's book he tells that lady that if he has little sympathy for Yale College, he has quite as little for her and her friends—indeed he cares nothing for the affair, it is a matter altogether among Protestants.

Called on Professor Emerson, and sat for half an hour. After-

wards an hour with Mr. Robbins of Middl[ebury] College. Returning at 12, drest, and at 1 went to Professor Edwards' to dinner.
Mr. and Mrs. Robbins there. Sat till nearly 3. Mr. Edwards wants
me to contribute an article by May for the *Bibliotheca Sacra* (must
write on Donaldson's *New Cratylus* etc.), also a page or two on
the best books for the study of Sanskrit, with general philology,
stating something as to prices.

At Henry's room from 3 to 6. Then to Professor Park's to tea.
Found Mr. Taylor, teacher—idem, minister. Park spoke of pro-
faneness in Germany, even among pious people. One minister
owned it was wrong and declared he never practised it. Within
5 minutes comes a procession in the street. "Ah God," says he,
"look there." Presently recollecting himself and feeling the need
of an explanation, "When I said God then I meant it—I did not
use it profanely."

Spoke also of looseness on the Sabbath. Higher classes do not
generally go to church. Hengstenberg and Neander very seldom.
Dinner at Neander's on Sunday—wine drinking and beer drinking
—continual cries of "Io." Tholuck preaches every other Sunday,
but on the alternate days does not go to church. Passing by some
workmen employed in building a church on Sunday, Park expressed his disapprobation. "What more proper," says Tholuck,
"than to contribute thus to *edification*." "Yet," he added, "do not
suppose that I dislike your sensitiveness on the Sabbath. I think
it a good thing." Traveling in Bohemia with a respectable Protestant clergyman who was consumptive, they came at Sunday to a
small village where the only church was Romish. The German
asked him where he should go. To the Romish Church, he said,
as there was no other. "Can you stretch your conscience so far? *I*
cannot," said his companion. Park did not dispute the matter with
an invalid. At dinner the clergyman was absent. At supper they
met again. "Where have you been?" "To the Romish Church. And
you?" "To the bowling alley," and with high spirits he recounted
the persons he had played with and the sums which he had won.

The Professor was so interesting that Taylor (minister) and I
would hardly have got away till morning, had not Kellogg, who
came in about 8, made a move at 9½. Went to Henry's room. Talk
with Whittlesey. Home at 10¼.

Tuesday, January 7. After breakfast, packed trunk, settled bill,
$5.00, received parting instructions from the fellows, lunched at

11½, and rode down at 12 to the station house (30 cents for two passages). To Boston, 55 cents. Park on board cars—to preach an ordination sermon on Wednesday. Some difficulty with my trunk at Boston. It did not come down with me, but in a train which followed some 10 minutes after. It had been checked too, but without any check being given to me. It was necessary to open it in order to prove property. Over to Worcester depot, .25. Ticket to Springfield, $2.65. Bought a number of the *Commonwealth,* from which I found that Charles Wadsworth has received from his people as New Year's present a casket containing $700. Ticket from Springfield to New Haven, $1.75. Arrived at 8. Hack, 44 cents. Started fire, unpacked, etc. Some trouble in warming up.

Wednesday, January 8. Afternoon, began upon first paper of Junior examination. Hyde came in and read me his sermon on temptation, so far as it has advanced. There were to be three heads, 1. temptation critical, 2. requires previous stock of principle, 3. must be met with fear of God—but the first had so spread out under his hands as to swallow up the other two. Advised him to condense it for this sermon, but afterwards, if he chose, make it the subject of a separate discourse. Attended prayers. Calculated remaining averages for 3d division. Bought small pair of tongs, .25. Rice called up and gave me a pocket knife, a handsome Christmas present from George Shepard. Began a letter to the Doctor at Buffalo. Grew sleepy and in three hours did little but wash my feet.

Thursday, January 9. President Woolsey came in just before 11 with Mr. Weed of Hamilton, Madison County, New York, who taught for some time in that place, but being compromised in the difficulties connected with the proposed removal of the College, went to Fairfield and was teaching there at the time of my visit to the place in September, though I did not then see him. He was dissatisfied there with the management of the Trustees, especially Porter, and disgusted, as I learned from John Chassell, with some scandalous gossip which connected his name with that of a lady music teacher. He had left his wife away on account of her illness and his own unsettled condition; and he had waited once or twice on this Fairfield demoiselle; and that was enough to set all tongues awagging. He complains also of the inhospitality of the people. At all events he determined to leave as soon as possible, and accordingly has just quit them. He is now going around on a tour of observation from college to college, picking up new ideas wherever he can find them. I took him to my recitation, though the exercise, being the first in the term, was a peculiar one; by no means a specimen performance. After recitation I gave my division a familiar talk, notwithstanding Mr. Weed's presence, on the primary and paramount importance of their college studies over all other objects. Gave them some hints however in regard to their English reading in case they should get any time for it. Took Mr. Weed to Professor Thacher, who invited him to a recitation in Tacitus at 4.

Some time on Junior examination papers. At 5½ Mr. Weed brought me a copy of Kendrick's Greek Ollendorff. It seems to me a carefully executed work, but with too much of unnecessary zersplitterung—not so bad in that respect as McClintock's work. It seems to me the best and easiest way to go over the general of etymology in the very outset, and not to give it out bit by bit without plan or method à la Ollendorff. In evening wrote to George, enclosing that Valentine and requesting him to send me back a copy. Studying awhile on dialects.

(Call on Larned. Greek not to begin until Court is over. Book undecided.)

Friday, January 10. First two divisions, all on hand at the first recitation. Several absentees from the third. Mr. Weed again present at 11. 12 to 1, at College Library. Afternoon and evening, some time on Junior examinations. Drafted a piece of a letter to Mrs. Curry.

Hair cut, .125. Pins, .0625. Comb, .33. Tweezers, .17. Matches, 12 boxes, .17. Cachous, .19. Subscription to Home Missionary Society, $5.00.

Saturday, January 11. No reporting this morning. 12 to 1, with Mr. Thacher. He says that the President will insist on a biennial examination at close of next summer term. I am a little afraid that we shall overset our calabash. He says the tutors have applied (to Prudential Committee last term) for higher wages. May they get them.

At 3, conversation with Mr. Warner about his son. The young man has not much stamina.

At Mr. Knevals' ordered a suit of clothes—also neck handkerchief. 10 shirts, to be made.

To Twinings' at 8. Returned before 11.

Thawing today and sloshy. Mr. Mitchell commences this evening a course of short lectures on the astronomy of the Bible. Can he give right ascension and declination for the morning-stars that sang together?

Bought shoulder brace for $2.00, and made myself for a short time an upright man. Found that in consequence I spoke more freely and clearly in the Chapel exercise.

Sunday, January 12. Studied and expounded John 4.43 to end of chapter. Luke 4.16–31. About a dozen present. Read Stuart on Daniel, chapter 4, and went over it at Twinings' in evening, not without some digressions. It seems to me that I must make some change, and at the risk of appearing stupid drop the character of sophist, which will become, I fear, habitual and natural to me. If I were giving decisions in College, the case would be different. I should be constrained then to assume the character of judge instead of advocate; to pronounce a just sentence according to the law and evidence, not devise a sophistical plea by the help of a perverse ingenuity; to approve the right and to condemn the wrong, instead of confusing the distinction between them and placing both on the same platform of unintelligible ambiguities. With this tether upon me to prevent my straying too often or too far, I might indulge without danger in occasional flights of fancy and excursions that should overpass the bounds of truth and soberness. But as it is, I am afraid of resting in my own negations, of losing my hold upon positive truth, of becoming thus unstable, light-minded, and inefficient. Lord, guard me and guide me, and deliver from all error of belief and practice; lead me into all truth, and may the truth make me both pure and strong.

Monday, January 13. Evening, wrote letter to Henry in great part, after having spent two hours or more on Junior examinations. Talk with Blodget about learning syntax in Zumpt's *Grammar*— fine print or not. Advised against an excessive minuteness. Read some in Niebuhr's *Rome*.

Tuesday, January 14. Finished letter to Henry. Call from Mr. Moore, who is a good deal disgusted with Dr. Taylor's pro-slavery tendencies, does not like his discussion of the doctrine of the Trinity, and charges him in general with want of personal dignity. At Pease's looked at Andrews' translation of Freund, which has just made its appearance—a very handsome book. Evening, Junior examinations. Call from Clarke, Sophomore, and talk on oblique cylinder.

Wednesday, January 15. Reading Ahrens on Aeolic dialect. At 11 Backus met me as I was going to recitation, said he had reseated the Freshmen, done it rather hastily but hoped there were no mistakes, and gave me the bills to read. I glanced at them in the recitation room and saw immediately that two or three of the shorter seats had the full complement of four men. If I had not known that it would be read in the other divisions, I would have refrained from reading it myself. After it was read a number of mistakes appeared: McConihe on the list, who has left the class; N. Smith, who sits in the gallery; no place for Reily or Stanton; etc. These I pointed out to Backus, who concluded to make out new papers. A striking illustration of "De more hashte, de lessh shpeed."

Senior party in the evening. Went at 7¾. Quite a crowd. Spoke with most of my lady friends, but gathered little news. Dr. Taylor thinks that Park and his antagonist have raised quite a fog between them. Mrs. Webster let me into the psychology of her son Eugene.

Thursday, January 16. Lazy today. Got over only 6 more of the Junior examination papers. Reading Ahrens.

Friday, January 17. Went at the examination papers with a real earnest. Worked upon them all day and finished them up. 10 have 3+; 32, 2+; 26, 1+; 19, 0+; rather more than half of them under 2.

Saturday, January 18. Reporting, 10–11. Residual examination at 2 to 4½. Nine present, all did pretty badly. Mr. Rice told me afterwards that he was ashamed to be seen in such a crowd. I am afraid that the rest will not think the crowd much more respectable for his being in it.

George Bushnell at tea with MacWhorter. Followed up to Mac's room. Larned came in, and the whole party adjourned at 7½ to hear John B. Gough lecture on temperance in College Chapel. All but me. I am afraid the man is a charlatan and I prefer not to hear him. At Twinings', heard of a Senior who, being introduced to Miss Anna just at the breaking up of the President's levee on Wednesday evening, remarked that "he thought he might as well be introduced to her as she was about the only one left." Said I,

"Who was it?" She felt unwilling to give the name, so I took to guessing. "Was it Sheldon?" No answer—hit the first time trying.

Sunday, January 19. Kirk in the morning, an exchange with Fitch. A good sermon—not quite his usual animation. He is not very well, did not preach in afternoon. G. Bushnell in Chapel—a large audience assembled to hear Kirk—disadvantageous position. Bushnell, however, did well. He is a straightforward practical preacher with a great deal of earnestness in style and in delivery.

Sunday lesson at 4. Miraculous draught of fishes. Demoniacs commenced, but not carried far.

Daniel, chapter 5, studied. Expounded at Twinings'.

Monday, January 20. Left *The Inheritance* at Twinings' with a few scribbled pages headed "Family Eclogues or Modern Deipnosophists," intended to introduce our family, our incommunicativeness on that subject having been ground of gentle complaint. Going to call on Mrs. Larned, heard loud music and the softly voice of Mr. John Henry Wilcox, and allowed myself to be frightened away from the door. Recollected that I had not been at the post office since Thursday last. Found a letter there, but clerks busy in sorting mail. Stopt in at J. G. E. Larned's. Found Mac. Talk on various matters: Senior party; Bushnell's backwardness about using the privileges of his position; Union speeches here, of which Union Committee in New York have ordered 5000 copies at their own expense; dangers of Taylorism, in regard to which Mac said very fairly that it was liable to overlook the capital importance of general rules for external action; etc. Came away just before 9. Found my letter to be a note from Professor Edwards, begging my article on Donaldson for next number of *Bibliotheca Sacra*. Mr. Short wants longer time for his on Aeschylus. Happy to gratify them, but it's quite "unpossible." Fighting for several days with a cold. Hardly know which will get the better—if the cold does I shall get the worse, I suppose.

Tuesday, January 21. Gave Mr. Eastman $5.00 for Tract Society, thus procuring change for my solitary $50. Joseph Silliman took coat and vest of mine to clean.

Heard remainder of Hyde's sermon on temptation. The fellows objected, he says, to founding it on the particular sin to which Joseph was solicited by the abandoned wife of Potiphar. They found fault also with the glowing language in which he described the seductions of the tempter. Goodrich agreed in those criticisms; not so I. It is a beautiful sermon—a little vague perhaps.

Wednesday, January 22. Called on Mrs. Larned in evening, afterward on Miss Sophia, about an hour with each. Talked on temperance with the latter, somewhat heterodoxly. J. G. E. Larned came in and vindicated Gough. Read some pieces to Mrs. Larned from a book of selections, *Memory and Hope,* lately published in Boston. One from Dryden which is singularly beautiful—must copy it. The great poets do better, a great deal better, than the small ones. Those few lines are worth half the book.

My cold appears to be going off.

Talk with Hyde about discussion on prison discipline just held in Rhetorical Society. Taylor was absent and they put Hyde in the chair. He said some good things which they do not often have a chance to hear.

The Beethoven Society are resolving on an organ, to be built by Hook of Boston, to cost $1200, to be mainly contributed I suppose by the Faculty.

Thursday, January 23. Letter from George (.12½), after long silence. Blue about College prospects and personal ones. Agitation for new Presbyterian College at Buffalo. Copy of my verses very neatly made.

Volume of *Literary World* drawn out from College Library.

Friday, January 24. Camp came in this evening from Washington. Has had a very lively pleasant time of it for the last 4 weeks. Seen and heard all the celebrities, participated in all the gayeties, talked politics with the men, talked fashion with the women. Small talk with all. It is very pleasant to me having him here again, especially as he has some idea of coming to board at the Tontine. I have been very mum there all this term, not a soul to talk with, and Kimberly opposite throwing the damper of his fastidiousness on any indiscreet sallies of conviviality, imposing a restraint which even Boardman feels. Dwight (Timothy) sits opposite with his mother at the Ladies' Ordinary, a place to which unfortunately I can advance no claim.

Found in the paper today an extract from Miss Brontë's preface to a late edition of *Wuthering Heights,* from which it appears that Ellis Bell = Emily Brontë and Acton Bell = Anne Brontë, her own younger sisters. Their novels, though written before *Jane*

Eyre, were not published until after it, and shortly after their publication Emily fell sick, declined rapidly, and died, December 1848. Anne was taken ill almost immediately after her sister's death, and after some months of suffering also died, apparently in the following year.

Saturday, January 25. In afternoon put on my new suit, which fits well. Tried, but in vain, to make a call on Miss Larned. To Twinings' at 8. Carried the notice of the Bells, as also some pretty lines of H. G. Arey from the same paper. Had some talk about the "Eclogues." They seem to like the treason, but despise the traitor. Read some in *Nathan,* and came away at 10½.

Sunday, January 26. Studied Bible lesson, chiefly demoniacs, and gave a tolerably good lecture upon it. Dr. Fitch on Creation. Talked about geology, and said some things ingeniously, but on the whole made a bad bungle of it. One who was familiar with the subject could understand what he was driving at. One who had not studied it must have been utterly in the dark. It is a great fault with Dr. Fitch's sermons that he often carries on a skilful fencing bout against an antagonist whom he does not bring out before the audience, so that his finest thrusts and strokes appear like mere pantomime. The afternoon sermon, on consecration to God, I was so unfortunate as not to hear. I was present bodily in the Chapel, but spiritually with Daniel in the den of lions, a subject which, having studied further after prayers, I expounded with manifold digressive talk at Twinings'. Back at 10 to a cold room, that is, moderately cold. There had been no fire in it through the day. The weather extremely mild and spring-like. Snow all gone.

Camp has quit the Union House and joined me at the Tontine. There at dinner and supper. A brave acquisition.

Monday, January 27. Call from Mr. Olmsted in the morning. He has been lecturing in Utica and Syracuse. He does not speak very highly of the latter, but was very favorably impressed with the former. He praises the intelligence and cultivation of the people, though he thinks them extra fashionable. He saw Professor Prentice, but fears that he offended him by a circumstance which was least of all intended to give offence. He says that Rexford of my class, a lawyer in Syracuse, died last summer. If so, we have lost three men during the year 1850.

Spent the evening at President Woolsey's in company with

Professor Peirce. Professor Salisbury and Mr. Hillhouse were also present. Mr. Peirce talked in a very animated and interesting way, with more of a religious turn, not prominent but shaded, than I should have expected. He asked me to call upon him at Cambridge if ever I should come there.

This morning Mr. Dana put into my hands the *Calculus of Operations* by Mr. Paterson of Albany, with a letter from Mr. Perkins of the normal school, and a sketch of the work by Mr. Paterson designed for publication in the *Journal*. Mr. Dana wished me to look at it, and say whether in my opinion it would be well to give it an insertion. The object of the book is to interpret the symbols and processes of algebra. His great idea appears to be the expression of x^0, x^1, x^2, x^3, etc. by a series of forces each of which is capable of generating the force which stands next below it and is itself generated by the one which stands next above it. I mentioned the book to Mr. Peirce in the evening. He gave no decided opinion concerning it, said it rested on a curious assumption and thought mathematicians might say that it was crude, a sort of groping round after a truth yet to be discovered.

Tuesday, January 28. Spent the evening at President Day's, being invited there by Professor Thacher to meet Dr. Wimmer from Saxony, a German gentleman who has communicated to the *Bibliotheca Sacra* within the past year an article on gymnasial education in Germany. He was invited on here to take the German tutoring in College. Apparently, however, he does not wish to teach, though he was said before he came to be extremely poor. He was fortunate enough, however, to meet with a railroad accident in Western New York, which broke a rib, collarbone, and shoulder blade, and through the kind interference of Professor Mason (brother-in-law of Professor Olmstead) has gained him, over and above expenses, the sum of $2000 from the Company. Mr. Wimmer is preparing a report on education in America for some people in his own country, and hopes to follow it back to Germany. We had a pleasant tea of it. Tutor Blodget one of the party. I talked detestably and made a fool of myself, which I should be sorry for if I had not by this time grown pretty well used to it. I wish I could get the secret of that "asanga" that Whitney and I used to read so much about in the *Bhagavadgītā*.

Wednesday, January 29. Change in the weather—growing colder. From 12 to 1, discussed with Dwight and Backus the results of our residual examination. Plunkett advised to leave. Chotard, Lathrop, and Thompson readvised more urgently to leave. Others, letters home.

Dialects in the evening.

Must take up supplementary nominations for ΦBK. Larned president of committee. Members, Porter, Thacher, self. Undergraduates, French, Hebard, Vose!!!

Thursday, January 30. Gave Johnny a dollar. Bought of Mr. Pease Bulwer's *Night and Morning,* together with a sort of story book—50 cents. Joseph Silliman brought back my coat and vest which he has been cleaning—$1.375 to be paid tomorrow at Tontine. They smell rather strong and are very little improved in appearance. On the whole it hardly pays.

Late in the evening took up Bulwer's *Night and Morning,* which laid hold of me with its charm and kept me up till 1 o'clock. About this time heard some rather uproarious talking, which I soon traced to Gaylord's room, and creeping to it, entered. Found Gaylord at backgammon with an unknown individual, Carter looking on, lemonade upon the table—a very moderate spree.

Friday, January 31. With Mr. Thacher from 12 to 1, inquiring about Seniors to be nominated for election into ΦBK. Saw Theodore Winthrop, who has just come back from Europe—*not* in the unfortunate *Atlantic*—is looking very well. Mr. Sobieski says that his evenings are engaged, promises to come in some Saturday afternoon. I am afraid he is not much of a gentleman, but fas est ab hoste doceri. Mr. Larned wished me to come up after dinner—is rather out of sorts—a troublesome diarrhoea—must keep his room for a day or two. Talk with Mr. Porter in afternoon; agreed upon a list of nominees. Saw Mr. Larned again in evening; talked on a variety of matters.

Read *Night and Morning.*

FEBRUARY, 1851

Saturday, February 1. Finished *Night and Morning.* It is a very grand novel—the characters forcibly drawn, but nicely discriminated and carefully sustained—the gradual progress of character extremely well developed, which is the most difficult attainment of the novelist. It is remarkably adventurous and daring: the author grapples boldly with every trying situation, every embarrassing combination of his subject. It is very sententious too, abounds in moralizing, and if it does not always reach the highest wisdom, it shows a great advance upon its author's previous works.

Another letter from Henry. Must be answering them.

Call from J. G. E. Larned. Says that he has tried several times to find me, but without success. Suspects I have been getting into a bad way. I could think of nothing very heinous except a visit to a dangerous neighborhood in Brewster's Building. He thought that might be pardoned if by going more frequently I should perhaps produce a salutary impression, but inquired archly whether my affections had not been entwining themselves about a fair object. I told him I had been engaged a year ago but supposed that I had got off. This was a new thing which I had never heard of before. He had heard of it 6 weeks or two months ago. I said that such rumors could do *me* no harm, but I was sorry for ladies who might be compromised or at least annoyed by them. He asked if I knew the lady referred to, and seemed to think that if the rumor were true I should have no reason to be sorry for it. I overbid his praise, and thus showed plainly enough that I was dégagé. He felt it so, for he inquired in all seriousness whether I had any purposes that looked however remotely to matrimony with any "weib person" whatsoever. I told him that my principles were sound and orthodox, but feared that my practice might not correspond with them. He said that he had never made any secret of his intention to marry as soon as he could maintain a wife. I said that I was spoiled by novels—I couldn't marry without falling in love first. "Falling in love," said he, "is a humbug, I think. Don't you think so too?" "Why yes," said I, "that's my rational judgment on the subject, but I am afraid that in the matter of action feeling might be more potent than conviction." Larned thinks that Bushnell's example and his own exhortations have had some influence even on the hard heart of MacWhorter. Etc.

At 8 o'clock, just as I was ready to take my accustomed start, Mr. Thacher came in to find Bellinger's room. He had received a telegraphic dispatch inquiring after his health and safety, and was trying to look him up.

At Twinings', read a little in *Nathan der Weise*.

Sunday, February 2. Communion Sunday. Oh for more of God's presence and his love. Studied Bible lesson—some miracles of healing—and expounded at 4. Miss Anna Twining was kind enough to send me word in the afternoon that she should not attend Monthly Concert in the evening, so that there was nothing to prevent our customary exercise. Accordingly, after evening prayers I shut and locked my doors and sat down to Professor Stuart on Daniel, 7th chapter. Fully agreed with him that the little horn refers to Antiochus Epiphanes. Got over his 30 or 40 pages by 7½, and then started off to find my pupils. They were rather reluctant to admit that the Pope of Rome was not specially aimed at in the prophecy.

Away before 10, and supposing my fire to be out, stopped at Camp's room from 10 to 12.

Monday, February 3. Call from Professor Putnam of Dartmouth, whom I had just seen yesterday in the Chapel. He came in before 10 o'clock, and attended my recitation at 11. Went with him to the College Library, where I drew *Pictorial History of England*, Volume 1, for Miss H. Twining, who finds her eyes wearied by the glare and blur of the American edition. Sent it over with my Cubi's *Spanish Grammar* for Miss Anna. At 2 went to Professor Thacher's room and consulted with Talcott and Kinne about Junior appointments.

In the evening, working at my paper on the Homeric dialect.

Tuesday, February 4. Junior appointments again at Professor Thacher's from 9 to 11. Settled them quite harmoniously for reporting to the Faculty.

Evening at my paper on Homeric dialect.

Wednesday, February 5. Working at the dialects. At Professor Thacher's from 9 to 11, on results of Junior examinations. Talcott, Kinne, and I were for recommending the excision of Este, McKissack, and Swift, and advice to L. C. Duncan's friends to remove him. King to be deferred for the present. At Faculty meeting in the afternoon F. Duncan was cut off. As to the others we shilly-shallied, changed our mind once or twice and at last put them over to next week. Appointments carried through. The intention was to surprise the class with them tomorrow morning, but the suspicions of the Juniors were awake, and were confirmed by some incautious expressions of Mr. Hyde. They commenced a rub-a-dub-dub with tin pans and trumpets and kept it up for nearly 3 hours, until about half past eleven they had the grace to adjourn and go to bed.

Thursday, February 6. Finished up my paper on the Homeric dialect and read it to the Philological Society. Rather ashamed of it, more especially as Professor Putnam was one of my auditors. I had not seen him since Monday and supposed that he had gone out of town, but he came in with the President. Of the members, Messrs. Gibbs, Hadley, Kingsley, (Larned unwell), Murdock, (Porter at Washington), Salisbury, Thacher, and Woolsey were in attendance, at Dr. Murdock's study. After my paper, which occupied about an hour, there was a good deal of interesting conversation, until half past nine, when we adjourned; next meeting at President Woolsey's, Professor Kingsley to officiate.

Friday, February 7. Call from Mr. Putnam in the morning. Wrote letter to Henry, setting forth a view of the relation between certainty and necessity. Talk with Hyde in the evening. Gave me an account of a speech he had just pronounced at nonsense meeting, in which he had expressed liberal views in regard to inspiration of Scripture.

Had received a note the day before from Hurlbutt requesting me to send a Triennial Catalogue to his classmate Titcomb. He also alluded archly to my engagement, apologizing for an injurious suspicion which he had expressed in regard to the lady when I met him in the vacation. He offered his congratulations but did not suppress his regret at the failure of his Albany schemes, and seemed to think he must now prosecute them on his own account. I wrote back this evening taking him to task for having *twice* injured my noble friend by his blunders—blunders alike discreditable to his professional skill and his sagacity in judging human nature—and finally bade him expect a dangerous rival for the affections of his Albany fair one.

Saturday, February 8. Another call from Mr. Putnam, who was to leave town at 11. The President came in and sat awhile. Wished me to look at ὅτι—ὁποῖον in 2d and 3d lines of *Antigone*. Read on Daniel, chapter 8. Sent off my letters to Henry and Hurlbutt. Sent Henry a copy of President Woolsey's most admirable sermon on ministerial authority. Forgot to enclose my decision on socialism.
  At Twinings'.
  Bought awl, 6¼. Soap, 11.

Sunday, February 9. Henry Ward Beecher preached at Eustis' church in forenoon and evening—very well, they say. Hyde there in the afternoon. His sermon on temptation caused some slight mirthfulness at first in Mr. Joseph Larned and others of that kidney, as well as some uneasiness in the female portion of his audience. Both soon passed away.

In Chapel we had an agent of the Colonization Society, not a man of very nice taste, but full of facts which to me were interesting. Glad to learn that the terrestial paradise of Liberia does not furnish quite so easy a passage to the celestial one as I had before supposed, that is, to the Negro. A white man can hardly live there more than five years.

Bible lesson as usual. Miracle at pool of Bethesda.

Read my sermon to Miss Anna Twining, which left only time to finish up 7th chapter of Daniel.

Some time at Camp's room.

Mrs. Larned wants me to write to Professor Stanley at Cairo and give him the College news.

Monday, February 10. Wrote to Mary and Mrs. Curry. I feel curious to know what this latter lady will say to my explanation on Women's Rights.

Felt strongly moved in spirit to write a Valentine that should express the idea of love content in hopelessness. Spun two verses and fell asleep on the third.

Tuesday, February 11. Nearly finished my "go"; only one verse, the twelfth, yet to be added. Saw MacWhorter at tea, just back from New York, apparently in good spirits.

Wednesday, February 12. Valentine to "the sex" at large or the "ideal woman" quite finished. At Faculty meeting decided to try McKissack, Este, and Swift still longer. Sophomores uproarious at declamation.

Yesterday President Day called upon me and proposed to me that I should assist him in getting out the new edition of his *Algebra,* now in course of publication. Professor Stanley had commenced and gone through simple equations, but as he was sick, or at least feeble, nearly all of last year, the work has been suspended for more than a twelve-month. President Day thinks it best to wait no longer, and as he feels the need of some help, applied to me. I told him I would do something, though I feared that I could not do all I would wish.

Hyde came into my room at 10½ and gave me an account of a discussion just finished in the Porter Rhetorical Society on the nature of virtue. The Doctor was much excited and gave a very long and unusually able decision.

Thursday, February 13. President Day came in and brought me a copy of his *Algebra*. I am to look over the subject of powers and roots, and see if anything is wanted. Commenced on the prize translations. Endeavored to make out a translation for myself, which occupied the evening or such part of it as I could rescue from sleep.

Sent my Valentine for Miss Baldwin to John Chassell with a note and copy for him. 10 cents.

Friday, February 14. After breakfast, a talk with Mrs. Larned about Chotard. She wishes me to call on Miss Whitney. Professor Porter having returned from Washington on Tuesday, our nominating committee for ΦΒΚ were to meet at 12 today at Professor Larned's room, that time being fixed upon expressly to accommodate Mr. Porter. He did not make his appearance, however—in fact was lecturing to the Seniors. Appointed meeting for Monday at 12.

Talk with Mr. Larned and Mr. Thacher till 1 on fugitive-slave law, President Woolsey's letter to Union Committee, question of new almshouse, Mr. Babcock, Whig candidate for Congress, etc. The Whigs are getting terribly rough here to put up such a fellow as that. Colin Ingersoll they say is to be the candidate on the other side. If so the choice will be a tough one, but it would give me a very genuine satisfaction to vote for any tolerably decent Loco in opposition to Babcock, a man every way completely insignificant. I wonder how often he must be beaten before the party will get tired of nominating him.

After tea went to Pease's and got new number of *Westminster Review*, a poor affair not really worth the taking. An article on the progress of the intellect (!) says that all unprejudiced critics regard the Pentateuch as a collection of fragments, the oldest not older than the time of Samuel. The man is fifty years behind the Germans whom he follows. Who is he? Newman?

At 8 went down to Beethoven concert, given to raise funds for an organ in College Chapel. The President had mentioned [it] at morning prayers, and we had given out half lessons for tomorrow morning, but I should think not more than a quarter of the students were present. Brewster's Hall was about half filled, which was pretty well for a rainy evening. Music simple and tasteful. Slipt out after first part, and called on J. G. E. Larned. He was going to Our Society at Blake's, and invited me in. I attended him up, but stopt at the outer door—with coat and pants both third-rate I dared not venture further. I was sorry, for I want to make more acquaintance there. On the way, Larned told me his "last." Why did Paul say 'twas better to marry than burn? D'ye give it up? Because he preferred (*high* men) Hymen to *low* women.

Saturday, February 15. Meeting at 12 at Professor Larned's room (the Professor being prevented by the rain, which poured during most of the day, from going as he had intended to New York) to nominate candidates from Senior class for election into ΦBK. Committee, Larned, President, Porter, Thacher, Hadley, Hebard, Vose (Taft absent). Made out our 12 nominations, harmoniously, concurring in 8 at first ballot and bringing in 4 at the second, one by an unanimous vote and the rest by four votes out of the six.

Unusual feat of extemporizing at morning recitation. Had given out a half lesson to second division, but wished to keep them up with the rest, and to enable them to get the longer lesson which this required, I gave up the recitation and myself read and commented on both the review and the advance lessons. The idea had only occurred to me as I was coming out of my room, and for 40 lines I had no preparation but what I was able to make during prayers.

At College Library read *Literary World*. Good on the Anglophobia of the *American Whig Review*. I do not know what to make of Whelpley—he is a man that may have his notions.

Called to see Miss Whitney at 7½. She was out. Met with the same fortune in trying to see Miss Larned. Found Miss Twining. Finished second act of *Nathan*. Recited my Valentine—made a bungle of it. My role was to seem unconscious and indifferent, but I saw that she was embarrassed, and that flustered me, so that with the utmost efforts I could not appear at my ease. It was plain enough that she suspected me of a personal reference, and I thought that she seemed agitated and affected by it, but I may have misjudged. It appeared to me also as if she meant to express a half reproach for having compromised her by the frequency of my calls. I was going to put down some of her expressions, but a man should be delicate even with himself, and not be at heart a coxcomb. Besides, I am quite as likely to be wrong as right in the conclusions that I drew. I have no confidence in them now. But at the time I felt them to be certain, and was a good deal perplexed, for in truth I had not expected it. I had meant only a disclaimer of the intentions which rumor has ascribed to me, supposing that such a disclaimer would be satisfactory to her, as showing that she had nothing to fear from me—no importunities, which it would be painful to reject, but impossible to accept and yield to. Finding, however, what then appeared to me evidences of interest that I had not looked for, I saw myself in a fix. I sat up two hours or more thinking what course to take, and it seemed to me that there was no way for it but to speak out the truth bluntly, that I *must* remain as I am for some years longer, and so leave everything to her. I have caught a little cold, and what with that and with this, I was pretty restless through the night, and seemed to myself, whether awake or asleep, to be always poring over the same subject. The morning light brought more of strength and courage, though that touch of cold keeps me still feverish and dumpy.

Sunday, February 16. Mr. Samuel Merwin in Chapel both fore-noon and afternoon, on an exchange, I suppose, with Dr. Fitch. He spoke extemporaneously with freedom and propriety, and with more of condensation and method than is common in extemporane-ous oratory. He quoted poetry too much, giving us the greater part of Longfellow's "Excelsior," which was a mistake. Yet on the whole I think he made a good impression.

Studied my Sacred Scripture lessons lazily, and expounded in much the same way. Bible class, on the doctrine of Christ concern-ing the Sabbath, did not stir a hair from orthodox ground, which implies either self-command or timidity or both.

At Twinings', on Daniel, 8th chapter. Felt pretty blue (not sky-blue either), but was considerably reassured by Miss Twining's un-concerned manner. She inquired whether I were ghost-haunted, and professed a willingness to relieve me of any spiritual presence which might be annoying. I hardly knew what to make of this, as it was very simply and frankly said, without any apparent conscious-ness. She even spoke of sending the so-called ghost to one who would be pleased with him. I gave a rather confused and ungracious assent and then came away. I hope to heaven that her peace of mind is not in [any] way involved in this business. I am coming to see more and more plainly how preposterous was the sort of familiarity which I thought of establishing with this people. But

> There's a divinity that shapes our ends
> Rough hew them as we will.

Monday, February 17. After coming away last night I sat down and copied my luckless verses and enclosed them in a note which was meant to be witty but perhaps succeeded only in being wicked. After this I glanced at my lesson for the morning, tried to wash out my cold, and went to bed at ¼ before two. Dull and heavy today. Recast my note of last night so as to make it worse than before, but at 2 received a note from Miss Twining in which she told me that her sister regarded her request as an improper one and she should therefore withdraw it for the present. This throws me back again into something of my former perplexity: and I believe that an explanation or understanding of some sort is absolutely necessary.

Received a long and most excellent letter from Whitney, who had not waited to receive mine. He speaks with great kindness of our intercourse last year: says that he finds trouble at Berlin from the crowd of Americans, who deprive him of all opportunity to learn German: means to go somewhere else in the spring, probably to Bonn. Is dissatisfied with most of his instructors, especially Bopp and Heyse—thinks very highly of Weber. Enclosed a note from Professor Franz, who proposes to open a boardinghouse for foreign students in Berlin and wishes to make me one of his references.

A good deal of talk during the day about Carrier, Senior, whose claims we had overlooked at our nominating committee meeting. He was absent last year when the appointments came out, and so received no part, but his marks bring him into the second-dispute range—his marks up to the end of Junior year—and this year he has been doing very well. Talk with Thacher, Porter, etc. Agreed to substitute his name for that of Hungerford. The Society meet this evening.

Call this evening from Whitney, Freshman. He has bad luck with his Euclid, going over the second book, but is getting on better now.

Working a prize translation.

Tried to collect my ideas and arrange my plans in regard to these unlucky woman-matters. I do not care for myself—my shoulders are broad enough to bear my own burden, even if it should be a pretty heavy one. But if I should have spoiled the peace and happiness of others, who were getting on so quietly and beautifully without me, I should hardly know how to bear it. But I will hope and trust and expect better things.

Tuesday, February 18. Spent some time on prize translations, and at 8 P.M. met Dwight and Backus to decide upon them. We read and compared four, and selected Dupee's for first prize, Alexander's for second, and Mitchell for the third. Letter from Henry.

More time still on the same subject, which perplexes me unaccountably.

Wednesday, February 19. From 12 to 1, talked with Clarke of my division about the suppression of infidel publications by law, the subject of the great prize debate in the Linonian Society, which is to come off some 4 or 5 weeks from this time.

Faculty at 3. Disturbances at Sophomore exercises in declamation. Resolved to go on with exercises.

Pretty much settled down on the course projected last Saturday night. Easier in mind, determined not to plague myself overmuch, let it go as it will.

Thursday, February 20. Wrote to H. D. A. Ward on organization of new Alpha of ΦBK in University of Michigan. Sent him Catalogue of ΦBK and one of College.

Attended lecture (.25) in the evening by Mr. Whipple on the American mind—had seen a report of it some time ago in New York paper. Very brilliant and striking, but I think hardly so interesting as that which we had from him a year ago. A large audience in the Baptist Church, although the evening was rainy. Back at 9½. In Dwight's room till 11½, settling prizes for 2d division. He read us seven, of which we set aside 3 very quick. They were all poor.

Friday, February 21. Short call in forenoon from my classmate J. A. Porter, on his way from New York to Boston. He says that he is getting to be pretty well acquainted in Providence, but has not yet commenced his courses. He begins in April. Chat with Professor Olmsted. Showed me a letter from Dudley in regard to Wade. Finds him well-meaning, unmanageable, and lazy, says he does tolerably well in Greek, and might do much better. Written with true Dudleian roughness—his connection with Miss Bates does not appear as yet to have exercised any peculiar softening influence.

From 8 to 10½ at Backus' room with Dwight. Settled prizes of 3d division: 1. Warner. 2. Cutler. 3. Lombard and Sparrow. 2d division: 1. Tracy. 2. Proctor. 3. Van de Graaff. Threw out Chotard (2).

* * *

Wednesday, February 26. Commenced a letter to Charles Long. Wrote farther on that to Henry, and very nearly finished the one to Whitney. Called again on Mr. Gibbs. He will let Mr. Whitney have those two first parts of the *Comparative Grammar,* but positively declines receiving any pay for them. Some talk with him on prophecy; it is curious to see how all questions are still open questions with him.

Faculty meeting; quite a stroke of business. Train, Sophomore, suspended for pushing against Mr. Kinne in going out of Chapel. Battles, Senior, suspended likewise for insult to him in College yard.

Mr. Silliman informed us that he should leave for Europe before our next meeting. In talking of introductions, Mr. Olmsted struck up, "Oh, Mr. Silliman, if you come to a place where you are not known, you are welcome to use any of our names."

Drest up and at 8½ went to Our Society. Talk with Mrs. Webster, Mrs. Winthrop, Miss Foster; Miss Twining was there, but went away before I had any chance to speak to her. Most of the company left at 9½. After some talk with Mr. Salisbury, I came away at 10. Going to MacWhorter's room, found J. G. E. Larned, and presently Mac himself came in. J. G. etc. gave an account of his lecture just delivered before the juvenile department of the Young Men's Institute, a world too deep for his audience, on the past and future of the laboring classes. It took him near an hour to give us the heads, though the lecture itself for a wonder occupied only an hour and five minutes in the delivery.

It was very interesting and valuable and I hope to hear or read it for myself. After finishing his account he began to labor with me and Mac on the subject of matrimony. He said it was an aggravation to a poor fellow like him who was only prevented by circumstances, to see chaps like us that could as well as not, yet would not be driven into it. He does not care whether I marry a certain lady or not, but insists only that I should marry somebody.

Came away at 11½, bringing with me the records, which I had

lent to Mac, of our class. He had copied and sent them to Joe Benton.

Thursday, February 27. Fast day for Colleges. Recitation at 7, not afterwards during the day. Prayer meeting at 2 in Rhetorical Chamber. An impressive speech by the President on the characters of a back-slidden church, followed by Taylor with an energetic appeal. Addresses by Fitch and Linsley, rather heavy. Not much disposition apparently to engage in active labor.

Call from Mr. Olmsted, with invitation to take tea at his house. Professor Andrews of Marietta College and Dr. Linsley, formerly President of that College, to be there. Went accordingly at 6 and came away at 7½, rejoicing that I had been prudent enough to take an umbrella, for it was just beginning to rain.

Made the first start in my review of Mure.

Friday, February 28. In the evening sorted some of my old papers, and committed a number to the flames. It gives me a certain pang, however, to destroy a paper. It always seems as if it would be interesting one of these days. But I do not expect to attain the years of Methuselah, or even those of "the many-wintered crow, that leads the clanging rookery home." I cannot wait to see my autographs invested with the interest of antiques. Read *New Englander,* which Larned had given me in the morning, Porter's article, and Woolsey's on Caucasians and their wars with Russia. In the first paragraph of the latter some fine remarks on the way in which we should regard the efforts of small communities to maintain their nationality.

MARCH, 1851

Saturday, March 1. Have come at last to our natal month, the first of spring. Commenced it with a coating of snow, a very thin one, which however kept its place in good part during the raw though sunshiny day.

In afternoon carried over to President Day some proof of *Algebra,* and suggested to him by Mr. Hamlen's desire the propriety of using the parentheses instead of the line vinculum. Mr. Stanley appears to have preferred the first.

Read *London Quarterly* (just obtained) on Grote's Socrates. It is very Grote-y for the *Quarterly.*

Paid bill at Tontine, $26.

At 7½ called on Miss Whitney, to speak of Chotard. Could not give a very encouraging report. Recommended a private tutor, Mr. Dwight or Mr. Camp. She expressed herself quite freely as to the Dwights, as she has a right to—they are connections of hers.

At 8, as usual. Read that fine apologue of Nathan, which however needs to be received with very careful qualifications—as to the equal perfection of the rings—it begs the whole question. Some talk about immediate decision. She feels too much the excitement and the suspense, finds it hard to sleep, or study. But after some consideration we agreed to abide for the present by the ground of Monday evening. With great delicacy she gave me a little statement of her circumstances. The amount is that we should have a home, and for the rest my salary. As to her small funds, they ought to remain untouched. We could get on fairly while well and prosperous and only ourselves—but if these conditions should change we might have trouble.

Broke truce and stayed till nearly 11. Soon after I had reached my room, Hyde came in. The tutors were to keep a lookout for an hour or two. The Sophomore class had escorted Train to the cars in the afternoon, and returning at prayers, had entered the Chapel in procession, somewhat tardy. It was feared that some outrage would be attempted. These apprehensions proved to be groundless. Everything remained quiet.

"There is no armor against fate." We move on, in spite of all struggles, slowly perhaps but surely, toward the inevitable verge. I scarcely know whether to hope or fear, to be joyful or sorrowful. Providence has hitherto done a great deal better for me than I have done or could have done for myself. I seem to see that everything in my life has been for good, for the best, that even what I feared has always proved for my advantage. All has thriven under my hands, the coming to College, the tutorship, the professorship, etc., and I will believe that Providence is not deserting me now.

If I were disposed to be superstitious, I might notice remarkable coincidences that look like intimations of the future and point to the same goal. I do not mean to float passively on the current, or surrender my personal reason and will; but I cannot help feeling a certain superior guidance, which moves me on to many results to which my own will and reason would never have conducted me.

Sunday, March 2. Dr. Fitch in forenoon; in afternoon, Professor Andrews of Marietta College on Cain and Abel, a smooth and elegant preacher, who treated the subject in a more pragmatical way than I should feel inclined to. I have no desire to run amuck with traditional beliefs, but I cannot practically receive the first five or ten chapters of Genesis as literal facts. Afternoon service at 3. Left me only half an hour for my Bible class. Four men in attendance. Continued Sermon on the Mount. After tea, called with Camp on Mrs. Larned and sat till 7½.

Looking over my diaries for March 1850. Objects then somewhat different. I believe that I give too much thought and attention to this business now, more than is necessary, more than is reasonable. I thought that I saw her going to the Chapel this afternoon, but I know not, for I did not dare to look steadily toward the place where I supposed her to be seated. Queer, is it not? And yet I cannot see that there is any strong feeling on my part, and if the whole thing should dissolve into thin air, there would be no great regret, I suspect, on either side. I have always been subject to a certain impatience and eagerness in view of any expected novelty, as for instance in going to College, entering upon an untried office, taking up a new study, etc. etc. It is a longing after decision and experience, a fermenting mixture of desire and curiosity and anticipation. And it is that which haunts me now. The imagination is not active, still less the enthusiasm. The halo and the glory are wanting, the canonization and apotheosis are yet to come. It is a little different with my noble friend. Her curiosity is piqued. There is something in the Protean aspects of a shifty vacillating nature which she cannot understand, it is so wholly foreign to her mind. She believes that there must be some unity and consistency in it all, and she wonders that she cannot find the key, that she cannot harmonize and account for the phenomena. She is thus interested and puzzled and perplexed. And here imagination does step in, and forms fine theories of the unknown character and throws an ideal splendor round a very common and very worthless object. I do not think however that there is any deeper feeling than this. At any rate there must be no more trouble about it.

Monday, March 3. Criticizing translations. Talk about Sophomore "bust" on Saturday. At 10 with Hyde and Blodget. At 12 with Thacher and Kinne. Professor Olmsted says that Mr. Silliman's companions (prayed for yesterday in Chapel) do not mean Mrs. Silliman. The story that he is to be married to Mrs. Webb tomorrow and take her with him to Europe is humbug. It has been generally believed here, and according to some authorities the arrangements were even made by the late Mrs. Silliman upon her death-bed. It would be no wonder, certainly, if Mr. Silliman should marry now; it is marvelous rather that he has not done it six months earlier. Talking with Mr. Thacher on this subject, I alluded to the reports which have circulated concerning me. He was eager to know if there was anything new. I described the rumors more particularly. He had not heard anything about it since the middle of last term, when he had spoken to me on the subject. I remember that he said to me then one day that he had heard a report which startled him very much: he thought it could not be true, it was so unexpected; and yet it was so particular and so confident that he was at a loss what to think. He had been disposed to say something to me about it, but was afraid of meddling in so delicate a matter. I supposed at the time that he referred to Miss O., for as to the more recent engagement, I neither heard nor thought of it till long after. It is pity that Mr. Thacher did not then speak to me; it would have served to put me on my guard. He went to the lady and questioned her about it, told her that President Woolsey had mentioned it to him and asked if it were really so, at a meeting of the Faculty—that was the first he had heard of it. The President apparently must have shared the feelings with which he regarded it himself.

It is strange that a man cannot go out among these womankind without making trouble for them and for himself. I have very serious thoughts of shutting myself up and living as a hermit, or rather as a monk, for the next five years, if I should last so long as that. At the same time I must contract my range of study so as to include only these three things: Greek philology, interpretation of the Scriptures, and history. And I must drive these with a vigorous and unrelaxing study, until my hair shall be wholly gray (it is now half way to that) and the incipient wrinkles have grown deeply furrowed on cheek and brow.

I *know* that this feeling of mine is not a real passion. It is a glow of curiosity and impatience, a temporary fever in the blood. And if I were alone involved I should understand well enough how to treat it. As it is, we may go on perhaps for the remainder of this term, but then we must look each other in the eyes and say farewell. And I must intimate something of this kind soon, so that it may excite no surprise or bitterness when the time comes. And thus shall we cross the arrangements of destiny, arm ourselves against Fate, nullify the intimations of Providence? I cannot tell.

Some time on Mure in the evening. Inexpressibly tedious.

Tuesday, March 4. Hyde came up at 2, with a letter from Henry. He thinks he shall not stay at Andover through the summer. Park will have gone over the most important parts of his course, and for the rest there is no great activity nor any special prospect of advantage. Hyde staid till 3, talking about his sermon on love toward a personal Savior. Talcott came in soon after to speak about the Sophomore difficulties, which he thinks should be vigorously prosecuted. Received proof of my essay on verb $\epsilon\iota\mu\iota$ from Professor Salisbury and read it carefully. At tea Mac and Sobieski came in, and the latter sat beside me. I felt a sort of reluctance to say anything to him, but overcame it so far as to treat him with civility. I did not, however, ask him why he had not come to my room as he promised, to imbue me with Becker; still less did I claim a fulfilment of the promise. After tea Camp came to my room to read the article on $\epsilon\iota\mu\iota$, and sat till 9. Hyde called again at 10 and read me a plan of that sermon. We had a long and interesting talk until 11½, when he took his leave. I made arrangements for washing, proceeding in a leisurely way and reading the *Quarterly* as an accompaniment, until 12¾, when I got to bed. After lying ten minutes, remembered that I had wholly forgotten my lesson for the morning. Started up instanter in great consternation, struck a light, and ran over the Greek until 1½, when I got into bed again.

I was soon asleep. But, speaking metaphorically, I believe that I am broad awake now, know my position, and cannot easily be driven from it. Quam paene vidi etc. What a narrow escape, and how much do I not owe to that noble friend of mine for her frankness and moderation. If she had been selfish or artful in the least, if she had prest me up to any movement instead of leaving me perfectly unconstrained, if she had not rather drawn back with true feminine delicacy from an object that had begun to interest her feelings, I should have been committed beyond the power of recall—and that without any real passion, without any positive intention, and contrary to all the suggestions of prudence, from mere flurry and blundering. But I am now clear, see the end fully and distinctly, and am determined to bring it about. How to save her feelings is the great point of difficulty, and one which really perplexes me, but I am elastic in confident anticipation of the result. I shall disentangle this snarl without creating anything more than a little temporary disappointment, slight probably at the time, and at all events certain to be forgotten in less than six weeks.

Wednesday, March 5. Called on Professor Salisbury at 8½ to return proof of my article and consult him as to my memorandum on Sanskrit books for Mr. Edwards. Returning at 9½, met President Woolsey, who brought up to my room Mr. Lampson of Quebec, with his son, a candidate for our Freshman class. His reading was too limited to allow his present admission, and after some little trial I told his father that he could not expect to enter Sophomore next fall. Advised that he should study with Mr. Dudley at Northampton and enter Freshman in September. The young man however preferred to stay here, under a private tutor, so I took them over to Camp, with whom after some negotiation they succeeded in making an arrangement. He is to recite before breakfast and pay weekly.

After dinner, was caught up by Reverend Mr. Miller of Newburgh, whose son has just concluded to withdraw from the Freshman class. The father will send him for the present to East Hampton, Massachusetts, and try him again as a Freshman in the fall.

At Faculty meeting resolved to change time of evening prayers to 5½ tomorrow, and morning prayers to 6 about the equinox. Battles reconsidered but left in statu quo. Sophomore Train-ing last Saturday discussed. Professor Kingsley very strong against meddling with it. We have sent off Train, have done what we wished. Let them talk. By going farther we shall keep alive irritation and, as so many are involved, shall only multiply the evil. Besides there is no need that we should know anything about it: it is a matter that we can ignore and it is our policy to do so. These sentiments after some discussion were pretty generally adopted, those who had before thought differently giving in their acquiescence. Experience is a great thing. As Professor Kingsley spoke I acknowledged at every step the wisdom of his words and was ashamed to think how shallow I had been before.

Difficulty at prayers on Thursday night, when Blackman had attempted to take down a Scull and Bone notice, and had been more or less abused by Crampton, Dana, Alexander, and Beman, Seniors of that Society. Admonitions to the offenders. Renew our rule of no notices in the Chapel. Resolved that all who come into

Chapel after the monitor has taken his seat shall be treated as absent.

25 cents to Newell Andrews.

At supper was accosted by Mr. Mitchell (class of 1802), who enquired about his grand-nephew, Thompson of my division. He had received my letter to his father, who is now in Italy, and he came up from New York to see what could be done. As the deficiency is in mathematics I took him to Backus, and we agreed that the best way was to put him under a private tutor for the rest of the term and give him the most thorough drilling. If that doesn't succeed, he *must* go.

In evening, read a little, slept more, and went to bed at 11½.

Called on Mr. Kingsley at 12 M. to see about meeting of Philological Society tomorrow night. Dr. Bushnell, we had understood, was to lecture before the Institute at that time. Concluded therefore to put our meeting over to April. Long account of Mix Mitchell family—talented and lazy.

Thursday, March 6. Returned volume of Byron to Linonian Library. Took out Eckermann's *Conversations with Goethe*. Was just going to College Library in afternoon when Mr. George E. Day came into my room. He inquired about Edward Whitney, and appeared much pleased with the good account that I was able to give of him. He said Mr. Dudley was anxious to know the truth of a certain rumor he had heard of me, Mr. Dudley's own consciousness of passages between himself and Miss Bates making him particularly curious in regard to similar affairs, real or supposed, of other people. I told Mr. Day that the mythus had run its course and ceased to be believed in New Haven; it was entirely indifferent to me, but I was sorry for the lady, and he might render her a service by denying it in Northampton. She was a noble lady, he said very frankly, and would be pleased, he doubted not, if the story were true; but if it were not so, she might not like to have it circulated.

After tea went to Camp's room and staid till 7½, when we went together to Dr. Bushnell's lecture on Connecticut (25 cents). The room was almost filled when we entered. We got placed, however, on the back seat. The discourse was mainly historical, describing and vindicating the glories of "our state": it was very interesting and instructive, and no less noble and patriotic. I grew quite proud of my adopted country: until I happened to think that her chosen representatives in the next Congress would probably be Chapman and Babcock and Ames and I know not who. Indeed Dr. Bushnell expressed it as his conviction that the least honorable period in the history of Connecticut is the present, and I quite agree with him on that point.

Friday, March 7. Talk with Fenn of my division about the piece for prize translation. Spent some time on the list of Sanskrit textbooks and began a letter to Mr. Edwards—decline sending him the article on Donaldson. Received in the afternoon a letter from Whitney, dated February 14. He has cut Bopp and is confining himself to Weber. Has given up Latin and Greek and nearly concluded to make Orientalism his great object. Will not go to Bonn, as Lassen is nearly disabled by pulmonary difficulties, and seems to be drawing toward the close of life: but to Tübingen to study with Roth, an eminent "Vedavid." Gives an account of the slashing work that Weber makes with Indian history and antiquities, bringing it all down below the time of Alexander. Has more to say about his own researches on English phonology, proposes to send them on to me, etc. etc. An admirable letter.

Tuesday, March 11. Bound up my diary of last year into a single volume of quite respectable dimensions. The record is hastily and clumsily made, and yet I rejoice in it. It proves more of perseverance than I had regarded myself as possessing; of my former journals none had continued beyond the fourth month, and only one I think beyond the fourth week. It was commenced, too, at a time of rather more than usual pressure, when Whitney was driving me with the Sanskrit and afterward the Moeso-Gothic. It is a curt and meagre affair, too much occupied with the physical, and very barren of ideas. In this last particular it falls short of the original intention, and short I hope of the future performance. I do not mean hereafter to be so full in regard to matters of mere daily routine, though things of this kind must come in more or less if I am to have here, what I would wish to have, a sort of daguerreotype of my passing life. On the whole I prize the record thus far with all its imperfections and only wish it had found an earlier beginning. It is a little curious that it commenced very soon after that course of operations which, without any intention or consciousness on my part, was to have, as it seems, so important an influence on my after life. And I suppose that both had their origin in the same vague longings and aspirations of the spiritual nature. Strange enough too, that soon after my intimacy with Miss Field, I began a similar chronicle, and kept it up till about the time when she left. Singular, that women not peculiarly spiritual themselves should so quicken the spiritual life of those around them. But tenderness and grace are gentle forces that, pressing on the calm ether of the masculine soul, set it to vibrating, and produce undulations which propagate themselves, far beyond the range of the primitive impulse, to the utmost verge of the nature.

I must be careful, however, not to spend too much time in these self-gossipings, a danger to which I am at present the more exposed from the tide of ideas and feelings which from the beginning of the work-a-day week to its end can only be expressed in this manner. It is not well in this short life to waste half your time in jotting down what you have done in the other half.

Mr. Olmsted came in while I was at work, and congratulated me on the unbroken quiet of my present life, conjuring up at the same time fearful images of the unrest, squalling babies, clamorous urchins, and I know not what more, of a different state. He reassured me, however, by giving the preference on the whole to this latter condition. With me I doubt if curiosity be not a leading motive—the longing for experience, the disposition to try a new sphere of life and feeling. So adieu to fears, and if harm come, let us say, "All times have I *enjoyed* greatly—have *suffered* greatly" —memoria praeteritorum etc.

Mr. Gibbs called at 12½ to enquire about Peck the shoemaker, who was member of the Freshman class last year, the first few weeks of their course, and then left in discouragement. Now proposes to enter the Seminary. Good fellow, though rather dull.

In afternoon wrote to Mr. Mitchell about Thompson, also to fathers of Marmaduke and Pierson. Looked at an old letter of Mary's announcing the obiit of my most dear brother and was affected to tears. It is strange how that pang lasts. I scarcely feel the softening influence of time. True, I forget—he is but little in my mind; but when he comes there, the old feeling returns in its old bitterness. And now my hopes and happiness seem to me almost an offence against the dead. What right have I to such fortune,

from which he, so much the worthier, was excluded, forced sadly
and despairingly to renounce it with the life to which he never
ceased to cling in fond hopes and fainting wishes.

After tea, at Pease's. Bought *Lavengro*, .25. Obtained *Edinburgh
Review,* new number. Was reading it sleepily when, at 9, in came
Mac and sat an hour and a half. The mantle of Gulliver, he says,
has fallen on Mr. George E. Day, who is now considered as one of
Mac's spies. Talked of Dr. Bushnell and his forthcoming work on
the Trinity, his ingenious way of proving himself on this subject
more orthodox than Edwards. This he does from an unpublished
treatise of that great divine. It is a master stroke and will paralyze
Goodrich, Hewitt, Hall, etc.

Wednesday, March 12. At 2 received a most unexpected call
from that rather strange fellow, Mason of Georgia, who was for
a time private pupil of mine. Afterwards two terms in the class
of '51, then one term in the class of '52—a good scholar in both,
but leaving both because he was not as good as he wished to be.
A year ago last summer he suddenly gave up the idea of going
through College and started for California. He sold his books at
auction, and I have now in my possession Müller's *Greek Literature,* Fishlake's Buttmann's *Lexilogus,* and Veitch's *Greek Verbs,*
which belonged to him and were bid off for me very cheap by Mr.
Camp. He has had a great variety of experiences in California:
dug at the mines with fair success, till compelled to leave by sickness; invested most of his money in San Francisco, on security which
was swept away in one of their great fires; made $800 by teaching
one quarter in San Jose; was next reporter to the legislature; and
lastly general agent to several papers. Has received an advantageous
offer to conduct a weekly paper in Los Angeles and thinks he shall
accept it. Speaks of Californian selfishness, unfriendliness, uncon-
scientiousness, general drunkenness, particular conviviality of
legislature, night "of a thousand drinks." When they adjourned,
a wag hung up an inverted brandy bottle as their emblem to
signify that they had drunk up every drop in the place and were
therefore gone home. The country will be densely populated in
the river bottoms, which however are subject to floods in the rainy
season and to parching droughts in the dry—no rain from latter
April to November, all rain the rest of the year. Chinese in moderate numbers—good citizens. 300 in San Francisco. Many Mexicans
and South Americans. Spanish the predominant language (that

of the majority) in San Jose, but not in San Francisco. Great uncertainty about land titles, source of immense risk and inconvenience.

At breakfast found Shaw Perkins seated opposite to me. He
is some 2 or 3 months back from California; was gone about 11
months. Pratt has returned since; is much soberer in manner than
he used to be. Perkins saw Benton at Sacramento City and heard
of Mulford, much the same man as formerly, in Stockton. Met
Huggins after prayers; he has left Natick, Massachusetts, where
he was preaching for a time; was there January 1, or rather was
just then at Boston, for I saw him at that date; is at present lying
on his oars without any definite engagement.

Had occasion to call at Knevals'. Found him gone from the old
stand, removed two days ago to a splendid store in the post-office
building. He seems to think he can still accommodate me as well
as ever. I shall stick.

At Faculty meeting. Appointed examiners for end of term. Am
to act with Mr. Talcott as committee of arrangements. The sessions to close on Saturday morning before end of term. Mr. Larned
desired some other plan for the benefit of the Junior Exhibition,
which suffers now from the absence of the students and the want
of an audience, especially in the forenoon; but we could not agree
on any change.

Discussed Mr. Thacher's project for the renovation of the
Lyceum. Estimated expense $1600[,] less than I had expected. I
do not know but we must come in to it, though I hate to lay out
a dollar on the old shell. It was said that when first erected it was
much admired for its beauty and regarded as quite a model of
college architecture.

Mr. Aitchison's wish to leave at the end of the term was considered. All wished to have him stay. As to the obligation there
was difference of opinion. Some thought him bound to stay until
Mr. Stanley's return in the summer. Others, myself among the
number, understood him to be free from any pledge as regards
time. He evidently wants to go and no doubt will do so.

In the evening, had an hour of geography with Camp. Cut
Reverend Henry Ward Beecher's celebrated lecture on character,
delivered before the Institute. Paid no heed to campanologian
chimes, but scorned their bells. Scorned also by way of impartial
procedure the belles of Mrs. Blake's party in Orange Street, sending my regrets by Camp. Read *Edinburgh Review*. Sleepy from

10 to 11. Rallied and read till nearly 1. Then to bed, but not to sleep. Heard the stroke of 1, 2, even 3. Nervous evidently, but not unpleasantly so. It was a kind of waking-dream process, with many thoughts that appertained little to the routine of daily business or the grand results of science. I cannot wonder that many natures are frantic with this intoxication, when one so earthy and prosaic as mine is partly shaken from its centre. But then reciprocation is the soul of it; without this, all would be desire and pain. But the idea of being one's self an object to another—cherished in pure thoughts, surrounded by kind wishes, watched with holy prayers, garlanded with gentle affections—it is this that goes farthest to make fools of us.

Thursday, March 13. Met the 3d division this morning and made them a pretty sharp speech on some disturbance last evening in going out of Chapel. It was on the south side. A large tall fellow whose back was towards Blodget sprung against the door and prevented its being opened. I suspect Perry and Van Sinderen, one or other. Fortunately both are in the 3d division, and the guilty one could not feel particularly flattered by my remarks.

Finished letter to Henry and carried it after tea to the post office. Stopt at Pease's on the way back. Think of getting at end of term the following works: Hume, *England,* $2.40; Gibbon, *Rome,* $2.40; Hildreth, *United States History,* $8; Bancroft, $6; Neander, *Church History,* $9; Grote, *Greece,* $6.00. (From Bohn's Series: Rabelais, 2 volumes; Count Hamilton, *Fairy Tales,* 1; *Early English Romances,* 1. Perhaps some of the Greek in the Classical Library—the 3 dramatists, Herodotus, Thucydides.) Letter from my classmate Porter, asking me to review one of Greene's Historical Series for *New Englander.* Long letter from George, much more cosy and spread out than usual. He rejoices in his new vocation, gives some scanty specimens of poetizing, etc. etc. Read Mure and *Edinburgh Review.* Abed at 12.

Friday, March 14. Hyde came in at 10 and read me the introductory sections of his sermon on love to a personal Savior. Handsomely written, with uncommon richness of thought and language; but perhaps a little too rich, the subject hidden under the weight of illustration; and certainly too impassioned for an exordium, insomuch that it would be difficult or impossible to secure the just progression toward the end. Mure: finished reading on Homer, and commenced writing. Perplexed in regard to the proper order of arrangement and development. Shall write on the topics that occur to me and leave the arrangement, the interweaving in one fabric, to the end.

Had a ticket to Stanley's Indian Gallery, now on exhibition at Adelphi building, a complimentary ticket sent me by the exhibitors, but have not yet availed myself of it.

Talk in the evening with Clarke, about that great Linonian question—fought pretty shy. Conversation with Norris about college ambition. Tired, and abed betimes. I do not sleep nowadays half so much as I ought to. I am getting into a foolish way of lying awake for an hour or two, thinking of course of one subject, but without any important progress of thought. If I were to think of anything else, I should drop away in a trice. There is a strange sort of exhilaration about this, which I cannot well account for; it is not reason and so I suppose must be nature, for "nater is a rum 'un, is nater," according to Mr. Squeers. Within certain limits it will do very well, for a man must enter with whole soul into an affair like this. But I am afraid that it may go too far, and interfere with present efficiency. I am determined to sleep a-nights, if I have to think metaphysics or Mure or metempsychosis or whatever else is most narcotic to effect it.

Saturday, March 15. Did much the same things as usual in much the usual way. Took with me in the evening those scape-grace verses which brought on the catastrophe, with the strange half-earnest, half-mocking note which I before wrote when requested to give a copy of them. Professor Alexander Twining is expected here very soon—probably now in New York. We read fifteen pages of *Nathan,* and then began to talk. After some conversation about Mr. Dudley, Mr. Field, etc. we came to ourselves (?), and I proceeded to shake the firmness of my friend by a glimpse into the escritoires of her female acquaintances, betraying thus, not without conscientious twinges, the confidence of Miss Blake and Miss Baldwin. My success was quite indifferent. She was a little curious to know where I found those pretty things—the one of last year she admired particularly—but on the whole jealousy appeared to be swallowed up in confidence. She was evidently very happy, and spoke and looked charmingly. Yet I kept my distance, and maintained a perfectly respectful demeanor. If everything should fail, she will not have the misery of thinking that the sanctity of her person has been violated by the slightest familiarity; her feminine delicacy and self-respect will be spared that bitterness. Nor even in words has there been any "liebkosung"; everything has been subdued and restrained: a good deal intimated, but very little spoken out. It is not easy to see how a thing could be carried so far, with so few plain words—with no irrevocable words. I have been exceedingly cautious, for an incautious man, to provide for the contingencies of ultimate failure. Not that I expect such an event. It is in fact out of my power to recede, even if I wished it, and that is far enough from being the case: though no irrevocable words have been uttered, yet I am bound in honor and in conscience, and will never be found wanting to the obligation.

Sunday, March 16. Reverend Mr. Strong in afternoon, on self-detecting nature of sin. Same subject that Mr. Egleston treated in the Chapel a few weeks ago. Both brought in McGaughey and Professor Webster, but on Foote they differed, Mr. Strong substituting McCory, who was recently hung in Rensselaer County, New York, for the murder of his nephews. One point of the sermon was that sin reveals itself by reacting on the physical frame, and as an example he instanced novel-reading, which makes the transgressor look sickly and sentimental. Had a good exercise in the Sermon on the Mount. Looked further at Daniel 11, and expounded the first 20 verses.

I wanted to talk with Anna but was reluctant to commence before Mary. She saw it and left, but not much before 10, so that my conversation extended to 11½ nearly, which was beyond all bounds of decency. I stated all the circumstances of my acquaintance with Miss Field, which moved her less than I expected. The truth is, she sees that I am her prisoner and understands pretty well that she is the first captor, but whether so or not she has me now and is sure of me. She says she has no feeling of anxiety or disquietude, does not particularly feel the anomaly of her position, enjoys the perplexity and mystification of some of her friends, is content with the status quo for the present. Wished to tell her brother Alexander, which I discouraged without vetoing. Asked me to a party on her niece's account on Wednesday evening. I rather begged off, but shall perhaps go. What I am most afraid of is that I should be tempted to talk too much to her, and should thus excite a suspicion not particularly favorable to our plans.

Monday, March 17. Writing hard most of the day. Made out 12 pages of MS in rough draft which will supply perhaps six pages of the review. What I wrote was all on the Homeric question, treated in the most superficial way and yet at the same time in a rather dry scholastic style. It is a consolation, however, to have dispatched so many pages, be the style and manner what they may. Had a call from Mason, who sat with me from 2 to 3. Rather advised him to cram for an examination, enter as Junior next September, and go on to a sheepskin and a B.A. He starts tomorrow for Georgia; has not heard from his mother for some time.

We have had a right stormy day of wind and rain. Coming in to my room after the evening recitation, I sat down by the warm fire and gave myself up to the current of pleasant thoughts. Was in full flood when the clock struck six. Heard the wind howling out of doors and the rain dashing in gusts against the windows. Balanced a little over the pro's and contra's. Soon voted that suppers, like taps, are all "wanity," and so sat contentedly thinking and dreaming till near 7. I believe I shall attend Miss Twining's party, and make myself very agreeable—not to her, but to everybody else. If I only knew what to talk about. I feel as though I had not fairly tried myself—as if with more *abandon* I could yet do wonders. Of course such expectations can lead only to disappointment, yet it is my nature to set them up again as often as they fall. Oh for a full fair view of the Archaeus.

Tuesday, March 18. Going out this morning, found snow several inches deep lying on the ground, or rather, under a high wind, whirling over its surface. Camp told me at breakfast that he had received an invitation to Miss Twining's party—was obliged to ask me where she lived. I told him that I had not received a note—I should think it a very ignoble revenge if I were left out.

Worked on Mure and made out again some dozen pages of MS, such as it is. Received a letter from Henry expressing his readiness to take Aitchison's place next summer, if Hodges will not. He has written to Hodges. Letter from Mr. George Kerr, principal of Franklin Academy, Delaware County, New York, asking about instructor for their school. Terms rather so-so. Not a word about Cousin Lucia, but that may have been because the letter was addressed in part to President Woolsey.

Wednesday, March 19. Talk with Hyde this morning, about Marvin, a young man, Sophomore, from Homer, New York, who died on Tuesday morning after an illness of only one day. He was to have competed in the Linonian prize debate this afternoon. He was a fellow of amiable character, and had distinguished himself in Society, though poor in scholarship. His disease was inflammation of the bowels, treated by a homoeopathic physician. We trust that this sudden and solemn occurrence may make an impression on the mind of the class. Report this evening that Mr. Herrick is dangerously ill. The mumps, which attacked him two or three weeks ago, have left a swelling and soreness of the limbs—an inflammatory rheumatism as they call it—and it is said that he is now in great distress, and has a high fever. God forbid that he should be taken from us; it would be an irreparable loss.

Davis of my division has taken leave of absence for the remainder of the term. He suffers under sore eyes, and finds it impossible to take the stand he would. He is going to the Law School at Ballston, where they make great professions in regard to rhetorical instruction. If he is satisfied with a few weeks' trial, he will remain there.

Faculty at 3. Reported on examinations. Mr. Thacher's plan for the renovation of the Lyceum discussed and (somewhat doubtfully) approved. Campbell, Senior, found guilty of some mean and violent conduct at the end of last term, dismissed, finally we hope. Cases of Sophomores who were kept in durance vile last Saturday night. There were a dozen of them, returning from Society between 2 and 3 A.M., all agog for a spree, and not very delicate in their sensibilities. They got an old Joe at corner of Hillhouse Avenue and carried it up to College. It was already standing on the green, with a Beethoven placard on it, and a boot-and-shoe sign in it, when the police set upon them, captured three of the gang, and dispersed the rest, an unheard-of act for the police, who generally regard the fence of our green as an impassable barrier. The fellows were locked up through the night, with Campbell, Senior, who at an earlier hour had been caught raising a false alarm of fire. In the morning Backus and Kinne were sent for to identify them. The Sophomores were J. Napier, dismissed at end of last term, Gillespie, and Martin. Of the latter two, we dismissed Martin, and gave Gillespie the second warning—a difference founded partly on difference of previous character and scholarship, partly on more or less prevarication in the present case. Curtis and Battles talked of, but nothing done.

Received Greene's textbook of mediaeval history, about which Porter had written me. It is a very fair-looking work—how well drawn up I have yet to learn.

I felt on the whole that it would be very mean in me to desert Miss Twining, that I was in duty bound to obey her wishes and lend what I could to the interest of her party, so I mastered my scruples, staid away from tea, drest, and went at 8½. Was afraid that the snow would keep everybody away, but the attendance was very fair. Had a pleasant conversation with Miss Sarah Hewitt of Bridgeport. Was introduced to Miss Rood, who attacked me in a very spirited way about Miss Julia Olmsted, and to Miss Wickham, whose bright eyes I have seen so often opposite me in the seat of Reverend Mr. Merwin, her grandfather. Miss Baldwin was there, just returned from New York, the varioloid in Judge Baldwin's family having kept her off for some time. Miss Larned said that she had thought of going West next vacation, an idea which I very strongly encouraged. Of other old friends, Miss Dwight, Miss Wells, Miss Forresta Shepard, Mrs. Bradley (olim Ruggles). Interesting chat with Miss Whitney. Miss Anna did the honors very quietly, and very charmingly, to Mr. Camp's perfect satisfaction— at least he expressed himself to me as highly gratified.

Professor Alexander Twining was there, come in from New York at 6 P.M., going to Boston tomorrow morning, in great hurry. Has got into business again as chief in the construction of a railroad.

Thursday, March 20. Called at Pease's after breakfast and got new number of *North British Review*, which Mac had mentioned to me the evening before. It seems to be a rich number. Read in the course of the day an interesting article on Arthur Hallam— certainly an extraordinary man—an appreciative review of Lyell's *Travels in America*, with good account of the illustrious author, and a rather fussy piece on the social position of woman, with sound doctrine foolishly expressed. Mr. Andrews told me that he was to spend the day with Mr. Herrick, whose state is very critical. President Day called in and left with me some sections which he proposes to insert in the article on quadratic equations. After dinner, had hair cut, .12½. At post office. Got a *New England Primer*, 3 cents, with a Catalogue of Princeton College from Rood (signed under the words ᾿Ω φίλοι, οὐ γάρ πώ τι κακῶν ἀδαήμονές εἰμεν). Called on Knevals to see about the shirts, which have been lingering long.

In evening, a little talk with Hyde. Paid him .12½ for postage paid at various times.

Worked a little on Mure tardily.

Friday, March 21. Had a talk with Kent (Senior) about taking the place of assistant in Mr. Kerr's school—will think of it. In the evening studied a little on Daniel, and wrote a little on Mure. A day of small accomplishment.

Saturday, March 22. Hyde came in at 9 to speak of subjects for prize compositions in Sophomore class. Professor Larned has turned over the selection to the class instructors. President Day called to reclaim the copy left here on Thursday and leave another piece, on ratio. Between 12 and 1, at College Library. Mr. Herrick said to be very low (it was Dr. Bradley that informed me; the Doctor had seen him the day before), yet keeps up his energy, and has done more or less business even during his worst times. Tried to find a piece of Greek or Latin for the prize translation of the Freshmen at the close of the term. Thought of a passage in Gregory of Nazienzen, sermon on St. Basil, where he describes student life at Athens in the fourth century. Afraid it will hardly do.

Letter from Henry, brought up by Hyde. Tutorship still balancing between him and Hodges. Very blue about sermonizing. Goes home in 3 weeks or so.

Call from Mr. J. P. Moore. He leaves us on Monday, may be back in the fall.

Drew from the Library two volumes of Grote's *Greece,* and had Eckermann charged over.

Kent will not go to Franklin. Try others.

At 8 as usual. Opened the German, but did not read it, had so much to talk about. Miss Mary came in at 9½ and insisted on departure at 10, as being a fair rule for the sparking of the parlor no less than of the kitchen. Discussed the matter till 11, when I was required to leave. Professor Twining had just come back from Boston, but I saw nothing of him.

Just as I got back to my room, Hyde came in and sat for an hour and a half. Abed at 12¾.

Sunday, March 23. Dr. Taylor in Chapel this morning, asserting a universal atonement and a possibility of salvation for all. Dr. Fitch in afternoon, a funeral sermon, eschatologic, transcended the bounds of our knowledge. Bible lesson on the Lord's prayer, very interesting to me. Expounded Daniel 11, verses 21–45. Saw Professor Twining; he goes West tomorrow. Beautiful conversation with Anna. We discovered that each had found it a relief and delight to pray to God for the other—a happy inauguration. "Nymph in thine orisons remember me"—where does that come from? Our veil of mystery I suspect is rather a thin one and will hardly outlast the coming vacation. If we could get along with the weekly calls, it might be kept up perhaps, but she complains that by Friday night she is nearly worn out, and my own feeling is not widely different. Then Mr. and Mrs. Magill are to be here during the summer, which must of course enlarge the number of our confidants. Home at 11 in the rain.

Mr. Storrs preached today at the North Church, 3 sermons.

Mr. Herrick very low, scarcely a hope of his recovery.

Monday, March 24. Prayers this morning at 6, and so henceforward. Began to work more in earnest on Mure but made scanty progress. More effort to secure a teacher for Mr. Kerr—small prospect of success. George Bushnell at Tontine in the evening, with Mac, no chance to speak with him. Spent a little while at the Beethoven, organ concert in Brewster's Hall; audience perhaps 250; singing very good. Tried to visit Larned, but failed.

Mr. Herrick no better. Great interest in town—everybody anxious and inquiring.

Tuesday, March 25. Talk with George Bushnell at breakfast. From 12 to 1, looked up a piece for Freshman prize translation, the oration of Dion Chrysostom on Socrates. Copied it out of text in College Library. Copied out in afternoon some of my verses for Anna, the Valentines to Miss Blake and Miss Baldwin, now to be given up to the rightful owner, to the one who was constantly present to the writer's mind, and gave him strength to endure the tedious toil of composing them. I am astonished now to see how completely true they were. When I wrote them, they appeared mere jeux d'esprit, exercises on imaginary themes, but I find them full of reality, showing that there was a reality, though unsuspected, in the author's mind. In regard to my four poetizings of the last 18 months, all of which were addressed truly if not avowedly to Anna, I am convinced that without a real passion not one of them would or could have been written. And anyone who knew us both would say that they were written not only by one in love, but by one in love with *her,* and by *me* in love with her, so truly do they fit the conditions of both minds. They are prophetic too, containing secret anticipations, which have been fulfilled in part already, and I trust in God will receive higher fulfilment hereafter. This is wonderfully the case with the Valentine of last year. The unconscious love which it represents and the unexpected awakening to consciousness have had a fulfilment which strikes me with surprise, almost with terror. If ever by many scattered intimations and directions leading all to the same point, the will of Providence was declared in any case of human conduct, I believe it to have been so declared in this. Thine, O Lord, be the ordering of all to come, and may the results of all lead to thy most worthy praise.

At 2 P.M. criticised Bingham's Greek piece for Junior Exhibition, left with me on Saturday. I had scarcely read it over, but it was very correct and needed little mending. Fortunately he was sensible enough to write in prose, which greatly lightened my toil.

Something more on Mure, though less than I had hoped.

A beautiful spring day. Mr. Herrick still in same condition. Oh that God would bring him back from the very jaws of death to a world that has great need of his generous activity.

Wednesday, March 26. George Bushnell again at breakfast. Copied prize piece for the press, supplying accents, and sent it over to Mr. Hamlen. Faculty at 3. Some discussion as to the expediency of giving any such prize. Vote taken. Several declined expressing an opinion. Of those who did, a majority declared against it. Professor Larned and myself appointed a committee to consider the subject. I have long felt that it was not worth while to have this competition more than once. Its efficiency the second time is very small. Professor Larned thinks that the money is more needed for the encouragement of classic learning than of rhetorical merit. He would make it a prize for proficiency in Latin. The President expressed himself quite strongly. He thinks that the whole current, in College and out of College, sets toward rhetoric and that sound scholarship is in danger of being swamped by writing and speaking. No doubt a great deal of *skinning* for this prize. Reported that one Senior wrote 3 translations last December, gave away two, and sold the third to J. C. Warner, who gained the first prize in his division. Curtis and Campbell reconsidered, without material change.

In evening, went out a little before 8 and called on Miss Elizabeth Baldwin. Found Governor Baldwin complaining somewhat of neuralgia. Had a pleasant half hour's conversation, which I broke off quite reluctantly to call on Miss Larned. She was not at home, nor Mrs. Woolsey—gone to meeting, I suppose. Mr. Kirk preached this evening in the Centre Church; preaches again tomorrow eve-

ning. Returned to a cold room, and wrote a page or two of my
article on Mure, and then went to bed before 10 o'clock.

Thursday, March 27. Mr. Herrick has been more ill today, and
his case regarded as altogether desperate. There was a report about
College at one o'clock that he was dead, and the students closed
their libraries. He revived somewhat, however, in the course of
the afternoon.

Wrote a letter to Mr. Kerr, reporting the failure of my efforts,
and adding a word for Cousin Lucia.

Made more progress today with my article, adding 8 pages of
my manuscripts, which will make up now about as much as 10
printed pages, ready for the press. Nearly half through—courage.

Washed and went to bed a little after 11. A mild and lovely
spring day. Thought a good deal about the approaching birthday,
which I must try to signalize in some way if I can.

Friday, March 28. Mr. Herrick no worse today, hanging in a
state zwischen Leben und Sterben. May God raise him thence to
continued life and usefulness. I suppose that if he should recover
he would not again be the man he was; his physical strength would
be greatly impaired. It is melancholy to think how unsparingly he
has treated himself, thrown away, as it were, a life so precious to
the world. He kept about 10 days after he was attacked with the
mumps. Went over to East Haven and was all day upon his feet.
Was out nearly all night, standing on the damp ground.

Progressing still with Mure. Added enough to make out fourteen
printed pages. Have therefore reached the summit level and shall
be on the descending grade. Shall slip along I hope more easily.
I have supposed that the Homeric question, with which I am now
occupied, would give me no great trouble. I am afraid, however,
that it will be rather drily treated. But, "vel, vot of it?" I am at
present in a state of mind in which nothing can trouble me very
much. Even Mr. Herrick's sickness, though it gives me terrible
twinges, does not steadily depress me, I feel almost in spite of
myself a joyous reaction of spirit.

Saturday, March 29. Written translations for the last time. At
2 to 3, with Dwight and Backus, arranging about matriculation.
Agreed on 63 men. Examined Wilson on studies of last term.

At 8 took over last four numbers of *Foreign Quarterlies* with those Valentines. Started at once with the German and read 18 pages before 9 o'clock. Talked till 10½. Came away. Found fire out, and went to bed before 11.

Anna told me that on Thursday Mr. Herrick had a long conversation with Mr. Dutton, in which he declared that from a child he had entertained strong religious feelings; that he had long cherished a hope in Christ, but had not been able to bring himself to a public profession; that he had been greatly troubled and dissatisfied with his position; that he should recover from this sickness, and that the first act of recovered health should be the open profession of his religious faith. He alluded to his habit of maintaining in conversation the side opposite to that of any person he might be conversing with. This had hindered him from speaking out to Christian friends. He had, however, some short time since, on reaching the age of 40, made a solemn consecration of himself to God, and this he should renew publicly so soon as health should be restored to him.

This is exceedingly gratifying to me, for though I regarded the man as a Christian in heart and life, I had feared that he was unsettled in his speculative opinions as to Christianity.

Sunday, March 30. My birthday. At waking in the morning I remembered the occasion, and endeavored to meet its natural and proper demands. I reviewed in general survey the mercies of God during my three decenniums of human life, acknowledging them aloud and thanking God for them. I then implored forgiveness for my imperfect use, my abuse of them. I next consecrated myself with all I have and am to God for the remainder of my days, and prayed for that divine assistance without which my consecration would be an empty form. Last I fervently thanked my Heavenly Father for the new help and hope which he has given me: for that beautiful alliance with a noble and pious soul, in which the hand of his Providence has been so clearly manifest: and I entreated him to bless our union to his glory and to our eternal good, that as one united being we might lead a more perfect life than would be possible to either singly. After a half hour perhaps spent in this way, the clock struck four, and I knew that I was not yet 30 years old, for my life rose with the sun.

Dr. Cheever preached in the Chapel forenoon and afternoon, an exchange with Dr. Fitch. Striking and impressive sermons both, one on last times, the other on the book of record. The last showed more the general fault of his style, the disposition to carry out a metaphor in an ingenious manner but to a tedious and tasteless extreme. There was a lack of definite and orderly progression about both discourses. Still I was much impressed by them. There was a hard, unyielding, unrelenting vigor about them that produces a powerful effect. Anna was present in the forenoon but not in the afternoon.

Hyde called upon me between 2 and 3. Was to preach for Dr. Cleaveland—the sermon, now finished, on love to a personal Savior. I excused myself from hearing the sermon, though desirous to do so, my Bible lessons being as yet very imperfectly prepared. For the Sermon on the Mount my study was very scanty, and I felt tired and listless.

*　　*　　*

APRIL, 1851

[April 1.] Found no Camp at dinner, though I waited patiently for him. Coming up, stopped at his room. "Slept over," said I. "Slept over what?" "Over dinner." "What," said he, "is it dinner time? I thought it was only a little after 11 o'clock. I was just going to start down for the paper." "Do you remember what day it is?" said I. We had been talking about Schiller's *Maid of Orleans* at breakfast. I praised it and spoke especially of the Introduction. Camp took it up to read at 10, and—that was the last of him. He took no note of time even by its flight.

Carried on Mure to end of page 22. Courage. Land ahead.

Wednesday, April 2. Took up Mure again in the evening and made out four pages of my manuscript. May add a little on general estimate of Homer. I wish to splinter a lance with him on the subject of love and courtship in modern fiction, but I shall have no time tomorrow, and I fear that it will be impossible to wait longer. And besides I am so completely out of humor with the whole affair that I would rather not put into it anything that I really care about.

I believe that I have caught cold, I hope not a hard one. I have reached the middle point of my week and am starting on the descending grade. Good.

Thursday, April 3. MacWhorter at breakfast. We made a rather long talk of it, and Camp did not wait for us. Coming back, met *her,* opposite the Blakes', going with her niece to the morning prayer meeting. Mac had left me at the corner of Temple Street, and I was hurrying on at a sound rate. The approach, the smile, the "good morning," the gay bow, were soon over, but they were strangely pleasant—made a sort of sunshine in my mind that corresponded to the beautiful springtime around.

Between 12 and 1, some talk with Backus about prize problems for Freshmen. Called at Professor Salisbury's a little before 1, and consulted him about *sant* or *sunt,* the Arabic name for the Acacia from which the gum arabic is obtained. Golius gives the form *sant.* Freytag and the French lexicographer (I forget his name) only *sanat* (سَنَط). None of them *sunt.* It is derived from سَنِط, imberbis fuit. Dr. Tully, for whom I made the inquiry, can probably explain the application of the name.

After dinner Kinne came in, and called on me for a dollar towards a purse for Captain Bissell. The watch have shown some disposition of late to do their duty to the College, and we wish to encourage them in it. While Kinne was with me, Hyde entered with a letter from Hodges at Pittsfield. He will probably come on as tutor next term, but does not wish to decide absolutely till he sees the young man, who will stop at Pittsfield on his way home. He is afraid of keeping him out next fall, and hangs fire on that. Says that Brace is again at Pittsfield, agent of Thompson and Company's Express.

Called at Tully's and Murdock's to leave notices of meeting of Philological Society. Tully was out, but Mrs. Tully made me come in and answer her questions about Mr. Herrick and Professor Stanley. Murdock is not well; laid up for several weeks with a hard cold, and a swelled face; thought he could not venture out in the evening. Room hot as blazes; wonder he does not have a cold all the time, cold from excess of heat, like "blind with excess of light" (Gray).

Call from MacWhorter, who sat from 4 to 4½. Says that the Whigs will run a split ticket here. Hubbard instead of Babcock. He thinks strongly of voting it. *My* mind nearly made up to vote for Ingersoll. I believe that the defeat of Babcock would teach the Whig party managers a useful lesson, and I think this worth more than the difference between the two candidates. Wanted to ascertain the age of Bushnell (George), natus December 13, 1818, and of Welch, natus January 1, 1820. If Bushnell had succeeded in his first design he would have been younger than his bride, though with the same advantage of hoary hairs as his illustrious successor. Mac says that Miss Kate Beecher is coming out with a new book on the true method of *righting* (writing?) woman's wrongs. What its particular aims and contents, is not known.

Looked over my article, and corrected it. Gave it to Mr. Larned after tea, promising to write the epilogue tomorrow. Said I wished to vindicate love and courtship in modern fiction against the aspersions of Mure. Professed to be orthodox on that subject. Mr. Larned says he is so also, believes in falling into it, though Mrs. Larned does not. I expressed my surprise to Mrs. Larned. "She had seen too much of the world," she said. "Love," replied I, "is not of the world, worldly."

At 7 went with Professor Larned to President Woolsey's to attend meeting of Philological Society. Present, Messrs. Gibbs, Hadley, Kingsley, Larned, Porter, Salisbury, and Woolsey. After a good deal of talk, Professor Kingsley suggested that perhaps we might as well organize. I said we had hoped to receive a communication from Professor Kingsley. Yes, said he, but the hopes of men are apt to be disappointed. He had excuses, but he would not give them like a Sophomore. The long and short was that he had nothing. So we talked on a great variety of subjects. Professor Lewis' views of metre. Rhyme in Latin hexameter and pentameter. Old English verse. Want of accent in French. Dr. Murdock's characters of his Andover colleagues. Nomination of Babcock etc. Mr. Porter told the story of a Negro, fugitive slave, at Springfield, who narrated his experiences to the public and then answered the questions that were put to him. Some one asked if his master was a Christian. No, he said, he was a member of Congress. Mr. Woolsey said it reminded him of a family on Long Island, belonging to the Episcopal Society. A new clergyman had come in and was going the rounds to see that all was right. He came to this family, and inquired if they had all been baptized. No, but they had all been vaccinated.

Walked up with Mr. Gibbs, reached my room at 10 o'clock, wrote journal, and went to bed at 10½.

For the last two or three days, Mr. Herrick has been free from delirium, and has rested very well. Strong hopes are entertained of his recovery, though the local difficulty remains much as it was, and will probably be very tedious at best in its leave-taking.

Friday, April 4. Finished my letter to Henry, writing with utmost rapidity. Hope it may reach him before he quits Andover. After finishing it, a little before 10 o'clock, called on President Woolsey, and begged the favor of a few moments for a personal inquiry. Asked him then whether there was any probability that my salary would be raised next August. I did not appear as a petitioner, but only wished to know the probability, that I might make my arrangements accordingly. He then said that he should have withdrawn sooner from the Greek department, but it would not do to have me Professor in full, while Mr. Thacher was an Assistant. But as Mr. Kingsley would resign at Commencement, he should then give up the Greek; that the department would devolve on me, and that I should properly receive full salary. This had been his confident expectation, and had entered as an element into his calculations and those of the Prudential Committee. I expressed the hope that he might change his purpose, so far as his connection with the Greek was concerned. He declared however that on this point he was immovable. He should always retain his love for Greek, but other fields were opening before him, in history and polity, mediaeval history, the feudal system. He had done something already, but more labor was necessary to make his previous labor fully available. Besides, he should probably be called upon more and more to preach, and he must have some time for writing sermons. He felt a great desire also to prepare some sermons for College students, with special reference to their peculiar circumstances and necessities. All this would require time, and he felt it necessary for himself, as well as better for the department, that there should be only one man responsible for it. On rising to go, I told him that I was not engaged as yet, and without some definite pecuniary prospect probably should not be. He then repeated that he had no doubt that some such arrangement would be made.

On my way to breakfast was met by Mr. Larned (J. G. E.), who said that his sister would leave today for Western New York, would spend 3 or 4 weeks there, and as I was unaccountably forgetful about offering my services, suggested that in returning I might put myself under her protection. MacWhorter, whom I found at the Tontine at dinner, told me that he had gone down to the cars to see Miss Larned off, but she did not come. Would leave at 4½ P.M. So at 3 I called at Miss Dutton's. Had quite a talk with Professor

Gibbs by the way. Found Miss Larned, but found that she had changed her intention and was not going till Monday. Talked awhile, mostly about Mr. Herrick.

After tea went to the Rhetorical Chamber, expecting to hear a preparatory lecture, but we had a church meeting, at which President Woolsey and Professor Goodrich made impressive addresses. Dr. Taylor preaches the preparatory lecture at the North Church, but I concluded not to go and hear him. Blodget came up to my room, and sat till nearly nine, in very interesting conversation. Some good things said.

Had my second exercise with Storrs from 12 to 1. While he was with me, Professor Olmsted brought in a letter which he had just received from Mr. Stanley, dated Cairo, January (February?) 18. He had experienced some benefit from the climate of Egypt, which he speaks of in the highest terms. Had visited the pyramids of Gizeh, riding 20 miles on a donkey. Should return to Paris about the first of April, reach home by last of May or first of June. I am afraid this is not very satisfactory. After dinner, gave the letter to Mr. Larned.

Saturday, April 5. Full of joyful impatience and much disposed to execrate the hours for their tardiness. Reported with Mr. Dwight at 10, and Mr. Backus, who happened to forget the hour, at 11. At College Library, reading periodicals. In afternoon, made a voluminous return to College Library, not, however, clearing off old scores.

Evening as usual. Read 10 pages or so of *Nathan*, leaving 20 more. I am to come in on Wednesday evening to read a part of the remainder, as it is absolutely necessary to finish up, this term. A world of pleasant talk till 11, when I came away, and soon after went to bed.

Sunday, April 6. Studied Sunday lesson (last this term), closing part of Sermon on the Mount, and expounded at 4½. Dr. Fitch, forenoon and afternoon, rather sleepy to me, but I allowed my mind to rest too much on our affairs. Read a little on Ecclesiastes, without really expecting to tell it in the evening. The arrangement was that I should come over, although this is the Sunday of Monthly Concert, and visit with Miss Mary, whose health does not allow her to go out in the evening—and if the weather should be stormy, then visit with both. I was much pleased, when I rose in the morning, to find it raining hard. I staid away in consequence from breakfast, expecting that Camp would do so likewise if I omitted to call him up. But I was mistaken.

At tea, Mr. Larned came and told me that Mr. Benedict was to go early in the morning to New York, and take down my article, and wanted to know if I had finished up the concluding page. I told him that I had been intending to give it to him in the morning, but I could get it ready earlier. Accordingly I promised to leave it in Camp's room, so that Mr. Larned could obtain it by calling at 9 or 10. I went at once to No. 105, spent half an hour in writing, drest a little, took my manuscript to No. 170, and went to 30 Elm Street. It was not storming exactly, but it was wet and drizzly and might pass, I hoped, for a stormy evening. I was mistaken, however. She had gone out, and I had what she was no doubt determined I should have, a long talk with her sister. I apologized as well as I could for the mischief I had done her. She spoke very kindly and nobly, but evidently felt more than she was willing to show. She let me know that myself, my conduct and my tendencies, had been patent to her for a long time, and that she might, if she had so chosen, have blocked the game which I was unconsciously playing. But she dared not interpose; dared not assume the responsibility of ordering the current of two lives. She told me that if I came into their family, I must be one of them. I answered that she might count on me for anything, if she would only tell me what to do and tell me very explicitly; but she must not leave me to my own wit for anything. She begged me not to praise her sister to our people at home. I told her I had my cue already on that subject and might be relied on.

At 9½ Anna came in from Monthly Concert, much pleased with a Mr. Bertram, a Scotch missionary from St. Helena, who had made a very animating address. Mary went out at 10, and I staid till 11. Heard some things that would make a sensation, if uttered in a whisper, as they never shall be in any voice of mine. I assured her that she had made a wise choice, for that I was the better man of the two.

Came back and was thinking over matters, when at 11½ Hyde came in. Talked about his sermon at Dr. Cleaveland's in the afternoon—on eternal punishment. Miss Mary, who had heard it, thought it excellent. He staid till 12, when I spent about 15 minutes on my lesson for tomorrow morning, and then to bed.

Monday, April 7. After breakfast went to the polls with Camp, who has just been made a voter. The place was already crowded, and in getting through I came very near breaking my cane. Later in the day there was great jamming and scuffling, coats torn, etc. I voted the Loco State ticket, Whig assemblymen. Camp went the split for Hubbard, Congress. At dinner Mac told me that the free-soilers here were voting for Babcock, led on by Joe Larned, who votes himself for Booth; cannot do less, since he nominated him as "our candidate," but employs all his influence to prevent other people from doing so. This is a strange sort of backing one's friends. Nobody seems to know what the result will be. I am strongly in hopes, however, that the Whig General Committee will suffer a salutary defeat.

Some talk with Mr. Heard, father of the Sophomore. He complains of us, that if this offence of his son was not the first, he ought himself to have been informed; if it were the first, that the discipline has been summary and severe.

At 12½ called on Mrs. Levere, asked for her bill. Then on Dr. Tully, who says the gum-arabic tree is very thorny; does not think the meaning *beardless* can be applicable to it. Says genus is much more prominent in the vegetable kingdom than in the animal.

Spent the afternoon and evening in writing to Mr. Whitney. My letter is equal to five pages of the *New Englander*. Rambling and gossiping, but not bad for a letter.

Tuesday, April 8. A rainy day. Staid away from breakfast. (Didn't I?) Made preparations for the examination. Attended to matriculation. Heard Storrs in Thucydides, last recitation for this term. In evening, made out averages for second and third divisions. Tired myself out, and went to bed at 10¼.

Received a letter from Hodges, written after seeing Henry, who it seems made a mistake about our terms here, and passed through Pittsfield on Friday. The matter is arranged, and Hodges will come in next term.

Wednesday, April 9. Sad news this morning from Mr. Herrick. He was attacked yesterday very suddenly with a terrible pain in his foot; it was the inflammation which precedes mortification. The limb is already black and scarcely a possibility of recovery is left.

Our examination commenced at 11. My two sessions lasted two

hours each. Mr. Bartlett of East Windsor was present at one, Mr. Rockwell of New Britain at the other. The fellows got on very tolerably, much better than at the examination of last term.

Camp came up after tea and read Goethe for a while at my room, until half past seven, when my engagements called me away. We read 11 pages of *Nathan,* leaving nine more for next Saturday evening. Had a great deal of charming talk, until at 10½, as I showed myself dilatory about going, I received a peremptory dismissal. A beautiful day followed by a beautiful moonlight evening.

Thursday, April 10. Mr. Thacher came in this morning at 7 to speak about Jones and Purnell. Mr. Herrick, he says, no better; reason to believe the mortification deep-seated. Had my three examination sessions at 8½, 11, and 3. In evening, calculated averages of first division and read *Pickwick Papers.*

Friday, April 11. Three sessions more of the examination. Sold Miles 24 copies of my Analysis for Mr. Wright of East Hampton —price $1.50. Miles gave me $2.00. I was unable to make change. This just sufficed to pay Mr. Greenough, Treasurer of American Oriental Society, who sent me his bill today. Received a letter from Henry at Geneva. George is there. A grand consultation to be held on the projects and prospects of the family when I get home. Mary has a bad cold. Henry, ditto.

Received 16 pages of my article in proof, and corrected it. Very well set up. Professor Larned called between 9 and 10 to get it. He saw Mr. Herrick this afternoon. His leg is a shocking sight. The doctors do not absolutely give him over, but the hope is a mere shadow.

From 7 to 9 in Dwight's room, making out results of examination and reporting absences.

At my own room, built up fire—it is a frosty evening—and, having finished up the proof of my article and transacted some other business, read *Pickwick* awhile, but grew sleepy. Combed, abluted, etc. Abed at 12.

Saturday, April 12. Last session of examination at 8½. Talk with Dwight and Backus about results. Only one (Hubbard) required to leave. Chotard and Hallock advised to leave. 12 or 15 conditioned.

To Twinings' at 7¾. Finished up the *Nathan,* reading nine pages. We did not like the conclusion of the story, in which Recha and the Templar prove to be "Geschwister." But really, in this play, the story is a thing of small account: the characters and still more the sentiments are the important elements.

I jested at starting about lovers' quarrels, and came about as near as we good-natured people are able to come to having experience of one. A mocking description of the way I should announce our affairs to the people at home gave her, not unreasonably, a good deal of uneasiness, which I was not able with the utmost effort entirely to dissipate. She is quite right in thinking that with our intentions and expectations it would be neither comfortable nor dignified to keep up an imperfect and ill-sustained appearance of mystery. And for me to deny, while *she* feels restrained from doing so, is horrible. But if we are going to confess, we may as well have something to be confessed. I am resolved, therefore, ready or unready, formula or no formula, to make a push, and do all that can be done without the blessing of a parson.

Back at 11 in the beautiful moonlight, and abed.

Drew today my salary, $287.22, diminished by the twenty which I borrowed two weeks ago. Check for the balance, $267.22, but have not got it cashed.

Sunday, April 13. Dr. Fitch in the forenoon. Mr. Dutton in the afternoon. Studied the first chapter of Ecclesiastes and expounded in the evening. Miss Mary left us at 9, and I then proceeded to carry out the plan of last night. I asked a series of questions, to call out what I considered myself pretty sure of before, and then solicited and received a definite promise, rendering in exchange the only thing I could return, a promise in the most solemn and soul-binding forms, to similar effect. It was an occasion never to be forgotten, another era in life. May the God in whom we trust grant us his blessing and lead us through our mutual love and union, upward to himself. Driven away reluctantly at 11.

Monday, April 14. Up at 6½. Proof of *Algebra*. Receiving prize translations till 7½. After breakfast, examined Grevemberg; marked o. Wrote notice of Greene's book on Middle Age history for *New Englander*. Made out examination averages for my division. At Treasurer's office exchanged my check for certificate of deposit of $200 and $67.22 in money. Returned Lessing to College Library. Mr. Herrick a little better. Mr. Henry White comforted him, when expressing dread of lameness, by referring to my case.

President Woolsey consulted Mr. Thacher and me about Junior

Exhibition tomorrow. Judge Daggett's funeral in the afternoon. Put last half or third of Juniors in evening. President expressed strong opposition to bands of music, especially at Commencement.

Paid Mrs. Levere for washing, $4.38. Paid Pease for *Tribune*, 6 months, $3.25. Bought Southey, last two parts, .50. $3.00 allowed on my analyses. Paid balance, .75. Left him 50 copies more of the Analysis.

Bought a dollar clock at Kirby and Brown's for Mother. Returning, met Camp, who gave me a letter from George, wanting *Index* to *Silliman's Journal*. Dinner. Court day and crowd— displaced me. At Fitch's bought *Kickleburys*, .125. Settled with Camp, $1.44. Bought his copy of *Night and Morning*, .25. Left him 50 cents for Miles. Called on President Day to give notice of my departure. On my way to see Lee, stumbled on Mrs. Pond. Lee quite sick with measles. Thought it best not to trouble him with the condition. Could not find Hallock; wrote him a letter. Journalized.

Call from John Orton, who leaves his wife now in N[ew] H[aven]. Late to tea. Talk with Dwight. Grevemberg diddled. Again at Fitch's. Bought the *Index* for $3.00. Settled at Tontine, $7.00. Dressed and called on Miss Baldwin at 8½. Found Camp. Staid in very pleasant conversation till 9½. Then to Twinings' with *Night and Morning*. Found Camp again there. He staid till 10, I till 10½. Came away and finished packing. Camp called in and gave me $13.00 to buy a Schiller and Andersen's *Tales*. Had already received a letter from J. G. E. Larned for his sister in Waterloo.

Tuesday, April 15. Up at 5½ and *fixed*. To cars, .25. Ticket, $1.50. Little dust, consequence of damp and drizzle. Gave my check to baggage-express man to take to Steamer *Empire,* and went with my carpet bag to Broadway Hotel (.25). Drest. Went to foot of Cortlandt Street. Bought ticket, $1.50, and berth in stateroom, $1.00. Name to be sent in to captain. Returning, saw John Chassell, much engaged with customers. Said Mrs. North of Fairfield (Martha Bryan) has been very ill, life despaired of. Getting better, but now worse again. At Fairfield, in old house—half moved out —recovery doubtful. Talked with Oakley for half an hour. Saw Spenser Shepard and dined with him at Western Hotel. Immense crowd. Accident with cranberry sauce. Repaired at Broadway

Hotel. Up to Lockwood's to get Béranger—only large illustrated edition. To Berard et Mondon's—expecting it daily. To Westermann's for Camp. Could not find the 12-volume Schiller he wanted. One for 6 dollars, cheaper set. Only this at Radde's. Went to Benedict's office in Spruce Street and gave him Professor Larned's message. Read proof of last ten pages of my article—well set up. Back to Westermann's. The Schiller afore mentioned for Camp, with right of return during the week. Added a Crusius, $4.50 ($2.25 per volume), and Andersen's *Märchen*, $1.50, a very pretty thing. Sent a line to accompany them.

Back at Hotel. Bill, 25 cents. Bussing all day, .25. Packed and off at 5½. Stopt at *Empire* boat office and asked if my name had been given to the Captain. "Oh yes, all right." Went on board and by advice of a hand called on Captain to speak about it. Forced my way up after a while but was repelled very gruffly; he knew nothing about it. So I returned to the agent, who swore a good deal, sent a man to inquire of the Captain, and at last started off himself, swearing as he went. Met messenger, who said the Captain declared he could not understand the matter. Agent proceeded and in a short colloquy settled the hash. I was much obliged to him, but he would not hear of it: should be much obliged to me if I would forget it. Went to my room, washed off the perspiration. Came out into saloon and had a pleasant two hours' chat with Alexander, Senior. He spends his vacation in Troy. Saw also Van Sinderen on board.

Went to bed at 9½. Sole occupant of my room. Rested pleasantly, but slept imperfectly.

A dripping day. No umbrella—slop and mud—feet wet—no damage. Glad that our Junior Exhibitioners, who have been so foolishly schemy, have at last got such a rebuff from overhead.

Wednesday, April 16. (Porter on boat, .125.) Reached Albany at 4 A.M. Rose and went on shore immediately. Luggage taken by carman to Delavan House, .25. Good breakfast at 5½ for .50. Porter, .125. Tickets for Syracuse, $3.25. Express train off at 7. Crowded cars, but not unpleasant—no dust. Cloudy day, but without rain. Lunched at Syracuse on apples and popped corn, .04. Called at Montgomery's office and learned the following facts as to Rexford's death. He died at West Granville, Massachusetts, September 19, 1850, on a visit to his wife's friends—his disease an affection of the liver which assumed a typhoid form. His uncle, or rather his wife's uncle, Mr. James Wadsworth of Hartford, Connecticut, was in the office at the time. He was going West in the same train of cars with me.

Reached Geneva without mishap at 3¼. Fare from Syracuse, $1.30. Cabman, .25. People all at home and much as usual. Mother with a heavy cold, the first this winter. Mary coughing badly. After talking an hour, went upstairs. Drest. Sat with George in library and commenced letter to New Haven. In the evening George and Henry went out to hear Mr. Chauncey Burr on the Rochester rappings. I staid at home with the women. Washed feet for fear of cold. With Mary in kitchen. Told her of our affairs, thinking it on the whole the safer course. Finished my letter in the library, and went to bed at 11½.

Received from George $3.00 for *Index* to *Silliman's Journal*.

Thursday, April 17. Mailed my letter, 10 cents. Took out one for Father, .05. Shaved etc. and went down to the cars at 9¾ to take the accommodation train for Waterloo. Train due at 10ʰ 8ᵐ. Bought ticket, .20, but waited (Henry and I) till 11 o'clock and then came away. It appears since that the cars of this train were detained by some breaking of machinery, so as to be about two hours later than their time. They (the engineer etc.) then resolved to follow close upon the express train, hoping thus to avoid collision with trains in opposite direction. With this view they came into Geneva at unusual speed. Coming round the short sharp curve west of the station house, they saw the cars of the express train, not yet gone. The engineer instantly reversed the wheels, but it was too late to do more than lessen the shock. The brakeman, it is said, was not at his post. At all events the moving engine struck the hindmost of the cars at rest and wounded several people standing on the back platform, one man fatally, so that he died in a few minutes, and two others quite severely. George must have been on the spot at the time. He had gone to take the cars for Rochester, to see about that new crutch, with Bushnell and with Mr. Curry, who happens to be there at present. Returning to the house, I began a second letter to "our folks," and made great progress with it. At evening, 7½, went with Henry to see Mr. Burr's second and last exhibition. It was very amusing and perfectly demolished the rappings. He continued till 5 minutes before 10, when the New England soap-man detained most of the audience (a small one at best) and made a diverting harangue on the virtues of his commodity. Returning with Henry, sat up till 11½, eating apples and talking on various matters.

Saw a copy of the latter prophets in Hebrew, Stephanus 1539, given him by Cousin Silas Blaisdale. A beautiful present.

Friday, April 18. At 10 A.M. took the cars for Waterloo, and arrived there in due season. Mailed my letter, .10. Found Miss Larned at the Waterloo Hotel, delivered her brother's letter, pressed her to go back with me to Geneva. She is engaged to go tomorrow to Aurora, will return on Monday evening. Has then an engagement at Waterloo which she has put off already and which I urged her to put off again. Perhaps she will; promises to let me know on Monday night. Had some thoughts of deferring her visit to Geneva until the close of the vacation. This I deprecated on her account and my own. I wish to have free space here for my own operations. I offered to escort her back to New Haven, and mentioned the necessity that would call me there in the week before the opening of the term. Found that she would ill like to lose so much of her vacation. I suggested then that the Greek and Latin examinations of the Berkeley scholarship might be transposed, so that setting out early on Monday morning, I might reach New Haven in time for my session on Tuesday afternoon. Being mistaken in regard to time, I hurried away from Miss Larned and her sister (a very pretty woman) and ran myself out of breath to reach the cars, which came along some 10 or 15 minutes later, at 11½, and brought me into Geneva at noon, for .20.

Met Mrs. Titus at dinner. Had a talk with Henry and by his consent wrote a note to Miss Larned proffering his escort to New Haven. Mailed it, .05. Out on the pier, somewhat damaged by the force of the water. Called on Dr. Crane, who could not spare any time next week but appointed the hour of 9 on the Monday following. In the evening had a good deal of conversation about George. Mary and I agreed that he was in immediate want of a wife and should be labored with on the subject. Henry, having come in from a call on Miss Wr[a]ggles, and having heard the case stated, acquiesced, though less warmly. Mother refused to have any part in the business. "She is willing," so she says, and cannot be brought any further. The laboring oar must be mine, and the great resource a serious, earnest, argumentative appeal. So let it come.

Saturday, April 19. Rain all day. Wrote letters home for the men of my division who were conditioned—all but Yung Wing.

Read Goethe and Burns. George came back from Rochester at 11. Not much prospect of the iron crutch. Henry read Tuel on courtship to the rest of us, greatly to edification. At 5½ George brought me a letter (.10) from *her,* written on Thursday evening, a gleam of sunshine, which made all light within me. Commenced a reply at 8 and wrote till 12.

Sunday, April 20. Rain all day. Mr. Hogarth, forenoon and afternoon. Easy and moderately interesting, not profound. Henry read aloud Professor Park's great sermon on a New England ministry. Continued and concluded my letter.

Monday, April 21. Clearing off today. Tired with three days' confinement in the house, I went out to walk and stumped about on board pavements for three quarters of an hour, after which I began to feel more comfortable. Read Goethe with Mary, and talked about *our* matters. In the evening went out with George. At Mrs. Hodges' from 7 to 8. Heard a letter from David Hodges on the Isthmus of Tehuantepec. From 8 to 9 at Mr. Curry's. Mrs. C. attacked me on Dr. Taylor's Compromise Speech. Back at home, talked awhile. After 10 began a letter, George reading *Lavengro* aloud to the rest. By and by they retreated, one after another, Mary, George, Henry, leaving me, who kept at my writing till 12¾, and then made the best of my way to bed.

Tuesday, April 22. Wrote till 9½. Went to Waterloo and returned with Miss Larned, .60—.10 to hotel carrier. Presented the Freiligrath. In evening, read *Kickleburys.* Finished my letter at 1.

Wednesday, April 23. Mailed my letter (.10). Expected one from New Haven, which reached me at last in a roundabout way (.05), through George Field and Dr. J. Hadley. George and I went over the College with Miss Larned and Mary. Tired myself with playing ball and graces. Commenced a new letter and wrote till after 12.

Thursday, April 24. George at work upon a new crutch. Finished the staff and shaped the head, of rosewood. He means to make a better head of lignum vitae. In the afternoon he started out walking with Miss Larned. They went to Mr. Brown's, two mile, cottage, and did not return till 6, so Miss Larned stays with us tonight. Very sleepy in the evening, but rallied at 10½. Finished my letter, which I had continued in the afternoon.

Friday, April 25. Mailed my letter. Escorted Miss Larned to Waterloo, .60. Saw her friend Mrs. Kendrick, a very pretty woman.

Saw Mrs. Green again. George had not understood that Miss Larned was to leave at this time; went over to Mr. Curry's to borrow a microscope for showing infusoria; lost his "good-by."

Professor Webster called home last evening by tidings of an accident to one of his children, which caused his death before morning.

Worked awhile on the rosewood top, abrading with steel scraper and burnishing with horn. But Mr. Curry, coming in at evening, told us that the proper way was to start the grain by immersion in water and then cut off by fine sandpaper, repeat this process as often as might be necessary, and finally polish with cloth, pumice, and rotten stone. Had a great washing and combing.

Calls from Mr. and Mrs. Curry, Dr. Coventry, etc.

Commenced a letter at 10½. Wrote till 12. I am not homesick, nor have I any feverish longing or fretful impatience. Still this writing gives me the greatest pleasure.

Saturday, April 26. Had a grand settlement with George up to date of March 15, 1851, and ascertained that the value of my share in his account with Sidney Shepard and Company was on that day $783.03. Received from him an acknowledgment in writing of the fact. Called with George on President Hale and sat for half an hour. He says that Professor Low is deranged—probably in hospital at Charlestown, M[as]s. Continued my letter. Afternoon occupied in treating the rosewood top according to the recommendation of Mr. Curry, with great advantage, and with looking on while George with a good deal of difficulty shaped another and a very handsome one out of a piece of lignum vitae which Mr. Curry gave him. After tea, invited George to walk down to the post office, alleging a great desire to see the semi-weekly *Tribune*. Found as I expected a letter from New Haven (.10) full of fine things, which I read several times in the course of the evening. Continued my letter, writing in the parlor; it was too cold in the library.

Sunday, April 27. Walked out with George at 9. Warm sun, air sultry. Took no umbrellas to church. About the middle of the service it began to rain hard, with thunder and lightning, and continued rainy for the rest of the day. Mr. Hogarth preached very well both forenoon and afternoon. George read over some old scraps of verse which he has gathered in from time to time—many good beginnings, seldom completed.

At evening finished up my letter.

Monday, April 28. To Dr. Crane's at 9, with a good deal of fear and trembling. The Doctor, getting to work at 9½, discovered and plugged four cavities in the upper front teeth. This was easy work. He then came to the back teeth, which I supposed to be quite carious, and expected a great deal of trouble in repairing them. But to my surprise and relief, he declared, after a short examination, that they were all right, with the exception of a little tartar, which he would proceed to remove. He dismissed me at 12, charge $6.00, paid. Bought 7 sheets sand paper for .14. In afternoon, having covered myself with dust, working on the supporters, came over to the house and had a pretty thorough wash up. Mr. and Mrs. Curry came in and took tea with us. Mrs. Curry calls me Mr. Two Sides. She brought in the ridiculous diatribe on Tennyson from Horne's *New Timon,* which the editor of *Littell's Living Age* stupidly attributes to Bulwer. They left at 9, and I commenced a letter, but made small progress. Abed at 11.

Tuesday, April 29. Supporters nearly completed. At bookstore, after dinner, bought Harlan Page for Ann, .15, and *Lalla Rookh,* .63. The wash up recorded for yesterday belongs to this day. The chronicle has fallen behind, and in bringing up several successive days, they are apt to get themselves mixed up together. Continued my letter quite industriously, but could not finish it in the evening.

Wednesday, April 30. Storm again. Finished my letter, the last of the series, not without emotion, and carried it to the office, .10. Opened it there to acknowledge the receipt of hers (.10), likewise the last in its series. Before taking mine down, I showed it to mother, who seemed surprised. Said she had had no suspicion, knew I corresponded with somebody in New Haven, but had no idea my correspondent was a lady. She asked Miss Twining's age, to which I replied that it was not far from my own: she looked younger than I, but was probably about as old. Mother made no complaint, but on the other hand expressed no joy, partly on account of a severe headache which she has had today, and partly because she knows that life is always a hard and thorny way and sees the care and trouble to which I may be subjecting myself. Went over to the College. The supporters at last happily completed —a handsome outfit. Paid George $2.00, 81 cents for expenses, the rest for Mr. Curry in return for the lignum vitae head. George's labor of a week and a half, I shall not be able to repay. He has done for me what I could not possibly have got an artizan to do.

Read *Lalla Rookh*. "Palace of Art" etc. Some sonnets of Mrs. Browning's that pleased me wonderfully. *Must* get her poems. Wrote a note to Miss Larned suggesting arrangements for her journey to New Haven in Henry's company. Mailed it, .05. Strolled out on Water Street beyond the Catholic Church and walked about an hour. Read newspaper. Talked. Felt lazy and went to bed at 11.

When I get to New Haven I am going to work *hard*. Such at least is my resolution. We will see how it holds out.

MAY, 1851

Thursday, May 1. A bright day for the most part. Have not commenced my industrial operations yet. Occupied most of the day in talking of the grand arcanum, which is at length fairly out. Mother told it last night to Father, who looked queer, and said after a little laughing, "So you're going to get one of your family married off at last." Mother herself shows less anxiety and indeed rather less curiosity than I had expected. She wanted to know how far away from College the people lived. "Next-door neighbors," I told her, "the courtship was an easy one." Talk with George after tea, in which I urged the "go thou and do likewise." He acknowledged the inclination but pleaded the constraining power of circumstances. Perhaps I may have given him a moral impulsion. Conversation with Henry, after the rest were gone to bed, from 10½ to 12 on the plans and prospects of both. He will not join the Episcopalians at present, but will probably connect himself with our College Church. Has given up the idea of preaching. Means to prosecute theology and paedagogy. Has received encouragement from Professor Park, who complained that there were no young men devoting themselves to such studies, and represented it as matter of duty in anyone who felt an impulse that way to make it his vocation.

Friday, May 2. Packed my trunk, took leave of the folks, and started off in the express train at 12. A cold day, but growing milder, and in the afternoon beautifully clear. The cars were sparsely filled, so that I had plenty of room. Dr. Hale was my compagnon du voyage. He carried with him the last number of the *Christian Remembrancer,* a Puseyite quarterly journal published in London, which he receives through the Appletons for $5.00 a year, less than the London price. It contained an article on the recent movements of Rome, which suggested a good deal of rather interesting conversation. Dr. Hale rejoiced in the appointment of Catholic bishops for England, because he thought it would offend many who were looking towards Rome and would thus stop the progress of the Romeward tendency in the Anglican Church. He lamented the present anomalous position of the Established Church, which he pronounced to be the only ecclesiastical body which cannot legislate for itself. The Gorham case was full of instruction on this point. The doctrine of the Church of England may be determined, not by any proper church authority, but by a court consisting perhaps of Socinians, Indifferentists, or Atheists.

At St. Johnsville I saw my quondam pupil Frank Lathrop, who is going to Mr. Wright's school at East Hampton. He introduced me to his brother-in-law, Mr. Bartow, a young lawyer of Leroy.

At Albany Dr. Hale and I walked over to the *Hendrik Hudson* and secured a pleasant room in the cabin, fare, .50, berth, .50. There is great opposition between this boat and the *Rip Van Winkle*—fare in the latter, .25. A handbill was circulated in the cars between Schenectady and Albany, announcing that the *Hendrik Hudson* had reduced to .25, but this appeared to be a mistake. Saw Dr. Carr of Canandaigua.

Felt sleepy and was going to turn in at 9, when one of our berths was found to be occupied already. A fellow had mistaken Berth 22 for Room 22. We called in the steward, who turned out the usurper and changed the sheets, which were rather unsavory.

Paid .25 for porterage at Geneva. $1.30 for fare to Syracuse, which I was obliged to pay over again, having somehow dropped my ticket. $3.13 to Albany. $1.00 down the river. About $7.00 in all.

Saturday, May 3. Hack and porterage, .75. In Canal Street just at 7. Took the accommodation train, which brought me into New Haven at 10. Fare, $1.50. Hack, .25. A beautiful morning. The drive to my surprise somewhat dusty. Got into No. 105 without serious difficulty. Spent an hour or two in furbishing, and then called on Camp. Went with him to Pease's and bought Miss Barrett's poems, $2.00. To Mansfield's; bought cap, $1.25. To post office, .24. Several letters. Most important one from Whitney. He declines the modern languages. Suggests Camp for the place and speaks of him in the highest terms. Defends his devotion to Indian archaeology. Vindicates the importance of Sanskrit, which I had rather called in question, and declares his resolution to "go it

strong" in Orientalism. Every man to his vocation. I am glad to
see his enthusiasm, and shall make no effort to turn him aside. He
will certainly do something pretty fine in the field he has chosen.
He has not forgotten linguistics, however, but is making and means
to make all his study subordinate to it. Has some excellent remarks
on the subject of phonetics. His arrangement of English sounds
will reach me in June or July. Note enclosed from Professor Weber
to Professor Salisbury. Called to deliver it, but Mr. Salisbury not
in. Mr. MacWhorter gone to New York with Dr. Forbes, whom
I had just met in the street. Will be absent for a week. Called at
Mr. Gibbs'. The Professor had gone out. Some chat with Mrs.
Gibbs.

I ate nothing from 11 A.M. of Friday to 1 P.M. of Saturday.
Whether in consequence of this or not, I cannot say, but I felt
pretty uncomfortable through the afternoon, took almost nothing
at tea, and feared that I might lose my call in the evening. Went
over at 7¾. Heard some noise in the east parlor. (Mr. Marshall
it appears has just returned *home*.) Was afraid of getting into a
crowd, but was shown into the west room, and there had a beautiful tête à tête of two hours. Saw Mrs. Magill for one moment.
Mr. and Mrs. Magill are going to keep house in the building opposite President Day's and are to take "the boys" under their charge,
so that only Kinsley and Harriet will remain with their aunts.
This will restore No. 30 Elm Street to something of its former
quiet. Anna told me of the progress of our story. She had a pleasant
session on Monday with Mrs. Thacher, received Mrs. Woolsey's
congratulations on Friday, had given her consent to the enlighten-
ment of Mrs. E. E. Salisbury, and also Mrs. Salisbury, Senior, who
will not let the secret mould for want of an airing, and had just
written to Miss Sarah Hewitt.

As regards the future, we are to see each other daily, either after
tea or at some early hour of the morning. We propose to read together. Had some difficulty in settling, what? History appeared
to have the best claim. I proposed Thierry's *Merovingian Era*.
(Schlegel? Humboldt's Philosophical Essay? *Historical Parallels* of
Useful Knowledge Society? Heeren's *Ideen?* Herder's *Ideen?*
Macaulay's article?) I started 2 minutes before 10, but Miss Mary
Twining was called in by her sister and kept me a not-unwilling
captive for half an hour. I am to have a longer talk with her tomorrow night, when Anna will be at Monthly Concert.

Made my bed and turned into it at 11.

Sunday, May 4. Communion. A good sermon from Mr. Egleston. Heard Dr. Croswell in the afternoon. His enunciation was better than I have known it for some time. Sermon on "ruins of sin and help in God" not without impressiveness. Cloudy all day; rain in afternoon; storm in evening. Anna was unable to attend the Monthly Concert, so that I had her to myself from 7½ to 9, and with her sister from 9 to 10¼.

Monday, May 5. Tried to get hold of Thierry's *Merovingian Era,* but in vain. Took from Linonian Library Schlegel, *Philosophy of History, Historical Parallels,* 3 volumes, and Becker's *Charicles,* all on Camp's name. Took the latter at 9 to Twinings', with Musäus and Adler's *Lexicon.* Read with Anna until 11, when we gave way to Mr. Ludden and visited the other people. Saw Mr. Magill.

Mrs. Levere cannot do my washing this summer. Refers me to Mrs. Bradley. Shall try her, but with doubts.

President Day gave me some manuscripts for his *Algebra.* Mr. Thacher congratulated me very briefly on recent occurrences, but very cordially. Informed me that Talcott had resigned, and that Henry would be wanted. Went to House's telegraph office after dinner, and left a dispatch for Henry, bidding him come on here Thursday morning. He might stay to Jenny Lind concert Wednesday evening, but no longer. They promised to send this immediately ($1.20 paid by Camp), but I suspect some failure, for I received no answer, though I requested one. If it does not reach him by 10 tomorrow morning it will be too late, as he leaves then to attend Miss Larned. Wrote a letter to George and sent it off.

In the evening, a call from Billings, who is come back, to be more quiet, I hope, than of old. Hodges came in soon after and sat for a while—more reserved in appearance than he used to be. Will take Aitchison's place, at least for the present. Selected and read over passages of the *Iliad* for tomorrow's examination. Went down at 10, closed and locked front door.

Tuesday, May 6. Berkeley examination from 10 to 12. William Winthrop the only candidate; did moderately well. Mr. Woolsey the only spectator. Sat through all, reading Professor George Anthon's account of his dismission from the chair of Greek in the University of New York, a pamphlet just published, spicily written. Mr. Woolsey told me of an interesting work by Koch on the Anabasis of the 10,000, or rather their Catabasis, which is much more obscure. Thinks that on some points Xenophon either forgot or never understood the real facts—likely enough.

Mr. Woolsey thus far makes no allusion to *our* affairs.

No answer from Henry. Sent a letter (.05) to John Chassell to intercept him on his passage through New York. Hodges wrote one or two similar letters to classmates of his. Letter to Dr. Robinson acknowledging the favor of his new Buttmann (.05). Letter to Mr. E. B. Jennings of New London on the Ollendorffian method in teaching ancient languages.

With Anna in the evening, 7–9. Some beautiful moonlighted conversation. Afterwards a gaslighted conversation for an hour with the family. Some interesting accounts by Mr. Magill of the way men live in Georgia, in the open air, and in groups of serious or merry talkers, much like the Greeks of old time.

Home at 10¼. Studied. Washed. Abed at 12.

Wednesday, May 7. At Seropyan's room saw Black's *Atlas,* which he sells for $11.00. Had great mind to get a copy, but forbore. To Anna at 9, and sat till 12, reading Becker and talking. She chanced to express her sentiments on whiskers, which I more than suspected before, and should have clipped mine in Geneva, but was ready to try the effect of a suggestion which Mother gave, that they made me look older. This I slipt into a letter, the last I wrote, but it seems to have made no impression. So they fell, a bloody sacrifice, before 1 o'clock.

Henry came, with Miss Larned, in express train. Had received my dispatch 15 minutes before starting, and did not stop to Jenny Lind concert. Some question as to priority among tutors; I thought it should be determined, as among professors, by College age; but it was decided to follow time of entrance upon actual service. So that Henry and Hodges come in last. Henry is to have my place, Greek with the Freshmen. They will hardly feel it as a change.

Afternoon and evening spent in various business, especially looking at my lesson in history, or rather geography, for tomorrow morning.

Call in evening from Edward Whitney. Says Mr. Dudley is being married. Wonder how he bears it.

Thursday, May 8. Up at 6. Met first and second divisions of the Junior class and gave them lessons. Heard my first recitation at 11 on geography of Europe. Made some long talk and occupied nearly an hour. Rest of the day mostly spent in making arrangements about optional classes. Am to have Elderkin *solum* in Greek —*Panegyric* of Isocrates. Would rather perhaps take a class in analytical geometry (Reynolds, Brewer, Hallowell, and Miller) who in Mr. Stanley's absence are going begging for an instructor. But my first care should be the Greek. Some talk with Mr. Thacher about displacing Mr. French, who spoils our study by putting his surveying class into the forenoon, and substituting Mr. Lyman. Said Mr. Thacher: "I could not think what made you look so peaked about the chin, but now I see. You are come under the same regime as I. You get however an excellent *quid pro quo.*" A class which was to recite in Justinian to Mr. Talcott are in sad perplexity about an instructor. Mr. Larned can hear them only twice a week. Wonder if he has got a new case.

With Henry to Twinings' at 8. Sat half an hour, and gave her a headache. At 9 Macy came in to bid farewell to Miss Ally, who leaves tomorrow. Came away at 10.

Paid Mr. Dow $3.00 for oil. He has retired from his establishment, and a Mr. Shedden, a druggist from New York, takes his stand.

Friday, May 9. Up at 5½, for the first time, but alas not the last, this term. Busied about nothing for great part of the day. Concluded to purchase Black's *Atlas* of Seropyan for $11.00. Newton, class of '50, has come to New Haven to study mathematics—with *me,* if he can. Should like to hear him, but believe it is impossible. My new textbook in history, my Greek optional, my labors in two biennial examinations and in that for the Woolsey scholarship, and beside all, the claims of a courtship nearing to its close will leave me little time for a study so arduous. Made out an examination paper for the Senior biennial, including a passage of Aeschines "Adversus Ctesiphon," which they have never read.

First recitation of Elderkin on *Panegyric.* Rather heavy.

Thunderstorm at 6, sharp lightning and heavy rain. Intermitted at 6½ to let me go to tea, returned again at 8, while I was with Anna. She says Macy was *satisfied* with what he saw of us, last evening.

She is urgent to have our people come out to the grand strike. I on my part will do what I can, but with scanty expectation of success. She seems inclined to make an affair of it and get together something of a crowd. I on my part will do what I can toward their entertainment, wishing only for that which will give her the greatest satisfaction. It is wonderful how much can be effected by some influences. Who could have believed that I should ever have endured without horror the idea of standing up thus before a crowd.

Visited the rest in the other room. Saw some new volumes purchased for the book club. Came away at 10½ by moonlight and studied till 11½ on my history.

Saturday, May 10. Camp was intending to bring up a Mr. Adami, a young German lawyer, traveling in this country, who has been spending a day or two in New Haven, but it appeared that he had left at 6. Camp dined with him yesterday at the Tontine. The German ate his way down the bill of fare like a regular trencher champion, and did not get away till a quarter after two—pretty well done, considering that he had breakfasted at 8½. He accounted for his heartiness by saying that in Germany the dinner was the principal meal. Of course he is bound as a patriot to eat a hearty dinner.

Mr. Porter again takes the Juniors in logic, Wednesday and Saturday forenoons, a convenient arrangement for me, though it is a pity to lose the intellectual impulse of the disputes. Staid with Anna from 9 to 12. Read some of Browning's finest things. Found one, "Christina," which I had never noticed before, that pleased us greatly.

In College Library, reading *Athenaeum*, but more of the time talking with Newton, whom I had seen at 9. He will study by himself, French first and afterwards mathematics. Advised him to procure Moigno's *Calculus*. Going to dinner, saw Fisher, just come in to spend a day or two with us before the opening at Andover.

Stopped in to look at the new hotel—very handsomely fitted up. Was going upstairs with Camp to look at the ladies' parlor, when the barkeeper, thinking us suspicious fellows, stopped us and we made off. Purchased Stuart on Ecclesiastes at Fitch's, $1.00. Read the commentary on chapter 2d. Very much in character. He thinks Koheleth would not have talked as he has, about knowledge, if he had lived in our day (of chemistry, exegesis, etc.).

After tea called on Mrs. Larned. Found Miss Larned with her. Had a pleasant chat of an hour. Miss Larned expressed herself well pleased with her journey to New Haven. She chanced to speak of Mr. Sobieski's present to Miss Mary Blake, a series of miniature German poets. Mrs. Larned suggested the idea that she had better get married herself. She replied that for such a present she might almost consent to take it into consideration. Poetry, I said, might no doubt do much to soften the asperities of a courtship. I did not happen to think just then of my own gift, the Freiligrath, and I certainly hope that she did not think of it, otherwise my speech might seem a peculiar one. I have since learned that I am beginning to be marked out as her future mate, while the Twining story has sunk into complete forgetfulness. Truly, our friend the public is a lady-sage.

Sunday, May 11. Hyde preached at the Centre in the forenoon, on love to a personal Savior. Fisher in the afternoon at the North Church, a fine flowing sermon, I understand, equably delivered, but a little wanting in energy. I heard neither. Dr. Fitch preached much as usual. Henry says he had quite forgotten that Fitch was so dry. Studied Bible lesson, "healing of centurion's servant, raising of widow's son of Nain, inquiry of John Baptist concerning Jesus," and expounded at 5. Some 12 or 15 present—more than I had expected.

Could not easily prepare myself on the Ecclesiastes, so took over Park's Election Sermon (Henry's copy) and read it through to them, from beginning to end. More than ever struck with its singular excellence. Anna gave me an account of her visit yesterday to Bridgeport. She described the deathbed scenes of Rebecca Hewitt in a way that made it impossible for me to restrain my tears. Is such faith attainable for me? I think not. It is a simple, child-like state, which people of education, with long experience of the world, and an acquired habitual distrust of themselves as well as others, seem to outgrow. Nevertheless we must try to become as little children.

Came away at 10½. Read Mrs. Browning. Assuredly she is not so great as her husband.

Monday, May 12. Lent Camp $2.00. Call from the President, who showed me a letter from Dr. Robinson in regard to Buttmann's Grammar. The Doctor wants us to state the facts about the book, to correct the erroneous impression that it has been superseded in Germany. I undertook to put together something of the kind. Talk with Whittlesey from 12 to 1. He has had a call to Bath, Maine, an excellent place, but has given no answer. Will remain in the Seminary till September.

Elderkin and Terry have concluded to give up the Greek, so that my afternoons are again free.

With Anna from 7 to 10. Was accused of unusual melancholy. Talked about the death of Miss Hewitt.

Afterward told the news from the planet Saturn, Professor Peirce's paper before the Scientific Association in Cincinnati, in which he asserts that the rings must be and are fluid, permanently two in number, but each of these constantly breaking up into new ones and again reuniting.

Tuesday, May 13. Long talk with Fisher at breakfast. Came up to Henry's room. Mac soon stepped in, and presently Whittlesey. The latter had heard a piece of news about me. The report had reached them at Andover some time ago, but nobody believed it. Last evening they had it very straight and there could be no doubt. I was curious to hear it, and accordingly it came out that I was to quit No. 105 and take lodgings for two at the Tontine or somewhere else. The public, I said, had done me the honor to connect my name with so many ladies that I really could not tell which was meant. Mr. Fisher hinted that it was a friend over the way. I said, that was not the last—they were behind the times. "Confess," said Fisher, "or you lose our congratulations." I was sorry, but must add that to my manifold afflictions. "Perhaps," said he, "we may congratulate you hypothetically—*if* it be true as reported, then we give you joy." "Great consolation," said I, "to know the felicity I *might* have enjoyed, if I do not." They gave it up as a bad job. Mac said Dudley was at the New Haven Hotel with his wife, ready to see his friends. I rushed over, and sat 15 minutes talking with Mrs. Dudley, who conversed well. She looks older than I supposed; is said to be six years older than her husband, but I should not have inferred it from her appearance. Dudley a shade and a half less wretched than usual.

Spent much of the day writing to Whitney. Showed him that if I had not attended to Sanskrit this year, I have attended to some other things. Finished at 4½. Went into the Library, drew Barante's *History of Dukes of Burgundy*, first volume. Went with my letter to the post office at 6, and found that I was just half an hour too late for the Cunard steamer tomorrow—must wait for the Collins of Saturday. Paid postage, 21 cents.

With Anna in the evening. Read a little in Becker.

Paid Mr. Seropyan 11 dollars for Black's *Atlas*, $2.10 for Gibbon's *Rome*, 6 volumes, 0.70 for Macaulay's *England*, 2 volumes—in all, $13.80.

Wednesday, May 14. Call from President Day, who brought in demonstration of binomial theorem.

With Anna from 9½ to 12. Told her what MacWhorter had said to me at breakfast, that Mr. Dudley had told him, that Mrs. Dudley had told *him,* that Mrs. Salisbury had told her that we were to be married. She said the secret was at length pretty fairly out. They had it yesterday at Dr. Fitch's, where it came from Mr. Charles Gould of New York, confirmed by Mr. Joseph Larned, whose sister had assured him of the fact—indeed he had seen there must be something in it last winter when he first broached the subject, I was so fearful it might reach Miss Twining. He prophesies, I suspect, post eventum. We finished the *Charicles,* coming quite to the bridal chamber. Came within an ace of a call from Miss Henrietta Blake, which might have been interesting. Mr. and Mrs. Magill move out today.

Report at Kinne's room today at 2. Faculty at 3. Meeting of examiners of Senior class. Was amused with Mr. Olmsted's simplicity in regard to a subject which was discussed before him in a committee perhaps a dozen times.

Sent Henry over to call on *our* people. Grew unaccountably sleepy over the *Westminster Review* and went to bed at 10.

Thursday, May 15. Call from Fisher, who leaves this morning. He was to have escorted Miss Baldwin to Worcester, but she stays on account of her grandfather's health. We talked about Mac's theory of infinite divisibility of magnitude; and on infinites in general, with good agreement. At 12 examined Heard—approved. Afternoon, prepared my examination paper for the press and sent it to Mr. Hamlen. Call from President Day. I had not looked at his demonstration, but read it while he sat in my room. He will suspend the printing at this point to await Mr. Stanley's arrival.

Did not get over to Twinings' till 7½. Anna came in presently, but our tête à tête was soon interrupted by the entrance of Mrs. Macy and her son. Camp called after a while. His mother a school acquaintance of Miss Mary's. Company left at 9½, and Anna explained how much trouble it takes for a woman to get married: poor things, I wonder they will ever undertake it. Question as to time, left a little indefinite. Grand explosion or not—I say nothing, determined that she shall not give up her wishes on my account, in fact caring little about the matter, though hitherto the notice of a crowd has been my uttermost aversion. We are now completely exposed, and Anna has been receiving any amount of congratulations from her friends. *Mine* say but little, though Mr. Sobieski made an attack upon me rather unsuccessfully at the supper table this evening. He came in with Mac. I wonder how Mac contrives to tolerate the fellow—it is great proof of his good-nature.

Had some instruction in regard to my future duties as a householder, of which carving seems to be the chief.

Friday, May 16. At 5½, went with Mr. Thacher to call on Mr. Herrick. Saw his foot dressed. The gangrened surface was reduced to two fifths of its original area. The toes are in a bad state, though it is not easy to see what will become of them. The sight and smell were almost too much for me. I felt very squeamish, the color fled, the sweat started, but I made a strong effort and stood it through. Mr. Thacher still comes twice a day to change the dressings. His assiduity and kindness through the whole have been wonderful, and not only Mr. Herrick but the people of New Haven owe him a great debt of gratitude. Mr. Herrick shows a little natural impatience after an illness so protracted. He sighs for the open air and the green fields and the stars of heaven. "This might have happened just as probably to anyone else in New Haven." "No one else," answered Mr. Thacher, "had abused himself so much." Mr. Larned came in, and we went off to tea together. He is going afishing tomorrow with Norton and his brother to Lake Saltonstall.

With Anna from 7 to 10, but not alone. Some time occupied by a call from young Gilman, who says his brother will soon be here. We started upon the *Historical Parallels,* but made no great progress. Mary was with us, and I believe enjoyed it. I hope she will not suffer any loss through our rich gain.

Saturday, May 17. Coming up from breakfast, Hyde stopped me, and said that he had been asked to preach at Colchester tomorrow; if he went, he should wish me to hear compositions for him at 11. The difficulty was that he had before promised Professor Goodrich to preach for Dr. Hall of Norwalk, but as he should receive an X at Colchester and a O at Norwalk, he hoped that the Professor might let him off. It went rather against the grain to give up an hour of my Saturday morning, but it is a shame to be selfish at any time, so I consented. From 9 to 11 read *Historical Parallels,* talked over our matters, and came away at 11, not sorry to give the slip to Miss Duncan of Montreal, who had been encouraged to expect sight of us any time before 12. Goodrich would not give up his claim, so I had the hour to myself. Wrote a letter to Abbot about Morris, and to Hurlbutt, begging for some missing averages, and announcing our expected change of condition.

Call from Hodges, who showed me Linonian circular just drafted, to drum up subscriptions for new Hall. J. G. E. Larned has gone to New York on same errand. Our people have already raised $2800; the Brothers, it is said, $3300.

At tea, Camp sat with Mrs. Larned. When Dwight came in I asked him to sit on both sides of me, for more efficient protection. Only a minute after, Sobieski entered with MacWhorter, but Mac was kind enough to place himself at my side, so that I got off this time. Mrs. Larned says that Mr. Artoni, before leaving New Haven, told her that Sobieski had learned his French within the last four years and spoke it very poorly. Spent some time after tea in her room, in pleasant chat. Mr. Larned came in, elated with his success in fishing, and declaring his intention to try it again. They handed me a pamphlet by F. A. Adams, A.M., proposing a new system of musical notation, which they wish me to look at and perhaps notice for the *New Englander*. Spent two hours at Henry's in a regular old-fashioned loaf.

Sunday, May 18. Dr. Bushnell at Centre, forenoon and afternoon. Mr. Atwater of Fairfield in the evening. Heard none of them. Dr. Fitch on demonology—much beyond the record. On deceitfulness of the human heart—a good sermon. Bible lesson at 5. Koheleth, chapter 2d, in the evening. Conquered my reluctance, and spoke to Anna of Hamilton's death. We had a good deal of conversation, in the old fanciful style; possibly after all "the golden crescent of our spirit hath not set."

Monday, May 19. Call from Mr. Henry Field, just before my 11 o'clock recitation. He has passed through the place, he says, several times of late on his way to New York, but without stopping, a neglect, however, for which he made ample apology by pleading his attachment to a lady of New York, whom he is to marry tomorrow (in Gramercy Park at 1 P.M.). She is a Miss Desportes, a sort of adopted daughter of Mr. Frédéric Monod, an orphan, has resided some years in New York, and appears from Mr. Field's description to be a very excellent and charming person. Distrusting his own judgment, he had confirmed it by that of his more critical, and in this case less interested, brother Mr. Dudley Field. He goes almost immediately to keeping house in West Springfield, Massachusetts, where he urgently invited me to visit him and his wife.[7] His brother Dudley goes to Europe—sails on Saturday. His family have been there for some time. Miss Mary will start with Mr. Cyrus and others on a summer tour to the West—Iowa, Minnesota, Lake Superior, etc. He has sent me, he said, a copy of his book, through Mr. Horace Day. It must have come during the vacation and has perhaps been brought to the College in my absence. He apologized for the binding; had not had time to get it bound as he wished. The Harpers told him that the book was going off well.

Heard that Hebard, Senior, died last night. He had exhausted himself, working on a catalogue of the Brothers Library, went home sick with a fever on Wednesday, and sank immediately. He was an ambitious man; little expected to be cut short thus in mid career, though perhaps it is no cutting short but the transfer to another scene of activity.

In afternoon, calculated averages for my Freshmen of last term, and wrote a letter to Mary, urging the duty of coming out here at the time of our crisis—for all at home, but especially for her.

Evening at Anna's. Continued our *Historical Parallels*. Some rather unsuccessful effort to develop in me a memory for practical matters. Came away at 10¼. Studied till 11, and went to bed before moonrise.

Tuesday, May 20. Talk with Hyde in the morning: account of his call on the ex-tutor and bachelor Mr. William Aitchison. Looked up Mr. Horace Day in order to claim my presentation copy of Mr. Field's book. Found him, after some search, at his father-in-law's, and got a promise that the volume should be forthcoming. Bought at Shedden's sundries to amount of 69 cents. Afternoon, wrote to D. P. Noyes an account of recent developments. Call from Mac, who took liberty or rather leave to offer his congratulations. Conversed on several points of philology: classes of roots, Grimm's Lautverschiebung, etc. Glad to see that he is traveling a little out of the beaten track of metaphysics.

Called on Mr. Herrick and sat ¾ of an hour. Talked of Van Helmont's Archaeus. Saw George Bushnell at supper and received his congratulations. Expressed none in reply. Poor fellow, he is to be married tomorrow. Dr. Bushnell to officiate; will come down (George said) with his head under his arm. The Hartford Central meet today and have before them the remonstrance of the Fairfield West. Will use their best endeavors no doubt to satisfy the remonstrants. At Twinings', most of the time with Mr. and Mrs. Magill. Read a little German. Driven off at 10½.

Wrote to Noyes a letter of announcement.

Wednesday, May 21. With Anna from 9 to 12. Read little in the *Historical Parallels*. Talked a good deal about our matters, stimulated perhaps by the neighboring example at Mr. Blake's. Received some account of projected arrangements as to house, furniture, etc., of which I made a memorandum at my room. Story about College that I was to be married in the evening—confusion between me and George Bushnell. Great interest among the Freshmen; talk of a serenade.

Faculty at 3. Talk about Presentation Day. No valedictory oration and poem. Class split up into a half a dozen factions, unable to choose, adjourned it sine die. Concluded to go through with the usual Latin exercises, and to have a cold collation. Appointed on committee with Mr. Thacher to consider question of Latin address before Senior examination. My examination in Senior biennial fixed for Thursday, June 5.

Wrote to Charles Long about recent occurrences, and began writing to Eaton.

Thursday, May 22. In afternoon, paid subscription to Foreign Missionary Society, $10.00. Called on Mr. Dana to inquire about possibility of sending Bopp's *Grammar* to Whitney at Berlin in package of *Silliman's Journal*. They send to Westermann, New York, and he to his correspondent in Brunswick, by whom the numbers are distributed. Can easily enclose the book; send next about the middle of July. Dana has a beautiful place, and seems to enjoy it.

At 6½ went over to Twinings' with Henry. They had a small circle: Mrs. Mumford and daughter from Rochester, the latter just entered at Miss Dutton's, Miss E. Baldwin and Mr. Camp, Miss Olivia Day and Mr. Thacher, with Mr. and Mrs. Magill. The evening passed pleasantly. Broke up at 10½. I staid till nearly 11. The lightning gleamed brightly as I came away, and the drops began to fall just as I entered North College. The shower was heavy and lasted I know not how long. I read my lesson half an hour, then lay in bed perhaps half an hour longer before I went to sleep, and it was raining then.

Amused to notice Anna and see how clearly the "engagée" appeared alike in words and actions, yet not more clearly than naturally, beautifully, and amiably.

Between 12 and 1, had a talk with Mr. Olmsted. He expressed the fear, which we all feel, that Mr. Stanley will never be able to act again as one of our number. We spoke of a successor, and he mentioned Mr. Loomis as having some valuable qualifications. My opinion of Mr. Loomis is high, though not quite so high as it was two or three years ago. He is an excellent man of business, a most industrious student, zealous in the prosecution of scientific research, but with less of originality than I once supposed. Mr. Olmsted fears in regard to himself that a growing dimness of vision, a progressive amaurosis, as he apprehends it, may ere long compel him to retire. I hope not. Finally he offered me his congratulations in a very handsome manner, the more pleased, he added, as my choice would not require him and Mrs. Olmsted to enlarge an acquaintance already too extensive, but would bind them more closely to a highly valued friend. He expressed his high esteem for the whole family, and especially for Mr. Stephen Twining, whom he described as a man of sterling integrity and very uncommon sagacity of mind. He mentioned an instance in which he had consulted him on a somewhat delicate subject—that of second marriages—and had received many valuable observations.

Friday, May 23. Received a ticket to the Wooden Spoon Exhibition, to be held in the evening at Brewster's Hall, or rather I received two tickets neatly enveloped, with a verbal invitation to attend. The same courtesy was extended to all members of the Faculty. Of course I did not go, and was not needed. The house was filled with a highly respectable audience—many ladies present. The performances, like the audience, were perfectly respectable, though too long—from 8½ to 11½—and on the whole rather tedious.

Got Henry Field's book at last, with a well-written note requesting me to notice it in the *New Englander* or somewhere else. Saw Mr. Herrick in the afternoon and sat for an hour in his company.

With Anna in the evening. Heard of some interesting conversations on an uninteresting theme: myself. Omne ignotum pro mirifico. Curiosity and admiration will wear away on acquaintance. Pleased to find, however, that I do not seem very labored and constrained in conversation. Easy, they say, and moderately fluent, but reserved—on that all agree—and according to Miss Baldwin severely critical? Talked and read till 10½.

Saturday, May 24. With Anna from 9 to 12. Time spent mostly in talking. Received a letter of gratulation from Noyes, a very handsome letter from a very noble man.

MacWhorter at tea. Came up with me to my room. Spoke of Martin Farquhar Tupper, who, as it appears, like his great proto-type King Solomon, occasionally uses spiritual elevators. A friend in New York proposed to introduce Dr. Bellows, the Unitarian preacher. "What," exclaimed M.F.T. (mufti), obviously under the spiritual influence before described, "What! the heavenly-minded Bellows," and then extending his hand with great cordiality, "Heavenly-minded Bellows," said he, "how do you do." Porter it appears got hold of the story in New York and vouches for its authenticity. Mac attended the Exhibition of the Wooden Spoon last night. Thought it rather heavy on the whole. Was pleased, however, with some things, particularly the question "whether the Russian serfs come from the sea," and the retort of one disputant to another, "If you don't like my premises you can leave them."

Sunday, May 25. Dr. Fitch on diverse subjects. Devils in the forenoon, concluding part, and heaven in the afternoon. Henry propounded for admission to our church. Went through my Bible lessons as usual.

Saw the Epistle of St. Leonard to the Congregationalists, quite apostolic. The grand result of his tour is that he likes Congrega-tionalism better than ever. Was it necessary, or as Mr. Weller says, "wuth a while to go so far and larn so little?"

Monday, May 26. Wrote a letter of announcement to John Chas-sell (postage, .05), and commenced writing one to John Foster. Called on Mr. Herrick, and found Mr. Salisbury with him. The latter gentleman congratulated me on news which he had recently heard. I told him he ought not to mention such things in the presence of Mr. Herrick. But he, nothing abashed, said that he had heard of it some time before, and that he could give the lady a character as he had known her of old. He need not, I replied, it was already too late. This reminded him of an Irish girl who asked a friend about the character of some young man. His reply was quite unfavorable, but she soon interrupted it. "Stop," said she, "don't go on. I've been married to him a fortnight." Mr. Herrick, however, could only remember of school-day times that she excelled in geometry. "She will take a turn now," said Mr. Salisbury, "and distinguish herself in linguistics." "The two things are not incompatible," said Mr. Herrick. "As we see from Mr. Hadley's case," returned the other. Etc.

Mr. Salisbury spoke of the recent meeting of the Oriental Society at Cambridge—small but pleasant. Mr. Beck gave up his place as Secretary of the Classical Section, and the Society did me the honor to confer upon me that responsible post. Meeting in October again in New Haven. Mr. Edwards has taken up the subject I had thought of, discoveries in Asia Minor. Said in a paper which he read that he could not obtain the books he needed in Boston or its environs and had been obliged to send to New Haven for them.

Judge Baldwin's death spoken of. He expired this morning at 2. In his 90th year. A man much respected and widely influential. Has seen affliction in his family: one son of brilliant talents died a drunkard; another is deranged, in the retreat at Hartford. Funeral on Wednesday.

At evening went over by previous arrangement to Mr. Magill's. Found Mrs. Thacher and Miss Day. Mr. Thacher came in soon after. All but our folks went before 9. We sat for an hour longer, and then I went home with her, the first walk in her company. Another Monadic experience past. Stopped in for a few minutes, but soon came away.

Tuesday, May 27. Recitation in mythology. Mr. Barrett said Aphrodite was goddess of love and domestic felicity. The remark made a sensation among the division, who appeared to think that I would follow up as usual with some explanation. But I did not. I only talked a little about Dionysos and Demeter. Went into Blodget's room and reclaimed my Bokum's *German Reader*. Worked two hours on a problem which he showed me in conics. This was from 4 to 6. Jenks (Senior) had been in my room with his solution of a problem which he had shown me some time before —an interesting question.

With Anna from 7 to 10, talking much and reading some, in German. Mary came in at 10, and I sat three quarters of an hour longer.

Russell, the elocutionist, is again in New Haven, staying at the Tontine. Henry is a member of his class.

Mr. Woolsey told me a strange story of Mr. Gray, the gentleman whom I saw last summer, a pupil of Rugby, who had the honor to be flogged by Dr. Arnold. He has just brought out a very complete and thorough edition of the *Ajax*. But has been obliged to quit his place in Cambridge on account of the impositions which he was detected in and indeed owned that he had practised.

Mr. Woolsey spoke again about editions of Greek classics for which no translations can be procured.

Wednesday, May 28. Faculty meeting at 8, on account of funeral in the afternoon. No business of consequence. Out at 9½. With Anna from that time till 12½. Heard another story from her unwritten diary. When the cycle is completed, I shall have to hear it over again, for I have already forgotten the earlier adventures.

At 2 to Kinne's for reporting. Mr. Thacher came in to excuse himself; he attends the funeral exercises at the house and must go there at 2½. The public service in the church commenced at 3. I staid away, supposing that there would be a crowd, and thinking that the old citizens of New Haven had a better claim than I. Read a letter from George, just received. He says that he did not understand my hints about the grand strike, took them for a joke, and was quite surprised, when I had left, to learn from Mary that it was all gospel truth.

Attended meeting of Connecticut Academy at Mr. Gibbs'. Thin attendance. Dr. Fitch presided. Some account of Foucault's experiment, which nobody appeared to understand. Fitch undertook to explain it and made a better case than I supposed he could, but evidently had no clear ideas in regard to it. The whole subject was committed to Lyman and Hillhouse. Mr. Dana gave a description of Becquerel's experiments on currents of electricity in plants, showing that they result from chemical action. Broke up a little after 9, but not before I grew desperately sleepy. Loafed an hour or so in Henry's room, and then abed.

Thursday, May 29. Had agreed to sit for my daguerreotype at 12, but forgot it and broke appointment. No matter; the day is a gloomy one, overcast, and insufficient in illumination for such purposes. There has been a great change in the weather, bright and warm yesterday, quite sultry even; today, just as people had donned their summer habits, it grew chill, and cloudy, and almost winter like. The daguerreotype was for Cooper, who has a singular idea of taking the series of his instructors. Jacocks came in about 9 to inquire concerning the locale of Professor Jared B. Swift, class of

1842, now teaching in Western Military Institute, Georgetown, Kentucky. Told me he had heard of Waterous as practising medicine and said to be doing well in York County, Pennsylvania, at Hopewell (nearest post office, Apple Grove?). Whether yet an honest man is doubtful. Had a letter from Windham, Connecticut, giving me an account of circumstances connected with the death of Gideon Bingham. Written by Samuel Bingham (query, brother of the deceased). He died in New Orleans of consumption, December 13, 1850.

Letter from John Chassell, who says he would congratulate me if I had not quitted the ranks of bachelordom, but, as it is, he cannot.

Saw Root at 2. Has been attending anniversaries in Boston. Stops here over night. Had not received my note. Likes his new situation very well. Has Sweet near him, also Knapp and Stone. He seems to be popular. Says one old lady to another as they were coming out of church, one Sunday afternoon, "A good sermon we have had this afternoon." "We don't never have nothing else," was the reply.

Edward Whitney brought me a letter written by his brother William to the people at Northampton, written from Frankfort and Heidelberg on his way to Tübingen, a long letter of 19 pages in very lively strain, and very beautiful illegible handwriting. Took it over to Anna in the evening, who read over great part of it with surprising facility, but stopt short before completing it, finding that it fatigued her eyes. I read her George's letter, which amused her greatly, as it had me. Read also most of Noyes'.

Friday, May 30. Made my visit to Anna at 3, as the evening was to be occupied with the preparatory lecture. Miss Day came in soon after and sat till tea time, when I went away. I had a better opportunity than ever before to make her acquaintance. Her appearance is striking, she shows a quick mind and a very ready wit, but I missed that desire to please which adds so much to the attractiveness of a woman. If thoroughly interested, however, and drawn out of herself into complete openness and unreserve, I can easily believe that she would become a very charming person.

Attended preparatory lecture in Senior Recitation Room, by Mr. Hyde—the sermon on love for a personal Savior. He pitched his voice too high for the room, and thus injured the effect of his delivery. But the sermon was one that could triumph over elocution much worse than that. Returned to my room at 8 and undertook to read on my history lesson, the reign of Alexander, but soon grew too sleepy to proceed. Concluded to talk discursively in the morning, and went to bed at 10 o'clock. I think I am not likely to suffer at present for lack of sleep.

Saturday, May 31. With Anna from 9 to 12. Reading at a dead stillstand. Heard more experiences of the past, not without ill-natured joy at the discomfiture of my illustrious predecessors. Went to Cowell's, and sat for my daguerreotype. The process is a little skeery, and I suspect the face will show an all too great intensity and fixedness. But the loss is Mr. Cooper's. Cowell showed me a fine effigies of Dr. Fitch, a highly successful performance.

Called at Pease's and obtained new number of *Edinburgh Review,* almost entirely political or economical, and to judge from appearances not particularly interesting. Was amused however by an article on Lamaism in Thibet.

Examined Potwin, Freshman, at 2½. He was sick at the regular time. Passed very well. The Senior biennial examination commenced this morning and went off very well. Two divisions, one in Attic of the Chapel, the other in Geological Lecture Room, each with two officers in superintendence. It was the Latin paper this time. Mine in Greek comes on next Tuesday.

Read *Athenaeum* and *Literary World* in College Library. Mr. Tayler Lewis is out on modern fallacies in regard to education. I recognize some of the ideas which I have heard from him in oral converse.

At evening, called on Miss Larned. Found her with Mr. J. G. E. Larned, just returned from New York, where he has succeeded beyond expectation. She gave a glowing account of her experience in the great conflagration of Tuesday night or Wednesday morning, when a barn burned down very close to the purlieus of Miss Dutton's school. They were greatly frightened, but fortunately quite uninjured; indeed they were really benefited, for that barn will never give them any more anxiety.

Called at President Woolsey's. Mrs. Woolsey alluded in very kind terms to events of recent date, or rather, recent discovery. Complained that on Mr. Thacher's positive authority she had contradicted the report in Philadelphia not less than three times during the vacation.

JUNE, 1851

Sunday, June 1. Dr. Fitch's sermon of the morning was followed by the Lord's Supper, peculiarly interesting to me in this instance from the fact that Henry united with our church. I hardly know what Mr. Pitkin will say to his stray sheep. He may perhaps turn Episcopalian one of these days, but the probabilities, I suspect, are against it. He never will, I am sure, so long as he remains in anything like his present circumstances.

In the afternoon the President, in compliance with a request from the Senior class, preached a funeral sermon on the death of Hebard. He had a large audience; it filled the gallery and compelled me to seek a seat below. The subject was the death of a Christian young man, the feelings it should awaken and the lessons it should teach. The discourse was simple, direct, and impressive, yet rich in thought and singularly beautiful in expression. The eulogy in particular was admirable—perfect—and excited a very strong feeling in the class.

Bible lesson as usual from 5 to 6. In the evening took over the *Edinburgh Review,* new number, and commenced reading to Mary the article on Lamaism in Thibet, but the reading was interrupted, as it is so apt to be there, by conversation, and we had not proceeded far when Anna came in from the Monthly Concert. She had been much struck with a new exhibition of himself which she had seen from Mr. Eustis. We continued talking until after ten, until in fact I declared it to be five minutes of eleven. I was mistaken, however, as I found on returning to my room—it wanted ten minutes to the hour.

Monday, June 2. Paid Mrs. Bradley for washing, $1.00. 17 cents still back. She worked for me two weeks and then turned me over again to Mrs. Levere.

Paid board at the Tontine, $13.50, May 3–31 inclusive. Called on Hyde at 9. Found him suffering from ague in the face—caught cold yesterday—one cheek much swoln.

Sat from 4 to 5½ with Mr. Herrick, discoursing of various matters.

With Anna in the evening. Camp called and sat for an hour. Returned with him to Henry's room and stayed there till 11.

Tuesday, June 3. My session in Greek with the Seniors. Sat in Chapel Attic with the President from 8 to 11. Henry with Professor

Porter in the Geological Lecture Room. No appearance of foul play in our department. They may some of them have brought in slips of paper, containing a scheme of metres or something of that sort, but they could not have used books to any extent.

Made out my paper for the Woolsey, and obtained Backus'. Mr. Thacher's tomorrow morning. Finished letter to George, and intended taking it to Anna in the evening, to see whether I had struck the right key in regard to our standing invitation, but happened to forget it.

Macy came in while we were together, and like a marplot as he is, started us in some conversation which, after he left, became, I suspect, a little annoying to Anna. I made too free with the established etiquette of marriage, which to her mind must have more of a positive and imperative authority than it has to mine. Things long familiar fix themselves in our thoughts; the uniform associations of the past become necessary and sacred. Habit is second nature—how should we always distinguish between first and second? Why should I exercise my skeptical criticism on things which must appear to her, if not as dear and holy, at all events as inevitable, and which as society goes are perhaps really so? And why in regard to trifles like these should I have any will, any opposition, any raillery even, nay, any lack of prompt and ready sympathy? I am quite ashamed of myself, and resolved on better things, determined to be watchful, considerate, helpful and above all, heartily cheerful. At all events I will not distress myself with vague fears and imaginary anxieties. I will hold myself in reserve for real afflictions. God may darken—and, if it be his will, may he darken—this bright sunshine which I now enjoy, but I will not disfigure it myself by looking through smoked glass.

Heard some strange things about announcement of peculiar situations, which pleased me well, as showing that I am not alone in my awkwardness. Heard also some unimaginable nonsense in regard to secret sorrows, hidden love pangs, where the subject is a young acquaintance of mine, the freest and most joyous man in New Haven, and the object a lady who might have been his mother.

Wednesday, June 4. Going to Henry's room at 7, Camp handed me a letter from Whitney, dated May 8th from Tübingen, with one for Camp in same enclosure. Henry said that Mr. Bailey, an old Fairfield pupil of mine, had called at his room the evening before and waited until half past 10 in hopes of seeing me. I found

him accordingly at the Tontine, and was honored with an introduction to his wife. He gave me some little account of himself and
his progress since we parted in 1840. During the 18 months before
that time he had made marvelous advance in Greek, Latin, and
mathematics—marvelous for anyone, but especially for a dull man
—so that from next to nothing at the start, he attained at the end
the qualification of a Junior in Rutgers College. Here he graduated
in 1842 with an honorable standing, and afterward studied theology
for three years in their Seminary. He was next settled in Guilder-
land, Albany County, for two years, from which place he went to
Schodack on the river, about 12 miles from Albany, where he still
remains. He married in 1847 and has two babies, one of them with
him. He has been on an excursion to Lyme, Coventry, etc., visiting
his wife's relations—traveling in his own conveyance—and is now
hastening homewards. I took them up to College. Showed them
the Trumbull Gallery (.50), the Mineralogical Cabinet, Mr. D. S.
Bigelow (Junior), whose family they had visited in Colchester, and
bade them adieu at 8¾.

Hyde had before called on me to hear his recitation in *Prometheus* at 11. Mr. Thacher had offered to go in, but unfortunately
no notice had been given them of a Latin lesson. I consented reluctantly, for it shortened my three hours' visit by two thirds, and
hastened to call on Anna. Some making up for last night, which
had affected her as I supposed. My letter to George, which I read
to her, appeared to be satisfactory, and was dispatched at once to
the post office. Meant to come away at 10, but did not get off till
20 minutes later. Had scanty time for preparation on the *Prometheus,* review lesson and advance, and knew little more about it
than the third division. They recited, no doubt, worse than usual,
partly because they are much occupied with the presidential contest between Boies and Crapo in the Brothers Society, and partly
because they were in hopes of getting off without a recitation. I
kept them three quarters of an hour and should have held on
longer if I had known more about the lesson.

Read Whitney's letter, very interesting as usual. Says that he
had been misinformed in regard to the extent of Lassen's illness. Is greatly pleased with Roth as a scholar, a teacher, and
a man. Has been studying a little Persian in preparation for the
Zend.

Mr. Andrews came in to level my bed. Had before paid him .125,
also .25 for his boy (yesterday).

Thursday, June 5. After dinner, drest and went out. To Dr. Murdock's to invite him to Philological Society. He was doubtful; is hard at work reading proofs; the printers after lying off for 9 or 10 months are just now waking up and beginning to press him. Up to Professor Gibbs' on similar errand. Overhauled Rice (Freshman) on the way, who presented me the respects of Cousin George Shepard, and wanted to know if I had any thoughts of going to Union College to supply the place of Dr. Nott. What strange ideas Freshmen *do* have. Mr. Gibbs had thought of attending Mr. Russell's Shakespeare reading. To Anna at 3, and sat till 6. She had been invited to go with Mr. Macy to the evening's exercise, was at a loss what to do. Seemed to think that my company would be as agreeable as Mr. Macy's, but soon gave up any such idea as that, shrunk from the sensation which our joint appearance in the Temple would be likely to occasion. Read Mr. Whitney's letter, slowly and with many pauses, so that it occupied two hours or so. Calls from Mrs. Winthrop, Mrs. T. Dwight, etc. My advice in regard to the evening was, "Follow your inclination." Whether she took it or not is more than I can say, but she went.

Saw Mr. Hamlen, just back from New York, about printing Woolsey exercises. He complains that he is not always treated as he should be when passing through the College premises.

To Mr. Woolsey's at 7½. Heard a letter from Mr. Silliman, Junior, to Mr. Dana, with an appended note from Mr. Silliman, Senior. They are at Rome, hearty and busy. Thought we should hardly make out a meeting. But the gentlemen dropped in one after another, Mr. Gibbs, Dr. Murdock, Professor Porter, and Professor Larned. The President showed us the first number of the *Zeitschrift* for Comparative Philology edited by Aufrecht and Kuhn, and read Curtius' explanation of the aorist passive in $\theta\eta\nu$. He then gave an account of Koch's work on the Anabasis. I read select extracts from Mr. Whitney's letter, which elicited a good deal of conversation, all however of philological bearing, which perhaps would not have been the case if Mr. Kingsley had been there instead of attending Mr. Russell's exercise. Mr. Thacher too was absent. With his brother George, I suppose, who is here from New York.

Returning, stopped at Henry's and stayed an hour. Heard his account of the Shakespeare reading. The audience was excellent, though not large, and the performances of the reader highly satisfactory.

Friday, June 6. Letter from Mary. Supplies the message she forgot for Anna. Her mind runs still on going South. Commenced the Roman history. The students are doing very well indeed.

Made a beginning on the examination papers, looked over half a dozen of them. Corrected proof during the day for the three Woolsey papers.

Had a call in the afternoon from the Reverend Mr. Street, father-in-law of Bolles, class of 1850, and classmate of Mr. Thacher, from whom he brought a note of introduction to me. His object was to consult me about the meaning of the preposition εἰς in Romans 5.18. He would explain it of tendency simply, not actual result, and so escape the apparent universalism of the passage. He found me a very complaisant critic of his view, and went away well satisfied.

Called on Mr. Herrick at 4. Dr. Knight went in at the same time with me. Mr. Thacher was there already. The Doctor proceeded to remove the dead matter from the toes (second and fourth), involving in the case of the second a loss of the extreme joint. The Doctor sat in cheerful conversation, and pineapple-munching, in which I did not participate, until I left at 5½. In the evening at Twinings'. Read Mary's letter. Showed some new specimens of autograph for card. Henry came in and sat an hour, until 10¼, when we came away together.

Saturday, June 7. Hyde, whose face has returned to its natural dimensions, goes to Colchester this morning, to preach there tomorrow. He had three places at his command this week, any one of which he would have liked for himself. Two he had filled by others, and had tried to find a man for the third, being afraid of the exposure in his own case. But every licentiate in the Seminary was engaged, and he must go in person. I consented of course to his request that I would hear the compositions of his division at 11. With Anna at 9. Mary told me of a possible situation for Sister Mary. She had some correspondence last fall with a Miss Sheddon of Natchez, Mississippi, who wanted an assistant in her school for young ladies. She knows Miss Sheddon very well, who was a warm friend of her mother's. Her age is not far from 60. In character she is somewhat irritable, but knows her own failings and struggles earnestly against them. She has excellent sense and excellent principles, and is a person of real and practical piety. On the whole, she is truly amiable and capable of very strong attachments. In her

school she aims at giving a plain substantial education. Miss Mary
Twining promised to write and find out whether Miss Sheddon was
supplied with an assistant, and if not, what offer definitely she
was prepared to make.

Heard compositions from 11 to 12, some quite good.

In the afternoon, went around to make arrangements for my
session of the Woolsey, Monday morning. At Mr. Thacher's, sat
awhile with his sister and Miss R. Bacon. After supper, called on
Mrs. Larned, who however did not come in until 8. Came away
a little before 9. Obtained at Pease's the last number of the *London
Quarterly*. Not very interesting, I suspect. Sat for an hour or more
in Henry's room, feeling rather qualmish and thinking that I might
have to take some medicine. But I did not. Went to bed at 10½
and succeeded in sleeping off the ill humours.

Sunday, June 8. Dr. Fitch in the forenoon. Text, "What must I
do to be saved?" An awakening theme, but a singularly soporific
discourse. Taylor in the afternoon. Subject, the gospel as appealing
to the consciences of men, one of his strong and heavy sermons.
Mac came up after the forenoon service and told me of an interview which he had yesterday with old Dr. Beecher. The Doctor
called at his room, and announced his business, his son's church
in Chillicothe. The people, it seems, are in debt $1200, and unable
to pay. Their house likely to be sold, and to the Catholics. Dr.
Beecher resolved to wear out his shoes in raising the sum; had
got $100 at Springfield, as much more in Hartford, and had now
come on same errand to New Haven. Mac came down with $50.
The tears started to the old man's eyes. "You give it," said he, "to
a grateful heart." Mac was quite upset and knew not what to say.
How would Kate feel as to her reverend father, if she heard of it
—accepting the price of blood, the money that ought to be Miss
Bacon's? Perhaps, however, she would look upon it as a righteous
spoiling of the Egyptians.

Bible lesson at 5. Talked a good deal about βαπτίζω. The more
I think of it, the more I am convinced that Luke 11.38 and Mark
7.4 cannot be relied on for the sense of "wash," that in neither
place is the word used in a common secular application, that it
denotes in both a religious rite, and that in Hellenistic Greek of
the New Testament time it had ceased to be used in any other way.

Made out nothing in Koheleth. Took over *Bibliotheca Sacra*,
with Mr. Adams' article on Neander, which I read aloud, some

parts of it not without difficulty, but with great interest and pleasure to all that heard it. Oh that God would enable me to gain but a tithe of the devotion which inspired the soul of that good and great man.

Monday, June 9. After breakfast, went round to Mr. Thacher's. Pulled twice at the door bell, without effect. Went in. Knocked at parlor door, looked in. Nobody there. Then at dining-room door. No response. Looked in: Mr. Thacher romping with the baby. He went after the documents while I paid my respects to Mrs. Thacher and Miss Day and told them how our College doors had been locked this morning. Hurried myself into a dripping sweat, but reached the Geological Lecture Room a minute after 8 o'clock. Found my 11 Freshmen in attendance, distributed rules and papers, and sat with them from 8 to 11, when Mr. Larned came to my relief. Returned after my recitation and took in the papers at 12.

In afternoon, criticised 24 Senior examination papers. Stopped flute in No. 126. Received call from Mr. Chapin, author of English *Grammar*. He asked me if I had received a copy of his work. I told him, no. He was surprised, had given directions that a copy should be sent me. I looked among my books and found that I had in fact received a copy—an awkward fix, which I squeezed myself out of as well as I could. He had heard a remark of mine reported, "that the Grammar of the English Language had yet to be written," and this had induced him to give me the book. He then opened the volume and began to explain some of his peculiarities: as to parts of speech, where definers take the place of adjectives and adverbs, predicatives of verbs, etc.; as to pronouns, under which he reckons only the substantive pronouns, using dictive, auditive, and abessive (!) for 1, 2, 3 person; as to tenses, where he gives regular place to "is being improved" and adopts a new terminology; and was just going on to mode, when I excused myself. He seems to be a thinking man, and has more common sense than is generally to be found among the innovators in English grammar. He has modesty likewise, a quality in which they are in general lamentably deficient.

Went at 4¾ to call on Mr. Herrick. Kept up a pretty steady stream of talk till after six. Mr. Herrick is just beginning to dress his own foot under Mr. Thacher's supervision. Expressed his great obligations to Mr. Thacher for his long and tedious service. "He had no special claim, no claim at all, upon him." Was a good deal struck with this expression. He feels, I presume, that he has no special claim on anybody, as no one has ever been admitted to any close intimacy.

A beautiful evening with Anna.

Tuesday, June 10. Brewer called in just after breakfast to inform me that Mason, the Californian, was to be married in Trinity Church at 12 M. to a Miss Woodward. He had scarcely gone when McKissack came to give me an invitation from Mason himself to appear then and there as a witness to the ceremonial. I responded courteously but staid away. From 12 to 1, read over about 20 Senior examination papers. In the afternoon, finding the weather uncommonly fine, I was seized with a strange desire to take a walk, and accordingly sallied out at 2¼. Went up Tutor's Lane, Powder House Hill, and so on to the turn which leads to Whitneyville. Arrived here at 3 or thereabouts. I gazed admiringly on the outside of the gun factory, and then thought of ascending East Rock. Missed the path and got myself entangled in a maze of brake and thicket, from which I emerged at last very heartily tired. Trudging slowly home, met Miss Baldwin a little this side of the village. Reached my room with great satisfaction just at 5 o'clock. Washed off the dripping sweat and sleeked myself generally. My walk was longer and more fatiguing than I intended when I first set out, but I think no harm will come of it.

With Anna in the evening. I took over Miss Barrett's *Poems* and read "Lady Geraldine's Courtship," which seemed to suggest *Historical Parallels*. Mary came in before 10, and we continued talking till nearly 11. The evening was wonderfully beautiful, and as I essayed to go, Anna seated herself in the doorway and barred my egress. Released at length from my imprisonment, I returned home and went to bed.

Wednesday, June 11. With Anna from 9 to 12, reading Mrs. Barrett Browning and talking.

Reporting from 2 to 3. Faculty meeting: monitors appointed; cent-pitching. Saw Professor Porter's portrait in Trumbull Gallery, painted by Huntington at expense of Senior class. Talked it over with Mr. Blodget and Mr. Thacher. It is a very handsome picture, but hardly anyone would recognize it at first view as meant for Mr. Porter. I do not doubt, however, that in the artist's studio, with the arrangement of light and shadow, the red hue thrown from drapery at hand, etc., our Professor, being withal better combed, shaved, and drest than usual, looked just as he is there represented.

Went with Henry to take tea with our folks. Fine fresh straw-berries from the garden. Mrs. Gibbs came in and sat for more than an hour. Anna had commenced translating for us one of Andersen's stories, "The Mermaid," when the lightning began to flash, and Mrs. Gibbs went home under Henry's escort. I remained, sat through a heavy fall of rain, and came away at 11.

Thursday, June 12. Completed a letter to Mary which I had commenced yesterday. Informed her of Miss Sheddon's wants. From 12 to 1, looked over examination papers of the Seniors. At 2½ sallied out for another walk. Went by Neck Bridge to top of East Rock. Coming back, went round at foot of Rock to Whitney-ville and thence by Ball Spring road to College. Got home pretty thoroughly tired at 5¼. Washed, drest, and at 6½ went with Henry to President Day's. Quite a little party, composed of the Twinings, Magills, Mumfords, Collins', and—that is all, except Mr. Hodges, and Mr. Beecher, with whom I had quite a talk. Saw less of Beecherism than I had looked for.

At 10 came away with Anna. Sat for a while in the garden, under the bright but rather chilly moonlight. Adjourned to the house, and had another beautiful moonlight session there. Plan for study-ing Spanish, Anna and Henry as pupils under my tuition. I, tutor in Spanish—what an idea!

Friday, June 13. At 12½ called on Anna to inquire whether she wished to attend Mrs. Bostwick's concert in the evening. She was not quite willing to adventure it, but proposed a drive to Laurel Lane, to which I readily agreed. Paid a visit to Mr. Herrick at 3½. Found a load of medical books which he had obtained from Dr. Knight to find out the precise nature of his ailments—mumps and swelled leg. He was somewhat exercised in mind by the thought that a proper mode of practice pursued through his first four days of illness would have saved him all the rest, but that proper mode he knew not and could not well be expected to know. Professor Salisbury and Mr. Macy came in, the former just returned from his trip to the West. Says the 2d volume of the Oriental Society Publications is just out. I can get a copy at his house. Dr. Knight's coming at 5 drove us away.

Engaged a carriage at Benton's. Called on Anna again at 6 to tell her I should come with carriage at 7, but she made me stay to tea and sent Kinsley in my place to the stable. We set off, accordingly, and drove through Fair Haven, Laurel Lane, East Haven, Water Street, etc. Home again at 9. The localities were new to me and interested me greatly. Fair Haven is a neat, thriving, pleasant village, Laurel Lane wilder than I had imagined anything to be in this vicinity. East Haven, with its whitefish smells, was an exception to the general agreeableness of the drive. The air was mild, and the full moon rose upon us in the middle of our journey. I took the horse and wagon back to the stable ($1.00), and went again to Anna, with whom I sat above an hour reading Mrs. Browning ("Legend of the Brown Rosarie," a very remarkable poem). Stopped at Henry's. Camp gave a favorable account of his picnic during the day at Roaring Brook. Henry and Camp had both attended the concert and were highly delighted with it, as were also a numerous and cultivated audience.

Saturday, June 14. Finished up Senior papers. With Anna from 9 to 12, alone. Read some sonnets from Mrs. Browning's first volume, with which we were greatly struck, but spent most of our time in talking. I find that reminiscences do very well, but forecasting is apt to be bad. Where it is anything but vague and fanciful, there is so much of suspense and uncertainty, so many unforeseen contingencies, so many uncontrolled possibilities, as to throw a sensible shadow on all our speculations. It is much the best on the whole to find our Arcadia in the present, which is bright to us if it ever were to mortals upon earth, with only shadow enough to relieve the otherwise too glaring brilliancy of the picture. May God fill us both with deep gratitude for his rich goodness.

At 1¾ went to Mr. Salisbury's, found him absent. Stole a copy of *Journal* of Oriental Society. Some time at Pease's bookstore. Afternoon spent in miscellaneous occupation, reading newspaper, reading Orientalia, reading Spanish, reading periodicals in College Library, etc. In evening, after some time at Pease's, who by the way is soon to return from his wedding trip No. 3, went to Mrs. Magill's —Mr. Magill has gone to Norwalk to preach there tomorrow—and sat till 8½. Saw Miss Victoria Cone, whom her father has contrived to establish there for the present. Coming away, bought ink at Shedden's, 15 cents. Loafing awhile at Henry's. Read *N.B.*, new College paper, very well got up. Severe on Seniors with reference to their failure this year in electing a Valedictory Orator and Poet; a fine parody on "Wanted a Governess"; a very sharp piece on the Monkey Roost at Miss Lynes'; etc. etc.

Sunday, June 15. Dr. Fitch in forenoon on means of salvation, well written and unimpressive. In afternoon, Dr. Dwight of Portland on God as hiding himself, a good discourse, but I was strangely sleepy and lost great part of it. Bible class at 5 on Luke 12.1–21. Only five present.

Staid away from tea to study Koheleth, chapters 4 and 5, but on going over at 7½ found that Mary had gone out to hear Mr. Léon Pilatte, the French Protestant missionary. Anna would have gone too, but as she was to be absent all next week, she chose to have her evening with me, and I hope did not regret the choice, as I certainly did not. Mr. Pilatte was kind enough to make a long address, of which Mary after her return gave us a brief synopsis.

Monday, June 16. A bright morning, but soon overcast, with a strong wind from the northeast—on the whole a very perplexing aspect of the skies. I could only conclude after a good deal of balancing that perhaps it would storm and perhaps it would not. Gave in my Senior examination marks to Mr. Woolsey and offered to help in casting averages, but he very generously declined. Looked a little at the *Spanish Grammar*. Took possession of my new recitation room on the third floor of the Lyceum, south room, a fine place, airy and spacious and sweet to smell, requires a somewhat higher pitch of voice than the old kennels. Jackson to open it in the morning, I myself at eleven, going there for the purpose five minutes before the hour. Lock the room myself whenever I leave it. The Sophomores at the same time come up into the second story. Repairs to commence immediately on the ground floor.

To Twinings' at 12¼. They had concluded on account of the wind to take up with the dust and go on the cars, when Miller came and told them that the boat had been detained. Sat down with them to an early dinner, but saved my appetite for Mr. Allis. Urged them not to neglect the commissions I had given. At length they set off, about 1, and I went down to the Tontine. After dinner, bought some white envelopes (15 cents), as Anna is determined to be no longer *done brown*. Tried to get some 5-cent postage stamps, but failed. Bought Dr. Ryan's book at Pease's for $1.50 and spent some time in looking it over. It is evidently a poor performance, but the poorest book may yield something, and from this I succeeded in gathering a few valuable hints. At 5 went to call on Mr. Herrick, but his mother met me at the door and told me that he had been for two days suffering from a severe headache, that he had shut himself in his room, closed the blinds, gone to bed, and directed that all visitors should be denied.

In the evening, drest, and went first to Mr. Thacher's to inquire about a further delay of the mathematics examination for Woolsey scholarship, as Dupee is not yet well enough to attend, though he may be so on Wednesday. Mr. Thacher said that Dupee was lowest in his Latin, and of course would be excluded by the terms from any chance of the prize, while the excitement of the examination might bring back his illness. Concluded to go on, tomorrow morning. Called to see Mrs. Mumford, but she was not in. Same fortune with Miss Larned. Probably they had gone to attend Mr. Goadby's Free Introductory Lecture, of which I had heard nothing, or had forgotten what I heard. Called on Mrs. Woolsey. Saw her mother-in-law from Philadelphia. Some talk with Mrs. Winthrop, pretty hard work as usual. Spent an hour very pleasantly with Miss Baldwin. Mr. Henry Blake came in and I withdrew. Returned to my room and wrote a letter to Anna, finishing at 12.

Tuesday, June 17. From 9 to 12, on Senior appointments. Potwin, valedictory. Little, salutatory. Crampton and Vose, philosophical orations. Winthrop (a good deal lower down) philosophical oration. 6 first orations, 10 second orations, 3 dissertations (all of them degraded orators), 8 first disputes, including Evans, 8 second disputes, and nine colloquies, all in one grade. In no one instance did we disturb the order of the marks; the only difficulty was to draw the line. The examination had exerted considerable influence on the standing, and of course on the appointments, of the men.

Faculty at 12. Passed the appointments. Talked about those who had in their examination fallen below two; no conclusion. Adjourned till afternoon. Townsend prizes from 2 to 3¼. Evans and Potwin best on imagination as an instrument of science. Little and Sheldon on relation of Christianity to art, the first neat, the last rushy. Winthrop closed up with a piece well written but without striking points and very poorly read. Faculty again. Long talk on the tail of the examination. After several propositions, concluded to pass the whole batch, as none fell below two, upon the whole, and as the class pursued their Junior studies without knowing what was to come—but to take some different course next year.

In evening called at Twinings'. All out. Met Harriet and Julia in High Street. Told them I had seen Mr. Charles Waring at the Tontine, and heard of our people's safe arrival in New York City.

Sat an hour with Mrs. Magill. Mr. Magill has gone to attend General Association at Bridgeport. Will probably visit New York in latter part of the week. Returned at 9 and commenced writing to Anna, but fell sleepy soon after 10 and broke off in the middle. A day of truly magnificent summer weather—for which I was most thankful on Anna's account.

Wednesday, June 18. From 8 to 9, finished my letter. Taking it to the office, fell in with Egleston going to Association at Bridgeport. So, Havens, Coe of Danbury, and Dr. Fitch, all of whom I saw. MacWhorter announced destruction of San Francisco by a still more terrible and desolating fire. Returning, stopt at Pease's. He has got back from his wedding tour. Called at all the bookstores in town to get Mrs. Browning's new volume, but in vain. Learned "Christina" by heart from a copy in Fitch's shop. From 10 to 12 on Woolsey papers.

12 to 1, journalizing, fallen lately in arrears. At 1 went to old Rhetorical Chamber and met the Faculty, thence to old Theological Chamber to meet Seniors, and then all together to Philosophical Chamber to meet the President and hear the Latin addresses. To Geological Lecture Room at 1½, where the cold collation was served in very satisfactory style. Adjourned at 2½ to President's Room for Faculty meeting. Rejected application for repeal of rule excluding members of secret societies from benefactions of College. Passed finally on College appointments. Second warning to Blakeslee and Bliss for breaking open the door of Potwin, monitor. A variety of other matters kept us till after 5. At 6, the Freshmen were on the qui vive, with broad shirt collars and other similar appliances. When the bell turned over I came down, stood on the front steps, and ordered off all whom I found thus disguised. Magill, DuBois, Drake, etc. At second turn Mr. Olmsted came out and sent the class into Chapel. Next year we must think to speak beforehand and punish all transgressors severely. As the Seniors held Saturnalia in the afternoon, the Freshmen had theirs in the evening, with shouting, tooting, and fireworks kept up till after 11 o'clock. Some talk among our people of an onset and an interference, but masterly inactivity carried the day. Such things are for the police of the city, especially as it always happens that a multitude of city fellows are engaged in them, fellows who are in no way under our authority and like nothing better than a chance to defy and insult us.

After tea, read over with Henry a list of theological works which he has thought of for the College Library. Staid awhile at 30 Elm Street [Twinings'], then half an hour at 87 Crown Street [Magills']. Came back at 9¼, and spent two or three hours on a letter to Anna.

Thursday, June 19. Mailed my letter in the morning. Spent forenoon on the history, which has been latterly too much neglected. At 1, received a beautiful note from Anna. She will probably remain in New York until next week.

Spent an hour or more in pleasant chat with Mr. Herrick, who has at last learned to put his lame foot upon the floor.

After tea, called at Twinings' to discharge a commission of Anna's, obtain a rag from an old dress as specimen of stuff. Stopped a few minutes at Mrs. Magill's to leave word of her sister, and report the failure of any direction as touching strawberries. To Temple at 8 (25 cents) to hear Dr. Goadby in the first lecture of his course on insects, with illustrations by oxyhydrogen microscope. He gave divisions of animal kingdom, characteristics of insects, classes of insects, modes of defence used by insects, sting and ovipositor, etc. He talks in an easy offhand way with much enthusiasm and some humor. The audience was small, but first-rate, and apparently well satisfied with the lecture. Home at 9½. Commenced another letter to Anna, but had hardly begun when Henry came in with a second note, as full of pleasantness and friendliness as it could hold. Finished my letter and went to bed at 12½.

Friday, June 20. George's birthday. Wonder if he is aware of it or can tell how old he is. If so, it is the only date in his life that he knows.

Spent some time in College Library, looking at Spanish books, a scanty show, far inferior to our collection of Italian classics. Concluded to keep on with *Gil Blas*.

Afternoon at 3, met Backus in Mr. Thacher's room to settle Woolsey prize. Added marks and found Fenn 8.05, Potwin 7.23, Alexander 6.92, Norris 6.10, the rest a good deal lower. The result will give no surprise to the class and will give unmitigated satisfaction to Fenn himself. I rejoice the more in his success as he is a South Carolinian.

Having been scant of sleep for two or three evenings, I lay down and rested (scarcely slept) for an hour.

In the evening, called at Mr. Magill's, and sat above an hour, talking on the associated divines at Bridgeport and other matters.

Went thence to the post office, but found no letter. Called to see Mrs. Mumford, but she was at Mr. Charnley's, in the great octagon, I suppose. Stopped at Miss Dutton's, though the clock struck nine as I entered, and sat nearly an hour with Miss Larned. Talked of Miss Woodward (now Mrs. Mason), who used to attend Miss Dutton's school. Miss Larned regards her with feelings not far removed from contempt.

Returning to my room, spent three hours in a leisurely letter to Anna, and went to bed at 1.

Saturday, June 21. I went to the post office as coolly as possible, for the day was a warm one, but found nothing there. Returning, stopped at Cowell's to look at my daguerreotype, but the artist appears to have abandoned his rooms. Tried in vain to find a copy of Mrs. Browning's late book. Coming into the Green was accosted by Professor, who invited me to the State House to see the pendulum experiment of Foucault repeated there by Hillhouse and Lyman. They had suspended the ball from the centre of the skylight by a line seventy feet long. The pointer underneath the ball showed a progress of one degree in every six minutes, a very perceptible motion. Most of our savants came in to witness it. Sent over Henry and Camp to enjoy the sight—Macy also, who wanted to know when our folks were coming back from New York. His mother is at Hudson, to return next week. He had thought of having her come in their company, but I could give him no definite information. Wrote again to Anna. Finished the letter just before prayers, but some time was necessary to enclose it and direct it, which made me too late at supper, and exposed me to the gibes of Camp and Dwight. I repelled them more feebly than usual, being a little troubled because no word had come from Anna since Thursday night. Mailed my letter, and came back to my room. Read *North British Review* till Henry entered a little before 9. Sent him to the office and obtained a note in pencil, which sensibly relieved my mind. "Very busy. No time for calls. Back on Tuesday or Wednesday."

Sunday, June 22. Dr. Fitch in forenoon on immateriality of soul, a disingenuous sermon. He did not acknowledge the difficulties of the case and much overestimated the strength of his presumptions. In the afternoon, on uncertainties of the future, elegantly written. Bible class as usual at 5; Luke 12, latter part.

Wrote to Anna in the evening. Expressed ideas which had been dwelling in my mind all day. I have been latterly unspiritual, ir-religious, forgetful of God, and thus have brought evil on myself. Even earthly love has suffered from the want of that elevating and ennobling influence which a thought of God and his eternal king-dom can alone exert. May God in his good grace enable me to live henceforth more devoted to him, and thus more truly devoted to her that is to be my future constant helper in his service.

Monday, June 23. At 12, commenced a letter to Anna, and con-tinued it with interruptions in the afternoon. Having finished 3 pages, at 4 P.M. called at 30 Elm Street to get some items. Was sup-plied by Harriet and speedily made out page 4. Mailed. 5 cents. Drest etc. At 6½, went by previous invitation to eat strawberries at Professor Olmsted's. No company, pleasant turn in the garden. At Dr. Goadby's second lecture (.25) a little too late. Sat with Mr. Thacher, who was much pleased with the performance. Showed some artificial paintings of stomachs, which were finely done, but not equal to nature. Jaws of beetles. Proboscis of tree bugs. Physi-ology of bedbugs. Came to London in wood used for rebuilding city after great fire of 1666.

Back by Henry's. Letter from Anna, or rather pencil note, an-nouncing her intended return on Wednesday evening. Enclosed note to Harriet, which I delivered immediately.

I neglected to set down the fact that on Saturday evening I lent Henry one dollar, the last emptyings of my pocket book.

Great prospect of rain, but as yet no fulfilment worth mention-ing. Carried umbrella all day with no use for it.

Tuesday, June 24. Called on Mr. Herrick and sat from 3½ to 5. His foot constantly improving; is quite healed over, though still un-serviceable for walking. Dr. Fitch came in, and I withdrew.

In the evening, called at 30 Elm Street and saw Harriet. She had received information of her aunts' return tomorrow evening. From 8 to 9 at Mr. Magill's. He undertakes to go down to the boat at 8½ tomorrow evening. Back to my room and tried to read a little in *North British Review,* but sleepy, and abed at 10.

Wednesday, June 25. Faculty at 3. More about Sophomore bi-ennial. Cases of Freshmen who dressed themselves for prayers last Wednesday evening. Admonished.

At tea Camp was late and apparently doomed to a tea out, so I proposed to Dwight the sharing of his strawberries, and actually made way with a moiety. Was just thinking of another dip when Camp himself came in. We had quite a laugh over it. Studied history till 8. Then went to Dr. Goadby's third lecture (25 cents), on suctorial apparatus of tree bugs, bees, butterflies, oxflies, etc. Why these insect bites so painful? Because the creature infuses his saliva into the wound, to dilute the blood and to destroy its vitality. Parotid glands of a goat moth. Acridity of saliva. That of rattlesnake, of dog, especially when rabid. Hydrophobia from bite of cat. Why sometimes more fatal than at others? Bite without infusion of saliva, predisposition to disease in human subject. It was a very interesting lecture. Present about one hundred.

Up by Elm Street. Found Anna returned in afternoon boat, attended up by Mr. Magill. She has been well except on Thursday afternoon, when she was obliged to go to bed. This circumstance accounts for the long silence of her notes. She was kind enough to get me Mrs. Browning's late volume of poems. We talked till 11 o'clock, when I rose to go, but was detained a willing captive to look at the carpet, knives, and white silk, in regard to all which I manifested a reasonable degree of stolidity, and came away at 11¾.

Thursday, June 26. Spent some time looking over syntax in Cubi's *Grammar*. At 3 took the book over to Anna with letters of George and Mary. She showed me in turn Lieutenant Smith's letter introducing Mr. Hébert, his brother-in-law, together with a note from the latter gentleman written yesterday, on leaving New Haven. Anna was telling me how she should proceed to see the young brothers, who stay, when the boys themselves came in, affectionate, homesick, and uncouth, evidently brought up on a plantation among Negroes. What a change shall we not see in the next eighteen months. They speak French as well as English, though not as easily, and have studied some Spanish; one of them accounted for his shortcomings in Latin grammar by the difficulty of distinguishing the Latin forms from the Spanish. They are intending to enter College in a year(?). Mr. and Mrs. Magill came in and sat awhile, and presently Miss M. Twining, and Miss Copp (sister of Mrs. Waring). Our progress in Mrs. Browning's sonnets was not very great. Staid to tea, giving Camp his opportunity for revenge on my strawberries.

Anna sent over for Henry to come and receive a Spanish lesson.

He held back till 8½, during which time I remained alone with Anna, cutting Dr. Goadby's 4th lecture on insects, without (I believe) any material loss of happiness thereby.

Mary came in at 9½ when Henry withdrew. I staid till 10½ and then left, after looking at a variety of chinaware articles.

Abed at 11. Waked at 12 by vivid lightning flashes and crackling thunder. Heavy rain, much needed to lay the dust of nearly 3 weeks. Rose to shut a window, then lay down again, and soon fell asleep.

George's letter received today announces Cousin Sidney's sudden marriage under singular circumstances. To think of a man so thoughtful of appearances, so fearful of criticism, so anxious to be regarded as comme il faut in all respects, and finally defying public opinion in this strange madcap way—there is really a sort of Nemesis in it. George forgot to tell us the name of the damsel. I feel curious to see the bait that hooked so shy a trout as Sidney.

Friday, June 27. To Anna at 12½, to learn her will for the evening. She declined attending Mrs. Bostwick's second concert and preferred a ride in case of fair weather. At 3½ called on Mr. Herrick. Found Mr. Thacher, who soon left to attend the funeral of Mrs. Hillhouse. He was one of the bearers. Mrs. Hillhouse has been for some time sinking with consumption, but her death, which took place early Thursday morning, was quite sudden and unexpected, the consequence of breaking of an abscess. I watched the funeral procession from Mr. Herrick's window, a very long one, perhaps forty or fifty carriages. Was somewhat conscience-stricken for staying away, as I have a little acquaintance with Mr. William Hillhouse. He has invited me more than once to call at his house and look at his library, but I have never done so. I have been introduced to Miss Mary Hillhouse, and shall soon become better acquainted with the whole family.

At 6½ called at Twinings' to report my coming at 7 with carriage; found Mrs. Macy. Anna was out. Refused invitation to tea and went to Tontine. Alarmed by clouds, moist, hot air, and east wind. MacWhorter at tea, but no special news. Excused myself and went to Benton's stable for carriage, with some misgivings for the clouds were dark and threatening. Beautiful ride up Powder House Lane, to Whitneyville, and thence along the Cheshire road. Air delightfully fresh and cool. Anna read a letter of her brother Alexander's, just come, filled with a various mélange of wit, science, and affection. Back at 8¾. Paid Benton $1.00.

Saturday, June 28. To Anna at 9. She complains of weariness, the consequence of her exertions in New York. Thinks she has had too much excitement of late, fears that she may fail in health and strength, just at a time when she would wish to be, as she has need to be, most strong and hearty. Proposes a return to that more restricted system which we had marked out for the summer, but which we have observed so ill, of shorter interviews, avoidance of late hours, etc. This morning she wished me to go at 10, there being a special reason in the present case, as it is the last day of Miss Copp's visit. I was much ashamed of myself for having been so thoughtless in regard to her health, and acquiesced most fully, though I can hardly say most cheerfully, in all her suggestions. This time I do not expect to be found delinquent.

At Knevals' in afternoon. Ordered coat ($25), pants ($10), vest ($5.50). Bought gloves (.50, not paid), waistcoats ($5.00, not paid), and gave commission for socks.

Evening, looked at Buttmann's *Grammar*. Read in Henry Field's book. It contains many fine things, but is, I fear, a little conceited and unmanly in its style.

Sunday, June 29. Dr. Fitch in forenoon on "aim of man's existence" (an unmeaning *lurry* of happinesses, in which the main point, the moral sense in man, was kept studiously in the background) and immortality of soul (argument from nature overstated). In the afternoon, on "seeking the praise of God more than the praise of men" (a good sermon, but without that immediate application to student life which, in this subject especially, is so important). Occupied with my Bible lessons, on Luke 12.54 to 13.9 and Matthew 13.1–23, to an audience of 6 persons, which is not bad perhaps for a sultry summer afternoon.

In the evening, from 7½ to 8 with Anna alone. Mary then came in, and we spent an hour or more on Ecclesiastes, chapter 4. Some talk as to times. Monday, August 18, suggested, day of opening Scientific Association at Albany. I rather held on to earlier time, though I care very little about it. It is hard to calculate, in the absence of certain and positive data. We wish to suit the convenience of people in Geneva, Buffalo, and Erie, but do not well know what that convenience may require. Was out of the house before the clock struck 10.

Monday, June 30. A broiling day. Mercury 94° in the shade according to somebody's thermometer. Collection of bigwigs at

Tontine, Judges Church, Storrs, Waite, and Ellsworth. Very little table talk among them, afraid perhaps of publicity, but such men ought to make a somewhat greater show. How can a mind of real strength and activity fail to rise at times above the commonplace?

Called on Mr. Herrick in the afternoon. Found Dr. Ives, the elder, quite infirm in his appearance, and Mr. Sanford, who has just returned from traveling in Italy, where he met with Dr. Bacon.

Ate cherries. Saw postage stamps for the new law, which comes into effect tomorrow.

Had invited myself to tea at our house, in order to finish up my visit by 8 o'clock and go then to Dr. Goadby's fifth lecture. Went to Tontine at 5 to assure myself as to the fact of his lecturing. (Found that one starting from New Haven in the morning could not reach Albany before 6 P.M.). Coming back, met Camp, and told him he and Dwight might divide my strawberries. He thanked me, but with little reason, for strawberries, like Troy, *have been*. Left Anna at 5 minutes before 8, and came to my room, bathed in perspiration. My courage failed me and I concluded to forego the lecture (more's the pity—it was on the nervous system of the insects). Kept cool as well as I could, and went to bed at 10. Lay reading Niebuhr's *Rome* till after 11, when I blew out lights and was speedily asleep.

JULY, 1851

Tuesday, July 1. Another hot day, less intense than yesterday, with a favorable change of wind at evening. Inaugurated the new postage law by two letters to Mary and to George, communicating our plans and asking as to any possible let or hindrance. Dr. Goadby gave his last lecture this evening, having changed his time from Wednesday to Tuesday, a concession to some Ethiopian minstrels. It was a question with me whether I should expose myself to the heat of the Temple, but my walk home from tea settled the matter in the negative. I went to Twinings' at 7½. Anna showed me a letter just received from Professor William Twining, announcing his intention to be present at the crisis. Call from three Mrs. Dwights (one from Clinton, New York), who sat till after 9. Mary had gone out, and for some time we had the ground to ourselves, but on the stroke of 10 I tore myself resolutely away. Met Mary and the Magills on the doorstep. Could not be induced to sit down. At my room tried to read Bunsen on hieroglyphics, but not succeeding on account of obstinate sleepiness, went to bed at 11.

Mrs. Dwight, Senior, told me that I talked like Dr. Fitch, and Anna confirmed the statement. "I had often reminded her of him."(?)

Wednesday, July 2. Woke shortly after midnight and found that a stomachic pain of which I had been conscious early in the evening had not improved during my short sleep. As it appeared to be increasing all the time in severity, I rose at one and took a Dover's Powder. The pain continued still, and at two I took another Dover, which made me quite comfortable, all but the dizziness and nausea. It would have been better for me if I could have vomited a little. As it was, I contrived to work through my recitation, without making any observations on the lesson, in about half an hour. At seven I went to breakfast, having slept in the interval. Got to the table before Camp and Dwight, but found myself obliged by returning nausea to leave quite precipitately. The doorkeeping Negro followed me down the steps, wanting to know if anything was wrong; he thought I was perhaps offended at failure or neglect in service. "It was nothing," I said, though I almost gagged as I said it. I hurried towards my room, afraid that self-restraint would be impossible. But when I reached the State House the flurry had passed away, and I turned again to the Tontine. Got through this time without remark from my companions. Lay down again, but rose at 8½ to make some change of dress. Henry, who came in to trace the wanderings of Paul upon the map, saw nothing strange. But Anna was sharper sighted and more inquisitive. I was obliged to confess my weakness, declaring however that I had quite recovered from the primitive difficulty and had only to recover from the opium. She said she had suspected me for several days, though I have thought myself quite well, except on Sunday, when I was aware of a peculiar lassitude. My appearance was unusually serious; she had feared that I was troubled by what passed on Saturday between us. Not really troubled, I said, only concerned for her health, and ashamed that I had been so thoughtless about it until then. As for this flurry, it was probably among the consequences of a cold, or what would have been a cold, if I had been as susceptible as formerly of such things. She had perceived, she said, on Friday night, as we were riding in company, that I had a cold. I took over a number of the *London Quarterly* (the last received) and commenced an article on Julius Caesar, but made small progress, the time being occupied chiefly in various talk. At 11 she sent me away, that she might return to her seam-stresses.

Spent an hour in journalizing. Called on Professor Kingsley and after some conversation agreed to defer the meeting of the Philological a week or two in hope of getting Mr. Whitney's article on the phonetics of the English language. Talked awhile on Dr. Jarvis and his last volume on Chronology. It appears that at some meeting in Oxford the work was mentioned, and something said about reviewing it, whereupon somebody declared that there were only two men in England capable of reviewing it. Very likely; such things are easily said. The editors of the volume seem disposed to admit that Dr. Jarvis was wrong in one particular, referring probably to the year of Christ's nativity. The calculation of Bianchini, which places the full moon of March A.D. 28 on Monday morning instead of Friday, is fully confirmed by Professor Peirce of Harvard, who was appealed to on the subject. But this one point was the centre of Dr. Jarvis' chronological system, as far as it was original, and everything else must fall with it. Professor Kingsley would write an article on the subject if unfortunately Dr. Jarvis was not in his grave.

To Henry's at one. Found Camp's trunk still there. He was going home today (returning Monday) to spend the Fourth, and make some settlement in regard to a European residence this fall. Was to go in the cars at one and a quarter, coming to the depot from Russell's and having his trunk sent down from 170, but if the carman called, he found the door locked. Henry forgot himself and staid away till 1. At all events the trunk staid, and Camp came in to dinner flushed and vexed, having lost a whole 24 hours by this untoward accident.

Faculty from 3 to 4. Recalled the sentence of suspension for remainder of the term passed against King and Alvord at our last meeting. King has shown great diplomacy, has been more industrious in calling upon members of the Faculty, stating his difficulties, announcing good resolutions for the future, than he ever was or ever will be in getting his lessons. Divisions to be addressed on tardiness at Chapel exercises, which has much increased of late and grown intolerable.

From 4 to 6, upon the bed, trying to sleep off last night's narcotics. Some squibbing at prayers. We must look to it. In the evening, drest cool. Had a call from Mr. Magill, sent over by Anna, who was still uneasy, thought I might stand in need of something. Pleasant chat of half an hour.

Thursday, July 3. From 8 to 9½ examined Little, the only applicant for the Clark, at my own room. He did wretchedly in his Greek; in Homer especially his performance was exceedingly discreditable. He stuck on the constantly recurring ἔκ τ' ὀνόμαζεν and rendered Ὀδυσῆος δαίφρονος the *wealthy* Ulysses. In the *Alcestis* he rendered ἂν Ορφεια κατέγραψεν γῆρυς "which Orpheus inscribed, *an old man*." My feelings were a good deal tried, and in the *Electra* I gave him in revenge one of the hardest places, the colloquy between Egisthus and Electra near the close, filled with ambiguities which were not very happily brought out in Little's translation. It is really a shameful thing when a salutatorian of Yale degrades himself by such an examination. I wish that some colloquist had prepared himself a little and appeared as a competitor; he might easily have carried off the prize.

Camp left at 1¼. Before he went, he called on me and asked me to draw in his place on Saturday for his share of the Boydell pictures. I told him that I would either do so or make some other arrangement for him. The difficulty in my case is that I know nothing of the collection. Mr. Macomber, when he brought them here two weeks ago, gave me a written invitation, sent up by Loomis, to call at his rooms in the Tontine and inspect them at my leisure, but somehow or other I have failed of doing so. A club has been formed here, with 14 or 15 members, to take one set—100 pictures for 100 dollars—the pictures to be assigned by lot. Among the participants are Mr. Thacher, Mrs. Larned, Henry Blake, etc., some taking 10, others 5 of the series. Camp, who is one of them, goes in for 5, as does also Mr. Thacher, and I shall probably ask Mr. Thacher to select for Camp as well as for himself, taking 10, the best that he can get, and dividing afterward with Camp.

At the two forenoon recitations, addressed divisions of the Juniors on their tardiness in Chapel, urging a reform.

At Henry's after dinner. He showed me the new number of the *Bibliotheca Sacra*, and read extracts from Park's second rejoinder to Hodge, a very strong and spirited affair. It seems to me the Princeton Doctor must tire of the controversy, for though his men will of course read only his articles, yet to have such articles as Park's read by anybody, even heretics, cannot well be otherwise than unpleasant to him. The Andoverian, on the other hand, evidently enjoys the *scrimmage*. He is perfectly sure of his position, and sees that the discussion, the longer it continues, instead of unsettling him, gives him a firmer and more impregnable stand. He is certainly far less attackable now, on the part of New England assailants, than he was two years ago. His convention sermon, as originally put forth and afterward vindicated in succeeding articles, is a most masterly stroke of theological warfare, and proved the author a consummate tactician.

At 4 went down to Common Council Chamber in Street's Building, to look at Boydell pictures. Found Mr. Thacher, Mr. and Mrs. Lyman, with two ladies (Mrs. North and Fitch) unknown to me. I ran hastily over the pictures in a most uncritical way, pleased with some, offended with others, but extremely indifferent in regard to most of them. Told Mr. Thacher what I should probably have to request from him. The gentlemen soon went away and left me alone with the ladies. Had a little broken conversation with Mrs. Lyman. By and by the ladies went also, and I too, having got through the heap (scarcely a hundred, I should think), took my departure.

Sat an hour with Mr. J. G. E. Larned, just returned (on Saturday last) from his tour of collection for the Linonian contribution to the New College and Society Hall; has met with fair success. I thought he would say nothing about particular matters, but at last he spoke up. "Mr. Hadley, it is always pleasant to a man when his advice is followed, and consequently I was very much pleased when I saw you follow the advice I gave you last winter. For the event followed so speedily that I made no doubt that you had gone at once and done as I directed." I did not deny the self-flattering idea of Mr. Larned, but suggested that he should use the same beneficent influence upon other friends. He confessed candidly enough that his success in my case was balanced by notable failure in that of MacWhorter. His best course, I told him, would be to allow Mac himself to take the initial steps, and then when he was pretty well advanced to pour in his advice *strong*. "Of course," said he with ready understanding, "you do not mean to represent that as a parallel case."

Went supperward together—he boards at Mrs. Hazard's. Back from the Tontine with Dwight. We were overtaken by a shower which had been threatening for some time, and with all haste were a good deal wet. Having repaired the damage and otherwise "sleeked up," went over to Twinings' at 7½. Found two Miss Fosters, who staid about an hour in pleasant conversation. Alone with Anna till 10, when I rose at stroke of clock and left precipitately.

Friday, July 4. The ever-memorable Fourth, celebrated according to long-established tradition, but with less squibbing than heretofore. Mayor Skinner had issued a stringent proclamation, which somewhat checked this exhibition of infant patriotism. The day was a beautiful one, especially in its postmeridian moiety. We had vivid lightning in the night, with loud thunder, which however I scarcely heard. The rain had begun to pour down before I went to bed, and must have continued more or less for several hours. I hardly know whether I heard the alarm of fire at 2 o'clock, my recollection of it is so confused and indistinct. A stable, it appears, was burnt in Orange Street. I was roused at sunrise by the morning guns and bells, and slept little after that, though I did not rise till nearly 7.

After breakfast, spent almost 3 hours in Henry's room, looking over notices etc. in *Bibliotheca Sacra*. At my own house, journalized etc. till 12¾, when I took my umbrella, for it had rained a little and was still dropping, and went upon the Green north of the State House. Mr. Hiram Ketchum of New York, the orator of the day, was already talking on our revolutionary forefathers, speaking extemporaneously and rather handsomely but, as it seemed to me, in an uninteresting way. It was the exordium of his speech, which lasted for an hour and a half, and was taken up, as most people expected, with saving the Union—a labored defence of the Websterian policy. I listened five or ten minutes and then went to dinner. After waiting some time, got a seat near the head of the table and then, by dint of patient effort, a plate of soup and a piece of blackberry pie, which with a few nuts and raisins constituted my dinner.

At Henry's again till nearly 3. Saw Hodges, who got off one of his best things. We saw the assembly on the Green break up, the oration having at length ended. I commiserated the unfortunates who had to sit it through, especially the Mayor, and said if I were to run for Mayor, I would make it a matter of express stipulation that Mr. Ketchum should not be Fourth-of-July orator. "You would not run *for* Mayor," said Hodges, "unless you could run *as* Mayor."

At my own room, studied history lesson and read Niebuhr, most of the time on bed. I have not quite recovered yet from the attack of Wednesday morning. Drest and at 6½ went down to tea. They were just setting their table; would be ready, they said, at 7. Sauntered slowly about town. Looked at preparations for fireworks, set up on north side of lower Green, unusually numerous and elaborate (cost said to be $1500). Back to Tontine at 7. Waited again for 10 or 15 minutes, and then walked off. Was crossing the lower Green, leaving a wide berth for the cannon, when a man cried out behind me, "Hallo you, Mister, they're agoing to fire the guns. You'd better go some other way." I considered myself safe enough and at first thought of pressing on, but it occurred to me that if by any unheard-of accident I should be shivered into atoms, it might aggravate the sorrow of my mourning friends to hear of my foolhardy neglect of the good-natured admonition. So I turned about, rather discontented and without thanking my monitor, which was wrong and contrary to what I have represented to Anna concerning myself, and left wider room for the artillery. I had reached the State House, however, before the roar commenced. It was nearly over when, at 7½, I went to Twinings'.

Found Anna in the new room, sewing busily, finishing up her long day's work. The Magills came in with Miss Cone (her father back today at the Tontine). Watched the people as they passed on their way to the Green. Soon they left themselves with the same destination, and Anna and I sat for a while in the garden. We were presently recalled to the house, as Mary was going, and we were left its sole defenders. Contrived to amuse ourselves by an occasional glimpse of the fireworks from the windows, as well as by our own conversations and taciturnities on the sofa under the fair moonlight, until the people came back a rushing torrent from the exhibition. Some saucy fellow threw in a torpedo, which did not explode according to intention, until it was picked up in the room and pinched sufficiently. At 10 of the clock, I started on the stroke and vanished instanter. After a little time in Henry's room, I sought my own, and went to bed before 11.

Saturday, July 5. My Saturday morning was put off this time until evening, in favor of a certain important vestment, which would require, it was supposed, the stitches of a whole livelong summer day. Sought Mr. Thacher to urge again my proposition touching Mr. Camp's share of the Boydell pictures. Could not find

Mr. Thacher at examination room or at his own house, where Mrs. Thacher met me, looking quite ill with a cold. Down to Street's Building to find out from Terry the arrangements for the drawing in the afternoon. Setting forth again near 1 o'clock, found Mr. Thacher at door of Lyceum. He acquiesced in my proposal.

No *Tribune* today on account of the Fourth. Read Goethe till 3, when I went to the drawing. Mr. Egleston had the first choice and took the "How sweet the moonlight sleeps" etc. Mr. Thacher the third, took the cave scene in the *Tempest*. I should rather have taken Ferdinand and Miranda at chess. Was glad to be free from the necessity of choosing, as my choices, I have no doubt, would have been accused of sentimentalism. Came away soon. Overhauled MacWhorter, who praised Ketchum's oration, and presently after, Sobieski, who wanted to know "when we were going to study Beckerism," and maintained the superiority of Schiller to Shakespeare.

At 5 called on Mr. Herrick. His mother came into the room and said she was going to a funeral, adding in an awful tone, "the funeral of a *bachelor*." Then turning to her son, she said, "He died alone." "Every man *must*," he replied, "no matter if he had a thousand wives." She endeavored to follow up the attack and produce a salutary moral impression, but apparently in vain; he parried all her thrusts, and remained unmoved, immovable. The funeral was that of Dr. Dow, a little withered man, who was said to have a good deal of science and skill in his profession. After she had gone out, the doorbell rung, and I hastened down stairs to answer it. Found Mr. Blake from New York, who was for some time here in the analytical department. Is now an assistant in the New Medical College there. Left at 6 to officiate at prayers.

To Twinings' at 7½. Mary met me. The day's work had been too much for her sister, who was seized at noon with a sick headache, which had put her hors du combat for the rest of the day. However she received me at length, in the new room, lying on the sofa, and I sat in moonlight until 10.

To Henry's. Found a letter from Mary. Everything at home agreeable to our calculations.

A number of the *Astronomical Journal* from Professor Stephen Alexander, containing a comparison of asteroids with comets of short period, showing many common points and looking strongly toward community of origin. Very ingenious and interesting.

Sunday, July 6. Dr. Fitch in forenoon. Sermon appropriate to Communion season. May God give me new consecration to his own blessed service.

Mr. Aitchison preached in the afternoon. "Why are the obstinately wicked spared in life?" A very fair sermon, level and respectable, much like his old Sophomore compositions. His late pupils in College gave him very good attention. The whole air and manner were those of an old hand, a minister of quarter-century standing.

Did poorly in my Bible exercise at 5, partly from want of preparation, partly because my faculties were somehow at a low ebb. Boggled even on the parable of wheat and tares, which should have been to me "familiar as household words."

Took with me *Bibliotheca Sacra* in the evening, thinking that Anna might perhaps have gone to Monthly Concert. But she has not been able to leave the house today. We had some time by ourselves. She taxed me with unusual seriousness and taciturnity of late, and I was much puzzled to assign the reason, for I could hardly deny that there was a foundation for the charge. I suspect that I have a sort of cold—what in other times would have been a hard cold, but now appears only in lighter symptoms—which saps my spirits and gives me a vague and nameless heaviness of mind.

We soon adjourned to the new room with Mary. Anna reclined upon the sofa. I sat down by the table and read part of Park's article. Anna objected with great good sense to his piecemeal quotations from *Biblical Repertory,* saying that by such a process any man might be made to say anything. In a pause of reading I had commenced telling a story, when the clock struck ten, and my tale was left like "the adventure of the bear and fiddle, begun, but broken off in the middle."

Monday, July 7. The President came in this morning and cited me to a meeting of the Professors at his house at 7½ P.M.

Cut out of my Owen's *Odyssey* passages from the 10th book, for the Juniors who have their Greek examination tomorrow, giving them about forty lines each, and requiring dialectic forms, derivation of words, and analysis of verbs for the first ten lines, together with mythic history of Ulysses. Carried these to Professor Kingsley, in whose room they are to work. Handed him also the obituary notices for members of my class deceased since last Commencement.

A little before one, called on Anna to mention my necessary absence in the evening. Left her at 1 and went to the Tontine. Tired of waiting for dessert and apprehending rain, I left the table in about 20 minutes. Met Dwight on the way. Heard a sound of rain as I approached the State House, which made me run as fast as I could. Got under cover of the trees and put in for the nearest port, the door of the Lyceum, without much damage. Duncan (Junior) soon came along and gave me the shelter of his umbrella to North College. The shower passed away in a few minutes, and left us clear sky for the rest of the day. Wrote diligently on a letter to Mr. Whitney; finished 7 pages; mailed it after tea (5 cents). It goes to Boston and thence across the water by the *Europa*. Had some thoughts of waiting for the *Hermann* next Saturday, which would have enabled me to pay full postage, but I have been so tardy that I wished to avoid farther delay.

Saw in the forenoon, a pupil of Mr. Dudley's, who thinks of entering here as Sophomore next year. Wanted to ask about the biennial examination on Freshman studies. His course of reading has been different from ours. I answered that we should be obliged to give him the same examination as the rest of his class. With perhaps five and twenty new men coming in, it would be of course impossible to examine each on his particular course of study. He speaks in the highest terms of Mrs. Dudley. She does a great deal for the comfort and advantage of the scholars. Mr. Dudley has had 22 boarders. This young man (I did not distinctly hear the name as pronounced by Safford, Junior, who introduced him) spoke of some difficulties at Northampton on the Fourth. The town authorities had prohibited squibs and crackers, and when the police attempted to enforce the rule against some offending youngsters, a fight ensued. Several arrests were made, and a good deal of excitement existed on the subject. Some of the transgressors were in Dudley's school, and he had intimated that he might feel it to be his duty, in giving them letters of recommendation for College, to insert some mention of this affair. My visitor had not participated in the disturbances, but he inquired on behalf of a friend, who had violated the rule of the city but had nothing to do with the fight, whose character and conduct in other respects, as he said, were irreproachable, whether this circumstance alone would debar him from College. It would be for the Faculty, I told him, to decide the question, and much would depend upon the circumstances of the case, but as I understood it from his representa-

258DIARY OF JAMES HADLEY

tion, I thought it probable that the decision would be favorable to the young man. Sent my respects to Mr. and Mrs. Dudley.

To the President's at 7½. Talk on some overtures in regard to a Professorship of History. No names were given. A proposition was made, it appears, to give a small sum for the endowment of such a place and then appeal to the public to make up the sum. The questions discussed were whether it is worth while to have a Professor of History, whether it is best to abridge so much the instruction given by the President, whether it is well to have a Professor of such limited range, whether it is desirable to give so much importance to the department of History. The discussion was rather rambling, but the conclusion was unanimous that, although it might be best perhaps to accept a complete endowment if one were offered us for such a purpose, yet it was not on the whole desirable to close with the proposition as it comes to us. Something was said likewise about the Treasury department. Mr. Warner has been nearly unable to attend to business for the last two years and a half. He is subject to confirmed hypochondria, and the probability seems to be that he cannot recover. It was felt that great delicacy should be shown to him, as he has conferred substantial service on the College, and as he supposes, though no doubt incorrectly, that by this service he broke down his health. Yet it was thought that unless signs of improvement should appear, measures ought to be taken soon with a view to his removal, say in a year from next Commencement. A few words of conversation in regard to the Professorship of Mathematics, in view of a contingency which we all deprecate, but cannot help regarding as too probable.

Back at 10 o'clock, by a beautiful moonlight. As we came to the corner of College and Elm Streets, my companion, Mr. Olmsted, urged me to go on a little farther and make a call, but I excused myself. Went to my room, and straight to bed, as one who must rise at 4 on the morrow.

Tuesday, July 8. Slept very imperfectly as one afraid of over-sleeping. Up at 4, drest, and started from my room. Met Mr. Hayes, the printer, at the door of North College and went with him to the office. He was obliged to go thence to Olive Street to start up one of the compositors who has some experience in Greek. Did not commence operations until after 4½. At 5½ or 5¾ Mr. Hyde came in, and I went to my recitation. Hurried through it as fast as possible, giving out my first set of subjects for review of history, and at 6½ returned again to the office. Found the proof nearly corrected by Hyde. Finished that and saw the first copies struck off, when Hyde came back at 7.20, and I went to breakfast. Got up to College in time to go in with Hyde at 8. Sat in the Attic of the Chapel with the last half of the alphabet. The paper was regarded as an easy, and few remained till 11 o'clock. Was well satisfied that some modes of gaining assistance which have been much talked of among the students are scarcely, if at all, practised. Heard my recitation at 11 in the second story. They were furring the ceiling under me, and the continual hammering made it very difficult to hear the exercise. From 12 to 1 read Goethe's minor poems. Struck with their wonderful freedom and variety.

In afternoon looked at Robinson's new translation of Buttmann's *Grammar,* with reference to a review of it. With Mr. Herrick from 4 to 5½. Talked somewhat on the principles of civil polity. Returning, spent half an hour arranging my Greek examination exercises in catalogic order. To 30 Elm Street at 7½, after an absence of nearly two days. Mr. and Miss Thacher came in and sat for three quarters of an hour. Mrs. Thacher and her sister with others have gone to Woodbridge today; will remain for several days. *We* talk of going out to see them some afternoon. Some time by ourselves, spent *not unpleasantly.* Mr. and Mrs. Magill came in at length with Mary, who played us a trick, however, coming in the back way and allowing us to be much alarmed at her non-arrival. Came off at 10.

Wednesday, July 9. Heavy rain toward morning. Heard the clock strike four and rejoiced that I could bid defiance to its summons. To Twinings' at 9. Read the article on Julius Caesar in the *London Quarterly,* and half of another on Poultry Literature. My conduct recently appears to be regarded as shameful, making others ashamed of me and of themselves. I could only acknowledge the fault, and say that, proceeding as it does from a radical vice of nature, it will probably be repeated. Faculty at 3. Subject of tutors. Nominated Fisk (with wry faces, but unanimously), Dwight with real alacrity. Hurlbut talked of, but we concluded to go no farther. I feel afraid of Fisk's malaprops, but if the rest of the Tutorial Board are good, I think we can carry him through. In the evening, looking at Buttmann. Etymology little changed. Syntax rewritten.

Thursday, July 10. Occupied most of the afternoon in writing my notice of Robinson's Buttmann.

With Anna in the evening. Macy came in and sat for a while, and then Henry till nearly 10. Extended my stay by special dispensation, or rather special command, to 10½.

Friday, July 11. Had a call from General Brandon of Mississippi, who brought a letter from my old pupil Brickell, now married and settled. General Brandon brings a son of his, with a young man named Sims, to enter Sophomore. Wanted to put them under my guardianship, but I declined the responsibility and spoke of Mr. Thacher. He had thought of him, but feared that he might be a relation of Judge Thacher of Mississippi, who is of northern origin, and a political and as I gathered a personal enemy of General Brandon's. I told him that there was no close connection, I believed, between our Professor and the Boston people. I gave him accordingly a note to Mr. Thacher, and let him go. He wants to put his boys with Dudley in Northampton until next Commencement or beginning of next term, but I told him that Dudley had resolved, as I understood, to admit into his school no more pupils of more than fourteen years. This determination was occasioned by the flare-up of July 4th, which had really almost disorganized the school. Wade was one of the rioters, and obliged to flee. General Brandon saw him in New York. He had given up all idea of College and was going South. Good.

At 4½ finished up the Buttmann, and concluded, as the weather seemed more promising than threatening, to take our trip to Woodbridge. Arranged to start at 6. Mr. Thacher gave me some letters for Miss Livia Day. At 5 called on Mr. Herrick. Found Dr. D. F. Bacon. Heard a good deal of spirited conversation—some account of the "Bacon hitch," ill-fitting boots, mortality of infants, etc. Mr. White came in, Mr. Macy, Mr. Francis Bradley, and I left at 5½. At 6 drove up to 30 Elm Street and started. We went slowly, lost our way twice but soon recovered it, and at sunset were passing the Woodbridge Church, when the horse appeared to act strangely and was disposed to run. He was, however, reined in without much trouble, and it appeared that one shaft was disengaged from the axle, the bolt having come out. Anna walked on toward the place of our destination, which was a quarter of a mile beyond. I staid until a good-natured man from the vicinity, whose wife was if anything more good-natured still, had replaced our iron bolt with a walnut rake tooth, which he tied as well as he could and pronounced safe for New Haven. Declined pay. Drove on to Mr. Hotchkiss's, found Anna and Miss Day just ready to come and look after me. It was then a little after 8. The people had gone to bed; were roused by Anna much to their surprise. They urged us to stay overnight, but we thought it best to return, and accordingly drove back slowly and cautiously. (6 cents toll.) (Borrowed .13. Case of conscience on a half cent.) Anna walked down the hill at Westville. Enjoyed the beautiful moonlight and other things. Reached home just before 10. Mr. Benton, of whom I engaged the carriage, had gone to bed. Spent an hour with Henry and Camp. Then home and abed.

It was a happy thing for us that our accident did not occur as we were going downhill: it might otherwise have been dangerous. Anna was perfectly collected, not in the least terrified.

Saturday, July 12. With Anna from 9 to 12. She complained of lassitude. Somewhat excited perhaps by the occurrences of last night. Read a few things from Goethe's minor poems. Mary was with us the last hour or more.

Looked at *Literary World* in College Library. In afternoon, long talk with Hughes, Senior, who brought in his autograph book and my *Antigone*. The latter I had missed and given up for lost. It was borrowed by Lyman, who, like a good-for-nothing careless scamp as he is, forgot to bring it back. Read Shakespeare, *Two Gentlemen of Verona*. Disagreeable in plot, but redeemed by many beauties. In evening went to see Powers' "Greek Slave," now on exhibition (25 cents) at Tyler Hall, and sat for half an hour, much struck with its calm and passionless appearance. Is it resignation or despondency? The scorn that some have spoken of is certainly a mere imagination. Shall go again.

Found at my room some clothes from Knevals, coat, vest, and pants, with socks, 12 pairs. My outfit for the times that are to be. Do not get much, because I have other tastes so soon to consult. Occupied somewhat with rearrangements of my stock.

Sunday, July 13. Fitch in forenoon and afternoon. First on Adam, much too favorable to his character; did not recognize the state of unstable equilibrium in morals. Second on practical atheism, completely spoiled by a number of practical inferences absurdly tacked to the end of it. Bible lesson, 5 to 6—half a dozen present. Parables connected with that of wheat and tares. Evening with Anna. Exposition of Ecclesiastes, chapter 5. Some complaint of illness. Mary thought of taking her to Woodbridge and keeping her a week away from New Haven and me, drinking milk and going to bed at 8 o'clock. Back at 10. Another delightful day. Lost the eclipse last night (from 1 to 4).

Monday, July 14. Talk with Hyde about Greek paper for tomorrow's examination on reading of Sophomore year. I had selected the passages and noted down the leading points. Gave him my brief to draw up the paper. He also attends to the printing, so that I shall be free tomorrow morning. Commenced a letter to Mary and wrote a page and a half. Called on Professor Thacher to give him portions of Herodotus, cut out of my Tauchnitz Edition, for the Juniors in their examination. He told me that his people at Woodbridge were to leave on Wednesday morning. Of course Anna will not think of going there.

Dressed and went late to supper, earlier than Dwight and Camp, who were too tardy for the raspberries. Of course I exulted over their destitution. Gave 50 cents to our waiter, a very good boy. At 7½ to Twinings'. I had been invited to spend the evening at Mrs. Macy's. Anna told me I must be sociable, which I pronounced an impossibility. We were to start at 8 o'clock, but overstaid our time. Contrived a conversation on the subject, which failed for want of opportunity. Our company consisted of the Magills, the Duttons, Miss Copp, and a Miss Tomlinson. Sociability very indifferent. Chiefly on Congregational order and the propriety of Christian dancing.

Back by full moonlight at 10½. Sat with Anna and Mary till nearly 11. Came home, washed, read newspaper, tried to charm away the evil spirit which had caught me and filled my soul with a complete despair. At last took up the Nala, and soon wearied myself, so that going to bed at 12½ I sank into deep sleep.

Mr. Olmsted called on me in the forenoon and said that news had arrived in some way, he did not really know what, from Mr. Stanley in Smyrna. He had got there much reduced in strength, so that he gave up the idea of visiting Paris and London and was to come direct to America: but so low was he as to give great reason for the fear that he would not live to reach this country.

Tuesday, July 15. Hurried through my recitation and went over at 6½ to relieve Mr. Hyde in the printing office. Found him a little belated from the tardiness of a hand. Corrected proofs with diligence, rendered the text immaculate, except a period in one place for a note of interrogation. Hyde went to breakfast at 7 and in 25 minutes came back to let me off, just as the paper was going to press. Henry sat with Hyde, Mr. Olmsted with Tutor Blodget, so that I was not called upon. The paper was regarded, not perhaps without reason, as long and hard.

Returning to my room at 8, I marked my shirts and stockings, the last a somewhat difficult job. At 9½ heard a knock and huddled my things out of the way (they were lying on the floor in bright sunlight). Mr. Woolsey came in to ask about beginning of examination. A minute after leaving he knocked again, entered. "I bring you a stranger," said he, and Professor Stanley, with oriental beard but otherwise himself, followed him into the room. Mr. Stanley *was* sick at Smyrna, worse than he has been any time since leaving us, but had grown better as he journeyed westward through Constantinople, Trieste, and by railroad through Germany to Paris, when he had become quite strong again. Stopped there a few days, and then a few at London—visited the Great Exhibition—and took the *Franklin* at Cowes. Had an easy passage. Will not come into College this term. Said nothing about the next. Took him to Mr. Herrick at 10 and sat there with him for about half an hour. Saw him again from 12 to 12½. He went then to call on Mr. Olmsted, who could scarcely believe the evidence of his eyes. He puts up at the New Haven Hotel, which he likes well. Goes to Hartford this afternoon.

Some trouble in my recitation at 11 on account of the gathering and noise of Sophomores under my window.

Finished letter to Mary in the afternoon—very meagre—and took it to the office. Obliged to wait some time for lack of a stamp. Paid 3 cents. Could not recollect number of our new box. Going back, spent half an hour in looking at the "Greek Slave." It grows constantly more and more beautiful, and the expression of sorrow becomes clearer and more unmistakable.

Evening with Anna. Call from Mr. Camp, who sat an hour. We went away together at 10.

Wednesday, July 16. Our morning extended from 9 till nearly 1. Mary refused to come and see us. The conversations of the last two evenings have been less than satisfactory; nothing very bad, but a little flighty or so. The objection could not be precisely stated, but the impression left was an unpleasant one. I know the difficulty well enough, though I would not mention it and hardly dare confess it even to myself: the devouring melancholy which has seized me in its clutches. Nearly two hours were necessary to make up for this désagrément, and then nearly two hours more passed in very cosy consultation on future plans and prospects.

Faculty from 3 to 5½. Subject of Townsend's Building reconsidered. Concluded that if Mr. Townsend will separate four rooms in front by an effectual partition, the remaining rooms under Mrs. Davies' charge may be occupied by students, provided that they are in fact efficiently controlled.

King up again for boarding at New Haven Hotel—to be warned. Burr, Sophomore, for bringing in a written slip of paper to the examination on Sophomore Latin. Detected by Henry and confessed. Examination null, and appropriation cut down from 11 to 6.

Thursday, July 17. After my recitation, went over to printing office, read proof of Sophomore mathematics paper, and relieved Hodges until 7.20^m. We get on finely with our figures engraved on wood. Sat with Blodget in Geological Lecture Room. No attempt apparently to evade our rules. Very few went out before I did, five minutes before 11. The paper, I understand, was regarded as difficult. The day is hot and sultry. It is fortunate that we are so near the end. Taylor, Sophomore, is thought to be dangerously ill with dysentery.

After recitation, D. S. Bigelow came in with a young man from Amherst, who wanted an examination for the Senior class. He is from Maine, cannot come to Commencement without great expense and inconvenience, and wishes to know his chance before the beginning of another term. I could not see, however, that there existed anything like urgent necessity in the case, and I therefore declined, quite as much for the sake of others as for my own.

Received a letter from George. Has some thought of staying away from the wedding. Do not wonder; he would have little time for quiet conference with me; surrounded mostly by strangers, he could scarcely entertain himself in a satisfactory way. Of course, however, I shall urge him to come on. The change of scene may be a benefit, for he is somewhat ill and very blue.

Down town at 5. Looked again at "Greek Slave" for half an hour, with increasing admiration but with the feeling that the artist's great design was little more than the production of a beautiful form and figure.

At Twinings' at 7½. Found Mary. Anna was out, but came in at 8 o'clock. Saw a letter from Mr. Charles Gould at New York, who will attend to the cards. Pretty much agreed upon the earlier day. Alone with Anna most of the time from 9 to 10.

Friday, July 18. Talk with Newton in the morning. He goes on still with his Duhamel. Spent several hours in looking over papers of Freshman Greek. Hyde had given me a list of 38 men whose standing is low, and I nearly finished them up. Some have done much better than I expected. No evidence of ponying. Gray called again, said he was already examined in Latin throughout by Mr. Kingsley and Mr. Thacher, and by Mr. Olmsted in natural philosophy and astronomy. Was willing to enter Junior; wanted the remainder of his examination. I said I could not examine but would try him a few minutes. He read a little in the *Iliad* and the *Odyssey* —got on pretty fairly. I told him I thought there was scarcely a doubt he could enter Junior if not Senior at the beginning of next term. And with that he left.

Article on Woman's Rights in the *Tribune* extracted from *Westminster Review*. Out and out in its radicalism; the strict politico-economical view of the subject, with rigorous exclusion of sentiment. Quite a marked and remarkable affair.

With Anna in the evening. Mary was out and we had our time pretty much to ourselves. Mary, it appears, considers me too much on good behavior in her presence, and thought last night, for instance, that my conversation was excessively stiff and just like a call upon indifferent persons. There may be something in this. It is well, no doubt, in general to keep our feelings in the background, but if they are likely to give pleasure, why not bring them forward occasionally? We may be selfish in our courtship by refusing all exhibition of it to our friends. It is natural that Mary should watch our progress with peculiar interest, as it affects a sister long and deeply loved, and has a direct bearing on her own daily household life. Would it not be kind and friendly to take her now and then behind the scenes, and give her some flighty and imperfect glimpse into our privacy? I must think of it.

Staid some fifteen minutes at the outside door till Mary came in from the Magills, and then some fifteen more with her.

Saturday, July 19. With Anna from 9 to 12¼, when I was required to leave. Endeavored to read a little in DeQuincey's *Biographical Essays*. Heard some new "experiences" from a book which

I had considered as nearly exhausted, one of them quite romantic in its character. Finished up the 38 Sophomores whose names were given and made report to Hyde.

Haldimand called in the afternoon and read me his oration on Americans the keepers of their own liberties. Mr. Larned had objected to some passages in which he referred contemptuously to the opposers of the Fugitive-Slave Bill, and the advocates of higher law. Mr. Larned's exceptions appeared to me perfectly reasonable. It looks as if Haldimand had a mind to make capital out of union and safety sentiment. His piece was splurgy, and ill hung. Tried to see Mr. Larned after tea to talk about it, but in vain. A half hour in Henry's room, after which I sallied out, defying perspiration, to call on Miss Larned, but she was not at home. Stopping on the way back found MacWhorter and J. G. E. Larned. The latter went soon, but I remained with Mac for more than an hour, in nimble talk. Came away at last from fear of the threatening storm. Lighted home by brilliant flashes of lightning. The rain began to fall some five minutes after I reached my room. One clap of thunder very loud and startling. Our summer is an electric one, much like that of 1845.

The Sophomores finished their examination this morning. Some of them, coming out of the Lyceum, flung their inkstands up against the building and left their mark upon its walls and floors. The class went out in the afternoon in a procession of carriages and with a band of music to East Rock, where they had a sort of picnic affair. Returned in the evening at 7 o'clock with loud vociferation.

Miss Adams of Keene, New Hampshire, who has been for several days sick at Mr. Blake's, died last evening at midnight. The disease, dropsy of the brain. She was a young woman of decided piety, though not a member of the Church.

Sunday, July 20. Dr. Fitch as usual. Studied my last Bible lesson for the term, the demoniacs of Gadara, and expounded it to *three* —Bristol, Hubbell, and Miller. Perhaps the first instance in College of a Bible class continued to the end of a year. I have not failed in a single instance since I commenced it last fall. My great object was to learn something about the word of God, and this I knew could be attained if I had to speak to empty benches. Grant, O Lord, that through thy grace and spirit the fruit of all this study may appear in heart and life.

Examined also Ecclesiastes, chapter 6, and commented in the evening. Read an article in *North British Review* on autobiography of Reverend William Walford. Familiar chat till 11, following up the idea of a desirable badness.

Monday, July 21. Hearing divisions round for the last time, and giving notices for the examination.

After tea, "Greek Slave" shut up. Pease's open. Went with Professor Larned to the President's at 7½. Assembled by 8. Subject opened: expediency of an immediate effort to increase the general funds of the College. Necessity of increase undoubted. Present salaries inadequate. Mr. Kingsley's experience. Mr. Porter's still more decisive, and somewhat alarming to an expectant householder. Mr. Kingsley has, during the forty years since his marriage, expended annually for living alone some 500 dollars more than his salary. Mr. Porter with all economy has exceeded his by $200 or $300, and has been obliged to use nearly half his available strength in eking out the deficiency. Apart from this, would have been worth twice as much to the College.

Difficulties in the way: College reputed to be rich; has been begging more or less for a year or two; new hall; Dana's professorship. Chief difficulty want of a suitable agent. Reverend Theophilus Smith of College Corporation excellent, but would he undertake it? Mr. Daniel Butler, class of 1835.

Advantages: General prosperity of the country; number and wealth of our graduates; etc. etc.

General and pretty clear conclusion to go on if a good agent can be found. Perhaps in first instance address a few wealthy men. Perhaps enlist the sympathy and help of some active business men in New York and elsewhere.

Mr. Olmsted urged the pressing necessity of an astronomical observatory. But the President said, "We must rise from our extreme poverty, before we can indulge in luxuries." Thought an observatory was little needed for the immediate object of the College, instruction—a point on which all but Mr. Olmsted appeared to agree with him. As we were returning, Mr. Olmsted remarked how much more had been given for chemistry than for philosophy. $500 recently allowed Mr. Silliman for buying apparatus, while his own demand for $500 to increase the apparatus of his department was refused. "Such," he said, "was the difference between one man and another."

Away at 9½. Stopt at Twinings' and staid till 11 with Anna and Mary, doing my devoir in the way of badness and of foolishness, as well as I was able.

Tuesday, July 22. Morning recitation for the last time this term. Commenced examination, with sessions at 11 and 4; went twice round with questions, first on Roman then on Grecian history.

Evening, with Anna, till 10½.

Wednesday, July 23. Sessions of examination at 8 and 11. None in the afternoon, as we put the optionals then. In forenoon from 10 to 11, read Merivale, *History of Romans*. It has been purchased for book club, and not being put into immediate circulation, was lent me last night by Anna. It is handsomely written, full of interest, and, though it does not inspire such confidence as the writings of Niebuhr and Arnold, full of instruction.

Drest at 3 and went to Twinings', intending to leave again at 5½ that she might go then to Miss Hillhouse's and perhaps spend the evening there. But the day was hot and she had a headache. So I staid to tea, and after tea till 10 o'clock, cutting the Connecticut Academy and Mrs. Professor Norton's party, to both of which I had invitations. In afternoon, read Sydney Smith's lectures on "Moral Philosophy," "Habit," and "Humor." In evening, the commonplaces of our situation.

Friday, July 25. Last session of examination from 8 to 9½. From 10 to 11, at Kinne's with Olmsted and Porter, reviewing examination. Nine or ten more or less conditioned. Faculty at 11. Passing on examination. Freshmen, as usual, a good deal winged. Some discussion. Put over to 3 P.M. Meeting of Professors to consider Professor Norton's application to our Honorable Corporation for degrees in his department (Philosophy and Arts)—likewise adjourned to afternoon. At 3, sustained the instructors of the Freshman class on nearly every point. Made arrangements for the work of Monday and Tuesday, to be done in the Geological Lecture Room; the gallery of the Chapel is now cumbered with the organ. Mr. Kingsley has a general superintendence, Mr. Thacher associated with him in making dispositions. Porter as usual took geography. Thacher suggested English grammar, as an addition, but Porter refused, whereupon Thacher chose it himself, for fear somebody else should take it as a mere get off. Thacher examines also in Sallust, and does not intend, I presume, to trouble himself much about English grammar.

Professors on degrees in fourth department. Mostly favorable; President rather adverse. Concurred in recommending to Corporation the appointment of a committee to examine the subject.

Petitioned increase of tutors' salaries. Occasioned something of an ebullition on the part of Mr. Kingsley, who styled it an impudent proceeding. Said the old tutors had board in hall as pay for taking care of the hall, so that, ceasing work, pay might fairly cease, and instead of 420 dollars plus board, there was no claim beyond the $420. The general feeling seemed to be that an increase of tutors' salaries could not be made without an increase in the permanent funds of the College, and that for the present, the professors' salaries are the most defective. It is less hard to live decently and lay up money for a tutor than for a married professor, and as Mr. Olmsted observed, turning towards me, "it is quite impossible to keep the professors from marrying." Has Mr. Olmsted really done all he could to prevent such a catastrophe?

Some directions to Henry about new schemes for the examinations—old ones exhausted, as it seems.

Attended Chapel, the last evening exercise of the term. Wilcox on the organ. Played without much reference to the singing. I am afraid that our music will be injured rather than improved by the innovation.

Exhibition of organ in the evening, attended by our *young* people. The instrument is said to be a good one. Whitmore prefers it to his in the North Church. Mr. Hook of Boston is the best organ maker in the country, and seems to have regarded this as a sort of advertisement or specimen, which he wished to make as good as he could afford to.

Alone with Anna. She complains of headaches, the result of overexcitement. Our conversation, however, was not particularly exciting: mostly on family statistics, to give me a clearer idea of the cousins to come. At her request, prayed with her before leaving; the first time, not by many, I hope, the last. Mary went to New York at 1.

Saturday, July 26. Still hot and sultry. With Anna from 9 to 12. Glad to be treated as one of the family, admitted to the ease and familiarity of a less elaborate costume. Headache still, which however did not prevent the busy motion of the needle. Carried over Merivale, but read nothing. Talk on financial matters—calculation for next year.

At breakfast saw Mr. Whitney, Senior, of Northampton, and talked with him for half an hour. He inquired after his son Edward, urged Mr. Camp in William's name to go this fall to Germany, and sought to ascertain the residence of Miss Julia Peck, the betrothed of Reverend Mr. Marsh, Missionary to Mosul. He left at 2 P.M. on his return.

At Henry's room from 2 to 3. Talk with Mr. Thacher on Mygatt's conditions. We do not agree exactly on this subject of examinations. Went over with Henry to printing office to look at new schemes; directed further alterations. Long talk with Tutor Dwight on examinations. He feels aggrieved with Mr. Thacher, who he thinks forbore to attack the discipline of the Freshman class while I was responsible for it, but came down on the three tutors, though they were only carrying out the same system. Of course he is wholly wrong in this idea. He was a little vexed too with Mr. Backus, who opposed before the Faculty the recommendations of the other instructors.

After supper, drest, and went up at 7½, according to previous arrangement, to Miss Hillhouse's. Stopt by the way to order carriage. Never before within the gates of this Hillhouse manor, a beautiful place. Found, beside Anna, Mr. Mayor Skinner and Mrs. Professor Porter, who soon left. Brinsmade (Senior) came in for his last Saturday evening; is thought to have more than a temporary connection with the house. Pleasant chat till 10, when the carriage came, a half hour too late. Staid with Anna till 11, which I ought perhaps to have forborne as she is still troubled with the headache.

Sunday, July 27. A perspiring morning. Attended at Centre Church and sat with our folks. Sermon by Dr. Bushnell, mystical, on participation in the divine nature. I believe in mysticism, a little of it, enough to constitute an acknowledgment of ignorance and wonder. But to dwell upon, and draw it out and make it into a system, is I think injurious to the mind. Staid away from dinner to avoid the heat. Change of wind in the afternoon, a fresh breeze from the west. Felt it too strongly in my place (the Tutor's box) in Chapel, but soon resigned my seat to Mayor Skinner. The service had just commenced when it grew dark in the room and a driving rain began to dash in at the open doors and windows.

It was a brief flurry, which soon gave place to clearer and cooler weather. Our expected new baccalaureate turned out to be an old one, elegantly written, but shockingly delivered. It had been expected that Dr. Bushnell would preach in the evening, but it proved otherwise and I spent the time with Anna.

Monday, July 28. First day of examination, overcast and cool. The Geological Chamber works finely; never knew an examination conducted with so much celerity and smoothness.

Three men from Russell's were rejected. Waring, in toto, a repetition of last year. Duncan and Gregory accepted in part.

Evening with Anna till 11 o'clock. Returned to room and read in Merivale till 12½. Near midnight heard a crash of broken windows, apparently in Analytical Laboratory, really in Divinity College—room of Willard, opposite to Camp. It was done no doubt by Russell's boys, who would have served Camp in the same way if they had not seen a light in his room. There were a number who had not read the *Anabasis* and were strongly urged by Camp and Russell, both, not to present themselves. Several complied, but the three who were just mentioned preferred to try their chance. They seem to have attributed their failure to the malign influence of their instructors. Camp perhaps did not take in all respects the most prudent course.

Dr. Bushnell delivered an address on sacred music in the evening at College Chapel, which of course I lost. Said by those who heard it to have been a great affair.

Tuesday, July 29. Examination finished. 57 Freshmen on our list, 5 of them from class above. 9 applicants rejected. Two applicants for Junior, neither admitted. Three for Sophomore, only one got in.

Conversation with Emerson of Beloit, full of interest and enthusiasm about his College. He inquired concerning a tutor for them in place of Joseph Hurlbut, also about William Whitney, his prospects, and his aptitudes for the wants of Beloit College. In regard to the latter point I could not give him a great deal of encouragement.

Drew my salary for the term, $246.12, of which I deposited $110, making a sum of $250 now on deposit in the Treasurer's office. I was in hopes that I might keep this unbroken to the time of my return from the wedding tour, but I fear that I shall not be able to do so.

At 6½, went by invitation to take tea at Mr. Dutton's. Present, Mr. Blanchard of Lowell with wife and daughter, Mr. Havens of Amherst, Mr. George Day, and two or three more. Miss Twining came in, a few minutes after I did. Nearly all went at 7½ to hear Dr. Atwater's Concio ad Clerum. Anna and I remained till after 8 in pleasant conversation with Mrs. Dutton. Was reminded that I had cut Mrs. Apthorpe's party. Returning to our house, saw a funny letter of Lieutenant Smith's to Anna, recommending some friends of his. Harriet and Mary Brayton came in at 10½ from a small party at Mr. Henry White's. I sat till 11, and parted with prayer, as for several evenings past. Read till 12.

Mr. Squier here from Geneva.

Wednesday, July 30. George Field back from Amherst. Saw Dana and Teele. Attended ΦΒΚ. A good deal of sparring about orator for next time. Imbroglio occasioned by the stand taken last year at the instance of Judge Cone in regard to William H. Seward. Acknowledged error, agreed to ignore politics, and elected Daniel Webster as orator, William H. Seward as substitute. Could not introduce Porter's name as honorary member for want of time, taken up in previous discussions. Talk with Learned, salutatorian of 1841, who thinks we snub the students. Cut the Alumni. Examined a Freshman. Went down town and cashed my check, $136.12. Returning, paid Mrs. Hemingway $1.25 for nightshirts. Caught the tail of the Alumni meeting. Eldridge. Bayne of 1847. Jack Robinson in his peculiar vein. Received a note from Anna informing me that Miss Cleveland of Middlebury was at Tontine and desirous to see me. Went down at 1, and after some waiting got a seat. Had a talk of half an hour with Miss Cleveland. She is attended by her brother Mr. George Cleveland. Had called at Twinings' to find Anna, but without success. Had there learned something of our affairs, and begged that word of her arrival might be sent to me. She told me of her father's death by paralysis in February, which I had not before heard of. She had just been at Boston to see Cleveland Keith embarked on a mission to China. Reuel Keith still at Washington. Cleveland Hicks at Hartford, a machinist. It was extremely pleasant to see her again.

Up at 2½. Spent 3 hours in examination, in Philosophical Apparatus Room. A wretched lot of fellows, mostly from East Hampton and Monson, nine in all, of whom we rejected four. Dwight,

Backus, Hodges, and Henry assisting. One man for Sophomore, likely to get in. Son of Daniel Lord, Esq.

Evening, to Twinings'. Found Mr. Camp. Professor William Twining of Indiana came in at 8, followed close by Mary. They had come in the cars together from New York without knowing it. Mr. Magill came in at 10½ and gave some account of the ΦBK oration by Mr. Lord and poem by Mr. Street.

Thursday, July 31. Cool and cloudy. Went down to church in procession at 8½, sat with Emerson, heard the opening exercises —very fair. Off at 9½. To Pease's. Settled for *Foreign Reviews,* $8.00. To Twinings'. Found Miss Thacher. Anna came in at 10, and we sat down to direct the cards of invitation. Raised an immense pile by 12, when we broke off. At 1 returned to room, and read Merivale till 1½. To Tontine for dinner. Tables filled. Mrs. Larned soon came out and proffered me her place. Waiters very scarce. Got a piece of apple pie, which with nuts and raisins constituted my whole dinner. Up to Henry's. Found Reverend Mr. Squier, who put into my hands an article of his on regeneration, intended for the *New Englander,* with directions to submit the same to editors. Settled with Camp by paying him one dollar, with Henry by receiving nine. I had lent him $11, but there was a dollar for half rent of Box 305 in post office for a year from July 1st, 1851, .50 for postage stamps, and .50 for money lent.

At 2½ went with procession to church, marching in company with Professor Coffin from Pennsylvania, but on arriving at church I dodged and returned to my room. Wrote a letter to George, urging him to come on to the wedding, telling him, however, to do as he liked about it. Letter received from Foster, inviting us to Schenectady. At tea, saw Skinner—same condition as at last report. At 7 had a call from William Richards. He will remain still at Cincinnati, though his success there has not been brilliant. He left at 8, and I went to Twinings', cutting the President's levee. Call from Mr. Lyman and his classmate Mr. Coe, formerly tutor.

AUGUST, 1851

Friday, August 1. Day after the fair. Up at 5. Morning quite chilly. Started fire, heated water, and bathed my feet to soak out a cold in the lungs which has been hanging about me for a day or two, making me intolerably crusty and morose.

Settled bill at Tontine for July, $15.50; obtained receipt in full. Gave Mr. Squier's article to Professor Larned. Constant succession of calls through the forenoon. From Mr. Franklin, Washington, D.C.; will place his son with Mr. Timothy Dwight. From Charley Stone of my class; just left Trenton, New Jersey; some thought of entering here in analytical department. From Mr. Russell of Gainesville, Alabama; will continue his son a year longer in College; talked very sensibly about slavery. From L. S. Wilcox, class of 1850, consulting me on choice of a profession, theology or medicine; advised the latter. From Elderkin to inquire about his standing through the term. From Hurlbutt, who told me my salary had been raised to $1140. From Emerson, who read me a paper by his brother Samuel, on a new mode of defining and treating positive and negative quantities. The paper showed ingenuity but was wholly wanting in clearness and development. Subject, the old difficulty about symbolical notation and methods of operation carried beyond their primitive intention. Advised that he should read Peacock's *Algebra* and Report to British Association, and that if he wrote he should do it very fully and clearly. Emerson has persuaded Potwin to go with him as tutor.

Had a fine long letter from Whitney, dated at Tübingen, June 30.

Saturday, August 2. Saw Thacher and Kingsley. The former says that Salisbury was with great reluctance induced to withdraw for the present the resignation which he had tendered to the President. He is morbidly modest and this plays the mischief with him. Wrote to Dr. Owen a letter of acknowledgment for his *Iliad*, which came to hand yesterday afternoon, a handsome-looking book. Gave 10 cents to a beggar. Over to Twinings' at 10½ to mark handkerchiefs. Anna did not come in till 11. Meantime read Dr. Bacon's account of his capture by the thievish and cowardly Kurds, very well written. Oh that he might have such an adventure to describe every week—what gain to the readers of the *Independent!* Did the business for which I came, but badly; the size was poor and the ink spread.

At dinner, introduced to Dr. Guentz, a German scholar, pupil of Zumpt and Hermann, who left his country 12 years ago, and has for three years been teaching an academy in Louisville, Kentucky. His school is firmly established: number of pupils limited

and every place engaged for three years to come. He showed me
a complimentary letter of Henry Clay, aus eigener Hands[chrift].
A pupil of his, Nicholas by name, is to offer himself for admission
here next term, to the Junior class. Dr. Guentz talked very well,
sensibly, though somewhat prosily. He sat for an hour in my room
until 3, when I directed him to Professor Kingsley's. He was to
start at 6 for Boston, going to see Professor Felton, with whom he
is acquainted. Proposed a correspondence with me, which I could
not well refuse.

Over to Twinings' to write notes of invitation for our wedding
guests. Did not begin till 4. Worked steadily till 6, when we finished
up and I left, opening the door to Mrs. Mumford as I passed out.
Found men locking up the buildings. Obtained a key to my entry
from Mr. Andrews, the same key which I had last vacation. Returning from supper, applied the key, but in vain—it would not
work. After some hunting found Dickerman, who told me a new
key had been fitted to the lock today—wards possibly a little
changed. Gave me his key, with which I was successful in effecting
an entrance.

At 8½ went to Twinings'. Found the girls. Rest all out. Sat
reading in silence till after 9, when I went over to Henry's. He
and Camp and Field had gone out on a drive in the afternoon to
Double Beach—fine time—plenty of oysters, etc.

Returned to room, read Merivale, enjoyed the dumps, and went
to bed at 11.

Sunday, August 3. A beautiful day. In forenoon went to Howe
Street Church. Mr. Love preached on the Christians of the first
two centuries, their belief and practice. Subject carried through
the day, a somewhat rambling sermon, easily made no doubt, as
sermons in vacation should be.

In the afternoon at Trinity. Two young men, both unknown to
me; one read service, the other preached. Sermon on the study of
the Scriptures. George Bushnell preached, I understand, at the
Centre, on hypocrisy.

Staid away from dinner, and did not get down to supper till
Camp and Dwight were through. With Anna in the evening, till 9,
when the rest came in. Left at 10.

Monday, August 4. A day of hard work. Read examination
papers all the forenoon and part of the afternoon, finished them

up. Called at Tuttle's and ordered pair of slips, to be done by the 13th. Wrote a letter to Mary, urging her to come, whether George does or not.

Symptoms of colic. Could only munch part of a biscuit for supper. Much ado to get through the evening at Twinings'. Henry came in at 8½, and I left with him at 10¼ in a good deal of pain. Took 2 Dovers, and became easy about 12½.

Bill at Tuttle's, including the slips, $4.50.

Tuesday, August 5. Moody and ferocious all day, effect of last night's drugging. Made out averages for second and first divisions of the late Junior class.

Wrote letter of invitation to Noyes at Brooklyn. Obtained Knevals' bill—present amount, $122.75. I am afraid that my first instalment of salary will be exhausted as soon as it comes, and that I shall be left without means to meet the expenses of a second term.

After dinner, bought *Wells' Lawyer,* 50 cents. Paid Henry for this year's *Bibliotheca Sacra,* $4.00, including 75 cents for lost January number replaced, and $1.00 for Bohn's Cary's Herodotus.

Copied out of diary the reports of meetings of Philological Society for 1850 and 1851. Fortunately there have been but nine meetings in that time, and my reports are exceedingly succinct and meagre, so the job was not a very long one.

A beautiful moonlight evening or what promised to be such, but soon grew overcast and hazy. At Twinings' did up residual invitations. The pack are to be issued tomorrow. As I came away at 10½ there was a cry of *fire* and a bright glow in the northeast, but I did not go to seek it.

Marriage of Mr. Austin and Miss Hughes this evening. The bridegroom, it is said, occasioned some alarm by decamping yesterday morning, bag and baggage, to parts unknown. He had conceived some offence, people say, but nobody knows. It was feared he would not return. He got back, however, today at 6 P.M., and "all went merry etc." A large party invited at 9. Great smash, some dancing. Broke up at 12. Another party for them tonight at the Bishops'.

Wednesday, August 6. Up at 6 after good night's rest. With Anna from 9 to 12. Mr. Thacher came in a little after 11 to hand me President Day's demonstration of binomial theorem for fractional and negative exponents. Talked of going to Woodbridge with his family tomorrow, and of taking Anna with them. I think it might be good for her to go. The self-torment of the wedding will make her sick.

At my room looked over the demonstration and corrected one or two little slips. Henry and Camp at work upholstering their old lounge, too busy to go for newspaper. Spent afternoon in finishing Merivale and looking at Niebuhr on same period. Evening (fine moonlight) with Anna. Henry came in at 8½. Brought letter from Mary, uncertain about coming to New Haven.

Henry left a quarter before ten, and I with him. Too perturbed for study. "Brooded silent" for an hour, and then to bed.

Anna has received a pretty present of silver from Madame Salisbury and Mrs. Woolsey. They are very friendly, and I rejoice in the feeling. But there is, perhaps, something a little humiliating in the idea of receiving presents which you are not able to return. I take them with a certain reluctance.

Thursday, August 7. Finished Niebuhr on age of Julius Caesar. Returned to President Day his MS on binomial theorem. With Anna from 10 to 12 and in evening from 8 to 10. Read Goethe in the morning. At night talked on theology with Professor William Twining.

Friday, August 8. Reviewing Merivale, with reference to Arnold. With Anna from 10 to 12, reading *Anne of Geierstein;* had occasion to notice the extreme weakness of my nerves—on some passages could scarcely command my voice. The first two chapters of that novel are unsurpassed by anything Scott ever wrote.

With Anna again in the evening. 8 to 9, in the garden. Mosquito bitten; washed my hands with salt and water. 9 to 10, with Mr. and Mrs. Magill in the house. The rest of the people gone aboating. Anna had thought of it, but given up the plan. Had proposed a ride to the lighthouse, but gave up this too, as I thought, with some concealed reluctance. The boaters came in at 10. Mr. Magill much discontented, and the rest in consequence rather uncomfortable.

Mr. William Twining took me aside and suggested the use of a will under my circumstances. I thanked him for his friendly advice, which was given with perfect delicacy. Said that I had the subject already in mind and should certainly attend to it.

Saturday, August 9. Drew up a will, bequeathing my scientific books to Henry, and all the rest of my property to Anna, and appointing Anna and Henry as my executors. Had intended to do it on Thursday next, when I should be able to describe Anna as my wife, but concluded that I might as well do it up now and have it out of the way. Took it to Mr. Olmsted for his signature, but he told me the three witnesses must be present at once with the testator and that this fact should be stated on the face of the instrument. I made the addition required, called Camp and Henry to Mr. Olmsted's room, and procured thus the requisite attestation.

At 11 carried the will to Anna, who approved of it in all particulars and laid it up in a place of security. We talked over our pecuniary prospects for the year to come. I suggested the expediency of calling in the $800 or so which I have in the hands of Sidney Shepard, in order to pay for Mary's share of furniture, $400 or $350, and Anna's recent outlay, $300, thus discharging debts and starting fair upon our housekeeping. After some calculation, decided not to do so, for the present at least, but try to work along until the spring and then see what is best to be done. We expect to use up $100 in our approaching tour, and shall then have $250, now on deposit at the College Treasury, to commence the fall with. The estimated total expense of the household during the time preceding January 1, 1852, is $400, of which $50 (grocery bill) need not be paid until that time, leaving $350 to be met from time to time. This exceeds my $250 by $100, for which we shall have $40, which can be a little anticipated, from Kinsley's board, and shall be able to make up the remainder, no doubt, by the help of friends. If to the $400 for family expenses be added $150 for my tailor's and shoemaker's bills which will then be presented, there results $550 total outlay by January 1, 1852. On the other hand we have $250 now on deposit, $400 my salary at Christmas, $48 from board of sister's, deducting rent, $40 from board of Kinsley, and $66 then coming in from Anna's funds, making our income to that time $804, and leaving a balance of $250 to start again upon a new term. This will be augmented by sums from various sources during the term, so that we shall pretty certainly be able to weather it without much borrowing till we reach in April my second instalment of $400, and can then look around us and form new calculations for the future.

We estimated our total resources for the year, excluding income of my deposit with Sidney Shepard, at $1740, or deducting rent ($160), $1580, with which we ought to be able to support our family of 5 persons and pay off a portion of our debt—so, at least, it seems to us.

ANNE TWINING HADLEY

Henry came in at 1, with the numbers of the Daily Times (a new paper just started in New York by Raymond, late of the Courier and Enquirer — we propose to take it in place of the Tribune, which wearies us with Socialistic vaticinations, Spiritual rappings, and windy correspondents. The Tribune we have paid for up to Sept 30, and shall drop it then. The Times is to be Henry's paper. The young man was persuaded to sit down and take his dinner with us. Our party was a small one, Many being at Pres. Day's hard at work, and Kinsley engaged in watching and counteracting the Sironian facts.

At the Faculty meeting, it was resolved to have an extemporaneous Catalogue got up in a few days, for the use of the Faculty. The subject of Euclid burials was presented and discussed — but every man appeared to be inops Consilii — and we concluded at last to maintain the same attitude as last year.

In the evening attended the wedding of Thomas Beecher and Olivia Day. The Ceremony was performed by Henry Ward Beecher. and was short, simple, and what one might perhaps have doubted of, tasteful — every way a perfect Contrast to the performance of last evening. The company consisted of 80 or 90 people, and evidently enjoyed themselves as well as could be expected — Broke up at 10.

Thursday Sept. 25, The Societies have come up nearly even — 61 accessions to the Brothers and 58 to the Sironians — so say the papers. It is better for the Seniors than I had expected — better than they deserved, if all be true that I have heard about their statement yesterday. One of their orators, Thomas, was

Off at 1¼ to Tontine. Read paper at Henry's, and went over to North College, but on feeling in pocket for the key, it was gone. Searched Henry's room in vain, and then in vain at Twinings'. But going to Tontine with Camp, it appeared that I had dropped it at the dinner table.

At 3 went over to Twinings' to propose to Anna that excursion to the lighthouse which, according to the confessions of today, was a source of some vexation yesterday. But this time Anna had really no wish to go, and I for my part was willing enough to stay. The conclusion was a fortunate one, for we had a smart shower between 6 and 7. Went to Mr. Magill's at 5 to ask his agency in procuring the pre-matrimonial publication of tomorrow. Found that he is to preach at Fair Haven for Mr. Hart, who, as I understand, lost only last week a child of about a year old. Returning, stopt at Mr. Andrews' to drum up my boy, who had forgotten me again. The people were all gone, and I was obliged to call on Henry, after reading with him some two or three pages of the *Wilhelm Meister*.

Drest and went over to Twinings' at 8. Had a long talk with Mary. Anna had gone to see Lieutenant Smith's friends from Louisiana, Lieutenant and Mrs. Stevens and Miss Hébert. She returned before 9 with Mr. Magill, much pleased with the people, especially Mrs. Stevens. To surprise them she enclosed the cards for Wednesday night, directed them, and sent them over by Mr. Magill to New Haven Hotel.

Sunday, August 10. Up at 5, soaked my feet, drest, etc. After breakfast journalized. Forenoon at St. Paul's. Heard new rector, Mr. Littlejohn from Springfield. A good voice tolerably managed —very little else. It was the time specially appointed to commemorate the 150th anniversary of the Church of England Society for the Propagation of the Gospel in Foreign Parts. Heard some interesting facts.

Staid away from dinner, filed letters, looked over papers. At 3 went down to Centre Church. Heard the announcement of our intended marriage. Anna and Mary had dodged; gone to Chapel Street Church to hear Mr. William Twining. I wanted to season myself, and also form some estimate of my fortitude for Wednesday evening. Conclude it will be small. The nerves are imperious and uncontrollable. If I get off without a suffocating palpitation and an aguish tremor, I lose my guess, and shall be happy to do so.

Evening with Anna till 9, when Mary came in, and presently

William. Staid till nearly 11. A most delightful day, cool and sunny, followed by a beautiful full-moon evening.

Saw no meteors, though I dare say they are careering in full tilt and frequent numbers through the sky. Let Mr. Herrick look to them. Mr. Olmsted has made himself dyspeptic, studying on a paper, which he is preparing for the Savants of Albany, on the connexion between the zodiacal light and the August and November meteors. He enumerated the principal points to me; they are certainly curious and interesting.

Monday, August 11. Mr. Olmsted read me this morning the concluding part of his article on the zodiacal light, in which he connects it with the meteoric showers. Seems to fear that it may be received with contempt and ridicule, like his theory of the meteors. With Anna from 10 to 1, and afterwards in the evening.

Bought a pair of kids at Knevals', size 8½. Looked for a cap at Mansfield's. Mailed a letter which I had written to Cousin Lucia, enclosing cards.

Mr. Alexander Twining came in the afternoon; saw him in the evening. He has thought out some curious things about parallel lines; also something on light of telescopes, which he intends presenting next week at Albany.

Mr. J. G. E. Larned called on Anna (and me) to say that he goes to Thompson tomorrow, and cannot be present here on Wednesday evening.

Tuesday, August 12. Mrs. Levere's little boy came at 7 to hand me my bill. Had picked up a full-length likeness of me in the College yard, a pencil sketch, with cap, whiskers, crutch, long heel, etc., not badly done.

With Anna from 10 to 12½. Showed her George's letter received this morning, declining our invitation. Mary's excuse was accepted; George's regarded as rather inadmissible, with some little unmuth. Showed myself wilful on the subject of a white cravat. Why not get full rid of all this sangâsanga, especially on so miserable a subject? Could not be induced to stay to dinner. Received a ring for the wedding. At 2 paid Mansfield $1.25 for cap received this morning. At 4 went to Twinings'. Paid for ring, $4.00. Could not get off from supper though I tried hard—a family gathering. Some talk about poetry with Mr. Alexander Twining. Calls from Mrs. Macy, Professor H. N. Day, with whom I had some discussion on phonetics, and Mr. H. H. Hadley. Returned with the latter to my room at 10¼. Abed at 11. Warm south wind—promise of hot weather for tomorrow.

Symptoms of diarrhoea in the morning, which I met promptly by the usual remedy. Divided a Dover into three parts; took one at 10, the second at 4, the third at 11. Much pleased with the stupidity and the indifference which they wrought. The forenoon, which passed before the narcotic had much effect, was a rather fidgety time, but the afternoon was tranquil, and the evening positively delightful.

* * *

SEPTEMBER, 1851

Monday, September 22. An equinoctial day in the teeth of Professor Loomis.

Measured our seat in Chapel. Found it very nearly 13 feet; wants about an inch. The adjacent and the opposite seats, 12 feet, wanting near 2 inches.

Calls in the evening from Mr. Hyde and Mr. and Mrs. Este. Most of the time alone with Anna. Mary is at President Day's. Read the German *Frithjof* (Mohnike's translation), which I had purchased in New York. It seems to be well executed, and certainly makes an interesting poem.

Tuesday, September 23. With Mr. Stanley from 12 to 1. He complains of the cold raw weather as giving him a little cough. Is thinking of introducing Loomis' *Analytical Geometry and Calculus* as a textbook into College. In the afternoon examined a fellow from Knox College, Tennessee, McMuntry by name, for the Senior class. He couldn't tell how much he had read in Xenophon, Homer, or anything else, from which I drew, as I am apt to do, an unfavorable augury. And it appeared in fact that he could not read a single sentence in any of his Greek, a failure which he accounted for by saying that he had not looked at his Greek since June. He had expected, he said, a different mode of examination; thought I should give him a page or two, and let him look it out with lexicon and grammar. I marked him 0.75 as an act of grace and sent him away—nothing loth, for, besides his indifferent scholarship, he was particularly unsavory, and it was some time before the room returned to its normal odor.

Call in evening from Mr. Henry Barnes. He has been spending a year at Princeton. Complains of the stagnation of the place. He is going to stay awhile at the New York Seminary in order, as he says, "to gain the good will of the firm." I was obliged to excuse our people and myself too, to go to the wedding. The evening was stormy and we rode up. The party consisted perhaps of about 60 persons. The ceremony was performed about 8½ by the Reverend Mr. Merwin. He commenced and ended with long prayers of the most unpoetical and even laughable description. He prayed among other things that "the affections of the parties might be strengthened and *consolidated* into a *friendship* of the purest and most refining order." Perhaps he had not full self-command; it was his last daughter, and he must have felt the separation. The bridegroom (Reverend Mr. Clark of Ridgefield) was a widower. His appearance struck me more favorably than I had expected. Mr. Reed first introduced himself to me with great friendliness, and then introduced me to his wife. I gained an introduction also to Mrs. Aitchison and her sister Miss Andrews.

The company broke up at 10 o'clock, in good time. The rain soon after began to pour down in a torrent.

Wednesday, September 24. Had my stove put up, and, though the weather was not particularly cold, put on a rousing fire to dry my books, which moulded a good deal in the damp hot weather of the vacation. The day was clear and fine, very favorable for the cattle show on the Green, which, however, is said to have been inferior to those of former years. The recitation at 11 was shortened to make way for the Linonian Statement of Facts. The facts must have multiplied alarmingly, for they were not fully stated until after 3 o'clock, and the Brothers, who had engaged the same room (Brewster's Hall), could not of course begin before that time. Fearing that some of *their* facts might go unstated for want of time, they sent up a request to the Faculty, praying that prayers might be put for once at 5½ instead of 5, and the Faculty, who were all Linonians (except the President, who did not vote, and Mr. Thacher, who was absent on wedding business), felt delicate about refusing the request. The attendance at Chapel, however, was sparse enough, scarcely more than a fifth part of our men making their appearance. But this it appears was not altogether the fault of the Brothers. President Boies had let out the men in time to be tardy at prayers, so that we might have had an unseasonable and indecorous rush but for a fortunate accident. The students in returning toward College had a sort of collision with the people on the Green, and for a time matters looked threatening, but the police presently interfered and restored order.

Henry came in at 1, with the numbers of the daily *Times,* a new paper just started in New York by Raymond, late of the *Courier and Enquirer.* We propose to take it in place of the *Tribune,* which wearies us with socialistic vaticinations, spiritual rappings, and windy correspondents. The *Tribune* we have paid for up to September 30, and shall drop it then. The *Times* is to be Henry's paper. The young man was persuaded to sit down and take his dinner with us. Our party was a small one, Mary being at President Day's hard at work, and Kinsley engaged in watching and counteracting the Linonian facts.

At the Faculty meeting it was resolved to have an extemporaneous catalogue got up in a few days, for the use of the Faculty. The subject of Euclid burials was presented and discussed, but every man appeared to be inops consilii, and we concluded at last to maintain the same attitude as last year.

In the evening attended the wedding of Thomas Beecher and Olivia Day. The ceremony was performed by Henry Ward Beecher, and was short, simple, and, what one might perhaps have doubted of, tasteful—every way a perfect contrast to the performance of last evening. The company consisted of 80 or 90 people, and evidently enjoyed themselves as well as could be expected. Broke up at 10.

Thursday, September 25. The Societies have come up nearly even: 61 accessions to the Brothers and 58 to the Linonians, so say the papers. It is better for the Linos than I had expected, better than they deserved, if all be true that I have heard about their statement yesterday. One of their orators, Thomas, was so regardless of propriety, and indeed of decency, as to ridicule the personal peculiarities of Professor Gibbs and appeal to College feeling against Dr. Fitch's long and abstract sermons. I am very sorry to hear that the Linonians have been soliciting contributions of books for the Library. It is a measure pessimi exempli. I hope it may never be repeated. A man who will give books could generally be brought to give money, and five dollars in money is worth a large lot of old, worn-out books, two thirds novels, and three thirds duplicates of works already in the Library. The truth is the libraries have outgrown the Societies; they are too large for the knowledge and the regulation of annual committees. A great library requires a permanent librarian.

Tinkered my clock with Henry's help, substituting fresh catgut for the broken string that held the alarm weight. I must take it to the house, for the morning bell sounds but feebly in our bedroom and I am perpetually afraid of sleeping over, an occurrence which just now would certainly be rather awkward.

Received a letter from Professor Edwards of Andover, enclosing a long German letter from Mr. Pischon, a friend of Edwards', and now secretary of Russian legation at Athens, in which he gives an account of certain interesting antiquities recently discovered there. Edwards wishes me to translate or epitomize it for the *Bibliotheca*.

In the evening received a call from Reverend and Mrs. Dutton, interrupted and succeeded by one from my classmate Whittlesey. He is soon to be ordained at Bath, Maine. He spoke in the highest terms of Mr. Woolsey's address at Andover, which he heard delivered. He says that Park admired it highly.

Henry came in a little after nine, to bring a letter which he had just received from Mary. Father had gone to Meadville. They had been living 3 women in the house for some days. Their solitude had been enlivened by a little hummingbird which was picked up in a half frozen state and given to their care and surgery. They warmed and fed it with good success and, continuing their charge for several days, had made the tiny thing so tame that it loved to sit perched on the finger of anyone that would hold it. I was surprised to hear this, for I had always regarded the hummingbird as perfectly untameable.

Friday, September 26. At 12 called on Mr. Stanley and invited him to tea. Anna had invited Mrs. Sherman Day—so it appeared when we came to compare notes—but, hearing what I had done, she sent her a note begging off and promising a call in the evening.

At 5¾ went home with Professor Stanley, who sat with us till after 8. Mr. Camp rushed in at 7 to report himself as off at 9. His passage is secured in the *Pacific,* his trunk which he lost in going home reclaimed and safe, and his box of books deposited with Westermann to send to Schneider of Berlin. Everything prosperous and promising. I can hardly help envying him the pleasure and the advantages of his three-years intended residence in Germany. Macy came in and stayed from 8 to 9. Some talk about dosing, which it was thought would strengthen him in bachelor ways.

Read *Frithjof's Saga* till 10, and then to bed.

Monday, September 29. Purchased Mr. Brewer's *Patmos* of an agent who called upon me. Thought more of the author than the book. Paid $1.50. Offered a dollar bill of People's Bank of Paterson, New Jersey, but was informed that the bank had burst, and Mr. Francis Bradley, of whom I inquired, confirmed the report. Must sell the bill to a broker for what it will fetch. Mr. B[radley] gives a good account of Thomas Hilton, the colored man who applied to me about a situation as College waiter. Ordered pair of shoes and got India rubbers at Tuttle's. Reviewed Mr. Pischon's letter with considerable care.

Paid $1.38 for stove. Gave Anna 45 out of the 50 dollars which I drew from the Treasury on Saturday.

In the evening called with Anna, first at President Day's and afterwards at Brother Magill's.

Home at 9. Read Grote. Abed at 10.

Beautiful aurora with brilliant red streamers.

Tuesday, September 30. Saw Mr. Thacher at 12 and reminded him of the cushion at Walker's, with good effect. A man made his appearance, or rather would have made his appearance, if he had not been hidden by two enormous cushions, 18 feet each, which he carried. This was at 6, and at 8 Mr. Thacher came in, and reported that he had purchased a cushion and a half for 6 dollars. We are to make our own cuttings.

While we were at prayers about 10 o'clock, Mr. and Mrs. Magill came in. They are going to New York early in the morning, rain excepted.

OCTOBER, 1851

Wednesday, October 1. H. E. Dwight called in and introduced a young Mr. Clark of Philadelphia, son of the late Reverend Dr. John A. Clark. He has been spending the summer with his mother and his mother's relatives in Fairfield. He brought a letter from Dr. Chassell. I examined him in Greek and marked him 2½, and afterwards, as Mr. James Dwight had no leisure till evening, I tried him in Latin and gave him the same mark. He was slow and rusty, but thoughtful and scholarlike. Henry gave him 2 in mathematics. He was at once admitted, assigned to my division, and enrolled upon our provisional catalogue, which is to be struck off tomorrow.

Young Bennett, recently admitted from the Junior class at Harvard to the same standing in our College, who passed so fine an examination on entering, called to consult me about Anglo-Saxon pronunciation. He has been studying Klipstein's *Grammar*. He sat 15 minutes before 11, and then came in again after 12 and staid till 1. He appears to have a mind of great intelligence and love of study, with a very amiable character.

Faculty at 3. President consulted the Professors as to an agent to solicit funds for the College. Theophilus Smith has declined. Talked of Mr. Calhoun, George Richards, Professor Goodrich. No decision.

In evening, call from instructor of DuBois, Freshman, who has been much discouraged about himself, and wrote so despondingly to his friends that his father and teacher came here to see about it. Talked encouragingly. Call from Lynde Catlin, evidently a good deal discomposed by the presence of a professor.

Friday, October 3. Upholstering on our church cushions. Read the *Ajax*.

Letter from Dudley, requesting ponies on *Antigone, Gorgias,* and Tacitus' *Germany* and *Agricola*. Obtained Mr. Olmsted's *conjectural* averages for the Juniors last term; his book was stolen near the end. Several hiatus valde deflendi. I presume, however, his averages will be quite as trusty as usual.

After tea, called at Fitch's and procured the ponies: *Antigone,* .38; *Gorgias,* .50; Tacitus (Anthon), .75; sum, $1.63. Mr. J. D. Whitney of Northampton came in at 7 o'clock. Left Mrs. Whitney at Tontine. She would have called, but not knowing either me or Mrs. Hadley, thought it contrary to etiquette. Talked about William and Edward. Gave Mr. Whitney the bundle for Dudley. He goes tomorrow at 11. Professor Kingsley came in before Mr. Whitney had left, followed soon by Mr. and Mrs. Magill, and finally by Hyde and Henry, who staid till 10.

Sunday, October 5. Contrary to general principles, attended Centre Church in the morning. Services in part by Mr. Egleston, who preached his farewell last Sunday. Sermon by Dr. Bacon, returned on Wednesday. "Grace and Peace," an old sermon it is said, and not a very interesting one. Prefatory and peroratory remarks in excellent taste. He looks wild and haggard as ever.

Afternoon at Chapel. Dr. Fitch on halting between two opinions. Cushion works well. Music good. Bigelow present with John Henry

Wilcox on the organ. In the evening, talk of attending Monthly Concert at Mr. Eustis'; given up. Read Stephen on Ignatius Loyola.

Monday, October 6. Saw Dr. Hoisington, the Ceylon missionary. Some talk about his lecturing in town.

In evening did not go to hear Mr. Whitney's imitations of great orators. Call from Mr. and Mrs. Olmsted. Professor disposed to be jocular about Sunday evenings.

Wednesday, October 15. Dr. Bacon called on our people in the forenoon, while I was out. They had some spicy conversation, in which the Doctor brought out plainly enough the grudge which since the year 1846 he has always cherished against Yale College. He made no great speculation in this instance, for our folks were on the alert, and took care he should get as good as he gave.

*　*　*

NOVEMBER, 1851

Wednesday, November 5. At Faculty meeting, talk about the Euclid affair, which it was understood would come off in the evening. No new counsels, although the threatened interference of the firemen, and the supposed attention on the part of the police to the subject, put a new face upon it.

Thursday, November 6. No disturbance last night. Students frightened out, it is thought, by fear of the police. Mr. Mayor Skinner, it is said, has got word to them that the authorities will be present with their posse, and if there is any disorder will at once arrest men and march them to the watch house, and keep them there until the Faculty *come to their rescue.*

Friday, November 7. Made our appearance for the first time in a standee, which Henry and Wickes united in declaring to be an improvement. Went over to the room 170 at half past nine o'clock P.M. and got the benefit of their criticisms.

Read the catalogue of Greek and Roman authors in Fiske's Eichenberg, poorly done, but convenient in extent.

*　*　*

Sunday, November 16. Opened Whitney's letter, found a long and animated account of his ramble in Switzerland. He had arrived in Berlin, and concluded to give himself up entirely to Oriental studies, determined to do this by the advice of his brother. Had Camp with him, who sent me a short note giving some account of his journey and his beginnings in Berlin.

Dr. Fitch in forenoon, on the Temptation. Blind and blinding —just up to the level of beginners at Sunday School. He has not the first conception of the moral condition of the Paradisaic man.

Dr. Taylor in the afternoon, on repentance. A long sermon, and delivered in a spiritless way, with very little of his ancient fire and energy.

Wednesday, November 19. At Faculty meeting in the afternoon, some talk about the Euclid affair, which was to come off, it was said, in the evening. No new counsel.

In the evening went out with Anna to make calls. Started at 6½, with Mrs. Herrick, thence at 7 to Mr. Olmsted's. Professor and Mrs. Dutton came in while we were there. At 8 to Mrs. Larned's. Mr. and Mrs. Asa Bacon of Litchfield came in upon us. They are just starting in their new house. Wound up with the Fosters; a pleasant chat. Sat up reading *London Quarterly* till 12. Had been some time asleep when the drum tap announced that the police and Sophomores were stirring. Feared that they would come round and salute us, but they did not. It seemed to be really a quiet sort of affair.

We have had but one serenade yet, on Tuesday night or rather Wednesday morning of this week, at 12½, a very pretty thing.

My letters home have brought on two anxious fathers, for both of whom I have done what I could in the way of advice and assistance. Mr. Wheeler of Easton called on me in the morning, Mr. Tomlinson of Woodbury in the evening.

The Catalogue came out today and was distributed as usual. While the Faculty were in session Mr. Hamlen's boy came in with a bushel basket full of them, all done up ready for direction, and dumped them down upon the floor, to the admiration and envy of all who were present.

Thursday, November 20. Looked a little at Döderlein's *Homeric Glossary*. Gloriously innocent of comparative philology. Went out again in the evening to finish up calls.

Dr. Bacon, it is said on good authority, allowed his son George to attend the Euclid. He would bite his own nose off if he thought it would spite the Faculty of Yale College.

Sunday, November 23. Dr. Bacon preached a long missionary sermon in the morning. Took occasion to speak a kind word of Yale College. What can it mean? But the afternoon brought an event more surprising still: Dr. Taylor preached in his ancient church. It is said that a reconciliation has been effected through the kind offices of Miss Delia.

MAY, 1852

Tuesday, May 11 [,1852]. Short talk with Mr. Woolsey. He does not wish to publish his address to the Andover Society, because there are points in it requiring more investigation than he is able to give them. He spoke of an article which he had written for the *New Englander* on the Waldenses. He had assumed like Neander and others the substantial genuineness of the Waldensian documents, but is now much shaken by a work which he has just seen, of Dieckhoff, maintaining that they are greatly falsified—stark interpolirt. Will perhaps write again on the subject for the *Bibliotheca*. He spoke of my selections from the Lachmann library for our College, and said he had struck off several works from my list because they were in his own possession. That must have been the case, I suspect, with nearly every book I marked, for my intention was in the main to note only works of high character and prime importance. He said that if he could see his way clear, he should give a large part of his library to the College, but he was not able as yet to do so. His books however ought to be used, and it belonged to me to use them. He wished that I would take everything I wanted, entering his Library freely at all times, and carrying off what I pleased, and keeping books if I chose until he himself should call for them. All he required was that I would make a memorandum on the spot of the works that I might take. He authorized me also to send any messenger to do what it might be inconvenient for me to do myself. I was very glad to have this conversation (as I said to Mr. Woolsey) because I have felt very much hampered and perplexed in regard to the increase of the Greek department in the College Library. I see now that the proper course for me is to get a perfect knowledge of Mr. Woolsey's library, the Greek part of it, and to keep it constantly in view in recommending new purchases for the College.

Spent some time in College Library, 12 to 1, looking out Pythagorean doctrine of planetary motions.

In afternoon made an unsuccessful attempt to see Dr. Murdock. Had a call from Professor Olmsted, who spoke of the reasons to apprehend a vacancy ere long in our Chair of Mathematics and to suggest to me the idea of taking it, as a possibility worthy at least of consideration. I mentioned some very obvious objections, but he would not admit them as decisive. It had been his desire from the first that I should have some place of the kind in connection with the College, and he had regretted that they had not at the time any such place to offer me. He seemed to think that I had more aptitude for mathematics than languages, that I should feel more enthusiasm in the study, and that I should stand a better chance in it to distinguish myself and add to the reputation of the College. I did not refuse to entertain the idea nor pronounce the thing a sheer impossibility—for who knows? I certainly feel that my Greek is likely enough to prove a failure, and though I do not rate my mathematical powers as at all superior, yet perhaps I might do better in this line. Still, as I should probably take the earliest opportunity for things still different, I do not know that it is worth while to make this change, especially as it would carry me from, rather than towards, what I have regarded as the goal.

Friday, May 21. Meeting of President and Professors at Mr. Silliman's study, 7½ o'clock. Present, Mr. Woolsey, Messrs. Silliman, Senior and Junior, Mr. Dana, Mr. Olmsted, Mr. Porter, and myself. Business, the new Engineering Department. Mr. Olmsted has received a letter from Mr. A. C. Twining, in which he declines appearing as a candidate for such a place. Reason, I suppose (Mr. Olmsted spoke guardedly on this), his ice manufacture. Concluded to give encouragement to Mr. Norton. Broke up at 9. Stopt at Mr. Dana's to pick up Anna, who had come with me so far. Saw the additional room which he has gained for his study, a very pleasant arrangement.

JUNE, 1852

Monday, June 14. Surprised by a ring at 10 or thereabouts. It brought a telegraphic dispatch from Alexander at Erie. It was in reply to one which we sent at H. White's suggestion on Saturday evening: "If you come here, a city committee will consult you about bringing water into town, possibly may engage you eventually." The answer was, "Should like that engagement, and will come soon, and telegraph you when." Very satisfactory in contents, though open to criticism on the score of superfluous words.

Tuesday, June 15. From 12 to 1 at President's room, discussing appointments. Only made a beginning. At Kinne's, quarter before 3, talking about monitors; amazing dearth of good timber. Passed them through in meeting of the Faculty, 3 to 5. Most of the time talking on results of Senior examination and especially on Bliss and Curtiss, who stood lowest (1.41 and 1.32) in biennial examination. They have been notoriously negligent during the year, and some of us were quite disposed to make a stand upon them. Mr. Thacher was inclined to slip them through on the ground of insufficient previous warning. As we talked, one by one went out, until there were only seven when the vote was taken: Olmsted, Thacher, Hurlbut for recommending; Hadley, Professor, and Tutors Fisk and Blodget against it. President would not interfere. Agreed to postpone the decision till tomorrow morning at 9. Heard Davies for the first time in the calculus. Made a good deal of talk.

Rough play in the garden and some discomposure. Warm day and prospect of warmer.

Wednesday, June 16. Ferociously hot. Faculty at 9. Hurried and confused about the two to be exscinded, but at last decided to reserve them. Over to Lyceum at 9¾. Met the Seniors in President's recitation room. Mr. Dwight read the Latin names, including Christophorum (pronounced with penultimate accent) Tigranem Seropyan but neither *Comem* nor Felicitatem (Curtiss and Bliss). Mr. Olmsted, who presided, remarked that two names had been omitted, reserved for subsequent consideration. Away to Chapel, where Mr. Dwight, after reading the first half dozen names, cut short the roll with "ceterosque juvenes quorum nomina in hac charta scripta sunt"—a very satisfactory alteration. Then came Mr. Thacher with a piece of beautiful Latinity in which he bestowed complimentary superlatives without stint on Mr. Kingsley, who bore them with becoming meekness. The President then pronounced his earnest and solemn address. Crapo's poem was neat and tasteful, but tame and commonplace, inferior to the expectations which I had formed of his earlier course. Sprague delivered an eloquent oration with his very beautiful elocution, easy, graceful, varied, and animated in an unusual degree. If his principles are up to his talents he will make an admirable man.

From 12 to 1 at house, with closed doors, employed in most assiduous fanning. At 2½ with Kinne, reporting. At 3 in President's room, working on appointments. Presented to Faculty and approved at 5. Bingham came out fairly ahead, 3.59 to Reynolds' 3.55. Brewer next, with 3.41, was made philosophical orator. I am heartily glad for him and his friends. Next came Allen, with 3.36, though he has been absent through the Senior year, and most of the time sick with what he regarded as a fatal malady. His biennial was the tiptop paper, 3.78, Bingham's being 3.72. Miller and Sprague came to the same figure, 3.34. Terry was introduced among the first orations, Safford degraded to a dissertation, etc. The changes from Junior appointments were numerous and considerable. I was most sorry for Odell, who came up two grades but stopt one peg short of an oration. He has been for the last year and a half a model of persevering industry.

We took some pains to guard against grotesque costume on the part of Freshmen in Chapel, but they did not adventure it. A heavy rain came up while we were in Chapel, which grew heavier and heavier until it came down in a perfect torrent. We supposed that our invited guests might be deterred from coming, but they made their appearance shortly after 7, having taken refuge from the storm in Mr. Olmstead's store on Broadway. Mr. and Mrs. Hyde came, and Mrs. Olmstead. Mr. Olmstead is not much given to making visits. Mrs. and Miss Emmeline Thacher were invited, but the rain deterred them from coming. We had a pleasant sociable time, with coffee, bread, and cakes early in the evening, and ice cream at nine, and broke up at 10. Mrs. Hyde appears extremely well, though not much of a talker, a point in which I fully sympathize with her.

The dinner at 1 o'clock was in the cold collation style, though in some respects a hot collation, and passed off on the whole very tolerably well. The President did not attend. Mr. Silliman presided and made a good-natured opening speech. The noise on the Green in the afternoon was rather less intolerable than usual.

The Freshmen were determined not to be cheated of their pow-wow by the prohibition of last Saturday. They mustered in procession with a band of music. But Professors Larned and Thacher, with most of the tutors, appeared upon the ground, and at about 11½ succeeded in dispersing them.

Thursday, June 17. Another oppressively hot day, scarcely less abundant than its predecessor.

Resumed my letter to Whitney, of which two pages were written a fortnight since, and added four to the number. Spoke of Professor Norton, who has just come here from Farmington considerably improved in health. Dr. Jackson of Philadelphia, a distinguished auscultator, declares positively that he has no organic disease of lungs or heart. But I fear the stethoscope may not prove itself infallible. Sleepy in the afternoon. Did not wake up even to see the grand funeral procession of firemen in honor of their deceased chief, Mr. Hemingway.

Another storm gathered at evening and began to pour down its floods while we were seated at the supper table. We had but just risen when, in the midst of the rain, Mr. Magill entered, having just come from Danbury. Announced the result of all discussion there, in the adoption of a report, drafted by a committee of one from each association, recommending that all obstacles should be removed, whether real or supposed, that stand in the way of settling Dr. Bushnell's case according to the established methods of procedure. It is supposed that Dr. Bushnell will in consequence be impeached and brought to trial before the consociation to which he belongs.

Call from Mr. Blodget, who spoke a little freely of the affair last night, as well as of Dr. Fitch's approaching resignation.

Friday, June 18. Still furnace heat. Talk with Mr. Thacher at 12 on the affair of Wednesday evening, which he is inclined to pass over without much severity of discipline. Took a delightful bath from 2 to 3. Finished up my letter to Whitney by adding six pages more and sent it off in all haste.

Went at 7½ to meeting of Professors at Mr. Silliman's. Got to work at 8. Heard a long and curious letter from Dr. Fitch in reply to that of the Faculty, declining to supply the pulpit statedly after his resignation but appearing to hold out obscure intimation that he might be willing to help others in the work. He suggested that the clerical members of the Faculty should take hold and supply the place until a satisfactory appointment could be made. But the letter consisted chiefly in a vindication of himself against the objections which have been made to him as a preacher and a minister. He alleged his utter incapacity for extempore speaking as reason sufficient for confining himself to the pulpit, which I for one would readily assent to. I should admit likewise the justice of his defence in regard to the predominantly didactic character of his sermons: the students, he says, require to be taught. Only the manner of teaching, I should say, was too abstract and unpractical. In regard to length of sermons, he pleaded that his lectures were not as long as those of his colleagues, an ingenious evasion rather than a fair reply, though the point itself is one of no great consequence. But in regard to unproductiveness and repetition, he was really disingenuous. He sought to convey the impression that his time and strength had been on the whole devoted to his work of sermonizing, that he had never been neglectful of his business in this respect, which is most certainly a false impression. These over-sensitive natures are nearly always self-indulgent; it is almost matter of necessity with them. We ought not to wonder at it, nor to blame them too severely, if in excusing it they show a little want of nobleness and honesty. Fitch, I should say, is too sensitive to be a thoroughly honest and noble man. He has not strength of nerve to face the truth just as it is, cut where it may, and act accordingly.

After hearing this document, we talked away with little result for an hour and a half. Discussed Doctor Adams, with many things said in his favor and one or two rather singular things against him, and adjourned at 10 to meet again next Friday evening on the same subject. We meet on Friday, in order that those who choose may attend Dr. Bacon's lectures on the East, which are delivered on Thursday evening.

Saturday, June 19. Less sultry today, though still warm. Hot work, President-making at Baltimore, where the Whigs, after long discussion about a platform, have at last come up to the mark, endorsed the compromise, and are voting patiently again and again on their three candidates, with very little alteration, running 130+ for Scott, ditto for Fillmore, and 30— for Webster. Webster's chance seems to me the best. I hope he may have the honor of the nomination, and the honor, which must certainly follow it, of being beaten by Franklin Pierce.

At 8½, met in the Chapel to hear the competition between Johnston and Sprague for the DeForest gold medal. The house was quite full below, and a number of ladies, even, graced the occasion. Johnston, who has not yet recovered fully from his fever, spoke rather feebly, though by no means badly. But Sprague appeared in the glory of an elocution which, though deformed occasionally by exaggerated vehemence, is seldom matched in College walls, or indeed anywhere else, distinct, various, graceful, impressing the idea forcibly on the mind of the hearer, and carrying the audience away by a sort of spell. (The President at the close declared the prizes. The Freshman scholarship was adjudged to Todd, Palmer standing second, though this was not publicly announced. Palmer stood first in mathematics and just enough so to balance the superiority of Todd in Greek, but fell a little short in Latin composition, where Todd made fewer mistakes though inferior as regards idiom. The rest were far behind.) After the speaking was finished, we had a Professors' meeting, Dr. Fitch attending also, in which the DeForest medal was awarded to Sprague. There was some difference of opinion. It was admitted on all hands that Johnston's composition showed the highest merit and that Sprague's elocution was decidedly the best, but how to strike the balance was the question. The President would give the preference to Johnston. So Dr. Fitch if he looked only at impression on his own mind, but otherwise if he looked at impression made on minds in general. Professor Olmsted was exactly on the balance. The rest of us inclined a little to Sprague, and so it went. Johnston however is to receive the Clark prize of 15 dollars for the best composition.

Drew seventy dollars, the remainder of my deposit, from the College Treasury. Drew also 50 dollars from the City Bank, from money forwarded by Alexander Twining. Deposited for Mary in Savings Bank, $104.50, reducing the debt to $200. At home found Anna returned from Jewish Synagogue, where she had gone with Miss Rood, much impressed at least with the politeness of her Sunday School scholars.

Tuesday, June 22. Wrote a letter to the Postmaster at Crab Orchard, Kentucky, soliciting information concerning the decease of my classmate Swift, who died there nearly a year ago. Asked him to give the letter to anyone who could send me the information desired. I believe the widow still resides there with her family friends.

Heavy rains in the afternoon, with some hailstones and with sharp lightning. One flash struck the sycamore tree back of South College.

Read a little in Pindar. At 7½ went to attend Professors' meeting at Mr. Silliman's, which was to have come on Friday but was put forward because Mr. Silliman is going out of town. Notice, however, was not given to all, and some who received it had apparently forgotten it, so that the Theological Faculty had no representative. Mr. Woolsey reported that the clerical gentlemen (himself, Taylor, Goodrich, and Porter) had talked over among themselves the possibility of supplying the pulpit for a year and had concluded that they could be responsible each for 8 Sundays, and had hoped that Dr. Fitch would undertake to do as much. Dr. Fitch, however, was not disposed to promise anything, though they derived some encouragement from his talk. Most of the time was spent in talking about raising money. Thacher was most pressing, but was strongly seconded by Larned and Silliman. The President took less part in it, though in his view there was nothing in the way but the want of a suitable agent. It was urged, however, that the present is a golden opportunity, when money is plenty, the country rich, everything prosperous, and that we must take hold now and make hay while the sun shines, agent or no agent. It was thought that a large amount might be obtained in New York City with comparatively little labor. The whole subject to be discussed again tomorrow afternoon after Faculty meeting.

Wednesday, June 23. Spent more time than I had intended looking at Navier's *Calculus.* Read a little in Pindar. Went to Mr. Kinne's at 2, but he had forgotten himself for once and was not on the ground. He however came soon after to my room, and we went through with our reporting. Faculty in session till nearly 6, occupied most of the time with the Freshman affair of last Wednesday evening. There seemed to have been a misunderstanding as to the terms of the prohibition. It was construed as applying only to disturbances in Chapel, and for other matters, as directed only against excesses. The men who were engaged in the affair came forward, nearly all of them, in a paper signed by 56 names, avowing their action but disclaiming any intention of disobedience. There was no design, they said, to have more than music and cheering. The procession was out of their calculation and counter to their wishes. It was concluded to adopt no discipline, but that the President should address the Freshmen and present our views at large, both as to their conduct in this case and as to the general expediency of nocturnal celebrations. W. S. King of St. Louis was to be informally apprized that his position in College is one of extreme peril. Norris of the Sophomore class, who behaved very shabbily in the matter, ought to have been dismissed, as he had already a brace of warnings, but mercy ruled the day and his father is only advised to remove him. Welch is to be restored at beginning of next term, through no fault of mine, I trust.

In evening, read Aufrecht and Kuhn's *Zeitschrift*, No. 5.

Saturday, June 26. Mr. Gilman called at 8½ to renew an invitation given yesterday to Anna by Mrs. Dana, to go on a picnic to Mt. Carmel, going and returning in the cars, from 11 A.M. to 7 P.M. Anna was rather disposed on grounds of general benevoience to join the party, but I alleged my engagement in the Chapel and succeeded in pleading off, as did also Mr. Dana and Mr. Larned, each on his own separate plea. Kinsley went, and Anna sent down by him some pounds of crushed sugar for the lemonade, as a sort of acknowledgment for the honor of the invitation. Meanwhile, at 9, rode out first to Mr. Elihu Sanford's on Fleet Street to engage his friendly services in securing our supply of coal, and this done, out to East Haven and, turning there, down to the lighthouse. After taking a look and sniff of the salt water we started back, and reached home at 11¾.

Sunday, June 27. Read from the translation of Neander's *Denkwürdigkeiten* etc., a club book entitled *Light in Dark Places*.

Anna was detained till nearly 7 P.M. at the Davenport School. They are again obliged to give up their school room and were looking around for another. Have a meeting of their teachers at our house tomorrow afternoon at 3 o'clock.

Monday, June 28. Warmer today. Made out subjects from Roman history for review of my class. Sat down today at dinner table four in number, the Twinings, all but Julia, having betaken themselves to their new home.

Wrote out a demonstration for the limit of $(1 + x)^{\frac{1}{x}}$, which occupied me for some time.

In the evening at Mr. Woolsey's. Present, Messrs. Olmsted,

Larned, and Thacher. Messrs. Silliman and Porter absent from town. The President read draft of a circular for new subscription, very forcibly and clearly drawn. Put deficiency of salary foremost among the necessities of the College. Mr. Larned had some question about the expediency of this. Thought people would say, "Oh, they'll work better if you don't give them too much money." Men would rather give money for something new. The majority however seemed to think the safest way was to tell the story as it is. No decision as to any immediate movement. Talk again after Faculty meeting on Wednesday afternoon.

Coming back by beautiful moonlight, with Professor Olmsted, stopt at the Fosters' to pick up Anna.

Wednesday, June 30. At work on Greek accent. Call from Mr. Olmsted, who inquired whether the Greek department might not be supplied from the younger graduates of the College. Spoke of Tutor Timothy Dwight, with some reference to his proposed solicitation of his neighbor. Interrupted by a call from Lewis, Junior, who showed me an ode of his on Light, in the style of *In Memoriam*, a very uncommon piece for a College man, with great ingenuity of thought and considerable copiousness and felicity of expression.

Reporting as usual at Kinne's room, there came up a shower with great suddenness, a little before 3 o'clock. Recollecting that the windows of my room were open, I was eager to get over to North College, and made several ineffectual attempts to borrow an umbrella in the entry. At length got one from Shackelford, already drenched, which proved but little better than none at all. When I reached North College, I was pretty soaky, which was the more vexatious as the rain just then nearly ceased, and my room had suffered no detriment whatever. At Faculty meeting, Weston and Phelps of my division came up for 12 marks. Getting through at 4¼, the Professors stopped, Silliman and Porter being among the number. The President read a shorter circular which he had prepared and then read again the one we had heard before on Monday evening. I took advantage of this to step over to the house and indue dry clothes, after which I returned to the meeting. Concluded to have the shorter circular printed, and in the meantime to commence personal effort with gentlemen of property in New Haven.

Anna went over in the evening to Professor Thacher's. Was escorted back by Mr. Thacher himself, who made a very pleasant little call.

JULY, 1852

Thursday, July 1. At 1, heard that Alexander Twining had just got into town. He ought to have arrived last night, but was detained by two collisions on the Erie railroad. About 3½, Henry came in with George. Mother and he were detained 2½ hours in New York by the lateness of the Albany boat. George was feeling rather wretchedly—out of health for some days before leaving home, and not improved by the journey. While he sat with me, Professor Porter came in to make arrangements for the examination. He is going on a trip to the White Mountains and wishes to prolong his stay as far as possible. May perhaps put over the examination to next term. Studying on my first lesson in review of Roman history, to be recited in the morning.

Returning home at 6¼, found Mother much improved in appearance since I left her in the vacation. Mrs. Twining and Eliza came in after tea and sat through the evening. After they had gone, Alexander came in from Mr. Timothy Dwight's and talked for a while in fine spirits. He is to superintend the preliminary explorations for water to supply the city. Goes to Erie tomorrow, but will return in a few days and set a party of men to work under his direction. His railroad operations will keep him busy for three months or more at the West.

Friday, July 2. Wrote to Henry Field of West Springfield and S. G. Coe of Danbury. Invited them to serve as members of our examining committee.

Wednesday, July 7. With George in College Library. Looked over contents of Poggendorff for several years back, with little result—more of physics than chemistry. Went in to Analytical Laboratory and looked at their books and journals, Gmelin, Pelouze, etc.

In Faculty meeting, Dulles admonished for absences. Meeting of Professors after it. The President showed us his circular in printed form. Some conversation which led away from the point rather than towards it. Mr. Olmsted and Mr. Larned thought it would be an unpopular move to solicit money for the support of professors, and were thinking of raising tuition to $50 and begging money for scholarships. Another meeting of Professors at Mr. Silliman's, Friday evening.

After tea, went out with George. Called at Professor Norton's.

Found him better than I had expected. Is confident that his case is one of bronchitis simply. Professor Silliman was out. At Professor Dana's we saw a beautiful microscope of Nachet's, price $150, belonging to Professor Silliman. Miss Larned was looking very well indeed. Told me that her brother Joseph was engaged to Miss Kendig of Waterloo. It was a piece of old news, she said. I had heard nothing of it before.

Friday, July 9. Professors' meeting at Mr. Silliman's. On way there, called at Alexander's place. Kinsley sick today; threatened with dysentery, but appears likely to escape. Mrs. Twining troubled with non-appearance of her furniture, which was sent from Erie, by Canal from Buffalo, and should have got here a week ago.

Of Professors, Mr. Porter out of town, Mr. Olmsted attending Dr. Bacon's lecture. Slow in coming. Much conversation on other topics. At last, near 9, took up the proper subject, and talked it over for about an hour. Mr. Thacher suggested the expediency of combining the two measures which have been talked of. Raising tuition to $45.00 to provide for immediate increase of salaries, and making a call for money on the friends of the College as a means of permanent development and progress. He urged with much reason that we cannot in any way make out a case of distress, such as we had in 1830, and that most of those who will give anything to the College, will give if we only say the College needs money, a contribution is essential in our judgment to the prosperity of the institution. These views seemed to meet with considerable favor. Mr. Silliman preferred $50 to $45 for the tuition, but otherwise came to the same point. We meet the Prudential Committee at President Day's on Tuesday evening.

Tuesday, July 13. Still very hot. Some water on the street this morning. Our regular waterman was "jugged" on the glorious Fourth for gloriously beating his wife. Since that time we have been very imperfectly sprinkled, and have suffered a good deal from the dust, but have now made a new contract. George left for New York in the cars at 9¼. Mother to follow on Friday morning.

Evening, at President Day's, meeting of Professors with Prudential Committee. Mr. Silliman expressed his views, urging an immediate increase of tuition to $50 per annum and an effort at the same time to raise funds for the College. President Day acknowledged the necessity, but was opposed to any raising of tuition which should carry it higher than $40 a year. Mr. Porter appeared to coincide substantially with Professor Silliman, but Mr. Theophilus Smith spoke clearly and strongly against any increase of tuition. Broke up at 9¼.

Thursday, July 15. Call from Rice, Sophomore, to talk about contemplated class celebration at close of biennial examination. I told him we would rather not have it—we thought it dangerous in tendency.

Wrote in the morning to Henry Field, inviting him and his lady to stay with us during the examination season.

Monday, July 19. Delightful ride with Anna in the morning from 8¾ to 10¾. We went down to Oyster Point and then came back zigzagging our way to West Rock, and thence by the MacAdam road to New Haven. From 2 to 3 at work, planning a new house, with indifferent success. Just time before 3 to get $36 from City Bank, with which paid taxes for self with J[ulia] and M[ary], a total of $30.39, our share $13.47. At 6 found Mrs. Hickok at the house. She went out with Anna in the evening to call on Mrs. Twining, and I sat alone reading Merivale, just brought in with a heap of club books beside from Mr. T. Dwight's.

Tuesday, July 20. Commenced examination at 11. Weather hotter than I had expected. Fourth subdivision. President Woolsey present. Fine reciting. Waited dinner for Mr. and Mrs. Field, but at length gave them up and sat down. Nearly finished when they came in. Had been detained on the way. Mr. Field attended my afternoon session with Mr. Joseph Eldridge of Norwalk. Good reciting. Call in the evening from Mrs. Hyde of Colchester with her two daughters. Much pleasant conversation till 9½, when we broke up. Mrs. Field is a woman of very ready wit and great powers of entertainment. Her manners are marked by a very charming vivacity and frankness, and everything she says indicates both high cultivation and strong good sense. My only fear is that she may be something too worldly—without those beautiful enthusiasms which make the glory of life. But of this I *know* nothing. She is certainly a very charming woman.

Mr. Hickok got in from Providence and Worcester just after 9 o'clock.

Wednesday, July 21. Sultry weather. At 8 had present Mr. Coe and Mr. Hickok. Good reciting. So at 11, with Mr. Perkins. At 4, with Smalley to Waite, had a dull and dragging exercise, but no witness. Calls in the evening from Mr. and Mrs. Gibbs, Mr. and Mrs. Strong, Mr. Horace Day. Mr. Field supped at Professor Olmsted's with examining committee. Reports 90° in the shade as maximum temperature of the day.

Thursday, July 22. Ferociously hot. Mr. Olmsted's thermometer gives 94°, higher than anything for last five years. Spectators at no session except the first, when President Day attended. Fair reciting all through. Mr. Porter began in logic at 11 and drew the whole committee to his room. His examination can hardly be very brilliant, I should fear. Anna went out in evening to make some calls with Mr. and Mrs. Field, while I excused myself and staid at home. At Mr. Dana's they found our new Professor Norton. Mr. John P. Norton, they say, had yesterday another attack of bleeding, by which his friends are greatly discouraged.

Mr. and Mrs. Grosvenor made us a call. Went out twice to engage a carriage for the Fields. They leave tomorrow morning, in the early train, at 5½, for New York. They consent to return to us on Tuesday or Wednesday of next week. Was somewhat relieved by the particulars of a conversation between Mrs. Field and Anna in which the former spoke of Mary Field and her recent marriage with Mr. Stone. This gentleman, it appears, is a young man of some property, a partner of Mr. Cyrus Field, likely to do well in the world, but without any decided mental superiority. Notwithstanding this last particular, Mrs. Field thinks it no bad match, and certainly equality in all respects is not essential to domestic happiness. The point, however, which especially interested me was this: that, according to Mrs. Field, my frequent calls upon her sister in the winter and spring of 1848, though they did not fail to suggest to her friends the idea and to some perhaps the desire of a closer connection, were never considered as pledging me in any way to pursue such a connection. Anna thinks, however, that if Miss Field had kept me for a year and a half, I should have been fixed beyond recall.

Friday, July 23. Still hot, though not so frightfully glowing as yesterday. Mr. and Mrs. Field left at 5½ in the train for New York. By particular request, we did not get up to see them off.

Closed our examination this morning. Meeting of instructors at Kinne's room at 10½. Did not condition very much. Faculty in afternoon from 3½ to nearly 6. Assigned parts in the examination of next week.

Alexander Twining came to town today. Called upon us in the evening. Staid while we were dressing for the party at Mrs. Whitney's, which we concluded to attend, though excusing ourselves to Mrs. Devereux and Mrs. John Sanford on Tuesday and Wednesday of next week. At Mrs. Whitney's from 9¼ to 10½. A young party. Mr. MacWhorter almost the only man of my sort. A good deal of dancing in one of the rooms. No great crowd. Weather unexpectedly cool. Fell in with Miss Martin and persecuted her with my exclusive conversation, till Anna came to her relief and called me home.

Saturday, July 24. Finished reading up the examination papers of Fellowes, Gibson, Hamilton, and Young, for Greek of Sophomore year—all poor enough. Faculty, however, regarded them mercifully in their meeting, 9 to 11. Gibson's standing put him out of danger. In regard to the rest, I had to notify Fellowes and Hamilton of their peril, while Mr. Kinne was to do the same kind office for Young.

Meeting of the Professors after the tutors had gone out, on the subject of tuition. Silliman, Olmsted, and Larned went for increase to 45 or 50 dollars, Larned urging again the creation of scholarships, from which he expects more than I am inclined to do, at present. Porter expressed himself doubtfully about any increase. Thacher went for 39 dollars, salaries to be put immediately at $1300, and raised as soon as possible to $1500. For my part I was inclined to oppose any raising of tuition, and to place the whole dependence of the College on the liberality of its friends.

Copied averages of second term into the average book. Came back to room at 2 o'clock. Call from B. A. Smith, who thinks of establishing himself here as a teacher. Call from J. K. Bennett, who is going back to Harvard, somewhat dissatisfied with his experience of Yale. He thinks there is more use of translations here than there and attributes it to the length of our lessons. He says also that our absenteeism greatly exceeds that of Harvard students, and thought it owing to the fact that in Harvard a student excused from attending recitation is still required to make up the lesson. He informed me that with them every excuse or petition must be presented in writing and must come before the Faculty. He made some valuable suggestions for which I was much obliged to him. He is a fine scholar, an excellent man and gentleman, whom I am sorry to lose from our number.

Monday, July 26. Sent a note to Alexander, who thinks of getting George to serve as his chief of engineers, asking what definite proposals we should send by Henry.

Examination today, much as usual, in numbers and in blunders. Not much very bad reciting. Dispatched during the day all the men who presented themselves, and made out 31 Freshmen. William Magill among the crowd.

Copious rain at noon, which will add much to our Commencement comforts.

Mrs. Sherman Day at tea and through the evening.

Tuesday, July 27. Finished up examination, with 55 admitted Freshman and 4 or 5 Sophomore. Two who tried for Junior from Amherst College failed miserably. One of them, Canfield, spent his first Freshman term under my charge. The other concluded to enter Sophomore. Rejections perhaps half a dozen.

Mr. and Mrs. Field came in during the forenoon. They have not been at Guilford. Mr. and Mrs. Magill made their appearance in the afternoon. The ministers went in the evening to hear the Concio ad Clerum, by Reverend Mr. Paige of Bridgeport, of which they gave on the whole favorable accounts. Mrs. Magill and Anna went to Alexander's, leaving me to very pleasant conversation with Mrs. Field. Charles Catlin came in with his two boys, one of them, Charles, just entered in College. Says his daughter Helen will make us a visit next winter.

Wednesday, July 28. Mr. Field off to Guilford at 8 A.M. Returned at 6 P.M. Henry started for New York at 9. Will probably go up to Albany with Mother in the evening boat. Dropt in at ΦBK meeting. Seward just chosen orator for next year. Judge Cone disposed to make a fuss about it on sectional grounds. Others (myself among the number) disposed the same way on different grounds of their own. Porter for reconsideration. Thacher against it. After much confusion, reconsideration carried 42 to 40. Seward ousted, Professor Park appointed orator and Professor H. B. Smith substitute. After this I came away.

Alumni meeting introduced with prayer by Reverend Dr. Field (1802), a very venerable-looking man. The dead roll, read by Mr. Dutton, was followed by a happy speech from Dr. Adams, in which he got off his "gloria frontis" story of Professor Kingsley. Mr. Strong (1831) made a fair speech. But when Mr. Merwin was brought forward, I thought it best to be off. At the house saw Hatty and Julia, arrived in safety last night. Returning after half an hour or more, had the pleasure of hearing Mr. Merwin's peroration. Horace Bushnell was loudly called for, but in vain. Finch of 1849 made a handsome speech. Came, who followed, did well, but hardly so well as his predecessor. A resolution complimentary to Dr. Fitch called out Goodrich, who with great tact and elegance spoke of Dr. Fitch, the circumstances under which he came here, his peculiar difficulties and trials, his deficiencies and the reason of them, his very distinguished merits as a pulpit orator, closing with the improbability of securing a competent successor for 1200 dollars and the necessity of larger endowments for the prosperity of the College. A resolution of compliment to other Colleges represented among us was responded to by Professor Silliman, who dwelt upon the commune vinculum, lamented the deficiencies of Cambridge and Oxford, where only eight men on an average attend the lectures on mineralogy, geology, and so on, and wound up as usual with the women, who ought to have, he said, the title of Mistresses not of *arts* but *he-arts*. President Thornwell of South Carolina College followed in a brilliant and eloquent harangue, in which he took occasion to counteract in a style of great delicacy the tendency of some of Professor Silliman's remarks, and insisted on mental discipline as the grand object of collegiate study. President Sturtevant made a very good speech in conclusion.

In the afternoon, engaged with Blodget, Hurlbutt, Fisk, and James Dwight, at the room of the latter, in examining eight boys, just come down to us from Mr. Clark of East Hampton. Among them was a son of Honorable Charles A. Mann of Utica. None of them failed of getting in, and some acquitted themselves remarkably well.

Wrote to Mr. Brickell of New Orleans, presenting the name of Lawrence McCully (Senior) for the place of teacher in the family of Mr. Harrison. Mr. Tupper (1850) called to say that he did not wish to take the place, preferring to get some situation at the North.

Examined Reynolds in the differential and integral calculus. He passed moderately well.

Our friends went out at 6½ to hear the ΦBK oration of Mr. Whipple and poem of Mr. Pierpont—both of Boston—but Anna and I staid at home and read Merivale.

The weather today has been perfectly charming.

Thursday, July 29. A fine day, though rather too warm for a Commencement occasion. Went down in the procession at 8½, but dodged at the first interlude of Dodsworth's Band and came off home. Call from Miss Hoover. D. D. Field with his daughter and Mrs. Brewer. Mr. Fowles of Philadelphia, a classmate of Mr. Magill's. Off at 12 to 105 to examine Brooks (Junior) on the history of winter term (3). Dined at home, having an insuperable repugnance to public dinners. Anna went to Commencement in the afternoon with Julia Twining and Julia Gibbs.

I studied the history of the class of 1842 and went at 3 to MacWhorter's room, where I found Whittlesey and Bushnell, C. L. Brace and Kingsbury, T. Cook and Sobieski. Beeman, Edwards, Fabrique, Skinner, and Teele did not honor us with their presence. Went over the list of the class and compared notes. At 5 came away with Bushnell, having the smell of smoke on our garments. Anna came in at 6¼, congratulating herself on the service she had been able to render to poor Miss Brewer, who nearly fainted away from weakness and exhaustion. The speaking is said to have been good—that of Sprague really remarkable.

In the evening went with the two Mr. Fields to the levee at Professor Salisbury's. Mr. Woolsey was not there. No great crowd—large rooms, airy and comfortable. Talked with Mr. Bradley from Amoy, President Chapin, Mr. Eastman, Professor St. John, Professor Bushnell, Mr. Pierpont, Dr. Field, President Thornwell, and so on. Mr. H. E. Dwight (grad.) very handsomely begged me to accept as a present the Armenian books which he lent me more than a year ago. Returning at 10, found Alexander, who sat till 10½, when we went off to bed.

Heard of a great steamboat disaster yesterday afternoon, burning of the *Henry Clay* on the North River, near New York—40 or 50 lives lost. Was at first afraid for Mother and Henry, but this boat was coming down the river and of course they could not have been on board. Apparently most criminal recklessness on the part of the authorities on the boat.

Friday, July 30. Mr. and Mrs. Field away at 7½. We have derived great enjoyment from their visit. At my room journalizing. Call from Mr. Talcott, late tutor, who sat for nearly two hours. Much interesting conversation. He says Professor Emerson is engaged to somebody in the neighborhood of New Britain. Wishes me to import some classical books for him. Went round from 11 to 12 settling bills. From 12 to 1, setting down accounts. In the newspaper today, found the testimony of Professor Bailey of West Point, before a coroner's jury, identifying the bodies of his wife and daughter, in which he speaks of two Miss Kinsleys of West Point as near him at the time of the disaster. These young ladies were nieces of Mrs. Alexander Twining, and Anna went to her house to break the news, but the two passed each other on the way, and Mrs. Twining heard the tidings at our house from Mrs. Magill. There are circumstances in this case which make the loss peculiarly distressing.

The Magills left about 6 and took Julia with them, leaving only 2 in the family.

Saturday, July 31. Journalizing at my room. Drew Justinian's *Institutes* (Vinnius) from College Library, with two first volumes of Savigny's *Heutige Römische Recht,* and began reading. Saw at College Library Professor Noyes of Dartmouth College.

Mr. Dutton came into our house with copy of *Tribune* of today, in which the two Miss Kinsleys are set down among those whose bodies have been identified, so that no doubt can any longer remain on that subject. It is a horrible thing, and makes me feel (as all terrible outrages and "indigna" do) that I should like to resign my appointment here. If it were not for others who would lament my retirement, I should be willing enough, it seems to me, to give up my place to any one of the unfortunates who were so rudely and shockingly ousted by the catastrophe of last Wednesday.

* * *

SEPTEMBER, 1852

Saturday, September 11. Going into College Library at 10, was saluted by my classmate John Henry Adam of Pottsville, Pennsylvania, who is on a visit to the Sampsons of Hillhouse Avenue, his wife's relations. Had quite a talk with him at the Library and in my room, going over the lists of our class and obtaining some valuable information.

At Library again from 12 to 1, looking for accounts of the Praslin murder. Fixed it for 1847, and then looked at *New York Spectator* for that year, our only newspaper authority of the time. Found an article on the subject by Mr. Poole, a correspondent of the *Boston Atlas,* then resident in Paris, and seemingly well acquainted with the subject. Nothing in it to inculpate Mrs. Field except the morbid suspicions and jealousy of the Duchess.

In the afternoon, obtained of Yung Wing the keys of the Brothers Library, and searched there for magazine articles on the same subject, but found none. At College Library again, looked more carefully at the notices in the *New York Spectator,* still with the same conclusion.

* * *

Saturday, September 18. Examined Harland in history and Greek of two terms. Went rather hard.

The President took the same view of Welch's case that I had done. Consulted me on a passage of *Alcestis,* the meaning of τοῖς μέλλουσι in line 50.

At 12 went with Professor Olmsted and Mr. H. H. Hadley to decide on the result of Stowell's examination. He is said to have stood third in his class at Hudson, but he got only 1¾ on Latin and less than that on mathematics, philosophy, and astronomy. Concluded that he could not come in at present. Two men from that College have already entered as Seniors and four as Juniors. Of the latter, Blodget says that only one passed a good examination. I hope that Stowell's rejection may do something to check the current which appears to be setting hitherward. The state of things at Western Reserve College is really deplorable, and the case of Mr. Pierce, their President, is in some respects a hard one. They have kept him begging for 6 years or more, and now complain that he is fit for nothing else. Mr. Olmsted having said something about the attempts of alumni in Amherst and Williams to dictate in regard to College matters, Mr. Woolsey said, "Mark my prediction: if our alumni meet together year after year, with nothing to do but talk, and time enough for that, they will be trying to govern us. You must shut their mouths with long addresses."

* * *

OCTOBER, 1852

Thursday, October 7. A busy day. Hard at work on my article for the Philological Society. Saw Mr. Gibbs in the morning and made arrangements for our meeting in the evening. Had some question with him as to Edward Twining, whom he all but insists on converting into a theological student.

Postponed Twining's recitation on Herodotus until tomorrow.

Finished up my essay after a fashion just before 6 o'clock. To Mr.
Gibbs' at 7. He had the *New York Observer* and wanted me to look
at two sentences, the difference of which was 20,000 dollars. They
were Dr. Parker as represented in *Uncle Tom's Cabin* and Dr.
Parker as represented by himself. I was a little puzzled at first to
bring out the difference, but after some trying I found it, and endeavored, though with scanty success, to make it clear to Mr. Gibbs.[8]
By and by other gentlemen came, and at last we had present Messrs.
Gibbs, Hadley, Larned, Murdock, Salisbury, Thacher, and Woolsey. Professor Porter is getting gas into his house and could not
come. Dr. Murdock was a good deal solicitous about the election of
officers, but at length we concluded to go on after the old sort, at least
until the next annual meeting. I held forth, reading through the 17
pages I had written, and was listened to with attention and apparent
interest. Mr. Gibbs made some remarks, dwelling upon his ideas of
internal inflexion, at which I protested as usual, but believe I must
write an article against them. Adjourned to meet at Dr. Murdock's
in November. Provision for the meeting to be made by Mr. Hadley.

Returning home before 10, looked at last new number of *Bibliotheca Sacra*. Not very rich; too much Stowe and Pond in't.

Thursday, October 14. The football game came off yesterday between the Sophomores and Freshmen, at 4 P.M., being deferred two
hours on account of a Sunday School celebration. Only two games
were played, the first a Sophomore victory, the second drawn. Great
tardiness at prayers. One of the Freshmen, Ward, fell down, was
trampled on, grew senseless, and bled freely at the ears, but soon
came to, and seems not greatly hurt—but the circumstance cooled
somewhat the ardor of the combatants. There is hope that the remaining games may be postponed indefinitely.

Saturday, October 16. Call from Mr. Lyman to speak of his plans
for an investigation of spiritual rappings. He had brought a me-
dium, a girl of 11 years, from Bridgeport and lodged her at Lucius
Fitch's, but the Irish servant girl was so much terrified, protesting
that it was the devil, and that she would not stay under the same
roof, that they were obliged to take her away, and the investigation
seemed likely to fall through from the difficulty of finding a place
for the subject.

Sunday, October 24. Two noble sermons by President Woolsey.
The first, on the permanent evil wrought by sin, I had heard before

in the Centre Church. The second, on the dignity of man's nature as shown by Christianity, is, I suppose, new. Mr. Thacher's infant boy was baptized before the afternoon service by the name of Edward Stanley. Some of the students, when they heard the child crying, thought it was the President's own boy, announced yesterday and a theme of congratulation for all the family friends. Some of the students thought proper to celebrate the occasion last night with a feu de joie in front of South College and with a sort of pow-wow generally. They had the grace, however, to leave off before Sunday morning.

About 4 A.M. we were waked up by a strange rumbling noise which shook the house and seemed like a mixture of cart and rail-car. It was repeated soon after, and being unaccompanied by human voices suggested to me the idea of an earthquake. It proved however to be a fire engine returning from a fire in State Street. The unusual stillness of the company was accounted for by a very melancholy cause, the loss of one of their number, who was killed by a falling beam. A more illustrious death had just before taken place: Daniel Webster, according to a telegraphic dispatch, departed peacefully at 22 minutes before 3 A.M. His age was 70 years and 9 months. Our three great statesmen are now gone. When shall we look upon their like again?

Tuesday, October 26. Talked with Mr. Dwight about noise last night and Saturday night. Midday walk up Elm Street to New Poor House and back by the MacAdam road. Edward at 2. Through in less than an hour. Journalized a while. Sent our divisions of the Freshman class to Chemical Lecture Room, to be addressed as usual by Mr. Silliman. Spent a while at College Library looking at the books we have purchased from the Lachmann collection. A fine dictionary of the old Frisic and Franz, *Elementa Epigraphices Graecae* interested me most. Some talk with Mr. Herrick and Professor Gibbs about the Beecher-Parker controversy. Mr. Gibbs has written the *Independent* about it; has made some good points, but hardly on the whole hit the nail upon the head.

Found Anna returned from Sewing Society at Mr. Root's. She was tired and sleepy through the evening. I commenced reading Wieland to her, but we were soon interrupted by a call from Dr. W. Hooker. Processions, first of Whigs with an illuminated face of Daniel Webster and a motto of "Men die but principles live."

Second of the Bhoys with "Pierce and King," "Firm as West Rock," etc. Wrote a letter long due to James Hoyt in New York. Read Grote to Anna when she waked up at 10.

Wednesday, October 27. At Faculty meeting, voted suspension to three Seniors, Jones, Skelding, and C. L. Thomas, detected in the bonfire of Saturday night. But the President objecting strongly, it was reconsidered and changed to second warning.

Dr. North was brought upon the carpet and some rich things told of his recent sayings and doings. He grows more and more crazy every year.

Mary returned from West Point and New York—got in at 7. Harriet and Julia Twining spent the evening with us. Unsuccessful attempt on Henry to induce him to attend the beehive.

Tried a little to read the 5th volume of Savigny.

Thursday, October 28. Mr. Gibbs came into my room about 10 o'clock, while I was working over the Herodotus, and said he wanted to consult me on a particular point—and the more, as my state of mind enabled me to view it differently from him. He then showed me a letter dated New York, October 25, and signed Joel Parker, which in the briefest and curtest phraseology called his attention to an article in the *Independent* signed G. and by rumor ascribed to him, inquiring whether he (Mr. Gibbs) was author of it and whether he authorized its publication in the *Independent*. To this somewhat formidable missive, he had drawn up a reply of about equal length. When I heard it seemed to me very good. We talked it over; several points were suggested, some rejected. When, after Mr. Gibbs had gone, it occurred to me that I would set down what I thought best, and I wrote accordingly, following to a great extent Mr. Gibbs' own sketch: "Dear Sir, I am glad that your attention has been drawn to a communication signed G. which I furnished, as I have furnished other articles on philological subjects, to the Editors of the *Independent*. I have endeavored in that article, perhaps without success, to set forth the *natural construction* of the paragraphs in question. What construction you yourself put upon them and particularly upon the one of which you are the author, I have not pretended to decide and I have not been able to make out with certainty. If there is any explanation of your meaning published, which you yourself approve and adopt, I should be pleased if you would refer me to it. If there is no such explanation, can you not present a statement of your views, which would give clearness to your friends and your opponents on this whole subject? Respectfully etc." Mr. Gibbs appeared to be pleased with this form in most particulars—how far he will follow it I know not.

NOTES

1. (March 3, 1848.) The Reverend Alexander MacWhorter (a classmate of James Hadley) and Miss Delia Bacon (sister of the Reverend Leonard Bacon; later famous for her Shakespeare-Bacon theories) for a time in 1845 showed marked interest in each other's company. When the affair ended, friends of Miss Bacon felt called on to defend her "delicacy" by saying that she would not have exhibited so open a preference if she had not been led to expect marriage. Friends of Mr. MacWhorter counter-defended that it was the lady who had pursued the gentleman. Thereupon Dr. Bacon charged MacWhorter before the county association of Congregational ministers with "slander, falsehood, and conduct dishonorable to the Christian ministry."

After receiving the majority and minority reports of the committee of investigation, the association adopted, 12 to 11, the following resolution:

"Resolved, 1st, That action in this case by this body is deemed unnecessary; by which we do not intend to imply that what the aforesaid licentiate has reported of the relative of the complainant is true.

"Resolved, 2dly, That as, in the view of some members of this Association, the aforesaid licentiate has been in a greater or a less degree imprudent, that a committee of three . . . give, with Christian and paternal kindness, such admonition to him, as in their view the case may require."

Miss Catherine Beecher (sister of Henry Ward Beecher and Harriet Beecher Stowe), who was a friend and former teacher of Miss Bacon, published, over Miss Bacon's protest, a 296-page account of the matter, entitled *Truth Stranger Than Fiction*. This book was dedicated to the Congregational pastors of New England, and took them to task for the stand of one of their bodies in the case of "Mr. A." and "Miss D." of the town of "N." James Hadley felt that it was directed especially against Dr. Nathaniel W. Taylor, who had for many years been a family friend of the Bacons and in whose household MacWhorter was living at the time of the crisis.

The affair caused a furor throughout New England and feeling ran high in New Haven. For example, though in 1852 Miss Henrietta Blake married Mr. MacWhorter, her father is said never to have addressed remarks directly to his son-in-law even at the family table.

2. (March 25, 1850.) Professor John White Webster, of Harvard and the Massachusetts Medical College, was convicted and executed for the murder of Dr. George Parkman of Boston. Webster had owed money to Parkman for a number of years, and the latter became incensed when he found that Webster had borrowed money from others on the security of a collection of minerals which had already been mortgaged to Parkman. By appointment, Parkman called on Webster in his laboratory in the medical college on November 23, 1849, to demand repayment of his loan. Webster slew him with knife and hammer, dismembered the body, hid portions of it in the vault of a privy, and burned other portions in the laboratory furnace. The prominent social standing of both murderer and victim intensified the public interest in the case.

A more detailed account will be found in *A Book of Remarkable Criminals,* by Henry Brodribb Irving.

3. (March 31, 1850.) Edwin Forrest, the actor, and his wife, the former Catherine Sinclair, separated in 1849. In 1850 Forrest sought a divorce, accusing his wife of infidelity and naming a number of men visitors to her house. His petition was denied. In 1851–52 Mrs. Forrest brought a counter-suit, and the jury awarded her a divorce and vindicated her character.

Among those mentioned in Forrest's suit was Richard Willis, a church organist and composer of music, lately returned from six years of studying sacred music in Germany. Richard Willis, his brother Nathaniel Parker Willis (the poet and editor), and Mrs. N. P. Willis testified that he was present at Mrs. Forrest's because she and her sister Mrs. Voorhies, the concert singer, desired to try some new music and he had several books of manuscript music not in print.

4. (May 25, 1850.) Beginning in the spring of 1848, members of the John D. Fox family of Rochester and Hydesville, New York, reported themselves plagued by spirits who rapped on doors and floors, walked about, moved furniture, pelted the family with vegetables or anything handy, and set up a racket that infuriated the neighbors. They further reported that, by means of a rapping alphabet, the spirits had instructed them to permit people to meet with them and communicate with the spirit world. Séances were held, and lectures on spiritualism were given.

Intense public interest and feeling arose, and many investigating committees were set up, in Rochester, Albany, New York, and eventually (1857) in Boston, where the committee included Professors Peirce and Agassiz. One of the prominent champions of the Fox family was Horace Greeley of the New York *Tribune.*

An account of the experiences of the Fox family was published in 1885 by A. Leah (Fox) Underhill under the title of *The Missing Link in Modern Spiritualism.* The New York newspapers of October 22, 1888, carried an account of the public exposé of the rappings by Margaretta Fox Kane, who produced raps with her big toe.

5. (August 25, 1850.) Henry Phillpotts, Bishop of Exeter, refused to institute George Cornelius Gorham to the living of Brampford Speke because Gorham denied unconditional regeneration in baptism. Gorham appealed to the Judicial Committee of the Privy Council, which decided in his favor (see *Report of the Judgment of the Judicial Committee of the Privy Council,* March 8, 1850). The case not only concerned the latitude of religious belief permitted within the Church of England but also stirred up dissatisfaction that spiritual questions should be decided by a secular court. It was the occasion of the secession to the Church of Rome of the future Cardinal Manning.

6. (November 1, 1850.) Taylorism. "The doctrinal system of Nathaniel William Taylor (1786–1858), professor of theology in New Haven, Conn., 1822–58, whose distinctive tenets were that man has the power of contrary choice, that virtue is the choice of the highest good of the universe, and that sin is not a propagated essential property of the human soul, nor the necessary means of the greatest good." (By permission. From *Webster's New International Dictionary,* 2d ed., copyright 1934, 1939, 1945, 1950, by G. & C. Merriam Co.)

7. (May 19, 1851.) Henriette Desportes (1813?–75), who became Mrs. Henry M. Field, was governess in the household of the Duke and Duchess of Choiseul-Praslin from 1841 to 1847, when she was dismissed because of the jealous suspicions of the Duchess. Two months later, in August 1847, the Duchess was brutally murdered, and all the evidence pointed to her husband as the slayer. The Duke died in prison of arsenic poisoning a week after his arrest, and the scandal of his being permitted, through negligence or connivance, to escape justice contributed to the downfall of King Louis-Philippe.

At the time of the murder Miss Desportes was arrested and questioned. Upon her release she took refuge in the family of the Reverend Frédéric Monod, founder of the Union of the Evangelical Churches of France. In 1849 she came to New York, where she taught until her marriage in 1851.

Her husband, Henry Martyn Field, was a clergyman, journalist, and author. He was a brother of Cyrus Field, who brought about the laying of the Atlantic cable, and of David Dudley Field, jurist and law reformer.

A novel based on the life of Mrs. Field, written by her husband's great-niece Rachel Field, was published in 1938 under the title *All This, and Heaven Too*.

8. (October 7, 1852.) In *Uncle Tom's Cabin,* by Harriet Beecher Stowe, a remark on slavery was attributed to Dr. Joel Parker at which he took offense because it differed from his actual wording. According to Professor Gibbs, Parker regarded the imputation of the sentiment "as an injurious and calumnious assault on his Christian character and professional reputation. . . . Dr. Parker himself estimates the injury at $20,000." The libel suit eventually was dropped. Henry Ward Beecher entered the controversy on the side of his sister.

A full account of the affair will be found in *Crusader in Crinoline,* by Forrest Wilson.

INDEX

Wheat, Dr. James B., 79

Wheeler, George W. (Y.ex-1855), 288; his father, 288

Whelpley, J. D., 59, 166

Whigs, 17, 129; state convention of, 37; local, 14, 165, 194, 199, 310; national convention of, 294

Whipple, ?Edwin Percy, 169, 305

White, 8

White (Y.1854), 89

White, Henry, 201, 260, 272, 291

Whitmore, 269

Whitney, Mr., 287

Whitney, Edward P. (Y.1854), 168, 177, 213, 227, 270, 286

Whitney, Elizabeth Fay, 165, 166, 172, 187

Whitney, Henrietta F. Edwards (Mrs. Eli Whitney), 57, 142–43, 303

Whitney, Josiah Dwight (1786–1869), 32, 270, 286

Whitney, Josiah Dwight (1819–96), 58, 67, 96, 109, 288

Whitney, Mrs. Josiah Dwight, Sr., 286

Whitney, William Dwight (1827–94), passim; European study of, 109, 168, 178, 231, 287; on JH as philologist, viii; JH studies Sanskrit and Moeso-Gothic with, 35, 58, 70, 86, and passim; plans of, 32, 178, 210–11, 288

Whiton, James M. (Y.1853), 73

Whittlesey, Eliphalet (Y.1842), 36, 62, 68, 71, 84, 90, 91, 149, 306; at Andover, 149–51, 216, 284; called to Bath, 216, 284; on JH's engagement, 217

Wickes, Henry (theol. student), 71, 149, 287

Wickham, Miss, 187

Wilcox, Mrs., 71

Wilcox, John Henry (Y.ex-1847), 156, 269, 286–87

Wilcox, Lucian S. (Y.1850), 274

Willard, James L. (Y.1849), ?149, 271

Willard, Samuel G. (Y.1846), 17, ?149

Willis, Mr. and Mrs. Nathaniel P., 314

Willis, Richard Storrs (Y.1841), 71; book of, of sacred music, 78, 132; and For-

rest case, 37, 44, 45, 314; JH's acquaintance with, 40, 68, 81, 87, 95, 136

Wilson, 107

Wilson, Joseph W. (Y.1854), 191

Wimmer, Dr., 159

Wingfield, John H. (Y.1851), 62, 87

Winthrop, Mrs. Elizabeth Woolsey, 170, 232, 240

Winthrop, Theodore (Y.1848), 16, 160

Winthrop, William Woolsey (Y.1851), 46, 75, 77, 85, 212, 240

Women's rights, 76, 164, 265

Woodbridge, Conn., 260–61

Wooden Spoon Exhibition, xi, 223, 224

Woods, Dr., 62

Woods, Mrs., 62

Woodstock, Pittsfield Faculty at, 5

Woodward, Dr., 4

Woodward, Judge, 112

Woodward, George W. (Y.ex-1854), 112, 128

Woolsey, Elizabeth M. Salisbury (Mrs. Theodore D. Woolsey), 111, 122, 142, 190, 211, 240, 277; on Beecher book, 41

Woolsey, Sarah Chauncey (Mrs. William Woolsey), 240

Woolsey, Theodore Dwight (Prof. Greek, 1831–51; Pres., 1846–71), passim; on alumni, 308; JH consults, about salary, 196; library of, to go to Yale, 289–90; plans of, 196

Wr[a]ggles, Miss, 205

Wright, Mr., school of, 200, 210

YALE COLLEGE, in 1850, ix–xi; New Haven relations with, 26, 78–79, 241, 283; 150th anniversary of, x, 34; see also Alumni; Fund raising; Salaries and wages; Tuition; and departments of instruction

Yale family (Newport), 108

Yale Literary Magazine, 64, 133

Young, Robert S. (Y.1853), 37, 303

Young Men's Institute, 66, 141, 170, 177, 181

Yung Wing (Y.1854), 145, 205, 308